Bordeaux

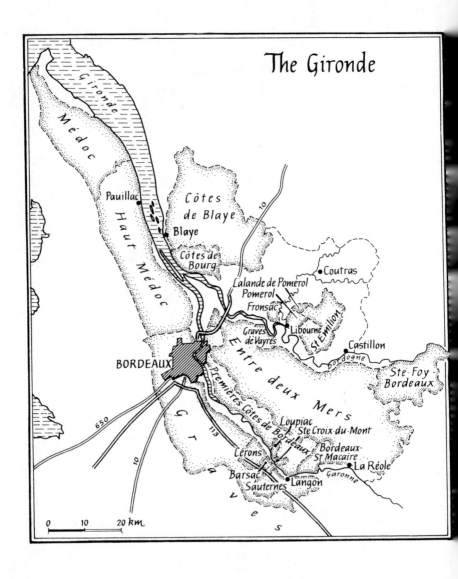

The Gironde

Gironde

Médoc

Haut Médoc

Pauillac

Côtes de Blaye

Blaye

Côtes de Bourg

Coutras

Lalande de Pomerol

Pomerol

Fronsac

Graves de Vayres

Libourne

St Emilion

Castillon

BORDEAUX

Entre deux Mers

Ste-Foy Bordeaux

Premières Côtes de Bordeaux

Graves

Loupiac

Ste Croix-du-Mont

Cérons

Bordeaux St Macaire

La Réole

Barsac

Sauternes

Langon

Garonne

Dordogne

650

10

113

10

0   10   20 km

BORDEAUX

DAVID PEPPERCORN
M.W.

faber and faber

First published in 1982
by Faber and Faber Limited
3 Queen Square London WC1N 3AU
Filmset by Latimer Trend & Company Ltd, Plymouth
Printed in Great Britain by
The Thetford Press Ltd, Thetford, Norfolk

British Library Cataloguing in Publication Data

Peppercorn, David
Bordeaux
1. Wine and wine making—France—
Bordeaux
I. Title
641.2'2'094471   TP553

ISBN 0–571–11751–1
ISBN 0–571–11758–9 Pbk

To my father, with affection and gratitude for
setting me on the right path, and to my
wife Serena for all her help and encouragement

Contents

Illustrations

Preface

This book is the fruit of twenty-five years of practical experience
in the wine trade, and of a first-hand knowledge of Bordeaux
which goes back to 1952, when I was still an undergraduate at
Cambridge. Claret was the first red wine I grew to appreciate at
my father's table, and Bordeaux was the first wine region I came
to know intimately. Between 1960 and 1973 I visited the region
over fifty times, and now go there regularly to learn, taste and
evaluate.

It is never easy for those actually working in the trade to put
pen to paper on the scale of a book of this size, as anyone who has
tried will know. This is why most of our books on wine tend to be
written by professional writers who have an interest in wine, and
not by professional wine people. I felt that the necessarily
distinctive perspective which an English wine merchant could
bring to a subject so dear to the hearts of wine lovers in the
English-speaking world would justify some sacrifice on my part.
So this is a book which has matured over some years, much of it
written during holidays in Spain and Italy, as well as over
numerous evenings and weekends.

My historical studies at Cambridge gave impetus to my interest
in the historical setting of the Bordeaux wine trade, the often
fascinating story of British merchants in Bordeaux, and the
development of the Bordeaux estates in their economic and social
setting. Reluctantly, I had to decide against the considerable
extension of the book which such a study would have involved. To
have gone into the history in detail would have greatly delayed
publication, and I have already tried the patience of my publishers
enough. Furthermore, much new material on this subject has
appeared in the last year or so and more is on the way, so this may
not be the best moment to attempt to summarize what is now

known about the historical background. But what I have tried to do is to set people and events firmly in their historical setting, whenever the narrative seems to call for this.

No one can write a book of this sort without incurring many personal debts on the way. Over and above the general acknowledgements, I would like to single out especially my father, who initiated and nurtured my interest in Bordeaux over many years. My first visit in 1952 was with him, and he was my companion on many other occasions. Then, I owe a special debt to W. & A. Gilbey and their successors, International Distillers and Vintners, for whom I worked from 1960 to 1974; my many visits to Château Loudenne gave me an incomparable opportunity of tasting new wines and learning how to judge them, while generous access to the private cellar gave me a marvellous opportunity to taste old wines. In particular, I should like to record my gratitude to my former colleague, Martin Bamford, M.W., for all his help and personal kindness, both when we were colleagues and afterwards.

Also, in Bordeaux, very special thanks are due to two of my oldest and most valued friends; Jean-Paul Gardère of Château Latour for much practical help and wisdom over twenty years, and Jean-Pierre Moueix, from whom I have learnt so much about St Emilion and Pomerol that could not have been learnt from anyone else. Nor must I leave Bordeaux without mentioning Bertrand de Rivoyre, whose breadth of experience of the whole region has been of great assistance to me over the last five years.

I wish to thank Kathleen Bourke for her kind encouragement which started me on the road of writing on wine when she was editor of *Wine Magazine*. Julian Jeffs, the editor of the Faber wine series, deserves a special word of thanks for his enthusiastic encouragement and monumental patience over a number of years. My final and very special thanks are due to my wife—even better known as Serena Sutcliffe, M.W.—without whose help, reading and constructive criticism of the manuscript, and constant encouragement, this work might never have seen the light of day.

I would like to acknowledge the help and assistance of the following people. Some responded to requests for written information, others provided informative tastings, but all have been invaluable in the preparation of this book:

14

Francis Dewavrin, Château La Mission Haut-Brion; the late Henri Woltner, Château La Mission Haut-Brion; Bernard Haramboure, Gardère-Haramboure S.A., Pauillac; Philippe Cottin, La Bergerie; Michael Broadbent, M.W., Christie's, London; Henri Binaud, H. & O. Beyerman; William-Alain Miailhe, Château Siran; Nathaniel L. Johnston, Nathaniel Johnston & Fils, Bordeaux; Cyril Ray, London; Ronald Barton, Château Langoa; Anthony Barton, Anthony Barton & Cie; Neville Reid, late of Reid, Pye & Campbell; the late Christian Cruse; Alexis Lichine, Château Prieuré-Lichine; Christian Moueix Ets. J-P. Moueix, Libourne; the late André Mentzelopoulos, Laura Mentzelopoulos, Château Margaux; Baron Eric de Rothschild, Château Lafite; Jean-Eugène Borie, Château Ducru-Beaucaillou; Jean Tapie, Château Branaire-Ducru; William Bolter, Bordeaux; John Salvi, M.W., Sichel & Cie; Peter A. Sichel, Sichel & Cie; Daniel Vergely, Maison D. Cordier, Bordeaux; Emile Castéja, Borie-Manoux, Bordeaux; Vincent-Noël Martelly, Mestrezat-Preller S.A., Bordeaux.

DAVID PEPPERCORN
London, 1981

1

Setting the scene

The ancient ties of history and commerce between the British Isles and Bordeaux are sufficient reason in themselves for the interest and fondness which the English, not forgetting the Scottish, Irish and Welsh, have long shown for the wines of this region. At the same time these ties make it natural for an Englishman to write about and interpret the Bordeaux scene, particularly one working in the English wine trade, which is justly proud of being the oldest and most knowledgeable to be found outside the wine-producing countries. From the ranks of the English trade have stepped, over the last two hundred years, a number of men who have played prominent roles in its Bordeaux counterpart.

The Bordeaux trade has passed through a number of distinct phases, and while it is right to be mainly concerned with the present and the future, the contemporary scene should be set firmly in the context of what has gone before. The first distinct era of importance for Bordeaux was the period of its allegiance to the English Crown. I express it deliberately in this manner because it would be misleading to describe this relationship in modern terms by saying that Bordeaux belonged to or was part of England. In the feudal world before the existence of the nation state, a man thought of himself more as a citizen of London or of Bordeaux, owing allegiance to his lord, rather than as an Englishman or a Frenchman. This period of allegiance lasted almost exactly three hundred years from Henry II's marriage to Eleanor of Aquitaine in 1152 until the final defeat of Talbot, Earl of Shrewsbury, in 1453. During this time a large export trade was built up with England, and while much of the wine came from areas not today counted as Bordeaux, such as Bergerac and Cahors, the vineyards of the present Bordeaux region were also developed and expanded.

With the departure of the English, there followed a barren period as Bordeaux suffered from the ills afflicting the rest of France. Hardly had her period of probation as a somewhat reluctant newcomer to the realm of France been completed, when France herself was split by the Reformation. Bordeaux became one of the centres of Huguenot dissent. The Wars of Religion divided France as bitterly as the Civil War did England in the following century, and their effects were far more harmful and long-lived. Whereas English liberties were restored from Tudor and Stuart encroachments and given a modern direction, in France the Wars of Religion fatally eroded decaying medieval liberties and opened the way for Bourbon absolutism. France did not fully recover her strength or sense of purpose until Louis XIV established his personal rule over seventy years after the end of the Wars. It is from this time, in the second half of the seventeenth century, that one can discover the beginnings of the movement which during the eighteenth century saw the rise and development of the great estates or châteaux, as we now know them.

This new epoch began in circumstances that were far from propitious. The wars of Louis XIV, coupled with the protectionist measures of Colbert, were harmful to the interests of Bordeaux. At the same time, new beverages, such as chocolate, coffee and sweet mistelles, gained rapid popularity in both England and Holland from the middle of the seventeenth century. The first Coffee House opened in London in 1652, and the period 1679–85 saw Coffee Houses become à la mode in London. One of the consequences of Louis XIV's succession of wars was that in 1697 discriminatory duties were levied against French wines imported into England, and these remained in force until 1786. Duties on French wines were now more than twice as high as those levied on wines from the Iberian peninsula.

Until this time, the large quantities of Bordeaux wine consumed in England had essentially been *vins de l'année* of ordinary quality. It was the new wine of the last vintage that was most sought after. But to surmount the formidable duty barriers now imposed, something better than *vin ordinaire* was needed. It was in these circumstances that 'New French Claret' was born and the notion of growths or *crus* which commanded a premium in price terms is first encountered. René Pijassou has now documented for the first time the full story of this remarkable revolution in drinking

18

habits. Of how the great Bordeaux landowners, like the Pontacs of Haut Brion and the Ségurs of Lafite, changed the face of the Médoc between 1680 and 1750, and how in the England of Queen Anne and the Hanoverians, an aristocratic and merchant upper class developed which demanded wines that were fine instead of ordinary. The copious records kept by men such as John Hervey, first Earl of Bristol, and Sir Robert Walpole, the first Prime Minister, show how the names of Haut Brion, Lafite, Margaux and Latour first made their appearance at prices well above other Bordeaux wines. The name of Médoc first appeared in 1708 in the London Gazette, and by 1714 we find the first mention of 'old' Margaux, to be shipped in bottle. Old, in this case, almost certainly means no more than older than the last vintage, since in this period the First Growths were still exported as new wines, that is of the last vintage.

France experienced a period of considerable commercial prosperity in the years leading up to the Revolution, and Bordeaux, with its growing and energetic middle class, played a leading part in this expansion. Not only was this a time of renewed activity in the vineyards, but great prosperity also came to the city through the development of its port, and particularly through its trade with the West Indies. Although relatively few of the famous châteaux belong to this period—Beychevelle is an outstanding example—it has left us a glorious memorial in the fine public buildings constructed at that time in Bordeaux, notably the Opera House and the Place Louis XVIII.

The Revolution swept away many of the old proprietors, who had been members of the *noblesse de robe*. Membership of this professional legal establishment was almost the only method of preferment open to those not of noble birth, under the *ancien régime*. Lafite, for example, came on the market when its proprietor, Pichard, president of the Bordeaux Parlement, had been guillotined—in fact, he was one of the very few in Bordeaux to suffer this fate. The estate passed to his daughter, who had fled the country, but was forfeit since all property belonging to *émigrés* was confiscated by the State. This was actually the largest single reason for changes of ownership in the Bordeaux region, where the Church was not a major owner of vineyards, as it was in Burgundy.

The places of the old proprietors after the Revolution and

19

especially after the Restoration (the re-establishment of the Bourbon Monarchy under Louis XVIII, brother of the guillotined Louis XVI, briefly in 1814 and then on a more permanent basis in 1815 after Napoleon's final defeat at Waterloo), went in many cases to a relatively new breed of men, the *négociants*, or merchants. In many cases their enterprises had begun during the eighteenth century as general import and export businesses, only gradually concentrating on wine. Often businesses had been launched by foreign merchants settling in Bordeaux to supply the needs of their home markets. Now that the protectionism of the *ancien régime* had gone and an era of freer trade was beginning throughout Europe, these men seized their opportunities. One such was Hugh Barton, who acquired a portion of Léoville from the family of the Marquis de Las Cases, as well as Langoa, while his partner, Pierre-François Guestier, not to be outdone, became his neighbour at Beychevelle. Although the Guestiers have now left the scene, their place has been taken by other partners of other firms, so that today a number of Bordeaux houses are also important château proprietors.

The Second Empire (1851–70) saw a new phase, the investment in Bordeaux properties by influential financiers from outside Bordeaux and the wine trade. The most notable of these were the two Rothschild purchases and that of the Pereires at Palmer.

However, viticulturally and economically the nineteenth century was equally a period dominated by the scourge of disease. The oidium of the 1850s proved a serious financial setback throughout Bordeaux, while the phylloxera and mildew period of the late 1870s and 1880s had a more profound effect still (see pp. 30–31).

While Bordeaux suffered far less from the French débâcle of 1870 (defeat in the Franco-Prussian War) than from the phylloxera, it was affected by general economic movements. This was certainly so in the depression at the turn of the century, accompanied as it was by a lack of really top-class vintages. There is surely no period so barren of notable vintages than the two decades that separate the great wines of 1900 and 1920. But perhaps the most serious setback came between the wars when severe economic difficulties again coincided with a run of poor vintages in the 1930s.

As if to compensate for all this, the post-war era began with a sparkling array of splendid vintages: 1945, 1947 and 1949 have certainly now taken their rightful places among the famous vintages of the past. Yet it was only very gradually that prosperity returned. Prices after the war were still historically low and the vineyards were in a rundown condition after the bleak years of the thirties, followed by the difficulties of the war years. As a result of this the area under vine was at a very low ebb and the existing vineyards were often old and in need of attention. It takes a generation and a great deal of investment to reconstruct a vineyard, and that is certainly one reason why Bordeaux, with its resources at rock bottom after years of depression and war, took a long time to recover.

Unfortunately, just as the tide seemed to have turned decisively in favour of prosperity, with the highly successful 1953s succeeded by the large yield and higher prices of the 1955s, the uncertainties of nature again stepped in with the disastrous early frost of February 1956. Wine lovers are so used to hearing wine growers, like farmers, cry 'wolf', that perhaps they may be forgiven for failing to appreciate just how significant that frost was to be. The repercussions were with us for over a decade and necessitated fresh investment on a large scale.

The great vintage of 1961 set a new level for prices which was not again to be reached until the 1970 vintage, except by the first growths. The 1960s were a period of reconstruction and growth. Symbolic of this time for me was the replanting of Larose-Trintaudon. What had been a great waste-land on the drive from St Laurent to Pauillac, now became the largest vineyard in the Médoc. The vineyard, uprooted in the 1920s, was replanted from 1964 to 1966 and now extends for some 180 hectares. The good vintages of 1962, 1964, 1966 and 1967 were tempered by the terrible vintages of 1963 and 1965, and the mediocre wines of 1968 and 1969.

It seemed at the time that the unusual vintage of 1970 had really ushered in a new era. The combination of yield and quality was something which had not been seen in the Gironde since 1934, and before that, one has to go back to 1900. It certainly marked the coming of age of the new plantings and was to be succeeded by a series of prolific years for red wines in 1973, 1974, 1976 and 1978, culminating in 1979. 1970 was really the year when proprietors began to reap the profits from their investments. But the boom was to prove surprisingly shortlived.

The much smaller 1971 vintage showed a dramatic price rise, but the wines were good and in short supply for a market now avid for Bordeaux wines—or so it seemed. However, when the very mediocre 1972s appeared, and higher prices still were asked for them, the market hiccupped, and then, under the influence of the energy crisis and world recession, it collapsed in a manner unknown since 1927. Somehow the idea had taken root in Bordeaux that prices always rose and never fell, and that the world demand was such that the relatively small quantities of top wines produced in Bordeaux must always find their market. In particular the belief prevailed that the American market would always buy the first growths at any price. The combination of economic recession and poor wines at record prices proved an indigestible one, and administered a very salutary lesson in common sense to the market.

I so well remember my own first tastings of the 1972s in January 1973. My conclusion had been that with such an escalation of price for such modest wines, this was the moment to stop buying. Unfortunately, within weeks the whole wine trade allowed itself to be sucked into a vortex of buying at absurd prices. When the market collapsed, these stocks of 1972s proved a major obstacle to the recovery of the market, because few *négociants* could afford to halve their prices, and there was no money to buy the cheaper and much better 1973s. I do not say that there would have been no crisis if the price of the 1972s had more nearly corresponded with their quality, but it would have been less acute and less prolonged.

This is not the place to go into the crisis of 1973–4 in detail. But it is worth remarking that one special factor was the activity of speculators outside the trade. Of course, there have always been speculators in the Bordeaux trade itself. Sometimes they have made fortunes and sometimes they have gone bankrupt. But in the boom years of the early 1970s, many people outside the trade were looking either for somewhere to place their money or even speculating with the help and often encouragement of the banks. I remember at least one instance of someone wishing to put £100,000 into wine, and this sort of thing was a very widespread experience at this time. In such a frantic atmosphere, prices easily escalated. But the writing was on the wall for those with eyes to see. One too often heard it said that so-and-so was selling his 1953 Mouton or 1949 Lafite because he could 'no longer afford to drink it'. The great Bordeaux had become something for buying and selling but not for drinking. The simple truth that a bottle of wine, unlike a painting or a piece of furniture, is not a joy forever, but only has true worth once—when the cork is drawn—had been temporarily forgotten.

The recovery was slow and painful. It was not assisted by the sheer volume of the 1973 and 1974 vintages, the first light and charming, the second sound but uninviting. It needed the magnificent 1975s to rekindle true enthusiasm for Bordeaux. Since then, the market has progressed soundly and steadily, to keep abreast of inflation, without running ahead of what consumers are willing and able to pay.

One other important trend has also been apparent during the 1970s. As the yields of red Bordeaux have risen to record levels, so the yields of the less profitable whites have begun to decline. There has been a steady reduction in the area under vine, as vineyards, especially in the Entre-deux-Mers, have been replanted to produce red wine. By the mid to late 1980s, we shall probably see a shortage of white Bordeaux.

Looking to the present, one is struck by the great post-war boom in wine drinking. This has been a phenomenon not limited to any one country. The USA, West Germany, Holland and the Scandinavian countries, as well as the UK, have all experienced a greatly increased demand for good quality wines as distinct from *vin ordinaire*. In France itself, the demand for staple *ordinaires* has stagnated and is now in decline, while the consumption of VDQS and AC wines grows steadily. Yet not until the 1970s did Bordeaux take full advantage of this movement. The comparison with its ancient rival, Burgundy, was particularly striking. Burgundy, with its much smaller production (approximately two to three times as much Bordeaux as Burgundy), saw its sales go from strength to strength, while Bordeaux was depressingly undersold. This did not, of course, apply to the best-known classified growths, but to thousands of small growths which form the backbone of Bordeaux.

Yet so much appears to favour Bordeaux. Its vineyards are arranged in relatively large and manageable units, while those of

Burgundy are notoriously fragmented. There are a good number of large properties able to produce wine in quantities sufficient to be promoted, something unknown in Burgundy. For the Burgundians this has meant that, apart from Beaujolais, only the village names of the Côte d'Or could really be promoted, but in practice this has led to each *négociant* promoting his own name, since this is the sole outward mark to distinguish his wine from what is offered by his neighbour.

In contrast, the Bordeaux *négociant* has tended to fall between two stools. On the one hand, few *négociants* have succeeded in widely establishing their own brands of generic appellations such as Médoc, St Emilion and Sauternes; on the other, they have sold a wide variety of château wines, mostly on a non-exclusive basis. In the 1960s a tendency developed for a few *négociants* to promote a number of châteaux on an exclusive basis, thus ensuring less cut-throat margins both for themselves and their customers, as well as a more effective and systematic distribution for the wines themselves. This system suffered a severe setback in the 1973 and 1974 depression, when many *négociants* were unable to honour their commitments. But the end result is that today the famous names of the past among the *négociants* have lost ground. There have been some important newcomers, but nobody has anything like a dominant position, and there are still too many very small firms. The Syndicat of Bordeaux *négociants* has 200 members.

It is this unique feature in the marketing of Bordeaux wines, that they are largely made and sold as individual properties, which has determined the shape of this book. Within each section, after dealing generally with the characteristics of the wines to be found in that particular region, I have listed the more important properties in alphabetical order with all the relevant information on each, the lesser growths being simply listed at the end with the latest production figures. I hope that in this way, information will prove easily accessible, and that the characteristics, production, and notes on past vintages of each particular property may all be conveniently found in one place.

Nothing stands still, and this is especially true of the reputation of individual châteaux. What I have tried to do here is to indicate both the general reputation in the Bordeaux trade and my own strictly personal view based on tastings over the years. I believe this is important because the opinions of experts so often differ, so that to give only a personal view could be misleading, while to present only the general view, though safe, could be monotonous. My aim has been to be informative and frank without being libellous, and at the same time I have tried to be fair and indicate my own preferences, so that the reader may discount them where appropriate.

On the technical side, I have tried to provide sufficient information for the serious student, while trying to make it interesting and easy to follow for the general reader. In describing the care of vineyards and the making of wine, I have been guided by what was clearly relevant to the end product rather than providing an exhaustive study.

2

Making the wine

THE VINEYARDS

The making of wine starts, of course, in the vineyard, and here nothing is more important to the end product than the selection of the correct varieties of vine, or *cépages* as they are called in French. It is rightly said that four vital and interlocking elements are involved in the production of good wine: climate, soil, vine and the skill of man. But if the first two are right, the difference between a mediocre wine and a fine wine will ultimately depend on the correct *cépage* and human skill. This is especially so in a variable temperate climate such as that of Bordeaux, where the *encépagement* of a vineyard must be selected to counteract as far as possible the vagaries of the weather.

Bordeaux, like the Rhône but unlike Burgundy, uses several different *cépages* to make its best wines, both red and white. A few dry white wines are today made only with the Sauvignon grape, but this occurs mostly in lesser areas for the cheaper wines and is not typical of the region as a whole.

Red

CABERNET SAUVIGNON is the classic *cépage* for red wines, especially in Médoc and Graves. This is a variety that does best on gravel. In St Emilion, where it is less widely planted, it is usually known as the 'Gros Bouchet'. It is generally less suitable for the colder soil of Pomerol. It produces wines which are fine, showing finesse and breed, and the small berries and thick skins provide plenty of tannin and a good colour. They ripen after the Merlot but are much more resistant both to *coulure* at the time of the flowering and to rot (*pourriture grise*) (see p. 31) before the vintage. They give a rather low yield.

CABERNET FRANC is known as the 'Bouchet' in St Emilion and Pomerol, where it is widely planted. This *cépage* is a cousin of the Cabernet Sauvignon, with similar characteristics, but produces wines which are less coloured and fine, but very perfumed. It is sometimes said to be halfway between the Cabernet Sauvignon and the Merlot, but in terms of yield and character it is nearer the Cabernet Sauvignon.

MERLOT, with the Cabernet Sauvignon, is the most important and widely planted red grape variety in Bordeaux. Today, it is probably more numerous, particularly in the smaller estates, than any other. Merlot thrives when clay is present, just the conditions that Cabernet dislikes. The yield is more generous than for the Cabernet, but it is very susceptible to *coulure* and also to early rot in wet weather. The wine is highly coloured, lacks the tannin of the cabernet, but produces a good acidity. The wines are also supple and full-flavoured, being higher in alcohol than the Cabernet. Although it is difficult to generalize about this factor, owing to the differing circumstances of age of vines and differences of soil, the difference is probably on average about 1 per cent alcohol by volume. On an average Médoc estate, when both varieties are properly ripe, the Cabernet Sauvignon will give about 11 per cent to 11·5 per cent, while the Merlot will give 12 per cent to 12·5 per cent. In great years, the final pickings will often produce alcohol levels as high as 14 per cent.

MALBEC is a variety which was never planted on a large scale, but most estates had 10 or 15 per cent. Nowadays, it is seldom replanted and few vineyards have more than 5 or 10 per cent, except in Bourg and Blaye where it still finds favour. It is early ripening, producing a high yield of soft, well-coloured wine—not unlike Merlot, but even more susceptible to *coulure*.

PETIT VERDOT, although not planted in quantity, is a very useful ingredient in the general make-up of a vineyard. Of medium yield, it produces wines high in alcohol and acidity which can be useful on light soils, or, where rather a lot of Merlot has been planted, as a corrective. It is a late ripener, and so seldom gives of its best except in the best years, when it makes a valuable contribution towards the completeness and complexity of a wine.

CARMENÈRE is included here for the sake of completeness. It is still found in some Médoc vineyards, but has ceased to have any importance. It is very prone to degeneracy.

White

SAUVIGNON. This is the same *cépage* that has become famous outside Bordeaux in recent years for producing dry, white wines which are distinctly aromatic in character. The best-known examples are Pouilly Fumé and Sancerre, but the vine is to be found in many other areas as well. In Bordeaux it produces both dry and sweet wines. It is noticeable that further north the character of wines produced from this *cépage* is so strong that it becomes difficult to distinguish regional characteristics. However, in Bordeaux, where more ripeness is achieved, a combination of soil and climate gives Sauvignon wines more body and breed, while preserving their elegance. The yield is low. In the best vineyards of Sauternes-Barsac and Graves, wines are hardly ever made from the Sauvignon alone but are a partnership of Sauvignon and Sémillon. This is found to impart the distinctive style and breed of Bordeaux white wine at its best. But in the lesser areas, such as the Entre-Deux-Mers, some properties are now specializing in producing light, dry wines made only from the Sauvignon; such wines are often prone to excessive acidity and suffer from a certain coarseness.

SEMILLON, the most widely planted and distinctive of white Bordeaux *cépages*, is more productive than the Sauvignon and less subject to disease. It is always blended with Sauvignon both in Sauternes-Barsac for sweet wines, and in Graves for dry wines, and is a much under-rated variety. It is interesting to note that some leading Californian estates are now planting it to blend with their Sauvignon, and there are some fine dry Sémillon wines from Australia.

MUSCADELLE is a good yielder producing a distinctive, perfumed wine. It is widely planted in areas such as Premières Côtes producing sweet wines, as well as in Sauternes-Barsac, but is not usually found in the best estates.

It is part of the genius of Bordeaux wines that they reflect first and foremost their origns. That is to say that each district produces distinctive individual wines, and that within each district

28

individual properties produce wines which can be readily distinguished from their neighbours. In other words, it is the soil and the wine maker who reign supreme here. The judicious mixture of *cépages*, creating the *encépagement* of a vineyard, is here the means of displaying the individuality of soil and place—it remains in the background. This is, of course, in marked contrast to Burgundy, where the Pinot Noir very much holds the foreground.

I have often heard it said that a certain claret has strong Cabernet characteristics. I think it truer to say that in Pauillac, where a high proportion of Cabernet Sauvignon is general, the wines have a most distinctive character. But this is as much the character of Pauillac as of the Cabernet Sauvignon which, as with other *cépages* in Bordeaux, enhances the character of the place rather than imparting in a general way its own character. This distinction can be most clearly seen when Bordeaux reds are compared with the single variety wines of other countries, notably California.

It is worth remarking at this point that perhaps the strongest single influence on the present selection of *cépages* in Bordeaux was the phylloxera. This great scourge of the European vineyards was first observed in the vineyards of the palus at Floriac in 1866, but its progress was slow, especially in the Médoc, Graves and Sauternes districts where the soil was less suitable for the spread of the disease. For this reason, the battle against the phylloxera was a long-drawn-out affair. At first, every sort of chemical treatment was tried and vineyards were even subjected to flooding where this was possible. But eventually it became clear that the only sure and permanent remedy was to replant on resistant American root-stocks. Whereas the European vines are of the type *vitis vinifera*, the American vines are of a quite different species—*vitis riparia* and *vitis rupestris*—which are resistant to phylloxera.

The major replanting of the Bordeaux vineyards took place over a period of some twenty years and was hardly completed before the turn of the century. Even after this, many ungrafted vines remained in some vineyards for years to come. It took some time to discover which root-stocks were best suited to the different soils and types of *cépage*. A list of American root-stocks now used in Bordeaux can be found in Cocks & Féret, 12th edition, 1969, pp. 43-4 (see Bibliography). But ultimately, it gave every vineyard owner the opportunity of re-selecting his *encépagement*, and led to a considerable reduction in the number of varieties planted—as a glance at any pre-phylloxera edition of Cocks & Féret will testify. It also meant that work in the vineyards could be mechanized. The old European vines were often propagated by taking a shoot from an existing vine and stapling it into the soil. As soon as it had rooted, it was detached from the scion. This method was particularly used to replace damaged or diseased vines in a vineyard. With the necessity for using only American root-stocks, this form of propagation became impossible.

The grafting itself is naturally a most important process. These days it usually takes place in a nursery rather than *sur place*. This ensures that only successful grafts are used, which is important in times of high labour costs. Matching incisions are made in both the American root-stock and the European cutting; these are then joined together and bound up. The grafts are then usually placed in sand-filled trays for some days to ensure that the European graft is above the soil, so that it cannot root itself and thus run the risk of becoming infected with phylloxera.

While the unique phenomenon of the phylloxera did bring some benefits as well as tragedy, the same cannot be said for other diseases of the vine. These are usually divided into three categories: fungi, animal parasites, and afflictions caused by weather conditions.

After the phylloxera, fungi have actually proved the most serious menace to the Bordeaux vineyards historically. The first to attack Bordeaux was the oidium. This fungus attacks all the green parts of the vine: the young wood, leaves and young, unripe grapes. Small whitish spots appear and rapidly spread. The effect is that leaves curl up and drop off, and grapes darken in colour, split and so dry up. It first appeared in Bordeaux in 1852 and made rapid progress, drastically reducing yields. But by 1858 it had been successfully mastered with the aid of sulphur preparations. Since that time there has never been any difficulty in controlling the disease, provided the weather is not so wet as to make spraying ineffectual. Nowadays, various chemical preparations are available which are more effective than sulphur, although some growers still prefer to use sulphur as certain chemical sprays appear to make grapes less resistant to rot in wet weather.

The mildew arrived in Bordeaux when the phylloxera was at its height, appearing first in 1883. As with the oidium, this fungus attacks the young green parts of the vine, appearing in white spots on the underside of the leaves and yellow-brown patches on top. But unlike oidium, mildew does not cause the grapes to be spoiled so that the yield is affected—rather, it ruins the flavour of the wine. As with oidium, the cure proved to be quickly at hand in the form of a copper sulphate spray, known as Bordeaux mixture. This distinctive bluish spray is now a familiar sight in every vineyard in France and elsewhere, and is still largely preferred to more modern chemical preparations because it is known to be harmless and deals with other pests at the same time.

Black rot is another fungoid pest which originated in the USA. It appears in the form of stems speckled with black on the green parts of the vine, and the grapes shrivel and turn brown. The vines are most susceptible to it in warm, humid conditions. In Bordeaux it has been chiefly noticeable since the last war and especially since 1952. The best treatment is again the copper sulphate spray.

Pourriture grise or grey rot is actually caused by the same fungus that is responsible for *pourriture noble*, that noble rot which produces the fine sweet wines, especially Sauternes. In conditions of alternating rain and sunshine, such as often occur in Bordeaux in September, this rot thrives. It was very prevalent in the sixties and was especially bad in 1963, imparting a sickly flavour to the wine which was also noticeable on the nose. The high incidence of this disease since 1958 had led many growers to believe that some of the chemically-based sprays used in recent years have lowered resistance to this particular disease by making the skins less hardy and so more liable to split. In consequence, many have returned to copper sulphate spraying, and new preparations have also been applied in wet weather specifically to allay the spread of this rot, with notable success.

The last disease in this section is a virus rather than a fungus. Infectious degeneration or *court noué* is today probably the most serious menace in the vineyards of Bordeaux. It is spread in the soil by the vector *xiphema index*. The symptoms are that the leaf turns yellow along its veins and in patches between them; the leaves then become misshapen, shoots bifurcate and multiply laterally and the flowers form double clusters. The disease will form in a small piece of vineyard and then spread slowly through it. The seriousness of the disease lies in the fact that it progressively shortens the life of the vine; it lives in the soil and so will attack a new vine as soon as an infected one is pulled up. At the present time there is no certain remedy, but it is being attacked on two fronts. New petroleum-based disinfectants are being applied to the soil, when an old vineyard is pulled up and before it is replanted. This appears to be meeting with some success, but it is too early to claim more. On the other hand, the Institut National de la Recherche Agronomique is endeavouring, through selection, to produce root-stocks which are resistant. Not surprisingly, it is a topic on which growers are usually reluctant to volunteer information unless asked directly.

The list of animal parasites, is, of course, headed by the phylloxera, the historical effects of which have already been discussed. The disease is caused by a louse or aphid which has a remarkable reproductive system. (See *Sherry* by Julian Jeffs, 3rd edition, Faber, 1982, pp. 169–73, for an excellent description.) It first of all attacks the roots of the vine and then the leaves. The vine withers and eventually dies. This louse is endemic in the North American vineyards where the *vitis riparia* and *vitis rupestris* are resistant to it, but when it was carried into the European vineyards during the 1860s, it rapidly spread, leaving a fearful trail of destruction behind it. As has already been mentioned, the grafting of European vines on to American root-stocks is the only sure remedy. It is usually claimed that this has shortened the life of the vine. One should say, however, that there are still some healthy vines growing in Bordeaux and elsewhere in France, which are first grafts after the phylloxera, planted in the last decade of the nineteenth century. Added to this, a great deal less was known then than now about the selection of the most suitable root-stocks. But the notion that grafted vines have a shorter lifespan than ungrafted ones probably rests mainly on the fact that it is only since the phylloxera that infectious degeneration has appeared—and this is today the major menace to European vineyards.

Next comes a group of three types of moth which produce larvae, which feed on the grape branches or the leaves—*cochylis* and *eudemis*, which attack the grapes themselves, and *pyrpalis*, which attacks both grapes and leaves. It was the *cochylis* which was principally responsible for the very small yield in 1926. I recall Baron Philippe de Rothschild telling me that at Mouton, where they sent out workers prior to the vintage to remove infected berries, several barrels were filled with this destructive grub. The cure today is really good husbandry, that is, spotting the trouble as soon as it starts and spraying immediately with one of the very effective insecticides now available.

Of increasing importance, recently, is the red spider, which attacks the leaves. The cause of its rapid spread is not really understood, but again, continual vigilance and early treatment seem the best answer.

The last group of hazards for the *vigneron* are those attributable to nature—that is, weather and soil.

Chlorosis is a yellowing of the leaves due to an excess of calcium in the soil associated with an iron deficiency. This occurs in Bordeaux on the calcareous soils, and the best remedy seems to be the selection of resistant root-stocks (*vitis berlandieri*).

Coulure is one of the most common problems to be found in the Bordeaux vineyards. It is the dropping of the blossom during the flowering, or of the tiny berries just after the flowering, and is caused by weather conditions. Wet and cold are the main causes, and *coulure* is the chief reason these days for small vintages. 1945 and 1961 are classic examples.

Closely associated with *coulure*, and sometimes confused with it, is *millerandage*. This is when one finds a bunch containing a number of stunted green berries about the size of a green pea. They are hard and never develop any further. This is usually an aftermath of *coulure* and is also caused by unsatisfactory fertilizing conditions during flowering. Like *coulure*, *millerandage*, of course, reduces the size of the crop, but poses an additional problem. Unless the stunted berries are removed when the bunch is cut, they will much increase the acidity of the wine.

Frost is not as dangerous in Bordeaux as in some other regions, but occasionally does very great damage. In more northerly areas, the great danger is spring frost, which just catches the first shoots. As so many of the Bordeaux vineyards lie near one of the great rivers which characterize the region, most of the important areas are generally immune. But areas like the plateaux of St Laurent and Pomerol, as well as parts of the Graves, do occasionally experience very severe frosts, which do great damage. These are usually the black frosts, when the temperature falls well below the normal winter level and freezes the rising sap, killing the vines.

This is what happened in February 1956 and to a lesser extent in March 1977—but the rarity of such occurrences may be judged from the fact that 1956 was the second severest winter in the Gironde since 1709, which was the year that the vineyards of Muscadet were destroyed and the wine froze on the tables at Versailles. Because of the infrequency of frosts, no general frost precautions are taken in Bordeaux.

Hail is not as serious a problem in Bordeaux as it is in the Beaujolais, for example. It is always extremely localized, and often one part of a vineyard will be affected and not another. The most usual time for hail is June and July. The damage is quite dramatic—vines stripped bare of leaves and the wood of the vine itself lacerated with smaller shoots often broken off. Severe hail damage not only greatly reduces the yield in the year it occurs but by damaging the wood, it can affect the following year's crop as well. A certain amount of success has been achieved by letting off rockets to disperse the hail clouds, providing that the local weather station is able to give sufficient warning.

The last major vineyard topic to be discussed in this section is pruning. Pruning itself is a highly technical matter which can only be made intelligible with pictorial aids. Fig. 1 illustrates the methods in use in Bordeaux. The actual work takes up most of the

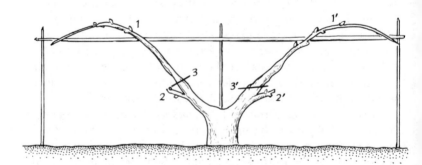

Fig. 1   Pruning methods

1 and 1' are the branches of the year kept after pruning which will bear grapes during the following Summer and Autumn. 2 and 2' are shoots left on old wood which will produce non-fruiting branches. After vintaging, instead of keeping one of the branches growing on 1 and 1', one branch will be selected on 2 and 2' for the following year's crop and the pruning will be done at points marked 3 and 3'.

winter months. Although one often reads in text books that late pruning is advisable to counter the danger of spring frosts, in practice there is too much to be done to leave the job until the new year. No doubt, on particular estates, any parts of the vineyard known by experience to be prone to late frost damage would be left until last. What is interesting about pruning, however, is not the technical details, but the influence it can have on the quality of the wine to be produced. The laws of *Appelation Contrôlée* lay down general rules about pruning for each region, and the *rendement* states how much may be produced in any particular vineyard which can bear the *appellation* and name of the growth. But, in practice, pruning allows the *vigneron* a fairly wide discretion in controlling the yield of his vineyard.

Of course, in a region such as Bordeaux, where nature so often takes a hand in limiting the yield with poor weather during the flowering (*coulure* and *millerandage*) and wet autumns (*pourriture grise*), to say nothing of other diseases, there is a strong temptation not to prune too severely to allow for natural hazards. Years when everything goes right, from the beginning to the end of the season, like 1970, are few and far between. What is undeniable, though, is that husbandry—the effective control of pests and diseases and general care of vineyards—has markedly improved since before the Second World War, and that, as a result, yields are generally higher. The figures show this unmistakably. My guess would be that most *vignerons* are pruning in much the same way they were thirty or forty years ago. It is not this aspect that has changed, but rather the other factors already mentioned. In other words, if all improvements are taken into account, pruning can now afford to be more severe than it was. But if there is a tendency to be discerned, it is probably in the other direction.

So what effect does yield have on quality? This is not a simple question to answer in the Bordeaux context. It is much easier to see that over-production of the Pinot Noir debases quality, not so easy to determine its effect on the more complex *encépagement* of the Bordeaux vineyards. It is evident, for example, that the Cabernet Sauvignon yields less than the Merlot, so presumably there must be an ideal yield which will produce a good quality under the best conditions. This is precisely where the per-mutations become complicated. It is clear that many vineyards in 1961 produced exceptional wines notable for their richness in

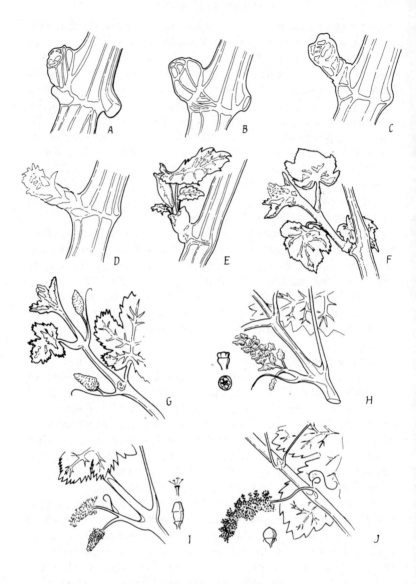

Fig. 2   Principal stages in the evolution of the vine

A. Winter Bud   B. Bud coming through   C. Bud turns green   D. Leaves visible
E. Leaves fully visible   F. Bunches on which grapes will appear are visible
G. Bunches clearly separated from leaves   H. Flower buds already visible   I.
Flowering   J. Setting of the fruit

extract, this with yields perhaps of between 20 and 30 hectolitres to the hectare—depending on the type and age of the vines. It is equally clear that some very disappointing wines were made in 1969 when many yields were also very low. On the other hand, in 1970 some vineyards made over 100 hectolitres per hectare and the wine was acceptable, if usually of very average quality, while some top growths made very fine wines with yields around 60 hectolitres per hectare.

I would suggest that this means that the ideal yield varies according to the conditions of the year. There is certainly some figure above which good wine could not be made in the most perfect conditions. On the other hand, in some years even an average yield will be too much to bring to a satisfactory maturity—given the particular weather conditions. So it looks as if this is likely to remain an inexact science, with the *vigneron* who prunes hard producing the most consistent results, even if the high yielders will sometimes do well.

Another reason for increased yields is the use of fertilizers. I remember being told by old Monsieur Dubos of Cantemerle in the early 1950s that it was his custom to manure his vines only every other year. Today organic manures are hard to come by and the use of artificial fertilizers widespread.

On the other hand, the revision of the *Appellation Contrôlée* regulations on *rendement* in 1974 has introduced both more flexibility and more certainty into this vexed subject, so that the worst excesses of over-cropping are now effectively discouraged, while the variations from year to year are reasonably allowed for.

THE VINTAGE AND THE VINIFICATION

The first and most important decision that has to be taken is when the picking is to begin. An examination of vintaging dates over the last one hundred years shows that, even allowing for inevitable variations, vintaging now begins later than it used to. This is because it is now possible to obtain a fairly accurate idea of the degree of ripeness attained at any particular time in various parts of the vineyard. But it should also be noted that, whereas today the time of one hundred and ten days from the time of flowering to the picking is taken as a reliable guide, nineteenth-century works usually quote ninety days as being the time then allowed.

37

That grapes were picked before they had achieved full ripeness can also be gauged from the alcohol levels obtained. Thus, first growths of the Médoc in the 1840 vintage only showed levels of between 8 per cent and 9 per cent (see Franck, *Vins du Médoc*, 4th edition, 1860), while some Ausones of the 1880s were still only around or below 10 per cent alcohol per volume. Conversely, this meant that the acidity in these wines was much higher than we would find tolerable today. This would also account for the need to keep these wines four or five years in cask before bottling.

Once the use of accurate hydrometers enabled growers to measure the progress of maturation over the weeks leading up to the vintage, there was a natural tendency for some to wait just that little bit longer in the hope of obtaining a better alcohol level. Most growers, however, have been happy to see a good average level and then begin picking while the weather held.

The result of this has been a tendency to forget that sugar content is only one half of the picture. For, as the sugar content of the grapes rises, so the acidity falls. There comes a point where these twin factors achieve an ideal harmony. If the picking is then further delayed, a degree of over-ripeness is reached which is likely to affect the balance and the development of the wine. This, in my view, is why some châteaux today—Lafite immediately springs to mind—are producing much softer but richer wines than they used to. This has much more to do with the degree of ripeness at the picking than with any of the changes in vinification methods which are usually cited as the reason for wines maturing more rapidly. Again, I must stress that this is very much a personal view.

One of the most interesting aspects of vintaging in Bordeaux is the variation in starting dates through the region. St Emilion and Pomerol are always the first to begin, the Graves and Margaux follow, and points in the Médoc further north begin a little later still. It should be emphasized that this is, of course, a generalization; the gaps can be greater or less depending on the conditions of the year. But in the Médoc, for instance, I have known ten days to elapse between the first picking in Margaux and that at Château Loudenne, the IDV property which lies on the boundary of the Haut-Médoc and the Bas-Médoc. 1978 was the only vintage of my experience when vintaging in the Médoc began at the same time as that in St Emilion and Pomerol.

All this is for red wines. The picking of the white grapes usually begins at about the same time as in St Emilion for the red wines, or even earlier. For the great Sauternes it does not usually begin until after the red grape harvest is finished. The most general time for the beginning of the vintage in recent years has been the last week in September. Anything before this is considered early. A start at the beginning of October is late. The Sauternes-Barsac vintage usually begins in early October, and in good years can continue until the early days of November.

What is interesting about all this is the light it throws on the micro-climates of the region. Even a cursory glance at the map will show how diverse it is geographically. The most striking feature is the river system, with the Garonne and the Dordogne converging to produce the Gironde. Then the districts themselves are strongly contrasting, with the flat, gravelly areas of the Graves often heavily wooded, while the Médoc is open and almost bare, with its low-lying slopes descending easily to the river. On the other side of the Gironde and Dordogne, the vineyards lie among much more hilly country, and hilly, attractively wooded country is also to be found in the Premières Côtes, across the Garonne from the Graves. It is therefore hardly surprising to find that vineyards on different sides of large rivers, on differing soils and with differing expositions, contrive to experience small climatic differences. These small differences of rainfall, sunshine and temperature can add up over a season to produce measurably different results, so that not only can a year which is outstanding in St Emilion and Pomerol be only average in Médoc—as was the case in 1964—but results in, say, Margaux can be different to those in St Estèphe, as in 1977. A further insight into the differences within even a small area, can be gauged from the experience of Chardon Père, the famous *régisseur* of Palmer, who used to supervise two other properties in the Margaux *appellation*—Siran at Labarde and Angludet at Cantenac. Over a period of some years, he found that the flowering in each vineyard always began at intervals of a few days from the others, and always in the same order.

The actual process of vintaging is straightforward enough. The pickers these days are drawn from a wide spectrum. Many Spaniards are brought in under contract in much the same way as hop-pickers from London were in England. But on many of the smaller estates, local labour predominates, interspersed with the

39

inevitable students. With the growth of Bordeaux University, the use of these students has much increased. Most of the larger estates both house and feed their vintagers, but those near to Bordeaux often return them there by bus every evening.

Certainly the most important development in harvesting over the next few years is likely to be the introduction of mechanical methods. Over the last five years, great improvements have been made in the design of mechanical harvesters so that it is now possible to use them in vineyards where the vines are still traditionally pruned and the old idea that vineyards would have to be replanted and the vines pruned high is no longer valid. This flexibility has meant that mechanical harvesting is likely to be introduced by many Bordeaux châteaux in the near future and not only by the large properties in the Entre Deux Mers, which are already using them. A demonstration was given at Château Loudenne during the 1979 vintage to show how machines could function in a Médoc vineyard, and it is clear that the flat terrain and large vineyards of the Médoc are particularly well suited to such methods.

Everyone, who has seen the results of mechanically harvested wines has, I think, been agreeably surprised by the quality that can be produced. Several points are worth making. Mechanical harvesting can enable the vintage to be brought in much more speedily. On a large estate, this can be very important and could result in a far higher proportion of the vintage being collected at optimum ripeness, as well as avoiding disappointments when the weather changes. It should not be forgotten that on a large property with a big vintage, such as 1970 or 1979, it can easily take 2–3 weeks to bring in the harvest. Another point is that mechanical harvesting will only remove ripe grapes. Unripe ones are left behind, thus ensuring a more effective selection than is often possible from unskilled hand picking. One of the early problems of mechanical harvesting was oxidation, particularly serious, of course, for white grapes. But now that it is possible to hold the grapes in a container on the machine under inert gas, this problem has been overcome and, indeed, the quality of those white wines which I have tasted from mechanical harvesting has been exceptionally good.

The pickers work their way methodically down the rows of vines, cutting the bunches of grapes and placing them in light wooden baskets called *paniers*. These are then emptied into larger containers called *bennes* carried on the backs of the workers, who walk up and down the rows of vines so that baskets may be emptied as required. When these large *bennes* are full, they are emptied in their turn into a container drawn these days by a tractor, which is waiting nearby. In some places one still sees the traditional round wooden tubs used for this final collection, but they are generally being replaced by a single large steel container. The exception is Sauternes-Barsac, where the smaller wooden tubs are more suitable for the reception of the over-ripe berries. When the container or the wooden tubs are full, the tractor proceeds with them to the vat-house, or *cuvier*.

In difficult years, when rot is prevalent in the vineyards, a system of selection, or *triage*, is carried out. To begin with, the pickers are instructed to remove obviously rotten berries from the bunches as they are picked. But, as many of the pickers are far from skilled, this alone is insufficient. A trellis is therefore set up at one end of the container and the carriers empty their *paniers* on to these trellises. Several experienced pickers then sort the bunches by hand, discarding all rotten berries. This process can also be carried out when the tractor arrives with its load at the *cuvier*, but it is easier and probably more effective when done as described in the vineyard, before too many rotten grapes have become squashed. The dire results experienced in 1963 led to this type of *triage* being used in 1965, and even more extensively in 1968. It is interesting to note that, although conditions in 1968 were similar to the other two years, far better results were obtained, and some wines even resembled the more successful 1960s.

The system for gathering white grapes differs only in the areas producing sweet wines. Here, on the best estates, the pickers go through the vineyard three or four times, selecting only the individual berries or parts of bunches which have been affected by *botrytis cinerea* or *pourriture noble*. This fungus attacks the over-ripe grapes, forming a furry coating on the skins, and has the effect of sucking the water content out of the berry, thus dehydrating it and leaving a far higher concentration of sugar.

When the grapes arrive at the *cuvier*, the procedure for red and white grapes diverges. The red grapes are emptied into a V-shaped receptacle with a large stainless steel screw running along the bottom of it. This draws the bunches into the *fouloir-égrappoir*, which destalks the grapes and gently breaks the skins. This is often referred to in English as a de-stalker and crusher, but this is rather misleading. The grapes are not really crushed so much as broken, just sufficiently to allow the fermentation to begin. The resulting pulp is then pumped into the fermentation vat or *cuve*.

The traditional Bordeaux *cuve* is wooden and cylindrical in shape (fig. 3). The top is covered by wooden sections which can easily be removed. In the 1920s, the first concrete vats lined with tiles were installed. One of the first was built at Loudenne in 1920. The latest innovation is the stainless steel *cuve*, first installed at Haut Brion and then at Latour.

Fig. 3   The traditional Bordeaux cuve

In most traditional *cuviers*, the wooden *cuves* are freestanding. This arrangement can still be seen at Lafite and Calon Ségur. But in the 1860s and 1870s, a series of *cuviers* was built where a wooden floor was inserted, level with the top of the vats. The grapes were then unloaded at this first floor level, which made the filling of the vats easier in the days before electrical pumping. This arrangement may still be seen at Mouton and Pontet Canet, amongst others.

Originally, the de-stalking was done by hand on a table with a sort of griddle top, the stalk of the bunch being held and the bunch rubbed on the griddle until all the grapes had been rubbed off. This practice only survives now as an occasional practice at Palmer and Pichon Lalande, principally as a method of *triage* in poor years. It is interesting to note, however, that Professor Amerine believes that hand *égrappage* is actually less efficient than with the present mechanical *égrappoir*, because it separates the berries from the stalk less cleanly, allowing a certain amount of oil and tannin from the stalk into the must ('The Golden Ages of Wine', lecture given in July 1969 to the Institute of Masters of Wine).

Once the grapes are in the vats, the fermentation begins. The natural yeasts which come from the skins of the grapes rapidly get to work, changing the sugar in the grapes into alcohol and at the same time extracting colour and tannin from the skins. For red wines, cultured yeasts are seldom used in Bordeaux. As more work is done in their selection, however, it is likely that cultured yeasts could come to play a larger part in wine-making in difficult years where off-flavours are a real problem.

When the fermentation is under way, the solid matter in the grapes, mostly skins and pips, rises to the top of the vat to form what is known as the *chapeau*, or cap. Great vigilance is now required on the part of the wine-maker. He must watch the temperature carefully and he must not allow the *chapeau* to become dry and hard. The very act of fermentation releases energy in the form of heat, but if this is allowed to rise too much, the fermentation itself is endangered. Just as, if the temperature is too low, the yeasts are inhibited from beginning their work, so if it rises too high, an environment is created where Aceto-bactea flourish, and vinegar will result. 35°C is regarded as the upper safety limit, and most wine-makers prefer a fermentation at around 28°–30°C. The other associated problem is that the *chapeau* gets a good deal hotter than the must below it, and if it is allowed to get dry and its temperature goes unchecked, bacteria rapidly breed and these can again produce vinegar. So the system called *remontage* is employed. This consists simply of drawing off the must from the bottom of the vat and pumping it to the top, where it is poured on top of the *chapeau* and so permeates it. If the general temperature is considered to be getting too high, the must will be passed through a simple device like a milk-cooler, where cold water flows over the pipes through which the wine is pumped. More sophisticated devices are also now in operation. Where stainless steel vats are in use, a thermostat can turn on cold water which runs down the sides of the vats to reduce the temperature. But one of the most ingenious solutions is that pioneered by Monsieur Henri Woltner at La Mission Haut-Brion. Here, after experimenting for several years with one or two trial vats,

Monsieur Woltner installed a complete system of vitrified steel vats in 1950. Painted white, their slightly corpulent appearance makes them look somewhat like ships' boilers. Their size and construction keep the fermenting must at a steady temperature by losing heat, and the *maître de chais* says that since their installation in 1950, the temperature has never risen above 30°C, so that other cooling methods have not been necessary. Curiously, this very successful system has yet to be copied elsewhere, although it is cheaper than the stainless steel favoured by Haut Brion and Latour. The submerged cap method, generally favoured in hot countries, is another solution. Here, the cap is held down by a wooden grill, and the carbon dioxide released by the fermentation forces the must up through a pipe and so on to the top of the cap. This has the advantage of controlling the temperature and moisture of the cap automatically, and of extracting colour more rapidly. The disadvantage is that there is some danger of oxidation. This method is now used at Branaire.

During the fermentation, a chart is kept on each vat, showing both the temperature and the progress being made in converting the sugar into alcohol. It is watched just as carefully as any patient's chart on a hospital bed. The time required to complete the fermentation varies considerably, both from year to year and from district to district. I have observed, for instance, that generally fermentation seems to be completed more rapidly in St Emilion and Pomerol than in Médoc. One year, when it was taking eight or nine days in the Médoc, it was generally being completed in four or five days the other side of the river. It is difficult to know what the explanation can be for this, unless it has something to do with the different *encépagement* of the vineyards.

Once the alcoholic fermentation has actually finished, the new wine is drawn off into the traditional Bordeaux barrels of 225 litres. Some châteaux do this almost immediately, others follow the more traditional practice and keep the wine in vat in the hope of extracting more colour and tannin from the skins. But whereas vatting for upwards of a month was once usual, now ten days to a fortnight is the maximum. Some châteaux now prefer to keep the wine in vat, at least until the malolactic fermentation (see p. 50) is complete. In difficult years, or when colour but not too much tannin are required, some châteaux heat the must. The results are inconclusive. I myself feel that such wines tend to flatter at first

44

but disappoint later on, just when one would expect them to be reaching their best.

The process for white wines differs in a number of important respects, and there are differences between the production of dry and sweet wines as well. To begin with, the stalks are not removed. This is because the juice must be quickly separated, so that no colouring is picked up, and retaining the stalks makes the pressing easier. To illustrate the point, I shall always remember Monsieur Jean Quancard telling a Study Course session for the Master of Wine Examination that, as a young man in the trade, he had wondered why the stalks were retained for white grapes. When first he was put in charge of overseeing the reception of a vintage, he thought he would experiment and de-stalk some white grapes to see what happened. When the grapes were put in the press, the must shot out all over him! This, of course, was the old type of hydraulic press now only used in some of the most traditional Sauternes estates such as Yquem (fig. 4).

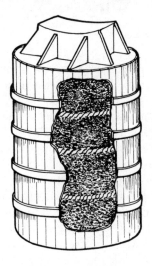

Fig. 4   The traditional hydraulic press

Most white wines are today made with the aid of the cylindrical presses (fig. 5) which are so familiar in Germany, on the Loire, and indeed for the production of most white wines. As the juice is run off, it is either pumped straight into casks or vats to begin the fermentation, or goes into a *cuve* for the process known as *débourbage*. This simply means that the juice is sulphured just sufficiently to arrest the onset of the fermentation, and then rests in a *cuve* for about twenty-four hours, during which time any solid matter can fall to the bottom. When the fermentation begins, it is likely to proceed more satisfactorily with a relatively clean must; also, the wine will not have to be racked so often, which is always an important consideration with white wines where handling must be kept to a minimum to guard against oxidation.

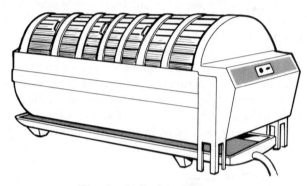

Fig. 5   Cylindrical presses

In Bordeaux, it is traditional for the fine Graves and Sauternes to have their fermentation in cask. But, with the increasing demand for white wines which are light, fresh and fruity, many properties now ferment in *cuve*. Loudenne, which makes one of the few white wines in the Médoc, has a model installation of this type. The *cuves* are of stainless steel and small in size (containing only 20 hectolitres each). By running cold water down the sides, the temperature of the fermentation can be controlled and kept down to a maximum of 18°C, far cooler than would otherwise be possible. This much enhances the delicacy and flavour of the wine.

For sweet wines, the process is slightly different. Again, the stalks are not removed. Since the grapes are already over-ripe, the pressure of the bunches tends to break the skins and cause the juice to begin to flow. The traditional process in Sauternes is for the bunches to be emptied straight into the presses on arrival at the *cuvier* where the weight of the grapes causes a certain amount of the juice to run off. The grapes are then pressed in the normal manner. Many properties today, of course, use the more modern type of press already described.

46

One important topic has not so far been mentioned: chaptalization. This is the adding of sugar to the must (i.e. the grape juice before it has begun fermenting) in order to raise the alcoholic strength of a wine. This process takes its name from Jean-André Chaptal, a noted French chemist, who suggested the idea at the beginning of the nineteenth century, although it was a very long time before his ideas were adopted.

It is only since 1938 that chaptalization has been permitted in Bordeaux, and then not generally. The authorities (l'Institut National des Appellations d'Origine, or INAO) take a decision each year, when growers make an application just before the vintage; this is in contrast to Burgundy, where there is general permission every year. There has been a definite tendency in recent years for permission to be given more frequently.

There is still a feeling in some quarters that there is something faintly indecent in sugaring the must. Nothing could be further from the truth, provided that it is not overdone. Chaptalization is desirable and necessary when the sugar content of the grapes falls short of what is normal for a good year—in other words, when the grapes do not reach perfect maturity. This can sometimes happen because there is a larger crop than usual and only an average amount of sunshine, or weather conditions may compel growers to pick earlier than they would wish, to save the crop. Whatever the reason, there can be no doubt that in recent years many wines have been much improved in this way. Most authorities in Bordeaux agree that the alcoholic content should not be raised by more than 1–1½ per cent by volume by this method, an example which unfortunately few Burgundians follow. Happily, there is as yet no fetish in Bordeaux about alcohol—certainly as far as red wines are concerned—and this limit is generally respected.

I have sometimes heard it suggested that in some mysterious way chaptalized wines have a 'sweet' taste which is discernible, in spite of the fact that all the sugar is, of course, turned into alcohol. The real cause of this impression is that chaptalization, by increasing the alcohol in a wine, changes its balance slightly and incidentally helps to precipitate cream of tartar. This makes the wine seem softer and less acid than it might otherwise be, and, incidentally, more agreeable to drink.

The system of vinification I have described is, in essence, the same as that used over very many years. What is meant therefore

47

when wine lovers speak darkly of changed methods of vinification? This is, of course, all part of that age-old belief that things are not what they were; and indeed, it is fortunate for the average wine drinker that they are not. It is very unusual nowadays for wines to be spoiled by volatile acidity, for example. In other words, wines are much more consistent than they used to be because the fermentation is better controlled. It is this ability to control more precisely which differentiates today's wine maker from his predecessors, and so serious mistakes are far rarer—the result, usually, of pure negligence.

The main differences, then, in the vinification of red wines in Bordeaux are the vatting of wines after the alcoholic fermentation has finished, and the control of temperature during the actual process of fermentation. Of the two, I would have no hesitation in saying that the control of temperature is by far the more important. This is not simply a matter of preventing the wine from spoiling by becoming too warm, although this is important enough when one remembers that as recently as 1945 half the crop at Cheval Blanc had to be pasteurized. Just as important are the positive benefits to be obtained by a cooler, and therefore longer, fermentation. Monsieur Henri Woltner at La Mission Haut-Brion was certainly one of the pioneers of what he called the *fermentation froide*. What this really means is a long, cooler fermentation with the temperature held at below 30°C. This seems to produce very well-balanced wines with plenty of colour, and sufficient but not excessive tannin, so that the wine can be drunk with pleasure when relatively young, but will have the potential for ageing as well.

Special mention must be made of Dr Emile Peynaud of the Station Agronomique et Oenologique of Bordeaux. His forty years of service to Bordeaux has done more than anything else to update this innately conservative region. It has been in the last twenty years that his labours have really borne fruit, and the culmination came when he was called in in the mid-1970s by Lafite and Margaux to advise them. It has become something of a standard joke in the Médoc for a proprietor to announce that Professor Peynaud is in charge. In fact, of course, it is more a question of establishing the right systems, seeing there is a competent manager, or *maître de chais*, to carry them out, and then just keeping an eye on things. The 1960s and 1970s have certainly been the Peynaud era in Bordeaux.

Balance is really the key word. The idea that wines will not last unless they have a lot of tannin, or that if wines are drinkable early they cannot last, is certainly erroneous. Very tannic wines may not be drinkable for many years, but will not be any the better for their long period of gestation unless they also have plenty of fruit and good acidity. Some 1928s have ultimately proved disappointing after a very long wait, and the same can be said of some 1937s and 1945s. To go back even further, contemporary writers reported that the 1900s were delicious at a very early stage, and for this reason it was thought that they would not last so well as the harder 1899s. My own experience of the two vintages in the 1960s, when I was fortunate enough to taste a number of bottles, is that the 1900s were still superb—I have never had a poor bottle— while the 1899s were fading and are now less consistent. Indeed, so-called light vintages nearly always seem to last well.

The part played by long vatting is doubtful, if the fermentation has been controlled in the manner described. I would suspect that with the longer, cooler fermentation, not much is likely to be gained by vatting for more than ten days or so.

Ultimately, this argument calls in question the basis on which we judge our wines. Is there any merit in longevity in itself? It is very fascinating to drink a bottle of claret which is 100 years old, but one must recognize that this is a curiosity and that it is not the object of the wine maker to produce a wine which will live indefinitely, since very few bottles indeed will have the opportunity to be tasted in this way. Rather, I would suggest that our judgement would be better based on some sort of hedonic scale, by which the prize went to the wine that could be drunk with pleasure for the longest time in the first twenty to thirty years of its life. On such a reckoning, the 1953s would clearly come out above the 1945s, as would the 1961s—the first vintage of this type to benefit from something approaching control.

HANDLING THE WINES FROM VINIFICATION TO BOTTLING

The French term for this process has always seemed to me very apt. *Elevage* carries the suggestion of rearing a delicate or perhaps difficult child. Applied to wine, it rightly implies the continued care and vigilance necessary.

We left the red wines with their alcoholic fermentation complete, racked off their fermentation vats. Although the tradition is to put them straight in cask, some properties keep the wine in *cuve* through the first winter, which tends to hold back the wines somewhat. When the wine is kept in cask, the loss through evaporation is, of course, more serious, and the wines are usually topped up every few days to keep them full to the bung, which at this stage is only placed lightly in the bung hole and is not driven home. For, although the alcoholic fermentation is finished, the malolactic fermentation now follows, during which a certain amount of carbon dioxide is given off, and the presence of some air is in any case desirable for this.

The malolactic fermentation is the changing of the malic acid in the wine into lactic acid. This greatly reduces the tartness, or apparent acidity of the wine, and is an essential process in its development. The actual process is chemically very complex and, until recently, was surrounded more by folklore than by science. What had been observed was that the timing and duration of the malolactic fermentation varied greatly from vintage to vintage, and even from property to property within the same vintage. As it now appears that no fewer than eighteen different amino-acids must be present for the fermentation to function normally, the complexity of the process may be more readily imagined. In a wine such as Beaujolais, the malolactic fermentation often occurs concurrently with the alcoholic fermentation. In Bordeaux, the process usually begins soon after the completion of the alcoholic fermentation and continues through the winter, finishing around March. Sometimes it is much slower to start, particularly if the weather in November and December is very cold. In such cases, it may not begin before the spring, and can continue into the summer months.

It is usual for the best growths to use new casks to receive each new vintage. These casks are made of oak. Before the war, the best oak was said to come from Memel in Lithuania; today, French Limousin oak as well as American oak is used. The use of new wood imparts a certain amount of additional tannin to the wine, as well as incurring a greater loss through evaporation. This loss of wine is an important factor in the cost of *élevage*, and is reckoned to amount to between 7 per cent and 8 per cent in the first year, decreasing to 4 per cent and 5 per cent in subsequent years. While it is normal practice for those who can afford it to put new wine into new wood, there are different opinions as to whether this is invariably the best procedure. That gifted and thoughtful wine maker, Monsieur Henri Woltner, believed that, in light vintages, new oak tended to mask the characteristics of the wine with its own. I have certainly seen cases where this has happened, while La Mission's remarkable run of good off-years is eloquent testimony to the success of Henri Woltner's approach. For purely economic reasons, many leading growers today only put between a third and a half of the new vintage in new oak.

Another important part of the maturation process is the racking of the wine. This is simply the drawing off of the wine from one cask, or *cuve*, to another, so as to leave the lees, or deposit, which have accumulated at the bottom, intact. In the process the wine is, of course, aerated to some extent. The amount of racking depends very much on the constitution of the wine. A robust, full-bodied wine will be racked more frequently than a delicate, light one. Traditionally, the first racking occurs in March, the second at the end of June—coinciding with the flowering—the third in October, after which the wine is placed on three-quarter bung, so that the bung is covered by the wine. A recent development is that some châteaux now put their wines on three-quarter bung in the spring, after the second racking, this has the advantage of reducing evaporation and thus costs. If things go according to plan, the malolactic fermentation will have finished just before the March racking, and the new wines may be properly judged for the first time when they have settled down after the racking.

The wine also has to be fined, a process which helps to remove unstable elements, so bringing it forward to the time when it may be bottled. The traditional fining is with white of eggs, and this is still done in many châteaux. But in *négociants'* cellars, where several thousand casks may have to be fined at any one time, this is hardly practical, and gelatine is used instead. Again, the number of finings depends on the constitution of the wine—two finings are usual, but three may be needed on occasion.

The decision when to bottle is clearly most important. These days, there is a tendency to bottle rather earlier than used to be the case; this helps to preserve the fruit and can make the wine agreeable to drink at an earlier stage without in any way affecting its keeping properties. The correct fining prior to bottling will ensure that the deposit which will eventually form in bottle in most years will not be any heavier than would have been the case had the wine been bottled later. It has thus become common for even classified growths to bottle in the summer or even late spring of the second year, instead of during the third winter, perhaps on average six months earlier. Even the first growths have now abandoned their tradition of bottling in the March of the third year.

My personal experience has certainly been in favour of earlier bottling. When, on occasion, I have seen wines which for one reason or another were bottled late, they invariably seem to dry up after several years in bottle. This would appear to confirm the belief that if wines are kept too long in cask, they may lose fruit and become tough in bottle. It is also important to maintain a flexible approach to the bottling time—vintages like 1975 required longer in wood to develop their characteristics than a lighter vintage like 1976.

Much has been written on the subject of English bottling versus château bottling. It should be remembered that if an English merchant announces his intentions to bottle in England at the time the wine is purchased, the Bordeaux *négociant* will invariably bring the wine into his own cellars for the *élevage*—so that this will not be identical with the wine to be château bottled. The process of shipping in bulk ages the wine to some extent and unsettles it. Certainly, the English bottling of robust wines is invariably more successful than that of light off-vintage years. But, finally, it means that there will be a number of different versions of the same wine, however carefully it is handled. This is why the leading properties now prefer to keep the bottling under their own control. When I have had the opportunity of comparing English against château-bottled wines from the same vintage, I have found the château-bottled ones to be almost invariably superior. The most noticeable difference is that the château-bottled wines have more bouquet, and more roundness and fruit on the palate.

The *élevage* of white wines has changed far more than that of red wines—as has their vinification—and for the same reason. White wines vinified to emphasize their freshness and fruit are usually not kept in cask at all now, but are bottled in the spring or early summer after only a single fining and racking. Some of the finest Graves, however, are still matured in cask, and are not normally bottled until the second winter or the following spring. Such wines, of course, develop more character in bottle and last longer. These very early bottlings, however, do provide fresh attractive wines which are very enjoyable and a welcome change from the general run of over-sulphured wines which for too long were synonymous with the cheaper white Bordeaux.

The great Sauternes, and indeed all the sweet wines to some degree, take much longer to clarify than either dry white wines or red wines. Because of the concentration of sugar in the must, and the inevitably dirty state of a must obtained by pressing grapes infected by *pourriture noble*, the actual alcoholic fermentation takes far longer than for other wines. In a successful year, a Sauternes must will obtain a Baumé reading of 20 degrees, and up to 24 degrees in exceptional years. The fermentation in cask progresses very slowly, sometimes for nearly a year, until the alcoholic level inhibits any further work by the yeasts. Even so, the top Sauternes growths can achieve 15 per cent or 16 per cent alcohol by volume, with anything between 4 degrees and 7 degrees Baumé of unfermented sugar left. But, if the grapes are uniformally botrytized, this inhibits the fermentation so that it can be successfully finished with only 13·5 per cent to 14 per cent alcohol. This produces a fruitier, better balanced wine than one with over 15 per cent. Failure to pick at the right moment can thus produce wines with an alcoholic 'burn' and a lack of finesse—as happened in 1975.

Traditionally, these wines remain in cask for three years, and the practice is still observed at Yquem. But, increasingly, growers believe that it is better to bottle after two years, preventing oxidation and preserving freshness. Many experts believe that the extra year in cask does not achieve anything useful now that better fining agents, such as bentonite, are available to correct any faults in the wine, and that it is better not to expose the wine to the danger of oxidation.

BOTTLING AND MATURATION IN BOTTLE

The traditional Bordeaux bottle has become so synonymous with the region, that bottles of this shape are referred to as Bordeaux bottles, even in other countries such as Italy. Its distinct and classic outlines are common to both red and white wines. The bottle holds 0.75 litres. The long, straight neck is ideal for holding the long, hard, straight corks for which Bordeaux is justly famous. Certainly, no finer corks are used anywhere, and their lasting powers are ample testimony to this quality. When wines are kept for very long periods, as in the magnificent private cellars at Lafite and Mouton, which certainly contain the finest libraries of Bordeaux wines in the region, the practice is to recork every twenty-five years. This is not to say that the corks will not last longer, but at this age all corks should be able to be drawn without problems—at a later stage there will be some which will have deteriorated. The oldest cork I have drawn intact from an old claret was a Latour 1909, which would then have been over fifty years old. Even more remarkable was the perfectly preserved cork in a bottle of Guiraud 1893. Something in the constitution of this great Sauternes seemed to have preserved its cork—perhaps the sugar and lower acidity than would be found in a red wine.

The actual bottling was until recently still carried out at many properties directly from the cask without any sort of filtration. This is, of course, a slow business, and now that compulsory château-bottling is becoming more general, more châteaux assemble their wines into bottling tanks and then gravity-feed through a light polishing filter. This is perhaps even more essential for white wines, which must be star-bright on bottling and remain so.

The maturation in cask is a relatively rapid business during which the wines find their equilibrium and dispose of unwanted impurities and unstable elements. Once the wine has been bottled, a much slower form of maturation begins. For the first few months after bottling, red wines often suffer from bottle sickness during which time it is impossible to judge them or indeed drink them. After this, the steady, even tenure of maturation continues, its timing and shape determined by the constitution of the wine.

The simplest way of explaining the life of a bottle of fine claret or Sauternes is in graph form (fig. 6). The initial stage of maturation is highly flexible. For some 1967s, 1971s or 1973s, it has amounted to as little as two years in bottle. On the other hand, in years like 1945 or 1937, and even in some 1961s and 1970s, this stage may have lasted for ten years. Two years in bottle for Bourg, Blaye, Fronsac and the lesser St Emilions and Pomerols is about average; three to five years for the better St Emilions, Pomerols, most

54

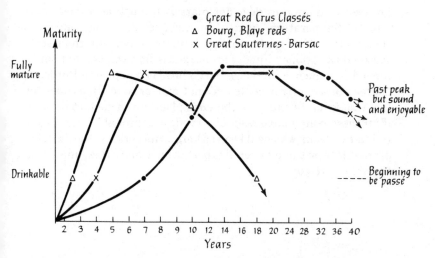

Fig. 6   Graph illustrating the life of a bottle of claret or Sauternes

Graves and Médocs is probably about right. At the end of this stage, the wine is enjoyable to drink, but its full potential has not yet been reached. This second stage may be longer than the first; on average it is usually rather similar. Then one can say that the wine is truly mature. The line on our graph here levels out, and most of the finest wines will continue steadily at about this level for twenty, thirty, fifty years, before beginning on a downward path. Of course, lesser wines, such as those of Bourg and Blaye, will seldom remain at their peak for more than about five years. The finest white Graves are usually at their best in about five years, and will keep for between ten and twenty years. The great Sauternes take longer to reach their peak, as the alcohol and sugar have to mellow and achieve harmony. This usually takes seven to ten years in the best vintages. But these wines may stay at their best, before beginning to lose fruit and sugar, for a further ten to twenty years, and in exceptional cases for longer still. Very luscious wines like Yquem sometimes mature more rapidly, and pass their peak more quickly.

Finally, it should be emphasised that storage conditions during this maturation in bottle are of supreme importance, and this is the principal reason why some bottles keep better than others.

Dryness or dampness does not matter so much as a reasonable steady temperature, which in turn means that an even temperature from night to day is more important than some seasonal variations. Equally important is that wine should not be moved too much. Whether a bottle has been kept in a Bordeaux château or a Scottish castle does not matter so much as does the fact that it has remained in the same place untouched. In the end, if all these points have been observed, it is probably true to say that a Bordeaux wine will keep as long as its cork. At the first sign of trouble from this quarter, it is best to open and drink, unless you are able to re-cork.

3

Classifications old and new

We are told that the desire to categorize is very French, but I suspect that to argue on the respective merits of well-tried favourites is a universal pastime. Horse racing has its form book, and cricket lovers spend the winter months selecting their World XIs or England pre-1900 *v.* England post-1920 XIs. The French being an essentially practical people, their classifications of wines have usually had a strictly commercial rather than a mainly esoteric purpose.

Classifications are first recorded in the eighteenth century in the Médoc, and also in Bourg, a district then more favoured than the Médoc. It seems clear that they were essentially the grouping together by price of the best-known wines. In the Médoc there were normally four categories: the first always extremely small, the second only slightly larger, then the third and fourth often merging into one another. Such lists were compiled by brokers (*courtiers*), merchants and by wine enthusiasts. What is noticeable, when comparing various lists compiled in the thirty years prior to 1855, is that while a fair degree of unanimity existed about the first and second categories, there were wide divergencies lower down the scale. There were also frequent comings and goings. Because nothing was official, nothing was fixed and this helped to keep interest and ambition alive.

When, almost by accident, one particular list received official status in 1855, the process of change and renewal received a setback, and a living tradition became ossified. This all happened when the organizers of the great Exposition Universelle of Paris invited the Bordeaux Chamber of Commerce to produce a representative selection of the wines of Bordeaux. This Exhibition was the first great *manifestation* organized to display the splendour of Napoleon III's new Empire. The Chamber of

Commerce decided that each commune should be represented by an example under a neutral label, but that the great estates of Bordeaux should also be represented. So as to decide in the most impartial way possible on such a selection, the brokers attached to the Bordeaux Bourse were invited to prepare a list. This they duly did, basing it on the state of the market at that moment. Certainly, it bears a strong resemblance to previous unofficial lists, but with many understandable variations in the lower echelons. Had this list not then become enshrined like some law of the Medes and Persians, it most surely would have continued to evolve and change, not in its essentials but in details, as is healthy and normal in any living body.

It is often said by supporters of the status quo that there is no need to revise the old classification, since it was essentially a classification of the soil, and this is something which does not change. Unfortunately this is only a half-truth. The actual composition of many of the classified growth vineyards has changed, often radically. This is because there is nothing to prevent one proprietor from buying new pieces of vineyard in times of prosperity, and another from selling up pieces in difficult times. After a hundred years, the name of a property may be the same, but the actual vineyard may be quite different from what it was at the beginning. In effect, it is the château name that is classified and not the vineyard. Another problem is that since every château wine is an assemblage from all parts of the vineyard, it is not easy to know what differing qualities each part of the vineyard produces. This is something probably only learnt with much experience by a *maître de chais* or a really knowledgeable and interested owner. In the end, therefore, we can only judge a château by the wine it actually produces. Even the price fetched over a period of years is not quite such a reliable guide as it once was, due to differing marketing methods employed by various proprietors. Price is a factor, however, which must play an important part in classifying a wine, and certainly cannot be ignored in any realistic assessment.

Let us now look in more detail at the Médoc classifications. The pre-1855 classifications were unanimous about the first growths— Lafite, Margaux, Latour and Haut-Brion. The second growths of two early classifications, in the possession of Ronald Barton, and that of Charles Cocks compare as follows:

58

1824	1827	1846	
Brane Mouton	Brane Mouton	Mouton	
Rauzan	Rauzan	Léoville	{ Poyferré Barton Marquis de Las Cases
Lascombes	Léoville		
Durefort (de Vivens)	Gruau-la-Rose	Rauzan	
Gorse		Durefort	
Léoville		Gruaud-Larose	
Gruau-La-Rose		Lascombes	
		Gorse	

As can be seen, the lists are remarkably consistent, the unfamiliar name of Gorse being the present Brane-Cantenac, and all seven names appeared as second growths in the 1855 list. But by then, the qualities of Pichon, Ducru-Beaucaillou, Cos d'Estournel and the newcomer, Montrose, were recognized as entitling them to a place in this elevated company.

Today, Mouton is officially a first growth, after being recognized as such for many years; indeed, Mouton's original position as a second growth was already rather anomalous in 1855, as its price was poised between the rest of the seconds and the firsts. The two Rauzans have rather fallen from grace in recent years, and it would be difficult today to place them among the second growths. The vineyard of Durefort has gone through so many vicissitudes that it can hardly be said to be the same wine that it was, and certainly at the moment takes second place to Brane-Cantenac. The same could be said of Lascombes, although for a brief period when Alexis Lichine was reconstructing the vineyard, this growth looked like taking its rightful place among the best ones again. But what growths would be added to the seconds? My own list would be Beychevelle, Calon-Ségur, Palmer, La Lagune and Lynch-Bages.

It has been suggested that a new classification should consist of only three groups instead of five. This was the formula adopted by the INAO in their abortive proposals of 1960. But although this would seem a simpler and tidier arrangement in principle, in practice I do not believe it is a solution which best accords with the facts. Looking back at the 1855 classification there is, of course, a very clear difference in quality between the seconds and the bulk of the fifths. But if one then examines the thirds and fourths, one finds certainly a few which could go down to the fifths. Equally, there are among the fifths a number of candidates for promotion, but while several are worthy of entry into an intermediate category, few indeed would be serious contenders for the seconds.

What I am saying is that there exists a substantial gulf in quality and usually in price, between the seconds and fifths, which demands an intermediary category. But certainly there is no real case for two intermediary categories, so that what I would favour is a classification into four groups. This is really one of my main criticisms of Alexis Lichine's classification. When one examines in detail his third, fourth and fifth groups, in so far as they concern the Médoc, one cannot help feeling that some of the distinctions are artificial and serve no real purpose. Having said that, I think that Alexis Lichine's action in preparing and publishing his classification was a bold and imaginative gesture, aimed no doubt at shaking the Bordeaux establishment from its lethargy. To those who say that no new classification is needed because 1855 is still fine—for the most part—the answer must surely be that it is good for every institution to be scrutinized and reformed from time to time. The 1855 classification was a historic landmark, but it is now a piece of ancient history and it is high time we moved on into the twentieth century before we find ourselves in the twenty-first. To those who say classifications serve no useful purpose, therefore why bother with them, I would say that they do provide a useful guide to the consumer, and if the proprietors did not think them important, there would not be so much wrangling on the subject. From the point of view of healthy competition, there is much to be said for clearing away the cobwebs and introducing a completely new classification, which would show some promotions and relegations compared to the 1855 list. There should then be regular reviews—as in St Emilion—again, with the possibility of promotions and relegations. This would certainly provide a most healthy stimulus for proprietors, especially for those lowly placed, who would be keen to improve their position, or to avoid being relegated at the very least, and for the proprietors of the best unclassified growths, who would at last have the possibility of recognition.

Having stated what I believe to be the case for a new classification, let us take another look at Alexis Lichine's classification. I have already said that I think four categories

ALEXIS LICHINE'S
CLASSIFICATION DES GRANDS CRUS

Crus Hors Classé (Outstanding Growths)

MÉDOC
Château Lafite-Rothschild
(*Pauillac*)
Château Latour (*Pauillac*)
Château Margaux (*Margaux*)
Château Mouton-Rothschild
(*Pauillac*)

GRAVES
Château Haut-Brion (*Pessac, Graves*)

ST ÉMILION
Château Ausone
Château Cheval-Blanc

POMEROL
Château Pétrus

Crus Exceptionnels
(Exceptional Growths)

MÉDOC
Château Beychevelle (*St Julien*)
Château Brane-Cantenac
(*Cantenac-Margaux*)
Château Calon-Ségur (*St Estèphe*)
Château Cos d'Estournel (*St Estèphe*)
Château Ducru-Beaucaillou (*St Julien*)
Château Gruaud-Larose (*St Julien*)
Château Lascombes (*Margaux*)
Château Léoville-Barton (*St Julien*)
Château Léoville-Las-Cases (*St Julien*)
Château Léoville Poyferré (*St Julien*)

Château Lynch-Bages
(*Pauillac*)
Château Montrose (*St Estèphe*)
Château Palmer (*Cantenac-Margaux*)
Château Pichon-Longueville
(Baron) (*Pauillac*)
Château Pichon-Lalande
(*Pauillac*)

GRAVES
*Domaine de Chevalier
(*Léognan*)
*Château La Mission-Haut-Brion (*Pessac*)
Château Pape-Clément (*Pessac*)

ST ÉMILION
Château Figeac
Château la Gaffelière
Château Magdelaine

POMEROL
Château La Conseillante
Château l'Évangile
Château Lafleur
Château La Fleur-Pétrus
Château Trotanoy

Grands Crus (Great Growths)

MÉDOC
Château Branaire (*St Julien*)
Château Cantemerle (*Haut-Médoc*)
Château Cantenac-Brown
(*Cantenac-Margaux*)
Château Duhart-Milon-Rothschild (*Pauillac*)
Château Durfort-Vivens
(*Cantenac-Margaux*)
*Château Giscours (*Labarde-Margaux*)

*These wines are considered better than their peers in this classification.

61

Grand Crus (MÉDOC)
continued

Château d'Issan (*Cantenac-Margaux*)
Château La Lagune (*Haut-Médoc*)
Château Malescot-Saint-Exupéry (*Margaux*)
Château Mouton-Baronne-Philippe (*Pauillac*)
Château Pontet-Canet (*Pauillac*)
*Château Prieuré-Lichine (*Cantenac-Margaux*)
Château Rauzan-Gassies (*Margaux*)
Château Rausan-Ségla (*Margaux*)
Château Talbot (*St Julien*)

GRAVES
*Château Haut-Bailly (*Léognan*)

ST ÉMILION
Château Beauséjour-Bécot
Château Bel-Air
*Château Canon
Clos Fourtet
Château Pavie
Château Trottevieille

POMEROL
Château Gazin
Château Latour Pomerol
Château Petit-Village
Vieux-Château-Certan

Crus Supérieurs (Superior Growths)

MÉDOC
Château Batailley (*Pauillac*)
Château Boyd-Cantenac (*Cantenac-Margaux*)
Château Chasse-Spleen (*Moulis*)

Château Clerc-Milon-Rothschild (*Pauillac*)
Château Gloria (*St Julien*)
Château Grand-Puy-Lacoste (*Pauillac*)
Château Haut-Batailley (*Pauillac*)
Château Kirwan (*Cantenac-Margaux*)
Château Lagrange (*St Julien*)
Château Langoa (*St Julien*)
Château Marquis d'Alesme-Becker (*Margaux*)
Château La Tour-Carnet (*Haut-Médoc*)

GRAVES
Château Bouscaut (*Cadaujac*)
Château Carbonnieux (*Léognan*)
Château Fieuzal (*Léognan*)
Château Malartic-Lagravière (*Léognan*)
Château Smith-Haut-Lafitte (*Martillac*)

ST ÉMILION
Château l'Angélus
*Château Balestard-la-Tonnelle
Château Beauséjour-Duffan-Lagarrosse
Château Cadet-Piola
Château Canon-la-Gaffelière
Château La Clotte
Château Croque-Michotte
Château Curé-Bon-la-Madeleine
Château La Dominique
*Château Larcis-Ducasse
Château Larmande
Château Soutard
Château Troplong-Mondot
Château Villemaurine

*These wines are considered better than their peers in this classification.

POMEROL
Château Beauregard
Château Certan-Giraud
*Château Certan-de-May
Clos l'Église
Château l'Église-Clinet
Château Le Gay
Château Lagrange
Château La Grave
Château Nenin
Château La Pointe

Bons Crus (Good Growths)

MÉDOC
Château Angludet (*Cantenac-Margaux*)
Château Beau-Site (*St Estèphe*)
Château Beau-Site-Haut-Vignoble (*St Estèphe*)
Château Bel-Air-Marquis d'Aligre (*Soussans-Margaux*)
Château Belgrave (*St Laurent*)
*Château de Camensac (*Haut-Médoc*)
Château Cos-Labory (*St Estèphe*)
*Château Croizet-Bages (*Pauillac*)
Château Dauzac-Lynch (*Labarde*)
Château Ferrière (*Margaux*)
Château Fourcas-Dupré (*Listrac*)
Château Fourcas-Hosten (*Listrac*)
Château Grand-Puy-Ducasse
Château Gressier-Grand-Poujeaux (*Moulis*)
Château Haut-Bages-Libéral (*Pauillac*)
Château Haut-Marbuzet (*St Estèphe*)
Château Labégorce (*Margaux*)
Château Labégorce-Zedé (*Margaux*)

Château Lafon-Rochet (*St Estèphe*)
Château Lanessan (*Haut-Médoc*)
Château Lynch-Moussas (*Pauillac*)
Château Marquis-de-Terme (*Margaux*)
Château Maucaillou (*Moulis*)
Château Les Ormes-de-Pez (*St Estèphe*)
Château Pédesclaux (*Pauillac*)
Château de Pez (*St Estèphe*)
Château Phélan-Ségur (*St Estèphe*)
Château Pouget (*Cantenac-Margaux*)
Château Poujeaux (*Moulis*)
Château Saint-Pierre (*St Julien*)
Château Siran (*Labarde-Margaux*)
Château du Tertre (*Arsac-Margaux*)
Château La Tour-de-Mons (*Soussans-Margaux*)

GRAVES
Château Larrivet-Haut-Brion (*Pessac*)
Château La Louvière (*Léognan*)
Château La Tour-Haut-Brion (*Talence*)
Château La Tour-Martillac (*Martillac*)

ST ÉMILION
Château l'Arrosée
Château Bellevue
Château Cap-de-Mourlin
Domaine du Châtelet
Clos des Jacobins
Château Corbin (*Giraud*)
Château Corbin (*Manuel*)
Château Corbin-Michotte
Château Coutet
Château Dassault

*These wines are considered better than their peers in this classification.

Bons Crus (ST ÉMILION)
continued

Couvent-des-Jacobins
Château La Fleur-Pourret
Château Franc-Mayne
Château Grace-Dieux
Château Grand-Barrail-
  Lamarzelle-Figeac
Château Grand-Corbin
Château Grand-Corbin-
  Despagne
Château Grand-Mayne
Château Grand Pontet
Château Guadet-St Julien
Château Moulin-du-Cadet
Château Pavie-Decesse
Château Saint-Georges-Côte-
  Pavie
Château Terte-Daugay
Château La Tour-Figeac
Château La Tour-du-Pin-Figeac
Château Trimoulet
Château Yon-Figeac

POMEROL
Château Bourgneuf-Vayron
Château La Cabanne
Château le Caillou
*Château Clinet
Clos du Clocher
Château La Croix
Château La Croix-de-Gay
Domaine de l'Église
Château l'Enclos
Château Gombaude-Guillot
Château Guillot
Château Moulinet
Château Rouget
Clos René
Château de Sales
Château Tailhas
Château Taillefer

* These wines are considered better than their peers in this classification.

would be more sensible than five. Apart from this, I would make two general criticisms. First, I feel that he has, on the whole, cast his net too wide. There are certain outstanding growths among the *Bourgeois* which should certainly be classified. But when one goes further than this, it is difficult to know where to stop, and when I look at some of the *Bourgeois* wines ennobled in the Lichine list, I can instantly think of others equally good which have been excluded. In other words, it becomes a list of personal favourites, and if a number of people were to prepare a joint list on this premise, it would be far too large and the classification would lose its purpose altogether. There is, after all, a good, up-to-date classification of *Bourgeois* growths in the Médoc.

My second general criticism is the comparing of the St Emilions and Pomerols with the Médocs. Actually, this was the most imaginative stroke of all Lichine's work, but there are, I believe, serious difficulties in making useful comparisons between these very different wines, or indeed, in fitting them into a form suitable

64

for the Médocs. If five separate categories were questionable for the Médocs, they are even more unsuitable for the St Emilions and Pomerols. Certainly, the INAO's 1954 St Emilion classification (this consists of two groups designated as *Premier Grand Cru Classé* and *Grand Cru Classé*; the first group contains twelve wines, the second seventy-two following the addition of eight growths in the last revision of 17 November 1969) contains in its large and unwieldy *Grand Cru Classé* section, wines of widely differing merits, so that there is a good case for saying that two categories are insufficient. But in the small and intensely cultivated area of St Emilion, the soil differences are well defined, and within the best areas, success or failure is very much a measure of the *vigneron*'s skill, and it is this which is largely recognized in the classification. So it is difficult to argue that three categories are not sufficient to meet the existing situation. On the other hand, I think there is much to be said for the idea of having a classification which groups the rather small number of classified Graves with the Médocs, and the at present unclassified Pomerols with the St Emilions.

As Haut-Brion has for so long been classified with the first growths of the Médoc, it is hardly a novel proposal to classify the two areas together. The wines are sufficiently similar to be truly comparable. Another good reason is that the INAO's classification only contains thirteen properties producing red wine, so that the number was too small to allow for any subdivisions to indicate the widely varying qualities. Among these wines, La Mission Haut-Brion has occupied a position not dissimilar to that of Mouton in the last century—hovering in a no-man's-land between the second growths and the firsts. The accolade of first growth is not one lightly accorded, and since the war, only Pétrus has really been accorded parity with the firsts of the Médoc, while Ausone and Cheval Blanc achieved this status only between the wars. The position of La Mission has been the more difficult because of the inevitable comparison with its neighbour, Haut-Brion, and the natural reluctance of Haut-Brion to accord parity to its neighbour and rival. The situation is very reminiscent of the rivalry between Lafite and Mouton, and indeed the contrast between the two wines is best expressed by comparing the style of Haut-Brion to Lafite and that of La Mission to Mouton or Latour. Certainly, today we should not hesitate to recognize La Mission as a first growth. Of the remaining growths, Domaine de Chevalier, Haut-Bailly and Pape-Clément would, without question, take their place beside the second growths of the Médoc.

The idea of grouping the St Emilions and Pomerols together seems sensible, because there is clearly a comparison to be made between them. In addition, such a classification might produce a more selective list which would be more manageable and usable. It is difficult to see what useful purpose is served by having one omnibus group of seventy-two wines such as the *Grands Crus Classés* of St Emilion now are. Even the twelve *Premiers Grands Crus Classés* are a curiously ill-assorted group. The two Beauséjours and Pavie are not really the equal of the others, either in general reputation or in actual quality. Among the top Pomerols, Pétrus would, of course, take its place beside Ausone and Cheval Blanc, while La Conseillante, L'Evangile, La Fleur-Pétrus, Trotanoy, Petit-Village and Vieux Château Certan would join the other *Premiers Grands Crus Classés*. This is a personal view, of course, and others might press the claims of two or three other growths, though few, I think, would challenge the names I have mentioned.

This would produce a list of the greatest St Emilions and Pomerols, which would read something like this:

(a) Ausone, Cheval Blanc, Pétrus
(b) Belair, Canon, La Conseillante, L'Evangile, La Fleur-Pétrus, Figeac, Clos Fourtet, La Gaffelière, Magdelaine, Petit-Village, Trotanoy, Trottevieille and Vieux Château Certan

So far, I have concentrated almost exclusively on the leading growths. This is because these are the wines which create the most interest and at the same time are the simplest to categorize. As has already been pointed out, the lines have always been much more blurred in the lower echelons, which is precisely why regular scrutiny and revision are necessary. The complexity of the task, however, requires special study, and so I do not propose to make any detailed analysis of what a third and fourth category might contain. Yet I feel that such a review of the state of play in the classification controversy would be incomplete without looking at some of the unclassified growths in the Médoc which could reasonably expect recognition today.

It should first be noticed that there now exists a gap in the classification system, in that a number of leading unclassified growths are not members of the Syndicat des Crus Grands Bourgeois et Crus Bourgeois du Médoc, with the result that they did not feature in that Syndicat's new classification of 1966 (revised in 1978) which was not unreasonably limited to its own adherents. These include four of the six wines classified as *Crus Exceptionnels* in 1932: d'Angludet, Bel-Air-Marquis d'Aligre, La Couronne, and Villegeorge. It is interesting to note in passing that Villegeorge is the only growth classified as *Cru Exceptionnel* both in 1932 and in 1966. In addition, the following leading growths are also in the same limbo: in Labarde—Siran; in Soussans—La Tour de Mons; in Moulis—Gressier Grand Poujeaux; in St Julien—Gloria; in St Estèphe—de Pez. This is not to say, of course, that all these wines or only these wines should be accorded the accolade of a superior classification. If I were asked to name the wines whose elevation would receive the widest support as distinct from my own favourites, I think I would give the following: d'Angludet, Chasse-Spleen, Fourcas-Hosten, Gloria, Lanessan, de Pez, Phélan-Ségur, and Siran. But there are undoubtedly other strong candidates, especially Bel-Air and La Tour de Mons in Soussans, and Gressier, Poujeaux-Theil, and Dutruch in Moulis.

I have already mentioned the classifications of the *Bourgeois* growths of the Médoc, and I want to conclude this chapter by looking at the classifications of 1932 and 1966 (*see* pp. 96–8). Although they are two very different beasts, a comparison does throw up some interesting facts about the position of the lesser growths in the Médoc today.

The 1932 list was drawn up by five *courtiers*, or brokers with the backing of the Bordeaux Chamber of Commerce and the Gironde Chamber of Agriculture. It consists of six *Crus Bourgeois Supérieurs Exceptionnels*, ninety-seven *Bourgeois Supérieurs*—all from the Haut-Médoc—and no fewer than 387 *Crus Bourgeois*, embracing both Haut-Médoc and Bas-Médoc. In 1962, the *Bourgeois* growths of the region formed themselves into a Syndicat, and this Syndicat then decided to establish a classification of its members to provide a guide of the current standing of these growths. The result was the 1966 classification, revised in 1978, with eighteen *Grands Bourgeois Exceptionnels*, forty-one *Grands Bourgeois* (including nine from the Bas-Médoc) and fifty-eight *Bourgeois*. In addition, there are six properties listed as being reconstructed.

As has already been pointed out, a number of leading unclassified growths who believed that they would or should be classified, did not join the Syndicat in 1962. It is also true that quite a number of smaller growths are not members. Nevertheless, the discrepancy in the numbers of growths in the 1932 list and those in the 1978 list does, to a large extent, reflect the contraction of the lesser vineyards.

The reconstruction that has occurred in the Médoc vineyards in the last decade is vividly illustrated by the fact that in the area as a whole, the area of AC vineyards in production rose by 37·5 per cent between 1970 and 1978. The largest increases were in the two smallest appellations of Listrac and Moulis, and the two largest, of Médoc and Haut-Médoc. But in Pauillac, the increase was as high as 27·5 per cent, although the largest communal *appellation* of all, St Estèphe, only shows an increase of 7 per cent. But a study of the Médoc *appellations* taken from the 1978 declarations when considered in conjunction with figures which show the number of proprietors, shows how vineyards are increasingly in fewer hands. They also show the predominance of the leading growths in the Médoc context. Thus, in Pauillac, 753 hectares are classified growths against 88 for *Bourgeois* growths, 13 for *Artisan* growths, and 185 for the *Coopérative*. In Margaux, the picture is 721 hectares of classified growths, 256 *Bourgeois* growths and only 87 for *Artisan* growths.

Will there be a new classification of the Médoc? The INAO has been very busy in Graves and St Emilion, but the Médoc has proved a stumbling block. Their carefully leaked proposals in 1960 met with a storm of protest, and have not been heard of since, despite numerous rumours that something was about to happen. The only event has been the decree of 1973, placing Mouton among the first growths—hardly a controversial topic. Perhaps one day, sooner or later, something will happen. In the meantime, I feel that Alexis Lichine has shown the best solution of all—to revise an old tradition of pre-1855 and make your own classification. It can be great fun!

68

4

The Médoc: Margaux and St Julien

The Médoc as we know it today covers an enormous area stretching from Le Taillan and Blanquefort in the south to Soulac in the north, a distance of 80 km (50 miles). The best vineyards extend along a fairly narrow ridge with a wider plateau of good but lesser vineyards behind and parallel to them. The area is divided into eight by the laws of *Appellation Contrôlée*. These divisions comprise the Haut-Médoc, within which are the separate *appellations* of Margaux, St Julien, Pauillac, St Estèphe, Moulis and Listrac, and Médoc, traditionally known as the Bas-Médoc. Until well into the second half of the nineteenth century, it was usual to find a rather different division applied, that of the *arrondissements* of Bordeaux and Lesparre. The boundary between these two administrative regions was drawn along the southern boundary of the communes of St Julien and St Laurent.

This is both the largest and most important red wine district of Bordeaux. Indeed, for many Englishmen, Médoc is almost synonymous with claret, an attitude which reflects both the ascendancy enjoyed by the region during the nineteenth century and our own traditional conservatism. It was the building up of large estates by wealthy Bordeaux families in the eighteenth century, and its proximity to the city and port of Bordeaux, that gave the Médoc such an advantage over its rivals when the claret boom of the mid-nineteenth century came. This flying start is something the region has never wholly lost, through all its vicissitudes.

HAUT-MÉDOC

I do not intend to go through this area in strict geographical order as in a travelogue, but will deal first with the six most important

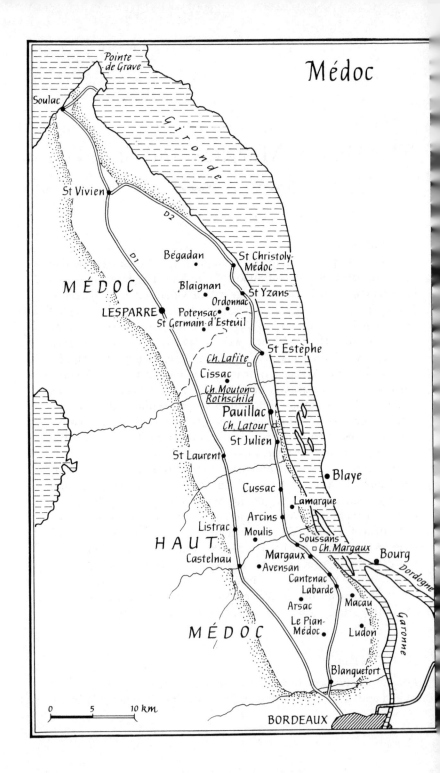

communal *appellations*. Although all the wines of the Médoc possess a certain family resemblance, it is possible nevertheless to find within its boundaries variations of style as great as any among the red wines of Bordeaux. The common denominator is a certain crispness of definition on nose and palate. The wines have rather less alcohol and less body than their cousins across the river, but they develop and sustain with age a bouquet of exceptional purity and subtlety. They are slow to develop at first, and even small growths in good years may require two years in cask and three years in bottle before shaking off the brusqueness of youth to reveal some charm and finish. Many wine ñovices have been put off Médoc wines by attempting to consume them too young, and it is often surprisingly difficult for the unpractised palate to perceive the delicacy and character which is to come when youth has mellowed into maturity.

As a general rule, it may be said that the first line of vineyards towards the river produces wines with the most finesse and breed, while those from the plateau behind have most body and vigour but are less fine. Similarly, the wines in the south of the area have less tannin and more delicacy than those further north.

MARGAUX

This is one of the few examples of the name of a famous commune being extended to neighbours producing wines of a similar style, a practice common in Germany and much approved by all who seek simplification and a degree of logic in wine laws. Unfortunately, such common sense is rare, local interests tending to favour subdivisions rather than amalgamations. Vineyards from the communes of Labarde, Arsac, and Cantenac to the south and from Soussans to the north are included now in the Margaux *appellation*.

The name of Margaux itself conjures up so many feelings and evokes such memories for any lover of claret. It is the only example in the region of a district whose name is taken from its most renowned growth. In the nineteenth century, the wines of Margaux were especially loved in England, and even today, with a new generation of wine drinkers, these wines have retained a special place of affection.

To capture the quintessence of the Margaux character in mere words is particularly hard. Its wines are delicately perfumed in youth and this perfume fills out and deepens in the years of maturity. On the palate, although lacking somewhat in body, they fill the mouth with flavour at once delicate, refined and subtle, full of nuances and finesse. Often in youth their charm seems too insubstantial to survive into age, but this impression is wholly misleading. As the years pass they broaden out a little and take on fresh colours and textures. It is a change of key, as in some exquisite musical development when the theme is subtly transformed during the exposition, the colours become richer, the tone more authoritative, but the quintessence of the originally simple theme remains.

The vineyards of Margaux immediately strike the visitor by their almost white appearance. This is due to a light, fine, pebbly gravel which is responsible in part for the finesse and delicacy of these wines. There is, of course, considerable variety among the wines themselves. Generally speaking, the wines of Labarde, Cantenac and Arsac are rather fuller flavoured, without quite the finesse of the wines from the exceptionally light, stony soil of Margaux itself. These wines might be described as the St Emilions of Médoc and it is often quite easy to confuse them with their cousins across the water, especially in youth. There is something of the same richness and softness of flavour—only their actual flavour when compared side by side invokes their true origin. Some growths in Margaux itself are even quite firm and powerful at first, but such individual differences will best be dealt with under the appropriate châteaux.

Château Margaux   First Growth in 1855 classification

Château Margaux has always been accounted a first growth since classifications began. Its wines are particularly mentioned as being in all the best English cellars by the first half of the eighteenth century.

The origins of this growth can be traced back to the fifteenth century when it was known as Lamothe. In those times the château was fortified, and belonged to the Seigneur Monferraud and later to the Seigneur de Durfort. It was in 1750 that the then proprietor, Monsieur de Fumel, made extensive vine plantations, and so the reputation of the château became more widespread. In 1802, it was bought by the Marquis de la Colonilla for 654,000 frs

THE OFFICIAL CLASSIFICATION OF THE GREAT GROWTHS OF THE GIRONDE: CLASSIFICATION OF 1855

	COMMUNE	HECTARES	TONNEAUX
Premiers Crus (First Growths)			
Château Lafite	*Pauillac*	88	300
Château Latour	*Pauillac*	59	200
Château Mouton-Rothschild*	*Pauillac*	70	250
Château Margaux	*Margaux*	42	200
Château Haut-Brion	*Pessac. Graves*	66	160

*Decreed a first growth in 1973

	COMMUNE	HECTARES	TONNEAUX
Deuxièmes Crus (Second Growths)			
Château Rausan-Ségla	*Margaux*	37	130
Château Rauzan-Gassies	*Margaux*	21	50
Château Léoville-Las-Cases	*St Julien*	62	330
Château Léoville-Poyferré	*St Julien*	45	200
Château Léoville-Barton	*St Julien*	46	200
Château Durfort-Vivens	*Margaux*	35	90
Château Lascombes	*Margaux*	100	375
Château Gruaud-Larose	*St Julien*	76	330
Château Brane-Cantenac	*Cantenac-Margaux*	115	375
Château Pichon-Longueville-Baron	*Pauillac*	27	90
Château Pichon-Lalande	*Pauillac*	49	200
Château Ducru-Beaucaillou	*St Julien*	57	300
Château Cos-d'Estournel	*St Estèphe*	60	275
Château Montrose	*St Estèphe*	49	200

	COMMUNE	HECTARES	TONNEAUX
Troisièmes Crus (Third Growths)			
Château Giscours	*Labarde-Margaux*	75	300
Château Kirwan	*Cantenac-Margaux*	23	100
Château d'Issan	*Cantenac-Margaux*	35	130
Château Lagrange	*St Julien*	39	190
Château Langoa-Barton	*St Julien*	17	50
Château Malescot-Saint-Exupéry	*Margaux*	26	80
Château Cantenac-Brown	*Cantenac-Margaux*	32	150
Château Palmer	*Cantenac-Margaux*	40	140
Château La Lagune	*Ludon*	55	220
Château Desmirail	*Margaux*	0	0

73

	COMMUNE	HECTARES	TONNEAUX
Château Calon-Ségur	*St Estèphe*	70	260
Château Ferrière	*Margaux*	—	10
Château Marquis-d'Alesme	*Margaux*	12	45
Château Boyd-Cantenac	*Margaux*	18	60

Quatrièmes Crus (Fourth Growths)

Château Saint-Pierre-Sevaistre	*St Julien*	17	60
Château Branaire	*St Julien*	43	160
Château Talbot	*St Julien*	76	340
Château Duhart-Milon-Rothschild	*Pauillac*	46	80
Château Pouget	*Cantenac-Margaux*	7	25
Château La Tour-Carnet	*St Laurent*	30	60
Château Lafon-Rochet	*St Estèphe*	40	160
Château Beychevelle	*St Julien*	53	275
Château Prieuré-Lichine	*Cantenac-Margaux*	57	260
Château Marquis-de-Terme	*Margaux*	29	170

Cinquièmes Crus (Fifth Growths)

Château Pontet-Canet	*Pauillac*	65	280
Château Batailley	*Pauillac*	40	100
Château Grand-Puy-Lacoste	*Pauillac*	30	125
Château Grand-Puy-Ducasse	*Pauillac*	26	100
Château Haut-Batailley	*Pauillac*	22	80
Château Lynch-Bages	*Pauillac*	59	250
Château Lynch-Moussas	*Pauillac*	16	18
Château Dauzac-Lynch	*Labarde-Margaux*	40	160
Château Mouton-Baronne-Phillippe (formerly known as Mouton Baron Phillippe)	*Pauillac*	50	200
Château de Terte	*Arsac-Margaux*	50	200
Château Haut-Bages-Libéral	*Pauillac*	19	80
Château Pédesclaux	*Pauillac*	15	50
Château Belgrave	*St Laurent*	35	100
Château Camensac	*St Laurent*	13	50
Château Cos Labory	*St Estèphe*	15	50
Château Clerc-Milon	*Pauillac*	27	100
Château Croizet-Bages	*Pauillac*	22	90
Château Cantemerle	*Macau*	25	100

(approx. £131,000). He pulled down the old château and built the elegant neo-classical mansion which is so familiar today, a building unique in style and importance in the Médoc. It was ready for the Marquis to move into by 1812. In 1836, it was purchased by a Spanish nobleman, Alexandre Aguada, Marquis de las Marismas, for 1,350,000 frs (approx. £260,000). Most of the extensive library installed in the château during this period remains to adorn its shelves today, together with much fine furniture of the Empire style dating from the Colonilla period. In 1879 it changed hands once more when the son of the original Marques de las Marismas sold it to Vicomte Pillet-Will. The Pillet-Will era ended in 1920, and for a few years it was the property of the Duc de la Tremoille, before a Société Civile, of which Fernand Ginestet was a partner, acquired it. Monsieur Pierre Ginestet, his son, gradually acquired this great property until he became sole proprietor in 1940. It was to remain Pierre Ginestet's home for the next thirty-five years.

In the aftermath of the Bordeaux slump, the Ginestet *négociant* business experienced acute financial problems which necessitated the sale of Château Margaux. At first it seemed likely that the new owners would be the American company, National Distillers. But this was vetoed by the French Government, and in 1976 it was acquired by Monsieur André Mentzelopoulos, through the supermarket group Felix Potin for 72 million francs. From the outset, Monsieur Mentzelopoulos took a keen personal interest in this new venture, and a very considerable investment has been made in restoring the buildings and vineyards, where the hand of neglect had become increasingly evident in recent years. Unhappily, after only four years as proprietor, André Mentzelopoulos died in December 1980. But already his impact on Margaux, and on Bordeaux as a whole, had been substantial, and he had at least had the consolation of seeing the 1978 and 1979 vintages acclaimed as exceptional. Madame Laura Mentzelopoulos, his widow, and her daughters are now the proprietors.

In the 1850s the production of the first wine only amounted to 80 tonneaux, but this increased steadily as the century progressed and the prestige of and demand for the great wines of the Médoc mounted. Thus figures of 125 tonneaux in 1874, 150 tonneaux in 1881, and 225 tonneaux in 1898 are recorded in the works of

Edouard Féret and his edition of Cocks. Today the production averages around 200 tonneaux, or 15,000 cases.

The wines of Château Margaux have all those qualities described as being particular to Margaux, and in the most exalted degree and perfect balance. The *courtiers* who compiled the 1855 classification placed Margaux in the first growths, second only to Lafite. It is not hard to see why. If we acclaim Lafite as the king of Médoc wines, then Margaux is surely the queen. Lafite may be the most complete Médoc, with its fascinating combination of delicacy and power: Margaux is a more feline and feminine wine, but it comes closest to Lafite in its finesse and breed, in its sheer beauty of flavour. The delicacy of the early years belies the longevity of the great years. I had a bottle of the 1875 on its ninetieth birthday and it was still beautifully preserved, one of the best bottles of old wine I have ever drunk, full-flavoured but light, sweet as only old claret can be, and still beautifully fresh. Undoubtedly one of the greatest vintages which still lives is the 1900. When sixty-three years old, its lovely colour was still unfaded, its bouquet was gloriously undimmed, a marvel of delicacy and penetration. The wine still had all those wonderful characteristics which words can only feebly sketch—great finesse, charm and a serene and perfect balance. This was, and no doubt still is, an ageless beauty and a fitting monument to the golden age of Margaux.

Although there were no great vintages between 1900 and 1920, some charming wines were made during this era, and I have had good bottles of the 1907 and the 1909. The period between the wars was a disappointing one in the history of this great wine. Neither in 1928 and 1929, nor again in 1934 and 1937 did Margaux rank with the best wines of the vintage. The outstanding wine of the period in my experience is the 1924. Ever since I first saw the wine at Lebegues' famous survey of wines of the Château in 1952 and was struck by its superiority to more famous years, I have never been disappointed by this lovely wine. Although now beginning to show its age, it was still graceful, charming and vigorous when last tasted in 1977. Since the war, the greatest years have been 1947, 1949, 1953, 1961 and 1978. The 1945 is a big wine, rather untypical of Margaux and lacking in breed. In lesser years, Margaux is inclined to produce a rather small wine with a rather limited future; the 1957 and 1958 were typical. But 1950, and to a much lesser degree 1960, produced wines of great charm with the breed and style of true Margaux, if not on the grand scale.

The 1962 is successful but rather dry; the 1961 is a great Margaux with a long life ahead of it and great depth and fruit. The 1960 is one of the successes of the vintage, a follower to the Margaux 1950. The 1959 is good but not outstanding, better than 1957 and 1955, but not in the 1947, 1953, 1961 category. The 1957 is sound and decent but unexciting, while the 1955 does not quite come off in spite of some promise—like many wines of this vintage. But after the great 1961 vintage, Margaux fell well behind the other first growths and indeed was often outshone by its neighbour Château Palmer. Respectable wines were made in 1966, 1970 and 1971, but they lacked the flair of the best that Margaux can do. On balance, the 1966 is probably the finest of these wines, combining finesse with lasting qualities. The 1975 has promise but is not among the front runners of this year. But with the new régime, there is hope of a renaissance. The 1978 seems to set the stamp on it, easily the best wine made since 1961, I thought, when first tasted in the spring after the soutirage. Subsequent tastings have shown it to be amongst the best wines of this vintage. Even in the modest 1977 vintage, an exceptionally attractive and stylish wine was made. The 1979 has opulence and a marvellous bouquet, which reminds me of the 1949 vintage here. So future years should hold many delights in store for Margaux lovers.

Some wines are immensely impressive almost as soon as they are made. Others hide their great qualities until their second year in cask or until they have had bottle age. Margaux was such a wine. When I first tasted Margaux in cask. I was quite unimpressed and indeed disappointed. The wine was usually more easily judged in its second year in cask, became disappointing again during the months preceding bottling, and only showed well in bottle after at least two or three years. But with improved wine-making and earlier bottling this is changing. It was customary at Margaux to bottle the wine only after the third winter, and I often wondered at the wisdom of this practice in any but the greatest years. The wines of light years seemed to take a long time to recover after bottling and in the interim period looked rather tired. Under the new régime, Professor Peynaud has encouraged a more flexible approach, and the 1977 benefited from early bottling.

Château Rausan-Ségla   Second Growth

This was one of the important vineyards owned by the Marquis de Rauzan in the eighteenth century. It became separated from his other property of Gassies in the nineteenth century. For a long period it belonged to the family of Durand-Dasier, and then for many years to the Cruse family, until its sale by them in 1957. It now belongs to the Liverpool shipping firm of John Holt, themselves now part of the international trading giant, Lonhro.

I have to confess that the wines of Rausan-Ségla have never greatly appealed to me. They are usually rather stubborn at first and seem to lack the delicacy and finesse of the finest Margaux wines. There is a small but charming château dating from the early nineteenth century. When John Holt acquired the property in 1960, the vineyard consisted of 37 hectares. Since that time, there has been a steady programme of replanting amounting to 16·75 hectares between 1960 and 1979. In 1979 the vineyard had reached 42·5 hectares and the final target is for a vineyard area of 46·6 hectares. The average production is 12,500 cases. At a tasting of 1975s in 1979, the Rausan was one of the best examples I remember tasting, perhaps a more hopeful sign for the future.

Château Rauzan-Gassies   Second Growth

This ancient domaine belonged to Gaillard de Tardes in the sixteenth century and to Bernard de Baverolles in the seventeenth century, before passing into the hands of Monsieur de Rauzan, the *conseiller au Parlement*, in the eighteenth century, who gave it his name. There have been many owners, but Monsieur Paul Quie and his heirs have been the proprietors since the last war.

More powerful than many Margaux and with nearly as much body as a Cantenac wine, at its best it possesses the delicacy and charm of the finest Margaux wines. Like Ségla, it usually takes rather longer to come round than most Margaux wines these days.

The 1875 was a very great wine which was still remarkably fine and well preserved when I drank it in 1962 and 1963. Of more recent vintages, the 1920 and 1926 were both very fine, very much in their prime still when I last had the pleasure of drinking them. Recently, 1964 was very successful, as were most Margaux in this mixed year. The 1962 is average for the vintage, with more depth than many; 1961 is a good specimen of this great year; 1960 was not one of the more successful wines of a year where selectivity was important; 1959 and 1957 were both fairly typical of the year; 1955 was rather light, but had more fruit and charm than most 1955s and was excellent for early drinking—a little past its peak now; 1953 was a delightful and typical 1953; 1952 and 1950 were both good wines in the style of their respective years; more recently, the 1976 looks charming and promising. To summarize, this has been a fairly consistent wine in recent vintages, sound if not at the moment quite in the top flight. There is no château. The average production is 4,500 cases.

Château Lascombes   Second Growth

This property was once part of Durfort and takes its name from the Chevalier Lascombes, an eighteenth-century *Procureur de Roi* at the admiralty. As late as 1860, it was still described as Domaine de Lascombes. At the time of the classification, it comprised only a small vineyard producing only some ten to fifteen tonneaux. This rose to thirty to thirty-five tonneaux under the direction of the Chaix-d'Est-Ange family who enlarged the vineyard. During the last thirty years of the nineteenth century the reputation and quality of Lascombes prospered. The period after the First World War was an unhappy one during which there were many changes of ownership. In 1951, Alexis Lichine persuaded a syndicate of largely American friends to buy the property, and after Lichine's departure from the company, Bass Charrington purchased control in 1971. By 1951, the château was in a poor state. The quality and reputation of the wines were at a low ebb, the vineyard neglected. The vineyard has now been both restored and much enlarged. There was a big initial improvement in the quality of the wines, but the combination of a great increase in production and the departure of Lichine seem to have depressed the quality in recent years.

The main part of the vineyard is situated in the best part of Margaux, the soil being light and stony. The wines at their best have real delicacy and finesse; those of recent vintages tend to be on the light side, probably due to the reconstruction of the vineyard. The château, a late nineteenth-century edifice with towers and turrets, has been restored and decorated in a startlingly modern manner. Lichine started, during the summer, an exhibition of modern paintings under the general heading of *La*

Vigne et Le Vin, which is one of the features of the Médoc and has happily been continued.

Some old vintages of Lascombes are charming and show the breed and style which the growth traditionally had. Of those I have tasted, the 1892 was particularly remarkable, with the depth of colour of 1928, but much browner. It had a superbly powerful and rich bouquet, and was a wine of amazing completeness and majesty, unbowed in its seventy-third year, comparable certainly to some of the 1899s and 1900s I have had. I shall always remember drinking it with Alexis Lichine in his charming dining-room at the Prieuré. He has always been the most generous of men with his great bottles. In later years, the 1926 and 1929 were both particularly fine.

Under Lichine, the 1953 and 1961 were the great successes. Both the 1964 and the 1962 promised much in cask but have been rather disappointing since they were bottled. The 1960 was light, but fruity and pleasing. I have been disappointed by the recent vintages, even the 1975. The average production is 35,000 cases.

Château Durfort-Vivens   Second Growth

This famous growth has also had a rather chequered history. It originally belonged to the family of Durfort de Duras, illustrious as a military family during the seventeenth and eighteenth centuries. Apart from Durfort, they also owned the fortified château at Blanquefort. The last member of the family was the Duc de Duras and the last Seigneur of Blanquefort. As general in command of the National Guard in the Gironde at the time of the Revolution of 1789, he made great efforts to keep this body loyal to the Royalist cause before being forced to emigrate. He finally died in England in 1800. In 1824, a new proprietor, Monsieur Vivens, added his name to that of Durfort and this has remained unchanged ever since. In 1895, it was acquired by Monsieur Delor, head of the Bordeaux shipping house of the same name. More recently, it belonged to the Ginestets who, in 1964, sold it to Monsieur Lurton, the proprietor of Brane-Cantenac, while they retained the charmingly unpretentious château, now the home of Monsieur Bernard Ginestet.

In the past, this growth has produced rather powerful wines, maturing fairly slowly, of the Rauzan type rather than the Lascombes type. Now, under the new proprietor, there are changes in the constitution of the vineyard and the wines have much of the elegance of Brane-Cantenac. The average production is 8,000 cases.

Château Brane-Cantenac   Second Growth

This has long been a very large and important growth. It was the only property in Cantenac classified as a second growth in 1855. It owed its fame and importance to the work of the great viticulturist, Baron de Brane, who was also responsible for the rise of Mouton. After the sale of Mouton in 1830, the Baron devoted himself entirely to the improvement of Brane-Cantenac and its wines. Before its acquisition by Baron de Brane, it was known as de Gorce.

It does not today quite maintain its former position as the best wine in Cantenac, a position yielded almost without dispute to Palmer, but under its present proprietor, Monsieur Lurton, great progress has been made. The property, always large, is now one of the most productive in the whole of the Médoc. It occupies a magnificent plateau behind Cantenac and Margaux, and adjoining Angludet and Le Tertre, while the stark whiteness of the soil typifies the best of Margaux. Partly because of the soil, partly because of young vines, the wine today is light but with a bouquet and flavour of great purity and beauty. This is a wine of real breed and distinction. The 1957 was one of the more agreeable and drinkable wines of that vintage, and the 1961 and 1962 were especially successful. They were followed by 1964, 1966 and 1967, while the 1970s have produced another string of successes. The average production is 35,000 cases.

Château Palmer   Third Growth

This is today not only the outstanding growth in Cantenac, but the best growth in the Margaux *appellation* after Château Margaux itself. It is now ranked among the best of the second growths, and regularly commands a higher price than any other.

The property has an interesting history, in which are mirrored many of the salient features of the history of the region. We are fortunate in having an excellent monograph on the history of Palmer by Monsieur R. Pijassou published by the Fédération Historique de Sud-Ouest in 1964 and embodying all the latest research, and the following is a summary of the most interesting parts of that history.

The property appears to have originated from a division of the ancient domaine of Château d'Issan among the heirs of the Foix-Candale family in 1748, when a portion seems to have passed into the hands of the de Gascq family. The members of this ancient and important family belonged, like all leading proprietors of the eighteenth century, to the *noblesse de robe* as *conseillers* of the Bordeaux Parlement, and several held important posts in it, as well as being noted patrons of literature and the fine arts. The wine from their property, known as Château de Gascq, became popular at the court of Louis XV. At that time the entire domaine only amounted to 50 hectares.

The end of the revolutionary period and the Napoleonic wars found Madame Marie Bumet de Ferrière, the widow of Blaise-Jean-Charles-Alexandre de Gascq, as sole proprietor. In 1814, Major General Charles Palmer, having arrived with Wellington's army, decided to settle in Bordeaux and invest his money in property. It seems probable that he had some introduction to one of the courtiers of the city, and his attention was directed to Château de Gascq, comprised then of a fine vineyard but no noble château. For this he turned to another property at Cenon. The price paid amounted to 100,000 frs (approx. £20,000). But for the next seventeen years, the General steadily augmented his original purchase and by 1831, he had invested 370,906 frs (approx. £74,200) in a domaine of 162 hectares, and Palmer could vie with her great neighbours Margaux and Beychevelle in size and importance. One of the most important of these acquisitions was the vineyard called Boston of over 30 hectares, situated between the communes of Cantenac and Soussans. In this first great age of Palmer, the estate was organized on the grand scale. Jean Lagunegrand, the *régisseur*, was one of the most highly paid in the Médoc, the equal of Joubert at the Bartons' domaine of Langoa-Léoville. At this period in the 1830s and 1840s, around 100 tonneaux a year were made.

Between 1841 and 1843, the General ran into financial trouble, and this in its turn was to affect Palmer's position when the 1855 classification was made. The high cost of running the estate was aggravated by economic difficulties in France and high duties detrimental to trade. After several poor vintages, in 1843 the

General was forced to sell to Madame Françoise-Marie Bergerac for only 274,000 frs (approx. £54,800), substantially less than his original investment. After the inauguration of the Second Empire in 1851, a more prosperous period began, and in this era the power and influence of the great bankers reached its zenith. In 1853, Baron Nathaniel de Rothschild bought Mouton, and his rival Isaac-Rodrigue Péreire bought Palmer.

The Péreires were a Jewish-Portuguese family who became financiers and were principally concerned in the development and exploitation of the French railways. They were also responsible for the development of Arcachon as a resort. The sum paid for Palmer was 410,000 frs (approx. £82,000) but Péreire had bought at a difficult time, for the Palmer vineyard was already wasting under the scourge of oidium, and by 1858 the entire vineyard had to be completely replanted. Soon the production rose again to 125 tonneaux, and as the vineyard was again increased between 1857 and 1887, so production rose still further. During the 1870s, it could average 170 tonneaux. This figure was halved during the phylloxera period of the 1880s, to emerge in the plentiful vintages at the end of the century at over 200 tonneaux. The charming château, which is such a familiar landmark on the *route de Médoc*, was built by Isaac Péreire between 1857 and 1860 on land known as the Palu d'Issan specially purchased for the purpose from Madame Lowick of Château d'Issan.

The Société Civile Péreire, which was formed in 1889, continued as proprietors until 1937–8. In the final period of the Péreire régime, Palmer, like many other Médoc growths between the wars, fell on bad times, and the vineyard at Boston was disposed of. Palmer was sold to a Société Civile in which there are three partners: Mahler-Besse, the *négociants*, of Dutch origin, who have over 50 per cent; Sichel, the English *négociants*, who have about a third share; and the Miaihle family, formerly *courtiers*, and now important proprietors, who have about 10 per cent.

For over 100 years now Palmer has been fortunate in having the Chardon family as *régisseurs*, and under the devoted attention of Pierre and his sons Claude and Yves the position of Palmer has been restored until its reputation is now as high as at any time in its history. In recent years, the 1949, 1953, 1955, 1957, 1959, 1960, 1961, 1962, 1966, 1970, 1971, 1973, 1975, 1976, 1978 and 1979 were all successful examples of the vintage. The 1953, 1960, 1961 and

1971 were accounted amongst the finest. At a blind tasting of 1961s, made possible through the generosity of Dr Taams at his home in Holland in May 1978, the 1961 was clearly placed first, ahead of all the first growths of the Médoc. The 1964 was on the light side and, while not one of the best wines of the vintage, made a very attractive bottle for early drinking. In the most successful years, Palmer is a very fat and generous wine to begin with, and has an almost Burgundian opulence which is very noticeable on the nose. This is due in part to the proportion of Merlot in the vineyard, and such wines can easily be mistaken for St Emilions. When tasting the famous 1953 with Allan Sichel, I recall his opinion that the proportion of Merlot at that time was excessive, and that more Cabernet Sauvignon was needed. While there has been some correction of the imbalance in the vineyard, the impression remains that Palmer is more Merlot than is usual for Margaux or the Médoc. But with maturity, the wines develop a bouquet of rare penetration and show all the finesse of a fine Margaux with rather more body and richness. The average production is 12,500 cases.

Château d'Issan   Third Growth

This ancient property can be traced back to the period of the English occupation. In the thirteenth century, a fortress called Château Lamothe de Cantenac was erected which was replaced in the seventeenth century by the present château. Before the Revolution, the property belonged to the ancient and noble family of Foix-Candale. It is interesting to note that in a classification of 1824, the château is referred to as Château de Candale. The rise in the value of vineyards is well illustrated by the various sales of Issan during the nineteenth century. Monsieur Duluc bought it from the Fox-Candale family in 1825 for 255,000 frs. It passed to his heirs in 1859 for 470,000 frs and was sold by them to Monsieur Gustave Roy in 1866 for 790,000 frs. After it became a Société Vinicole, the château continued to be administered by the Roy family until it was purchased by the Cruse family, and is now the home of Madame Emmanuel Cruse whose husband had to undertake the complete restoration of the château in 1952–3 when the ancient fabric threatened to collapse.

The vineyard and château are situated just below the *route de Médoc* as one leaves Cantenac for Margaux, and part of the vineyard is surrounded by a fine old stone wall. The château itself is certainly one of the oldest and most interesting in the Médoc, and above the gateway of the château is carved the proud motto *Regum Mensis arisque Deorum*—'For the table of the King and the altar of God'.

The wine of Issan has always been considered rather untypical of Margaux, due to the particularity of the soil. Edouard Féret described it as having the power, fleshiness and colour of a St Julien, and the same is true today. This growth, the favourite wine of the Emperor Franz Josef, was also very popular in England, but of recent years has seldom been seen in this country. The production, which by the end of the nineteenth century had risen to 150 tonneaux, decreased to 80 tonneaux in the 1920s and to as little as 30 tonneaux just after the war. The average production is now back to 130 tonneaux, or 11,000 cases.

Château Kirwan   Third Growth

This is another property in Cantenac; it takes its name from an Irish family who, like the Lynchs, hailed from Galway. It had belonged to the Seigneur de la Salles until a Kirwan married his daughter in 1750, giving his name to the property. He was the first proprietor to take a personal interest in the running of it. Unhappily, Kirwan was a victim of the Terror, being guillotined in 1792. The château acquired a great reputation in the nineteenth century, being placed at the head of the third growths in 1855 and subsequently achieving prices comparable to a second growth. In 1881 the proprietor, Camile Godard, died leaving the property to the city of Bordeaux. In 1901, the firm of Schroder and Schyler acquired the monopoly of the crop, and purchased the vineyard in 1925. It was here that the first of the many artesian wells were successfully drilled in the Médoc, where there had always been a great shortage of water. Its depth is 85 m (approx. 225 ft).

Kirwan was one of the last classified growths never to be château-bottled, the wine being kept and bottled in Schroder and Schyler's Bordeaux cellars. The reputation of this growth has suffered in the last forty years, and the wine no longer occupies the exalted place it held in the nineteenth century; it is seldom seen in England nowadays. Since 1972, Schroder and Schyler have carried out extensive replantings and improvements. Perhaps this will mark the beginnings of a more distinguished chapter in the history of Kirwan. The average production is 8,000 cases.

Château Cantenac-Brown   Third Growth

In the 1855 classification, no mention is made of Cantenac-Brown, but only of Château Boyd in the commune of Cantenac. In 1860, part of this vineyard was sold to Monsieur Armande Lalande and from thenceforth, the property has been known as Cantenac-Brown and remained the property of the Lalande family, who at that time also owned Léoville Poyferré. The Lalande family have an ancient and continuous history in the Bordeaux wine trade and were *courtiers* before and after the Revolution; Armande Lalande then founded the firm of *négociants* which still bears his name. In 1968 the château was sold to the firm of de Luze, which soon afterwards was bought by the British paper firm of Bowater. It now belongs to Rémy Martin.

Although the production of Château Boyd was only given as 35 tonneaux in 1860, by 1881 the separated Cantenac-Brown was making 130 tonneaux, and in 1893 achieved 250 tonneaux. Now the average is 150 tonneaux, or 13,000 cases, and the château has lost some of the considerable importance it formerly enjoyed. The wines today lack the elegance and finish of the best wines of Cantenac. There is a large and complex Victorian mansion which serves as a château.

Château Boyd-Cantenac   Third Growth

This growth has had a strange and chequered history. It was classified as a third growth in 1855 and had appeared as a fourth growth in earlier unofficial classifications of the 1820s. In 1860, it lost the major part of its vineyards, which then became Brown-Cantenac. Soon after 1874, Château Boyd, now classified as a Margaux rather than a Cantenac, was bought by Monsieur Abel Laurent, owner of the château of the same name. He proceeded to sell its wines under the name of his own property, which then enjoyed a good reputation. But in 1920, the then proprietor, Monsieur Marcel Laurent, again claimed and won the right to sell Boyd-Cantenac separately as a third growth after a gap of some forty-five years. So it reappeared as a separate entity again in the 1922 edition of Cocks & Féret with a production of 25 tonneaux. Subsequently it was acquired by Monsieur Ginestet who, having sold the building to Château Margaux, made the Boyd wines at

Lascombes. It now belongs to Monsieur Guillermet, proprietor of Château Pouget and the wines are now made there. The wine today is rich and supple in style, with the most successful of recent vintages being 1970, 1971, and 1978. This is an attractive well-made wine; if no longer of third growth quality, it does at least justify its position as a classified growth once more. The average production is 4,500 cases.

Château Malescot-St-Exupéry   Third Growth

At the time of the 1855 classification, Malescot was an ancient but very small domaine, producing 20 tonneaux on average. It had long been the property of the Comtes de St-Exupéry until sold by them in 1853 to Monsieur Fourcade for 280,000 frs (approx. £56,000). The new proprietor proceeded to reconstruct the domaine so that the production by 1874 had risen to 150 tonneaux. The vineyard of Philippe Dubignon, which had also been classified as a third growth in 1855, was added to Malescot at this time and then disappeared from the list of classified growths. An attractive château was also constructed in the village of Margaux, which has only recently been completely renovated and restored.

Since the time of the First World War, the estate has again been reconstructed, and production now averages 7,500 cases. Between 1912 and 1955, the château belonged to the English company of W. H. Chaplin (subsequently Seager Evans), who then sold it to their manager, Mr Paul Zuger. His sons now manage it. The wine today again enjoys an excellent reputation, and is noted for a bouquet of exquisite fragrance and delicacy. It is a wine of real breed and finesse, with sufficient body.

Château Marquis d'Alesme-Becker   Third Growth

A very small but very ancient property in the heart of Margaux. Its history has been traced back as far as 1616 when vines were first planted here. Little is known of its early history except that before the Revolution it belonged to a Marquise d'Alesme. For simplicity's sake, it was usually referred to as Becker in the nineteenth century. At the time of the classification, the production was only 5 tonneaux; by the end of the century, 25 to 30 tonneaux were achieved. In 1919, it was bought by the then proprietor of Lascombes for incorporation into this growth whose vineyard it adjoins, but the plan was not carried out, and the property was sold again to W. H. Chaplin who ran it in conjunction with Malescot, being sold to Paul Zuger at the same time as Malescot. The wine is not well known today, but is a good and typical Margaux with an average production of 3,500 cases.

Château Giscours   Third Growth

This important property lies in the commune of Labarde. The records go back to 1552 when Seigneur de la Bastide sold it to Pierre de l'Horme. Before the Revolution, it belonged to the Saint-Simon family but was confiscated by the State during the Revolution. In 1793, it was acquired for two Americans, John Gray and Jonathan Davis of Boston.

The great era of Giscours as a vineyard began when it was purchased in 1845 by J. P. Pescatore, a banker, for the sum of 500,000 frs (approx. £100,000). In 1847, he secured the services of Pierre Skawinski to manage the estate. This remarkable man was one of the great agriculturalists of the Médoc in the nineteenth century, and it was largely due to men like him that such strides were made in the region during this period. Skawinski himself was a Pole born in Lublin in 1812. He studied at the Ecole d'Agricole under Grignon, and then managed a property on the Loire near Montrichard. For fifty years, first under Pescatore and then under the Cruses, he managed Giscours, and it was under his management that Giscours became one of the finest and most sought after of the third growths. He invented, in 1860, a special plough for the vineyards, which bore his name, and in 1882 he began the first experiments in combating mildew. The extent of his influence may be gauged by the fact that his three sons managed at various times Pontet-Canet, Léoville-Poyferré, Cantenac-Brown, Léoville-Lascases, La Couronne (Pauillac), Lamartine (Cantenac), Senailhac (St Seurin de Cadourne) and Laujac (Begadan).

The château itself was built by Monsieur Promis in 1837 and replaced an ancient and important château of historic interest. Later, under the Cruses, a large range of farm buildings and a new cuvier were constructed. During this great period Giscours consistently made about 100 tonneaux. The Cruses having sold the property in 1913, Giscours, like so many others, went through a bad period between the wars and by the post-war period production had fallen to 20 tonneaux. In 1954 the present proprietor, Monsieur Tari, acquired Giscours, having formerly been a wine-maker on a considerable scale in the Oran district of Algeria. Under the new régime, the vineyard has been reconstructed and enlarged to such effect that an average of 275 tonneaux, or 28,000 cases, has now been reached. In 1974, an agreement was made with Gilbey-Louderme for the exclusive world-wide distribution of the wine, a great act of faith in the future, given the situation at that time. An interesting feature of the agreement is that one third of the crop is sold in instalments over two years. This protects both buyer and seller from speculative movements of the markets.

At its best, Giscours is a most attractive wine distinguished by a delicately perfumed bouquet of elegance and finesse. The 1899 and the 1929 were both fine examples of these great years. In more recent years, the 1953 was delightful and the 1955 more attractive than many wines of this vintage. There followed a period when, with the greatly increased production and rather young vines, the wine was not always consistent and sometimes lacked the distinction of past vintages, but as the vineyard acquired maturity so the wine improved, and the growth once again occupied an important place in the Médoc. The excellent 1966 was followed by a good 1970, an especially fine 1971, an above average 1973, while 1975 and 1976 both promise to be fine in their different ways. 1978 and 1979 look like being another outstanding pair of wines, each representative of the best features of these vintages.

Château Ferrière   Third Growth

This old vineyard in the heart of Margaux now has the distinction of being the smallest surviving growth of the 1855 classification. Others have been smaller but are now larger, like Marquis d'Alesme, or were small and have been absorbed, like Dubignon, but Ferrière has always been small and remains unaltered. In 1860, an average of 10 to 15 tonneaux was recorded. After the phylloxera, 20, and then 25, tonneaux were made, but the production has now returned to an average of 10 tonneaux (only 900 cases).

One remarkable feature of the growth is that it has been in the possession of only two families for over 200 years. The Ferrière family owned the estate to which they gave their name from the middle of the eighteenth century until 1914. Dutch in origin, they were an important and wealthy family of Bordeaux merchants. Gabriel Ferrière, who was a *courtier royal* and *officier des chasses du Roi*, left the property in 1777 to his cousin of the same name. He and his brother Jean were bourgeois of Bordeaux but also held a number of official positions; they were imprisoned under the Terror, but in 1795 Jean became Mayor of Bordeaux. Henri Ferrière was the last member of the family to own the property.

The purchaser in 1914 was Monsieur Armand Feuillerate, the proprietor of Marquis de Terme, and he gave it to his daughter in 1921, who is now Madame André Durand, the present proprietor. In recent years the vineyard has been leased to Château Lascombes where the wine is now made, but it is quite separate from Lascombes, and the wine is distinctly different. It is characterized by a most distinctive and powerful bouquet, being full flavoured and yet elegant. The 1961 and 1962 were particularly successful and were made available in England for the first time in many years. The 1847 has long been one of the legendary wines of Bordeaux.

Château Pouget   Fourth Growth

This property in Cantenac has ancient origins, the vineyard having originally been the property of the abbey of Cantenac. The growth is mentioned in all the old classifications during the first half of the nineteenth century.

The average production of 1,800 cases has not varied very much during the last hundred years. Now the property of Monsieur Guillermet, who runs it jointly with Boyd-Cantenac, the wine, no doubt on account of its small production is seldom met with in England. But the quality has improved under its present ownership, and the wines are rich and supple.

Château Prieuré Lichine   Fourth Growth

The charming old château was once the Prieuré for the monks of Cantenac, and backs on to the parish church of Cantenac. After the property was bought by Alexis Lichine in 1952, he completely restored the château in the most original and decorative fashion.

The reputation of the vineyard goes back some 300 years, although it did not appear in classifications prior to 1855. Since the change of ownership in 1952, the vineyard has been enlarged and reconstructed, so that on average 260 tonneaux, or 25,000 cases, are now made instead of the 30 tonneaux previously achieved. The wine is much improved and is rather fuller in body and rounder in flavour than Lascombes, more typical indeed of the wines of Cantenac. Recently, the 1973 and 1977 were above average in these years, while fine wines were made in 1975, 1976, 1978 and 1979.

Château Marquis de Terme   Fourth Growth

This property lies at the back of Margaux and is extremely well kept. It is of ancient origin and appeared in all the old classifications. Its vineyards lie in Margaux and Cantenac. The name comes from an eighteenth-century proprietor who acquired it through marrying a niece of the celebrated Marquis de Rausan. From the era of the classification, Oscar Sollberg owned and improved it for many years until it passed into the hands of Frédéric Eschenauer under whose care it continued to prosper. The present owner is Monsieur Pierre Sénéclauze.

Production, which at the time of classification amounted to 45 tonneaux, averaged 100 tonneaux by the end of the century and now stands at 170 tonneaux, or 15,500 cases. The wine is attractive and consistent if not in the highest class; it possesses the Margaux characteristics, is rather generous, but has some delicacy and usually develops quickly. The wine is usually kept in *cuve* for the first winter and then spends two years in cask, rather longer than is usual for most Margaux wines these days.

Château Desmirail   Third Growth

Mention must be made of this growth because it still appears in lists of the 1855 classification, although no wine is now made under this name, the vineyard having been sold to Château Palmer. This growth is effectively absorbed in Palmer, while the château belongs to Monsieur Zuger of Château Malescot.

The property was formerly part of Rauzan but formed the dowry of Mademoiselle Rauzan de Ribail when she married a Desmirail. The château is a remarkable building of the 1860s in what was described as the style of Louis XIII.

Château du Tertre (or le Tertre)   Fifth Growth

This vineyard occupies a very fine position in the commune of Arsac, of which it is the only classified growth. The château stands in an elevated position commanding a fine view of the plateau on which the vineyard is planted. This is fine, pebbly soil with views towards the vineyards of Giscours and of Cantenac. *Tertre* means a hillock or rising ground.

By the 1840s, under the ownership of Charles Henri, it had a good reputation and was in demand in Holland. This reputation was greatly increased after its acquisition by Henri Koenigswarter in 1870. The production now rose from 60 or 70 tonneaux, to 100 and up to 160 tonneaux. The reputation and production fell away considerably after the Second World War, but happily it was bought by Monsieur Philippe Gasqueton, one of the partners in Calon Ségur, in 1961. He, together with his Belgian partners, have steadily restored both vineyard and château. The production has been restored from about 25 tonneaux to 200 tonneaux, or 18,000 cases. The wine now being made resembles a Cantenac, but has a particularly brilliant colour and a beautifully perfumed bouquet with a very fine and elegant flavour. The 1964 and 1966 were the beginning of a line of attractive vintages worth following in the future.

Château Dauzac (formerly spelt Dauzats)   Fifth Growth

This is a growth which did not assume importance until the middle of the nineteenth century. It is not mentioned in Cock's classification as late as 1846, but was classified a fifth growth in 1855, when it belonged to a Monsieur Wiebrock and produced between 50 and 60 tonneaux. At an earlier date, the château, a building of pleasing proportions, had been the home of Jean Baptiste Lynch, although the vineyard does not seem to have excited much attention at this time. The great age of Dauzac came when it passed into the hands of Nathaniel Johnston, a member of the famous family of that name of Irish-Scottish ancestry. In this period, the firm of *négociants* was actually run firstly by his father, and then by his brother, Harry Scott Johnston. Nathaniel Johnston was a notable figure in the Médoc of his day. He had qualified as a civil engineer and was very active in the Société d'Agriculture de la Gironde, whose gold medal he was awarded. He was also the proprietor of Ducru-Beaucaillou and ran this property and Dauzac in harness. It was here that Bordeaux Mixture was first successfully tried to combat mildew, the scourge of the 1880s. In spite of his great interest in these properties and in all matters connected with viticulture, Nathaniel Johnston also found time to stand for the National Assembly in 1871, to which he was duly elected. During his proprietorship, wines from this estate were used to make a well-known sparkling wine known as Royal Médoc Mousseux.

From the description of the wines of Dauzac at this period they seem to have resembled those of other wines of the commune such as Giscours. In recent years, however, the wine has been rather atypical of Labarde or Margaux, a little firm and austere, lacking the mellowness and fruit usually associated with this region.

In 1965, the property was acquired by Monsieur William Alain Burke Miaihle, the proprietor of the neighbouring Château Siran, whose wines now have a better reputation than those of Dauzac. Monsieur Miaihle is also part proprietor of Pichon-Lalande and a partner in Palmer. At this time he managed his family's interest in all these properties. As the vineyards of Siran and Dauzac are contiguous, the advantages of running the two estates as one seemed obvious. But the venture proved a disappointment, and within a decade Dauzac was again on the market. The average production is 15,000 cases.

Château Siran

This growth is officially classified as a *Bourgeois Supérieur* but was included in the INAO's proposal for a new classification published in 1961 as a *Grand Cru Classé*, an opinion confirmed by its inclusion in the Alexis Lichine Classification (see Chapter 3).

For many years, this property belonged to the Comtes de Lautrec, but was sold by them in 1848 to Monsieur Leo Barbier who greatly improved the vineyard, so that by 1874, Féret could write that Siran was by then one of the best *Crus Bourgeois* in the Médoc. The present proprietor, Monsieur W. A. Miailhe, is descended from Leo Barbier, and the property has greatly benefited from continuity of management.

The vineyard is very well tended and the wine is consistent. It is gently perfumed, delicate and on the light side, but with a delicious flavour which fills the mouth. It is very typical in style of the type of Margaux one finds in Labarde and Cantenac. Of recent vintages, the 1953 is very fine, and is holding up very well; the 1960 was very light but a wine of great charm and freshness; the

1961 is outstanding; the 1962, 1964 and 1966 all highly successful. The average production is 11,500 cases.

The château is small but charming, and the small park is noted for its sea of cyclamens at vintage time. It lies just to the west of the *route des chateaux* (D2) where it is joined by the D108.

Château la Tour de Mons

This is another excellent property which is today ranked as a classified growth, both in the INAO proposal and by Lichine. It is an estate of very ancient origins; the château can be traced back to the fifteenth century and was much restored around 1615, at which time it passed into the family of de Mons through the marriage of Pierre de Mons with the only daughter of Baron de Soussans. Catherine de Mons took the property as her marriage portion in 1740 with J. B. de Secondat de Montesquieu of La Brède, the son of the famous author of *L'Esprit des lois* and *Lettres persanes*. The son was himself a distinguished naturalist, becoming the director of the Académie de Bordeaux in 1736 and a Fellow of our own Royal Society. He had no children and bequeathed the property back to the Mons des Dunes family. Since this time, the names of the proprietors have changed from time to time, but the property has remained in connecting families, passing through the female line on several occasions. It now belongs to the heirs of Pierre Dubos, for over forty years the proprietors of Cantemerle as well as La Tour de Mons.

For over ninety years it has been regarded as one of the leading growths in Soussans, and in recent years has been generally acknowledged as the best wine in the commune. It is a wine of race and breed, a little firm at first but developing finesse and delicacy with ageing. It is the monopoly of the *négociants* H. & O. Beyermann, who are now owned by Atkinson Baldwin, the wine side of Drambuie. The production, which formerly reached 200 tonneaux, now averages 100, or 8,500 cases.

Château Bel-Air-Marquis-d'Alègre

This is the second of the Soussans growths which was proposed both by the INAO and Alexis Lichine for classified growth status. Earlier, it had been named as one of the six *Crus Exceptionnels* of the *Crus Bourgeois*. By the end of the nineteenth century, wines of Bel-Air were highly esteemed and fetched prices on a par with

94

third and fourth growths. The vineyard, beautifully situated on a plateau of light, pebbly soil, after reconstruction by the present proprietor, now averages around 4,250 cases. The wine is being very carefully made now; an elegant wine of breed which should be worth following in the future.

Château d'Angludet

This is an example of a growth which was once regarded as a classified growth, failed to be classified in 1855, and is now once more making a come-back to classified growth status. In 1874, Féret records a melancholy state of affairs. The property, formerly one large and important growth, was divided among three different proprietors. Before the Revolution, it had been in the Legras family and was regarded as a fourth growth, but when the head of the family died in 1791, it was divided among four sons. It is significant that it was not mentioned in the best classifications of the 1820s or in Cock's list of 1846. A revival began when two of the four portions came into the hands of Paul Promis, grandson of a former proprietor of Giscours, and by 1880 he had raised the production of his share from 25 to 45 tonneaux. At this time one part was called Domaine d'Angludet and the other part, now reunited under Jules Jadouin, was again known as Château d'Angludet. In 1891 he had the satisfaction of reuniting the property exactly a century after it was first divided.

By this time, the excellence of the wines of Angludet was firmly established again, and the growth fetched prices equal to those of classified wines. It was recognized that, with such excellent soil, the property had only missed classification through its unhappy division. During the period of this renaissance, England is frequently mentioned as one of the best markets for Angludet. At this time the production amounted to 150 tonneaux from the excellent vineyard which lies at the back of Cantenac and is partly framed by trees, offering prospects towards Giscours, Brane-Cantenac, Kirwan and Le Tertre.

After the Second World War, Angludet fell into a sad state of neglect, so that production declined to a few tonneaux. Happily, in 1961, the Sichel family acquired it and it became the home of Mr Peter Sichel. The château itself is a single-storey building dating from the eighteenth century, with some very interesting equestrian tapestries in the salon which have been fully restored.

CLASSIFICATION OF *BOURGEOIS* WINES OF THE MÉDOC AND HAUT-MÉDOC: 1978

Grand Bourgeois

Château Agassac	Ludon	*Exceptionnel*
Château Andron Blanquet	St Estèphe	*Exceptionnel*
Château Beaumont	Cussac	
Château Beausite	St Estèphe	*Exceptionnel*
Château Bel-Orme	St Seurin de Cadourne	
Château Brillette	Moulis	
Château Capbern	St Estèphe	*Exceptionnel*
Château La Cardonne	Blaignan	
Château Caronne Ste-Gemme	St Laurent	*Exceptionnel*
Château Chasse-Spleen	Moulis	*Exceptionnel*
Château Cissac	Cissac	*Exceptionnel*
Château Citran	Avensan	*Exceptionnel*
Château Colombier Monpelou	Pauillac	
Château Coufran	St Seurin de Cadourne	
Château Coutelin-Merville	St Estèphe	
Château Le Crock	St Estèphe	*Exceptionnel*
Château Duplessis-Hauchecorne	Moulis	
Château Dutruch-Grand-Poujeau	Moulis	*Exceptionnel*
Château Fontesteau	St Sauveur	
Château Fourcas Dupré	Listrac	*Exceptionnel*
Château Fourcas Hosten	Listrac	*Exceptionnel*
Château La Fleur Milon	Pauillac	
Château Du Glana	St Julien	*Exceptionnel*
Château Greysac	Bégadan	
Château Hanteillan	Cissac	
Château Haut-Marbuzet	St Estèphe	*Exceptionnel*
Château Lafon	Listrac	
Château Lamarque	Lamarque	
Château Lamothe	Cissac	
Château Laujac	Bégadan	
Château Liversan	St Sauveur	
Château Loudenne	St Yzans	
Château Mac-Carthy	St Estèphe	
Château Malleret	Le Pian	
Château Marbuzet	St Estèphe	*Exceptionnel*
Château Meyney	St Estèphe	*Exceptionnel*
Château Morin	St Estèphe	
Château Moulin à Vent	Moulis	
Château Le Meynieu	Vertheuil	
Château Martinens	Margaux	
Château Les Ormes Sorbet	Couquèques	

THE MÉDOC: MARGAUX AND ST JULIEN

Grand Bourgeois

Château Les Ormes de Pez	St Estèphe	
Château Patache d'Aux	Bégadan	
Château Paveil de Luze	Soussans	
Château Peyrabon	St Sauveur	
Château Phélan-Ségur	St Estèphe	*Exceptionnel*
Château Pontoise-Cabarrus	St Seurin de Cadourne	
Château Potensac	Potensac	
Château Poujeaux	Moulis	*Exceptionnel*
Château La Rose Trintaudon	St Laurent	
Château Reysson	Vertheuil	
Château Ségur	Parempuyre	
Château Sigognac	St Yzans	
Château Sociando-Mallet	St Seurin de Cadourne	
Château du Taillan	Le Taillan	
Château La Tour de By	Bégadan	
Château La Tour du Haut Moulin	Cussac	
Château Tronquoy Lalande	St Estèphe	
Château Verdignan	St Seurin de Cadourne	

Bourgeois

Château Aney	Cussac
Château Balac	St Laurent de Médoc
Château Bellerive	Valeyrac
Château Bellerose	Pauillac
Château La Becade	Listrac
Château Bonneau	St Seurin de Cadourne
Château Le Boscq	St Estèphe
Château Le Breuil	Cissac
Château La Bridane	St Julien
Château De By	Bégadan
Château Castera	St Germain d'Esteuil
Château Chambert	St Estèphe
Château Cap Leon Veyrin	Listrac
Château Carcannieux	Queyrac
Château La Clare	Bégadan
Château La Closerie	Moulis
Château Duplessis-Fabre	Moulis
Château Fonreaud	Listrac
Château Fonpiqueyre	St Sauveur
Château Fort Vauban	Cussac
Château La France	Blaignan
Château Gallais Bellevue	Potensac
Château Grand Duroc Milon	Pauillac
Château Grand Moulin	St Seurin de Cadourne
Château Haut-Bages Monpelou	Pauillac

97

Bourgeois

Château Haut-Canteloup	Couquèques
Château Haut-Garin	Bégadan
Château Haut-Padarnac	Pauillac
Château Houbanon	Prignac
Château Hourtin-Ducasse	St Sauveur
Château de Labat	St Laurent
Château Lamothe Bergeron	Cussac
Château Landon	Bégadan
Crû Lassalle	Potensac
Château Lartigue de Brochon	St Seurin de Cadourne
Château Le Landat	Cissac
Château Lestage	Listrac
Château Mac Carthy Moula	St Estèphe
Château Monthil	Bégadan
Château Moulin Rouge	Cussac
Château Panigon	Civrac
Château Pibran	Pauillac
Château Plantey de la Croix	St Seurin de Cadourne
Château Pontet	Blaignan
Château Ramage la Batisse	St Sauveur
Château La Roque de By	Bégadan
Château Saint-Bonnet	St Christoly
Château de la Rose Marechale	St Seurin de Cadourne
Château Saransot	Listrac
Château Soudars	Avensan
Château Tayac	Soussans
Château La Tour Blanche	St Christoly
Château La Tour du Mirail	Cissac
Château La Tour Haut-Caussan	Blaignan
Château La Tour Saint-Bonnet	St Christoly
Château La Tour Saint-Joseph	Cissac
Château des Tourelles	Blaignan
Château Vieux Robin	Bégadan

Vineyards at present being reconstituted

Château Les Bertins	Valeyrac
Château Clarke	Listrac
Château Lariviere	Blaignan
Château Lavaliere	St Christoly
Château Romefort	Cussac
Château Vernous	Lesparre

Production increased as the vineyard was reconstructed, and now averages around 9,750 cases. The wine is characteristic of wine from a new vineyard, very light in colour, but with finesse and breed which one would expect from soil of this quality. Undoubtedly, Angludet will produce fine and worthy wines in years to come.

Château Paveil-de-Luze *Grand Bourgeois*

Before the Revolution, the property belonged to the Bretonneaux family. In 1862, it was bought by Baron Alfred de Luze, who in 1820 had founded the Bordeaux *négociants* of that name. It has belonged to the family and firm of de Luze ever since. Production, which was 125 tonneaux in the 1870s when the domaine spread over the communes of Soussans, Arcins, Avensan, and Moulis, fell after the First World War to 25 tonneaux and has only of late revived, so that at the present time average production is 55 tonneaux, or 4,700 cases.

This is a wine included in the Lichine classification but not in the proposal of the INAO. I must confess that, while I find the wine good and sound, it is to my mind rather anonymous and I cannot really regard it as being of classified growth standing.

Château L'Abbégorsse de Gorsse (Margaux)   950 cases
Château Labégorce (Margaux)   8,500 cases
Château Labégorce Zédé (Soussans)   5,100 cases

Because of the confusion which these three very similar names are bound to cause, it seems sensible to deal with them together. There can be no doubt that at one time they formed a single property, the origins of which have been traced back to the fourteenth century. Deeds show that it belonged to the noble family of La Bégorce in 1332. It passed through a number of noble hands before the Revolution, including the de Mons who took the title of Seigneur de Labégorce in 1728. By the middle of the nineteenth century we find Capelle, formerly Abbé Gorsse and de Gorsse, the property of the widow de Gorsse, and Zédé, the property of Emile Zédé, all at Soussans, while in Margaux, l'Abbé Gorsse was also the property of widow Gorsse. The mixture of Soussans and Margaux seems to have been more a question of the position of the houses rather than the vineyards. There are vineyards in both communes, and even in the case of Zédé, much of the vineyard is in fact in Margaux.

The present Labégorce is descended from the Capelle formerly Abbé Gorsse, and its prosperity principally dates from its acquisition in 1865 by a Monsieur Fortune Beaucourt who greatly improved the vineyards and the buildings so that the production rose from 50 to 60 tonneaux in the 1860s, and to 80 to 90 tonneaux at the end of the century. After Monsieur Beaucourt's death, production gradually declined, although the château maintained its excellent reputation.

L'Abbé Gorsse de Gorsse remained in the possession of the widow de Gorsse and then of her daughter until nearly the end of the nineteenth century, when it was bought by Edouard Peres who remained the proprietor until the Second World War. The production here rose to 50 tonneaux under Peres, but has now declined again.

Labégorce-Zédé belonged to Admiral Zédé and his heirs until the inter-war period, and the production has now been restored to a figure approaching what was achieved in its heyday at the turn of the century. Recent tastings of these wines suggest that Labégorce is now the best of the three. It has the finesse and distinction of a fine Margaux.

There are a number of lesser properties in Margaux which, while not meriting detailed treatment, can nevertheless make excellent wine. Some may be found on *négociants'* lists, others may be sold by *vente directe* at the door. These days fewer go into generic blends, since Margaux is now such an expensive *appellation*. It is interesting to note, in this context, that compared with 721 hectares of classified growths in the *appellation*, there are only 256 hectares of *Crus Bourgeois*.

Finally, there are three excellent growths: Château Martinens, *Grand Bourgeois* (production 4,250 cases); Château Tayac, *Bourgeois* (production 2,250 cases) and Château Marsac-Seguineau (production 2,550 cases), which is unaccountably absent from the classification of bourgeois growths.

ST JULIEN

This is the smallest of the four great communes of the Haut-

Médoc, and the *Appellation* limits the name to wines produced within the commune. The gravelly soil of St Julien resembles that of Margaux but contains more clay. This results in a wine with something of the finesse and breed of Margaux but with some of the vinosity and body of Pauillac. The bouquet of these wines is especially fine and develops early, and while they are in a sense somewhere between a Margaux and a Pauillac, this is a very inadequate description because it takes no account of their exceptional individuality. One cannot do better than to quote what Franck wrote to them long ago when speaking of their incomparable flavour which, he said, 'cannot be well compared to that of any other claret. They combine all the qualities which constitute the very best wines.' (Traité sur les Vins du Médoc, 4th edition, 1860.)

Within St Julien itself one can discern a distinct progression in the style of the wines. Those vineyards situated on the slopes along the river-front produce the wines with the most pronounced bouquet and finesse. Here are to be found the best parts of vineyards such as Léoville-Lascases, Ducru-Beaucaillou and Beychevelle. As one moves inland towards the plateau of St Laurent, the wines become more full-bodied, more highly coloured and richer. Gruaud-Larose is an example of the best type of wines in this category. There are, of course, many variants between the two extremes because, apart from other factors, many vineyards are to be found in different parts of the commune and on differing soils.

St Julien used to be the most popular generic or district name for claret. Unhappily, wines sold under this name alone had to be viewed, especially in England, with a certain degree of suspicion. This was because a high proportion of the wines of St Julien were already sold under the names of individual châteaux and, apart from poor years, the quantity of genuine St Julien available for sale under the generic *appellation* was not large, and was certainly never cheap. Of a total of 746 hectares under vine, only 96 are *Crus Bourgeois* and 91 *Crus Artisans*; all the rest belong to the classified growths. Now, generic St Julien is essentially a thing of the past.

It is one of the curiosities of St Julien that, while the percentage of fine wines produced is exceptional, and the quality of its wines represents much that is best in claret, no first growth is to be found here. But it must be said that in some years its best growths

101

produce wines which equal, or can indeed surpass, the first growths.

Château Léoville-Lascases   Second Growth

This great growth must take pride of place among the wines of St Julien. It represents the major portion of the pre-Revolution estate of the Marquis de Las Cases, and its label still proudly, if rather confusingly, proclaims its lineage 'Grand Vin de Léoville de Marquis de Las Cases'.

Before the Revolution, this was one of the greatest estates in the Médoc of the eighteenth century, extending from Château Latour to Château Beychevelle, its vineyards broken only by the village of St Julien, and situated on the unrivalled slopes above the *palus* (the alluvial, low-lying land by the river) commanding a fine prospect of the river. The present estate comprises half the original domaine, a quarter having been sold to Hugh Barton and a quarter to Baron de Poyferré in the 1820s. It has remained unchanged since that time, and is comprised mostly of a single vineyard stretching from Latour to the village of St Julien. The whole is enclosed by a fine wall, and the main entrance is marked by an arch, recently repaired, which is a notable landmark on the *route des châteaux*, and has long adorned the château label. It is one of the largest vineyards in a single piece in the Médoc.

Until 1900, it remained in the hands of the Las Cases family, from whence it passed to a Société Civile. After the change of ownership, the estate was entrusted for some years to the management of Monsieur Théophile Skawinski, son of the famous agriculturalist whose career has already been touched upon under Giscours. It is now under the direction of Monsieur Michel Delon who.has recently followed in the footsteps of his father, the third generation of his family to supervise the property, so that a remarkable degree of continuity has been achieved from the eighteenth century through to the present day. Although, like his famous father, Paul Delon, before him, Michel Delon is a rather controversial figure in the Médoc, there can be no doubt that he is one of the most capable proprietors in the region today. With a passion for quality, he controls all with a precision that commands admiration.

Over the years, with certain exceptions, Lascases has maintained its position as the finest wine in St Julien. There was certainly a period before the war when Poyferré was often its equal and sometimes its peer. Again, there was a period in the 1950s, when, due to a preponderance of young vines following extensive replanting, the wines failed to achieve their usual excellence. But from 1959 onwards, even in off-vintages, Lascases has consistently been one of the best second growths in the Médoc. The essence of Lascases is a bouquet of great elegance and suavity and an incomparable flavour which is almost silky in texture when mature, very long but at the same time firm and well balanced. A good Lascases is a very complete wine in the fullest sense of that word.

A word about the historic Vintages may be of interest. The 1899 was still well preserved when I was last privileged to drink it in 1963. But much more remarkable was the 1900. On both occasions when I drank this wine in 1962, I thought it one of the greatest clarets I have ever drunk, the equal of any first growths. The bouquet was still wonderful and continued to expand in the glass, while the flavour was delicious, a perfection of breed and finesse and perfect harmony, without a trace of decay. In 1971 I tasted a bottle from the cellar of Glamis Castle which was every bit as fine and vigorous. This is truly one of the immortals. Next, one must mention the 1928. The Lascases of this vintage was the best wine of the year, superior to any of the first growths. When last drunk in 1979, it was in a state of complete perfection, a wine stunning in its sheer beauty. Its fascination is that combination of the bouquet and finesse of a great 1929 coupled with the power and solidity of a 1928, and in so doing, it far outstrips its contemporaries which seem dry and harsh in comparison.

One has mentioned the lean years in the 1950s. Before this, good wines were made in 1945, 1947 and 1948. The 1959 was a very fine comeback and has lived up fully to its early promise. The 1960 was a most attractive wine and was one of the best Médocs of the vintage, while the 1961 was one of the best wines of this great year. Along with Palmer, Ducru Beaucaillon and Gruaud Larose, it is one of those on a similar plane to the first growths, as has been clearly shown in recent blind tastings. The 1962 was also one of the best wines of the year, which has continued to develop in complexity and interest over the years, and the 1964 was one of the most successful Médocs in a year when the region generally failed to live up to its early reputation. The 1966 was excellent, and the 1967 one of the best wines of a mixed vintage, and which, unlike most Médocs, has not dried up. The 1970s have produced another string of classics: a great 1970, an elegant 1971, an above average 1973, great 1975s and 1976s, and a beautiful 1977, while 1978 promises to be one of the great wines of the decade. 1979 is yet another success, with more solidity than most wines of this year.

In conclusion, it should be said that today Léoville-Lascases, because of its quality and consistency, is one of those top Médocs, separated from the first growths only through the rigid traditions of Bordeaux's ossified classification system, and its price. As such, it represents wonderful value—a wine enabling connoisseurs to enjoy claret of first growth quality at half the price. The average production is 30,000 cases. Mention must be made of the second *marque*, sold as Clos du Marquis, which maintains a very good standard.

Château Léoville-Poyferré   Second Growth

The growth began its separate existence when it was purchased from the Las Cases family by Baron de Poyferré, and comprised a quarter of the original domaine of Léoville. In 1866 it was bought for one million frs (approx. £200,000) by Monsieur Armand Lalande and the Baron d'Erlanger. The property then passed in the 1890s to Edouard Lawton and, after the First World War, to the Bordeaux *négociants*, H. Cuvelier & Fils. During the second half of the nineteenth century this growth enjoyed an exceptional reputation as one of the very finest of all the second growths, and Biarnez's poem was often quoted, where he proclaimed: 'Et je ne comprends pas quel expert inhabile a pu dans les seconds classer le Léoville', the inference being that Poyferré should have been a first growth.

At its best, the style of Poyferré was essentially similar to Lascases, as might be expected. The greatest Poyferrés I have seen were the 1928, which was second only to the Lascases in that vintage, and the magnificent 1929. It is interesting to find Morton Shand, always a lover of old wines, echoing the nineteenth-century view of Poyferré still in 1920 in finding Poyferré the best of the Léovilles. I have not seen enough examples of the wines from the inter-war years to express an opinion as to whether this was generally true in this period, but in recent years, Poyferré has in general been well behind Lascases in quality. It is usually supple and attractive but lacks the breed, distinction and consistency of Lascases. Without doubt the raw materials are as good as ever, the problem lies in cellar-work. The average production is 18,000 cases.

Château Léoville-Barton   Second Growth

Like Poyferré, Léoville-Barton is a quarter portion of the original Léoville domaine. It was purchased in 1826 by Hugh Barton, an Irishman whose grandfather had first come to Bordeaux in 1725. In spite of this, the Barton family then and now remains an Irish family with close ties with their homeland. Having acquired the neighbouring property of Langoa in 1821, Hugh Barton was able to use the *chais* of Langoa for housing the wines of his portion of Léoville, so that there has never been a separate chais, or château, for this property. These two properties have been in the ownership of a single family for longer than any other classified growth in the Médoc, for Hugh Barton's descendant, Mr Ronald Barton, today owns and runs Langoa.

The production of this portion of Léoville has increased in recent years: it is recorded at 50 to 60 tonneaux in 1860 and is around 125, or 18,000 cases, today although in the prolific vintage of 1893 it reached 164. The reputation of Léoville Barton has remained very consistent over a long period and, as might be expected, has long enjoyed a considerable following in this country. Ronald Barton succeeded to the family inheritance as a very young man in 1927, after his father, Bertram Hugh Barton, was killed hunting in Ireland; he had joined the family firm of Barton & Guestier only three years before his father's death. Ever since, he has very much been the resident proprietor, closely supervising his wines and setting the highest standards for them.

I have not seen any very old examples of this château in fine years, but the 1929 was a fine wine, if not quite the equal of the Poyferré of that year. This is a wonderfully consistent growth; very attractive wines were made in rather mixed vintages such as 1934 and 1948, while the 1949 and 1959 were particularly successful. More recently, classic wines were made in 1961, 1962, 1966, 1970, 1971, 1975 and 1978. Unusually, the 1974 is to be preferred to the 1973. While Léoville-Barton will not usually match a great year of Lascases, it will seldom disappoint either, and is usually one of the best wines of St Julien—a shade richer and fuller-bodied than Lascases, and a little less elegant and fine.

Château Ducru-Beaucaillou   Second Growth

This charming property adjoins that of Beychevelle, and indeed both châteaux are rather similarly placed, commanding a fine view across low-lying meadows to the river. As a building, Beaucaillou cannot, it is true, equal its neighbour, but with its elegant terrace and its pleasing proportions, this rather distinctive Victorian mansion has an attraction all its own. The château is unusual for Bordeaux in having its *chais* situated beneath it and its *dépendances* in large underground cellars.

In the early part of the nineteenth century this growth was known as Bergeron, but when it came into the possession of the Ducru family their name was adopted, together with that of Beaucaillou, the name given by them to the place itself. The fame of Beaucaillou dates from the care and improvements effected by Monsieur Ducru, and subsequently by Nathaniel Johnston who acquired the property in 1866. Under him, it was usually known simply as Beaucaillou.

The reputation of Beaucaillou declined between the wars, but since the property has come under the management of Monsieur Jean-Eugène Borie, whose father had bought Beaucaillou during the last war, a renaissance has occurred in its quality and reputation. Monsieur Borie is a devoted enthusiast, and one of the relatively few resident proprietors among the top growth Médocs, so that visitors to the château are frequently welcomed by the proprietor in person; he is also one of the best-liked and most respected proprietors, a man of engaging modesty about his own wines, and always a generous judge of his neighbours'. He is also a much-travelled ambassador for Bordeaux wines abroad.

The vineyard itself, lying beside that of Beychevelle and south of Léoville Lascases, produces a wine typical of the best of St Julien. Beaucaillou has the elegance, lightness and breed of a wine from a vineyard near the river, a superb bouquet and a flavour which fills the mouth. Compared with Lascases, it is a little softer and lighter and lacks the richness of growths like Gruaud Larose which lie further inland. There is, interestingly enough, a small parcel of vines in the neighbouring commune of Cussac.

I have seen few examples of pre-war vintages, and of these two were worthy of note: the 1920, which was still very fruity and generous, typical of its year, sound in wind and limb when drunk in 1963. The 1928 was curious for being already faded and light in 1958. The vintage which did more than anything else to re-establish the reputation and standing of Beaucaillou was 1953. This has developed into a really delicious wine with an outstanding bouquet and an almost silky texture on the palate—one of the top 1953s. The 1955 is more attractive than most, the 1957 one of the most approachable wines of this vintage. The 1958 and 1960 were both charming wines, light, elegant and flavoury, at their best when about five years old but holding up well afterwards for several years. The 1959 has been a great success, with more length in middle life than many wines of this vintage; it has consistently lived up to its early promise, one of the few 1959s that can stand beside the 1961. The 1961 is one of the great examples of the extraordinary qualities of this vintage with its phenomenal power and depth. In a blind tasting in Holland in 1978, this wine was placed first among ten leading growths of the year, and was then placed on a par with some of the first growths in the second half of the tasting. The 1962 is outstanding for its attractive ripeness, while the 1964 was one of the best Médocs in a disappointing year. Since then, a string of successes have followed: 1966 and 1967, 1970 (exceptional) and 1971 (an outstanding example of the vintage), 1973 and a 1974 with more charm than most, a great 1975, a fine 1976, a 1977 of charm and a 1978 that promises to be great. 1979 looks one of the top wines of the vintage. All this goes to show that since 1953 Beaucaillou has consistently produced fine wine and is today undoubtedly one of the jewels of St Julien.

The vineyard and production remained remarkably constant over a long period. Charles Cocks gives it as 100 to 120 tonneaux in 1846, Franck as 80 to 100 tonneaux in 1860. Today it averages 300 tonneaux, or 28,000 cases, after M. Borie's years of improvement.

Château Gruaud-Larose Second Growth

This is another example of a large estate which was created during the eighteenth century by a wealthy and enthusiastic proprietor, Monsieur Gruaud. It was in 1757 that he combined three properties, Tenac, Sartaignac and Dumarle, to form this important growth which was at first known as Fonbedeau before

107

assuming that of Gruaud, or Gruau as it was sometimes spelt. Gruaud made a name for himself both as an enthusiastic viticulturalist and as something of an eccentric, for to live on one's estate and personally supervise its management in every aspect was hardly the norm in the France of the *ancien régime*. He even built a tower especially so that he could observe work on all parts of his large estate, and from the top of which he would fly a flag whenever a vintage had been successfully gathered in.

On his death in 1778, he left the estate to Monsieur de Larose, a member of the *noblesse de robe* which played so important a part in the development of the Médoc in the years before the Revolution. He was Lieutenant-General of the Sénéchausée of Guyenne as well as being president of one of the law courts. The château now became known as Gruaud-Larose and the fame of its wine became more widespread, so that it found its way on to the greatest tables in the land. It was during this period that it boasted the proud device which has for long appeared on its labels, 'Le Roy des Vins, le Vin des Rois'. When the heirs of Monsieur Larose disposed of the estate in 1812 for the sum of 350,000 frs (approx. £70,000) it was bought by the house of Balguerie, Sarget, Verdornet & Cie. The driving force in this enterprise was the remarkable Pierre Balguerie-Stuttenberg, one of the most successful and colourful figures of Bordeaux. His history is typical of the vigour and enterprise which characterized Bordeaux commerce at this time. His family having been ruined by the revolution on St Dominique, he began by working for the drapery business of Diré and Verdornnet. His aptitude for business, combined with his industry, intelligence and loyalty, so impressed his employers that he was taken into partnership in 1805, at the age of twenty-nine. Two years later he married a Mademoiselle Stuttenberg, the daughter of a Hamburg merchant who had offices on the Chartrons; when his father-in-law died soon afterwards, Balguerie-Stuttenberg took over the running of the business, and thus his connection with wine began and he became associated with the future Baron Sarget. For Balguerie-Stuttenberg, wine and Gruaud-Larose were very much a side-line left in the capable hands of Sarget, while he occupied himself with the affairs of a rapidly growing shipping and trading business which was to extend as far as China and South America. He and Sarget were both concerned with the project for building the bridge across the

Gironde at Bordeaux. He was also instrumental in improving the port of Bordeaux, established a telegraph between Royan and Bordeaux and became well-known for his charitable works as well.

After Balguerie-Stuttenberg died in 1825, worn out by his remarkable industry, Sarget became solely concerned with the management of Gruaud-Larose and acquired a considerable reputation as a viticulturist. All the early classifications of the nineteenth century are unanimous in placing Gruaud-Larose among the then rather small group of second growths, and this was confirmed in 1855. Although the Sarget family maintained a very long connection with Gruaud-Larose, unfortunately they divided the estate in two, selling the other portion of it in 1867 to Edouard and Charles de Bethmann and Adrien Faure. The two Bethmanns came of a German family of Frankfurt who had settled in Bordeaux in the eighteenth century. Their father, as noted for his philanthropic work as for his banking, was in fact Mayor of Bordeaux at the time of the purchase. In this era many gold medals and diplomas were awarded to both growths, and in 1879 Sarget was awarded the Gold Medal by the Ministry of Agriculture for the best-kept vineyard in the Gironde. New *chais*, cellars and *cuviers* had been constructed in the 1870s.

After the First World War the Sarget family sold their property to Désiré Cordier after a connection of over a century with the growth, and in 1934 Monsieur Cordier had the satisfaction of reuniting the property, when he purchased the Faure portion. The house of Cordier is now one of the most important in Bordeaux; Gruaud-Larose is meticulously run and is something of a showplace. The garden is one of the finest to be seen in any Bordeaux château although, unlike some other châteaux, it does not encourage visitors without specific trade introductions. Monsieur Cordier believes that too many visitors can interfere with the work of a château. One unusual feature of the *chais* are the large wooden *cuves* of around 60 hectolitres each, where the wine undergoes a part of its maturation. Wine is also kept in the traditional 225-litre barrique bordelaise, but this is carefully monitored according to the constitution of each individual wine. It is felt that these large *cuves* enable a slower maturation to be achieved, enhancing the fruit of the wine, which is such a feature of modern vintages of Gruaud-Larose. The production has always been one of the most consistently large in Médoc and now averages 30,000 cases.

The wine itself epitomizes the rich, generous, fleshy type of St Julien. Of recent vintages, the 1959 was very successful, fulfilling its early promise sooner than most. The 1961 is an outstanding example of this great year which, while ready earlier than some, has continued to develop and last well. The 1962 is a classic of this year. Unfortunately, the *chais* was severely damaged by fire in 1965, causing some loss to the 1964 crop. Since then, successes were recorded in 1966, 1967 (above average), 1968 (very good for the year), 1970 (an outstanding wine), 1971 (a wine of great charm), 1973 (forward but delightful), 1974 (better than most), 1975 (promises to be one of the top wines of the year), and 1976, which has great promise.

Château Beychevelle   Fourth Growth

This beautiful property has a long and interesting history. It can be traced back to the fourteenth century when it was a feudal castle and one of several important properties belonging to the de Foix family. This family became known as Foix de Candale after one of them, Jean de Foix, had refused to sign the surrender of Bordeaux in 1451 and had fled to England, where he was rewarded for his loyalty by being given the title of Kendal. This he mysteriously kept after his return to France and submission to Louis XI in 1463, when Kendal became Candale.

The property passed to the Duc d'Epernon when Marguerite de Foix-Candale, one of the greatest heiresses in France, became his third wife in 1587. Jean-Louis de Norgaret de la Vallette, first Duc d'Epernon, was one of the great men of his age, deeply involved in the politics of the turbulent period in which he lived. He was the confidant and favourite of Henri III under whom he became an Admiral of France as well as a Duc, and was in the coach with Henri IV when the king was assassinated. He has been described as ambitious, vindictive, haughty, insolent but brave to the point of recklessness, and recognizing no bounds to his power—the last personification of the old nobility before the age of Versailles destroyed their virility. It was through the Duc d'Epernon's position as Admiral of France that Beychevelle acquired its name. Ships passing by on the Gironde were required to lower their sails as a salute when passing the residence of an Admiral of France.

Beychevelle is a corruption of *Baisse-Voile*, *baisse* meaning lower and *voile* sail.

After the death of the second Duc d'Epernon without heirs, Beychevelle reverted to the Crown, who sold it to pay off the debts left by the Duc. In the eighteenth century, Beychevelle was still very much a feudal property, probably with a good deal of mixed farming as well as vines. In the period prior to the Revolution it belonged to the Marquis de Brassier, and was a very considerable estate extending over six parishes and including Lamarque and St Laurent as well as St Julien, where the seignorial rights and jurisdiction of the Marquis held sway. The income from this property was as much as 400,000 *livres* in rents, dues and feudal rights.

The Marquis being an *émigré*, the State seized the property during the Revolutionary period and put it up for sale. It was purchased by the Marquis's sister, Madame de Saint-Harem, who soon resold to Jacques Conte, a prominent Bordeaux ship-owner. But the fame of Beychevelle as a great vineyard must be traced from the time of its purchase by Pierre-François Guestier in 1825 for 650,000 frs (approx. £130,000). It is interesting to note that while Beychevelle does not feature in classifications of the 1820s, it does appear on Charles Cocks's list of 1846, and was classified as a fourth growth in 1855, as was its neighbour, Branaire.

Pierre-François Guestier was an important figure in the Bordeaux of his day. Because of the Revolution and his father's friendship with the Bartons, he was largely educated in England. Apart from his activities as a partner in Barton & Guestier, of which he was one of the founders, he was keenly interested in all agricultural matters. Thus he established a plantation of cork trees at Beychevelle, which excited considerable interest and was responsible for his being presented with the Gold Medal of the Société d'Agriculture de la Gironde in 1845. It was not until 1866 that the same Société awarded him a Gold Medal for the cultivation of the vine at Beychevelle. No doubt because of liberal sentiments acquired in England, Monsieur Guestier was much in sympathy with the régime of Louis Philippe and was active in politics during this period. He was first Deputy Mayor of Bordeaux, then Conseilleur Général, and finally representative for Lesparre in the Chamber of Deputies. In 1847 he was made a peer of France, but took no further part in public life after the 1848 Revolution.

111

On Monsieur Guestier's death in 1874, the property was sold to Armand Heine, and on the death of his widow, it passed to her son-in-law, Monsieur Achille-Fould, in whose family it has remained ever since. The Achille-Foulds have maintained the interest in public affairs which has marked former proprietors, the father of the present proprietor having been Minister of Agriculture in one of the inter-war Governments of the Third Republic, while his son was for many years a Deputy representing the Médoc, and held ministerial office.

The château itself, which commands a prominent position on the *route des châteaux*, has a fair claim to being the most beautiful in the Médoc. The present building dates from 1757 and the era of the Marquis de Brassier. It follows a classic Bordeaux formula which was often repeated, though never with such effect, in the nineteenth century. This provides a central single-storey building in which is the principal salon, and twin-storey towers at each end. The perfect proportions of the building are beautifully set off by delightful wrought iron railings and sumptuous flower-beds, which invariably attract the attention of the passing motorist. On its river side is a beautifully laid-out garden and lawns running down to and commanding an unrivalled view of the Gironde.

Beychevelle has long enjoyed a great reputation in England, and today its quality and prices place it among the second growths. It is one of the largest estates in the Médoc and has always had a considerable production. This averaged between 160 and 180 tonneaux by the end of the last century, although in years such as 1889, 1893 and 1900, well over 200 tonneaux were made. A small piece of the vineyard lies in the neighbouring commune of Cussac. Today 275 tonneaux, or 26,000 cases, are average.

There is a saying that a good year for Beychevelle is a good one for Bordeaux. It is true that this wine usually succeeds very well in the best vintages but is seldom very distinguished in small years. This slight inconsistency, however, is really the only reservation to be made about a wine which is, at its best, a very beautiful and charming St Julien. It has a bouquet of great elegance, and its ripe, fresh flavour is usually evident very early on, so that it often makes delicious early drinking.

Among old vintages, the 1928 was a rather typical wine of the year in taking a long time to come round, but then made one of the most enjoyable and sublime bottles of the vintage. The 1933, on the other hand, was a delightful wine, one that in the old days would have been called ideal luncheon claret—soft, delicate, fruity and quite charming. The 1945 was a fine wine, slow to mature, the 1953 was a beauty, all charm and almost too pretty in its first youth—it then filled out and deepened like an enchanting treble who to everyone's surprise turns into a first-rate tenor as well. The 1954 was a pleasing wine for the year, but the 1955 was a disappointment. The 1957, on the other hand, was one of the best wines in the Médoc. Neither the 1958 nor 1960 were very good, but Beychevelle has continued to do well in good years and was particularly outstanding in 1961, followed by a pleasing 1962 which was somewhat reminiscent of the 1953. Then came 1964 (above average), 1966 (a fine classic), 1970 (one of the early developers in this slow year), 1971 (really magnificent) and 1975 and 1976 both promising to be classics of these two very different years. 1978 and 1979 promise to be another fine pair, with the 1978 especially fine. All in all, it can fairly be said that the wines are as pretty as the place.

Château Branaire   Fourth Growth

This charming property faces Beychevelle across the road and looks out over vineyards and the S curve of the *route des châteaux* towards Ducru-Beaucaillou. The château itself is well worthy of mention. Its beautiful classical bearing is unusual in the Médoc for its elegance and simplicity. Built in 1780, it is a monument to that renaissance of prosperity and good taste which beautified Bordeaux in the decades just before the Revolution. The fine *chais* include magnificently cool, sunken cellars for the maturation of cask wines in their second and third years. This plays an important part in the fine development these wines always show in cask. There is also a charming orangery, recently restored for the entertainment of visitors.

There is a notable history of continuity at Branaire, for although its name and those of its proprietors have changed, it remained in the possession of connected families, so that there is an unbroken link from the 1740s until the time of the First World War. During this time, the property was known successively as Duluc, Branaire-du-Luc, and finally Branaire-Ducru. It is mentioned in classifications of the 1820s as a fourth growth, but its eminence really dates from the stewardship of Louis du Luc from 1825 onwards.

In the 1855 classification, it was placed among the fourth growths, but already by the 1860s its wines were fetching the prices of a third, and sometimes of a second growth. It was at this period that Branaire passed, after the death of Louis du Luc's widow, into the hands of a relative, Monsieur G. Ducru, whose family had just sold the neighbouring Beaucaillou, to which they had also given their name, to Nathaniel Johnston. It was under Ducru that the property reached the zenith of its reputation in the nineteenth century, although for a time this was well maintained by Ducru's nephew and heir, the Marquis de Carbonnier-Margac. After the death of the Marquis, the ownership was in the hands of a number of heirs, and it was from these that Monsieur Mitel bought Branaire after the Second World War.

As with many other properties, the affairs of Branaire languished just before and just after the Second World War, until Monsieur Tapie acquired it in 1952. Since then, he has gradually reconstituted the vineyard, always being careful to preserve a good proportion of old vines, but ensuring that new plantations were maturing to take their place, so that a correct rotation was re-introduced. In the *cuvier*, Monsieur Tapie introduced the submerged cap method of vinification, familiar in North Africa. This seems to give colour and generosity to the wines while keeping them supple, and there is some evidence that the results that have been achieved here are more encouraging than the practice of heating the must, which is employed at some other properties. The combination of a good Médocain *maître de chais* and a proprietor with Algerian experience, who is neither afraid of new ideas nor unmindful of what tradition has to impart, has proved remarkably successful. The production, which throughout the history of the property has been very consistent, has now been restored to something like 14,000 cases, close to the average attained at the end of the last century.

The reputation of this growth has also revived considerably since its acquisition by Monsieur Tapie. Fine wines were made in 1953, 1959, 1961 and 1962. The 1960 was exceptional for the year, while the 1964 and 1966 were very good examples of their respective years. In 1966, Monsieur Tapie decided to launch a non-vintage wine, the object being to improve the quality of the

114

off-vintage wines by blending them with some wine from the best years. As a corollary to this, only the best years were to appear as such under the Branaire label. This was a bold move at the time, designed to arrest the debasement of the 'vintage' wine which had been an unhappy feature of Bordeaux in recent years. As a result, 1963, 1965 and 1968 were not sold under a vintage label. But with the changed circumstances of the 1970s, the experiment came to an end. In more recent years, a very fine and characteristic 1970 was made, a charming 1971, and outstanding 1975. The 1976 has great promise, 1977 is one of the successes of the year, and 1978 again bids to be top-flight. The 1979 is a most attractive and typical example of this year.

The wines of Branaire have a marked individuality. The bouquet is very powerful, with an almost Pauillac assertiveness. The wine is rich, generous and supple with a most distinctive flavour. It has rather more body than most St Juliens. This particular personality is probably due to the fact that a part of the vineyard is on the plateau of St Laurent and, though not large, lends its personality to the whole. Amongst his other gifts, Jean Tapie seems to have a special touch when it comes to the *assemblage*. I have, on a number of occasions, tasted the constituent parts of a new vintage with him before the final *assemblage*, and it has been fascinating to see how the various elements have been fitted together to achieve a whole more satisfying than any of the individual consituents—the true test of any blending of wines of different *cépages*, and from vines of varying ages and soils.

This is one of a number of examples in the Médoc of classified growths with a part of their vineyard in a commune other than that of their *appellation*. As these anomalies are nearly always of long standing, the *Appellation* authorities do, in fact, give special permission for such wines to be incorporated in the final blend without in any way affecting the right of this blend to its traditional *appellation*.

Château Langoa-Barton   Third Growth

Nowhere perhaps does one see such a handsome collection of châteaux in so short a distance as around the tiny village of Beychevelle-St Julien. Beychevelle and Branaire face each other across the road, then Beaucaillou is to be seen away on the right across the vineyards, and finally, as one leaves the village for St Julien itself, there is the more massive but distinctly fine château of Langoa. It has the distinction of having been in the Barton family continuously since 1821, longer than any other classified growth; at that time the property was known as Pontet-Langlois. Perhaps English mispronunciation soon turned Langlois into Langoa. The advantages of continuity are evident as soon as one steps over the threshold, for this is a château that has been continuously occupied by the same family apart from the interruption of war, and indeed some of the hangings and decorations go back to Hugh Barton's time. At the entrance there is a most pleasing staircase, so that one mounts to the ground floor at first floor level, this being built over the private cellar—a charming arrangement.

The extensive *chais* houses the wines of both Langoa and the Barton's portion of Léoville. It is one of the curiosities that the wines of Langoa were never château bottled until 1969, but were removed to Barton & Guestier's cellars in Bordeaux and bottled there. The wines of Langoa maintain a good standard; they somewhat resemble those of Léoville-Barton in style, but are rather lighter and seldom quite match up to it in quality. In other words, it is a thoroughly reliable wine, a true St Julien and deserving its present reputation. Among the recent vintages, the 1970 produced a classic St Julien, 1971 is outstanding, better in my view than the Léoville, 1973 is already showing age, but the 1974 is unusually attractive for the year, better than the 1973 and better than the Léoville. 1975 is typically rich and tannic but with plenty of fruit and fat; it should mature more quickly than the Léoville. The 1976 showed better than the Léoville in the early stages but here one must wait and see. The 1977 is a success for the vintage and the 1978 very promising. It should be said that the present proprietor, Mr Ronald Barton, has also taken a very keen interest in his vineyards and his wines, and believes that quality is not to be sacrificed for quantity. The average production reaches 4,500 cases.

Château Talbot   Fourth Growth

This well-known growth has long been popular in England, not least because of its English name derived from that Earl of Shrewsbury who was killed in the last important action of English arms before the loss of Gascony to the English crown. Curiously enough, there seems to be some doubt as to whether the property ever actually belonged to him. Two families have dominated the history of Talbot: those of the Marquis d'Aux, and of Cordier. The wines of Talbot first became well known when the d'Aux family were proprietors. Surprisingly, it did not feature in unofficial classifications of the 1820s, but appears in Cocks's list of 1846, and in 1855 Talbot, Branaire and Beychevelle were all placed among the fourth growths. The vineyards of Talbot lie further inland than those of the other two, on that rising gravelly plateau which reaches back towards St Laurent, and its neighbours are Gruaud Larose and Lagrange. During this period of its history, the property was usually known as Talbot d'Aux or as d'Aux Talbot, or Château Marquis d'Aux. Throughout the nineteenth century, production remained fairly constant between 100 and 120 tonneaux. Today 340 tonneaux, or 32,000 cases, are made.

The property left the d'Aux family at the end of the nineteenth century, and was acquired by George Cordier after the First World War from Monsieur A. Claverie. The Cordiers have in recent years done much to improve and modernize, especially in the *chais*. The wine itself is a true St Julien—elegant, soft and distinctive. It is always interesting to compare its wines with those of Gruaud Larose, its neighbour and now under the same ownership. The style of the two wines is remarkably similar, but the Gruaud is nearly always the better of the two, with more body, more bouquet and concentration of flavour. The comparison between the two is rather similar to the Léoville-Langoa relationship on the Barton estate not far away, although of course the marriage is far more recent.

Lovers of Talbot will have happy memories of the 1929 and 1934, both delightful and typical wines, the 1934 being more attractive and enjoyable than many wines of this vintage. In recent years, the wines, as at Gruaud, have been noticeably quicker to mature.

The 1959 and 1962 were both successful years which made pleasant drinking early but have stayed the course well. Since then, the most successful years have been 1966, 1970, 1971 and 1973, while fine wines are promised for 1975, 1976 and 1978. It is interesting to note that here, as at Gruaud Larose, large wooden *cuves* of around 60 hectolitres are used for part of the maturation. I used to feel that these Cordier properties flattered early but then disappointed in the middle life. However, the development of the vintages since 1959 has, I think, shown this fear to be unfounded.

Château St Pierre   Fourth Growth

This property is one of ancient origins. Its archives go back to 1693 when it was known as Serançon and belonged to the Cheverry family. In 1767 it was acquired by a Monsieur St Pierre who gave the estate his name. His family's connection continued until after the Second World War.

The division of the estate, and the confusing nomenclature which resulted, took place in 1832 due to its being divided among different members of the family. About half the estate remained in the hands of Lieutenant-Colonel Bontemps-Dubarry, a grandson of Monsieur St Pierre, so that the name of Bontemps-Dubarry was then added to St Pierre to distinguish his portion from the rest. Some time later the largest part of the remainder came into the hands of the daughter of Bontemps-Dubarry from whose estate it was purchased by Monsieur Leon Sevaistre. This was how the second portion of the St Pierre estate came to be known as St Pierre Savaistre. The other part of the estate continued in the hands of Lieutenant-Colonel Bontemps-Dubarry, then of his son and his son's brother-in-law, Monsieur Kappelhoff of the Bordeaux house of Journu Frères & Kappelhoff. Monsieur Kappelhoff's son then became proprietor and was known as Bontemps-Kappelhoff. The Sevaistre part was sold to the Antwerp firm of Van den Bussche just after the First World War, and they acquired Bontemps-Kappelhoff's part just after the Second World War, thus reuniting the property after over a hundred years of division. Unfortunately, although the property is now reunited in name, the years of division have taken their toll. There were a number of small properties owing their origins to St Pierre; these, with one exception, have been absorbed into other growths. On the other hand, other properties, notably Gloria and du Glana, contain important portions of the original St Pierre vineyard.

In the classification of the 1820s, St Pierre appeared among the fourth growths. The divided property was placed among the fourth growths in 1855. Today the wine is light and pleasant but lacks the weight and style of the best St Juliens and is usually surpassed, for instance, by the *Bourgeois* growth of Gloria. The average production is 6,000 cases.

Château Lagrange   Third Growth

This château has a somewhat exotic history, mirrored perhaps by its fanciful label with its Don Quixote-like figures. The vintage used only to be discovered inscribed rather shyly on the pennants those martial horsemen carry.

The property is of ancient origin. In 1287 it formed part of the Manor of the Templars at St Julien. In 1669 it was called Pellecahus. On the dissolution of the Templars at the beginning of the fourteenth century, it had passed into the hands of the de Cours, *seigneurs* of Pauillac and Lagrange. From then until the Revolution it had a succession of noble owners including Baron de Brane of Mouton. In 1832 it was purchased for 650,000 frs (£162,500) by a Monsieur Brown, and then sold by him in 1847 to Comte Duchatel for 775,000 frs (£193,750). Comte Duchatel, whose father had been a prominent administrator in the Gironde, under the Consulate and Empire from which the title derived, was then Minister of the Interior. To emphasize the wealth and importance of the new proprietor, a massive tower was constructed at the château. The edifice dwarfed a decent, sober, classical portico and mansion of modest but comfortable proportions. This monument to wealth and ostentation is constructed in a parody of the Italian style, much in vogue during that period.

It was then that Lagrange, which had not featured in any of the unofficial classifications of the 1820s, was rapidly promoted in the hierarchy of the Médoc. Already, by 1846, Charles Cocks placed it among the fourth and fifth growths, and in 1855 it was placed among the third growths. In the 1880s, it was bought by the Louys family, and between the wars was acquired by the Cendoya family, who came from northern Spain and still maintain very close links with their native land. Indeed, the atmosphere at Lagrange today is decidedly and delightfully Spanish.

Lagrange is a very large property, although not as large today as during its prime under Duchatel, when there were 300 hectares, 100 of which were under vine, so that an average of 200 tonneaux was the rule and 300 tonneaux were made in years like 1874 and 1893. Later, a number of subsidiary *marques*, such as Château St Julien, were used, and the production of the *Grand Vin* diminished accordingly. Today there is a legacy of vast *chais* and the names of forgotten brands.

The vineyards themselves lie on the gravelly plateau which rises above St Julien on the road to St Lambert behind Gruaud-Larose, and the wine has some of the body and firmness of St Laurent. The wines in the immediate post-war period did not have a good reputation. Many vintages of the 1950s were tough, stalky and coarse in style, with the 1957 one of the most outstandingly unattractive wines of the year. Then a distinct improvement began, and in 1961, 1962 and 1964 wines with more fruit and balance and more St Julien elegance were produced, which suggested that more careful vinifications and selection was being practised. For some years till 1977, the château was under contract to Lichine and so disappeared from the market. I did not see the wine during this period, but its reputation was good. When I visited the property again to taste the 1978, I found it to be excellent, fleshy but with real St Julien vinosity and charm— certainly a growth on the way up again and once more worthy of its old classification. The average production is 17,000 cases.

Château Gloria

Gloria is not a name which will be found in any old book of reference, for it has been created in the space of a generation by Monsieur Henri Martin. The project began from small beginnings just before the war. Monsieur Martin purchased the *chais* of St Pierre, but did not have the money then to buy the brand, hence Gloria is not a classified growth. Instead, he set out to build up a vineyard which would be acclaimed for what it was and judged solely on its own merits.

The vineyard is, in fact, in the best part of St Julien near the village of Beychevelle and contains parcels of land bought at various times from Léoville-Poyferré, Gruaud-Larose, St Pierre and Duhart-Milon, and the average production is now 17,000 cases. The proprietor, Monsieur Henri Martin, is one of the leading personalities in the Médoc today. Mayor of St Julien, he was for many years President of the Comité Interprofessionel and is still one of the leading figures in the Bontemps de Médoc. More recently he has played an important role in the new management of Château Latour.

The wine itself is a fine and typical St Julien of the more

generous kind, combining true finesse and breed with a fullness of flavour and richness of body—the Gruaud Larose type rather than the Léoville Lascases or Beychevelle style. It is very consistent and was included in the INAO's proposal for a new classification in 1961, an opinion also endorsed by Alexis Linchine. In recent years, the 1953 was worthy of the vintage, the 1961 was fine if not so relatively outstanding, and very successful wines were made in 1962, 1964, 1966, 1970, 1971, 1973, 1975, 1976, 1978 and 1979. In recent vintages, the price of Gloria has edged up to that of the classified growths, and indeed this is well warranted by its own intrinsic merits. The names of Haut-Beychevelle-Gloria and Peymartin are used as subsidiary *marques*; the former is now to be found in England, and the latter, the product of younger vines, in America.

Château Du Glana   Grand Bourgeois Exceptionnel

This is another property which is of relatively recent importance, although its origins go back a little further than Gloria's. It was the creation of the Kaelin family who built it up in the early years of the century from an obscure *Artisan* growth making only a few tonneaux to an important property which today produces some 25,500 cases on average, and is, with Gloria, the most important growth after the classified ones in St Julien.

Unlike Margaux, Pauillac and St Estèphe, there are remarkably few Bourgeois growths in St Julien, where as much as 75 per cent of the vineyards are classified growths. This explains why good St Julien generics are so hard to find and why the name was in the past so often the victim of fraud.

Among those of interest is Château La Bridane, now classified as a *Cru Bourgeois* (production 4,250 cases).

Then there are three other growths worthy of mention although not included in the classification of *Crus Bourgeois*: Château Terry Gros Caillou, now making an excellent wine of real distinction (production 6,800 cases); Château Moulin-Riche, formerly of greater importance—its vineyard is well placed (production 1,600 cases); Château Hortevie, a name which will be familiar to members of the Wine Society (production 1,000 cases).

5

Pauillac and St Estèphe

PAUILLAC

This is the most important commune in the Médoc, both in terms of size and the sheer volume of fine wines it produces. While the sign-board at Margaux proudly proclaims 'Vins rouges les plus célébrés du monde', Pauillac's boast is simpler and more complete, 'Les premiers vins du monde'. Yet the curious thing is that the name of Pauillac itself is not so well known. One hardly ever sees generic wines simply sold as Pauillac; Margaux and St Julien are much better known and more sought after.

The fame of Pauillac lies in its great growths, which stand as sentinels at either end of the commune; Latour at the southern end adjoining St Julien, Lafite to the north, looking across a marshy brook to Cos d'Estournel and St Estèphe on its neighbouring hilltop. The variety and individuality of these wines is such that any generalizations about Pauillac wines are extremely difficult. On the whole, they are more powerful than other Médocs with slightly more body and firmness than the bigger St Juliens. The lesser wines lack the finesse and breed of St Julien or Margaux, or the bouquet of St Estèphe, and are sometimes a little mean at first. But the best wines have a regal quality which is unsurpassed among Bordeaux wines for its combination of power, elegance and individuality. They age superbly and are amongst the most long-lived of natural red wines.

The town of Pauillac, know to Ausonius as *Pauliacus*, is the most sizeable in the Haut-Médoc, but its river-front has a curiously desolate and run-down quality, like a seaside resort perpetually out of season. Yet in the days of sail, when the journey on to Bordeaux took valuable time, this was an important port, and it was from here that Lafayette, once a magnet of Francophile feelings on the other side of the Atlantic, set sail in 1777 to champion the cause of the rebellious colonies and hasten England's discomfort. The headquarters of the Commanderie du Bontemps de Médoc is housed in Château Grand Puy Ducasse, a pleasant Empire building situated on the front, together with a wine museum. Except for special investitures during the three *fêtes*, which punctuate the Commanderie's year, new members are usually invested here. The pastoral tranquillity of Pauillac has now been somewhat shattered by a Shell refinery, small by the standards of such things, but looming large in this low undulating landscape. Nevertheless, it has found a new use for the port.

Pauillac itself incorporates a number of very small communes which once had a separate existence, sometimes of some importance. St Lambert was at one time a separate parish before it was united with Pauillac—Latour and the Pichons lie within its boundaries. Other villages are Artigues, Bages, Milon, Mousset and Le Pouzalet.

Château Lafite   First Growth

Any account of the wines of Pauillac has to start at its northern extremity with the most renowned of all clarets, Lafite. The history of Lafite is almost as interesting as the wine.

As with most Médocs, although mention of the property first occurs in 1355 and the wine itself is first mentioned in 1641 (only among the *vins de Graves et du Médoc*), the fame of Lafite first dates from the eighteenth century, when it was the property of Nicolas-Alexandre, Marquis de Ségur. In 1707 it is mentioned in an advertisement in the *London Gazette* along with Latour and Margaux, and we know that Sir Robert Walpole regularly shipped Lafite in the 1730s. After the death of the Marquis de Ségur in 1755, it took some years to settle the estate due to its considerable extent and complexity, as well as to the competing claims of the heirs. Eventually, it passed into the hands of Nicolas-Pierre de Pichard, President of the Bordeaux Parlement, who retained it until the Revolution.

The ownership of Lafite in the eighteenth century mirrors very faithfully the economic and social pattern of the period. Ségur was an immensely wealthy man who owned Latour, Mouton and Calon Ségur, as well as Lafite; he was a provost of Paris as well as being President of the Bordeaux Parlement, and a man of letters who was a member of the Bordeaux Academy. In spite of his great interest in the region, he spent more time in Paris than in Bordeaux, and it is interesting to note from the inventory of his property made eight years after his death that Lafite is referred to simply as a *maison noble* and not as a château. Pichard's family was old and noble but not as aristocratic as that of Ségur. His interests were more completely centred in Guyenne. Born in Bordeaux in 1734, he became Avocat-Général of the Parlement in 1755, and its President in 1760. He was one of the relatively few proprietors guillotined in the Revolution, being executed in Paris in 1794.

It is often said that the Duc de Richelieu was responsible for popularizing Bordeaux wines, and especially Lafite, at the Court of Versailles. He was appointed governor of Guyenne in 1755 and is said to have recommended and served Lafite at Versailles on his return. The story is universally reported and seems reasonable enough, so that I can see no good reason to doubt it. Certainly from this time onwards, Bordeaux wines were in fashion at the court of Louis XV, and both Madame de Pompadour and Madame du Barry are reputed to have regularly served Lafite at their tables.

Before the execution of Nicolas-Pierre de Pichard, his sole heir, Anne-Marguerite-Marie-Adelaide had fled the country with her husband, the Comte de Puységur. This meant that as an *émigrée* she was proscribed and unable to inherit, so Lafite became the property of the State and was put up for auction on Fructidor 15 of the year V of the Republic, better known as 2 September 1797. The buyers were a Dutch syndicat, who sold again in 1803 to one Ignace Joseph Vanderberghe for 1,200,000 frs (£240,000).

It is at this stage that the history of Lafite's ownership becomes extremely complicated. Fortunately the puzzle has now been unravelled by Cyril Ray in his excellent history of the property (see Bibliography). Vanderberghe was a grain merchant, financier, army contractor and at this time Napoleon's Head of General Supplies. He was an associate of Ouvard, a notorious speculator, and the two of them went into bankruptcy in 1808. Vanderberghe's battle with his creditors was still dragging on at the time of his death in 1819. The year before, he had taken the precaution of transferring Lafite to his former wife, Barbe-Rosalie Lemarie, for 1,000,000 frs, in spite of the fact they had been

124

divorced as long ago as 1800. It has always been said that Vanderberghe was Dutch, but Cyril Ray has shown that he was in fact a Frenchman of presumably Flemish origins, born in Douai in 1758, the father-in-law of Napoleon's General Rapp.

In 1821 Barbe-Rosalie Lemarie apparently sold Lafite for the same sum she had paid for it to Mr Samuel Scott, an English banker. From this date until 1868, it was generally supposed that Mr Scott (who succeeded to his father's baronetcy in 1830), and after his death in 1849 his son, also named Samuel, were the owners of Lafite. But in fact they were simply administrators, having bought the property on the account of and with the money of Vanderberghe's son. This transaction was kept secret lest it should fall into the hands of his father's creditors, for it was not until 1856 that the Tribunal Civile de la Seine formally declared the Vanderberghe inheritance free from further claims. The real situation was finally revealed on the death of the younger Vanderberghe in 1866, when the bank registered a formal declaration that it had bought and administered Lafite on his behalf, and Lafite was now put up for auction for the benefit of Vanderberghe's heirs.

It was thus that on 8 August 1868 Lafite was knocked down to the agents of Baron James de Rothschild for 4,440,000 frs (£880,000). But the sale was not without incident. A syndicate of Bordeaux merchants had been formed in an attempt to save Bordeaux's most precious jewel, following Margaux and Mouton, falling into the hands of Parisian bankers. For some unexplained reason the first auction on 20 July failed to produce a result, the reserve price of 4,500,000 frs not being reached, although both sides claimed to have resources in excess of this figure available.

The unique value set on Lafite may be gauged from the fact that Nathaniel de Rothschild had paid 1,125,000 frs for Mouton in 1853, and the neighbouring Cos d'Estournel had changed hands in 1852 for 1,150,000; while exactly a year later the pride of Burgundy, the Clos de Vougeot, was bought by Baron Thenard for 1,600,000 frs.

Following the sale of the property, a remarkable sale took place in the *chais* at Lafite of a wonderful collection of old vintages of the château. It is interesting to note that Cyril Ray, relying on Bertall, described this as a sale of the wines belonging to the château itself, whereas Maurice Dubois in *Mon Livre de Cave*

125

states categorically that this was the sale of old wines in bottle which had formed the collection of Monsieur Goudal, the father of the then *régisseur*, Emile Goudal. This sounds reasonable, as the elder Goudal had been *régisseur* from 1798 until 1834. In all, according to Dubois, 5,252 bottles were put up for sale and realized more than 110,000 francs, while six barrels of the 1865 vintage were sold for 3,000 francs each. At today's value, this means an average price per bottle of around £19, an unheard of price in those days. The record price was fetched by the 1811, the famous wine of the Comet. The twenty-one bottles available were auctioned in two lots, the first of eleven bottles fetching 976 francs, while the remaining ten bottles went for 121 francs each, or around £109 each in today's terms. No wonder this was spoken of as the greatest wine auction that had, up to that time, ever been seen.

Within three months of the purchase, Baron James de Rothschild was dead, and the new jewel in the Rothschild treasure went in equal parts to his three sons, Alphonse, Gustave and Edmond. Today, the property is divided into six shares, of which Baron Guy de Rothschild as head of the family has two; the remaining three great-grandsons together with the widow of a grandson, have one each. After the Second World War, it was Baron Elie who was entrusted with the running of the property. During this period, one has the impression that the Lafite-Rothschilds were never really close to Lafite and its wine. It remained one amongst many interests and concerns to be visited and supervised as necessary, enjoyed but not perhaps loved in the way that Baron Philippe has loved Mouton and its wines. However, a new and promising era opened in the seventies with the appointment, in 1977, of a member of the next generation of Rothschilds, Eric, the son of Baron Alain. Before that, in 1975, Professeur Peynaud had been asked to act as consultant, and Monsieur Jean Crété was appointed *régisseur*. The arrival of Monsieur Crété was in its way even more important than Professeur Peynaud's advice. With his experience of Léoville Lascases under Monsieur Paul Delon, he could have received no better preparation for the great responsibility now vested in him. Already all the signs are that a new golden age for Lafite has begun.

With 80 hectares under vine, Lafite is the largest of the first growths in terms of area and production. The fluctuations in its

126

production, however, have been very marked. In the heyday before the phylloxera, for instance, 195 tonneaux were made in 1865, 189 in 1870 and 246 in 1875. After the phylloxera, 224 were made in 1888, 210 in 1893, 145 in 1899 and 213 in 1900. Then came a period of much lower yields: only 63 tonneaux in 1920, 160 in 1924 and a meagre 40 in 1926, when the wine was superb but greatly reduced by disease. 1928 and 1929 both yielded 150 tonneaux, but 1934 was the best inter-war year for yield (apart from the disastrous 1925), with 190 tonneaux. The great 1945 only made 90 tonneaux; 1947, 107. 1950 was the first decent, if not great, year since 1900 to exceed 200 tonneaux with its 247, and this was the beginning of much higher yields: 202 in 1953, 236 in 1955, 158 in 1959, 218 in 1962, 318 in 1964 and finally 323 in 1966 and 335 in 1967. This gives a good example of how difficult it is in Bordeaux to speak of an average. In the decade 1957 and 1967, the production at Lafite has varied from 116 to 335 tonneaux. On five occasions it has been under 200 tonneaux, on three occasions over 300. The average production is now given as 300 tonneaux, or 22,000 cases.

And what is one to say of the wines of Lafite that has not already been expressed with all the gloriously extravagant rhetorical fantasies of bygone days? André Simon, Maurice Healey, Warner Allen, Morton Shand have all sung its praises, vying with one another to convey its ethereal qualities. I will only say that factually Lafite, together with Margaux, is lighter in body than Latour or Mouton, and is a softer, more feminine wine than any other Pauillac. Its successful and great years are not so frequent of late as are those of Latour, and its lesser years tend to be exquisitely pretty but decidedly small wines. But a great vintage of Lafite is the quintessence of all that claret aspires to; a bouquet at once perfumed, delicate and powerful, in texture rich but elegant, in flavour subtle, silky and long. Because of its higher proportion of Merlot, Lafite is always a softer wine than its neighbours, but this is deceptive because its great vinosity and power enable it to last and improve much longer than seems likely early on. The 1953 is proving to be a case in point, provided one is fortunate enough to get the right bottling.

The longevity of Lafite is proverbial. The only vintage I have ever drunk which was in a state of decay was the 1858, and I dare say I was unlucky. The following decade produced some very great years for Lafite, notably 1864, 1865 and 1869. Those fortunate enough to have drunk them have testified even quite recently that they were still very much alive and enjoyable. These were followed by the famous 1870—a giant of a wine even now, crude beside other Lafites and still the most commonly found old Lafite—1871, 1874, 1875 and finally 1878, the last fine pre-phylloxera wine. From then onwards, the mildew combined with the phylloxera to give Bordeaux the most disastrous sequence of vintages in its history. Although there were decent wines made again in 1888 and 1889, it was the 1893 that really set the seal of success on the vineyard's fight back to prosperity. The 1893 Lafite was a very fine wine which was still at its best when I first drank it in 1957, although the last bottle I saw in 1962 was fading.

My own introduction to old Lafites was a most fortunate one. That great wine lover and master organizer, Mr Tony Hepworth, managed in 1954 to stage in Yorkshire a remarkable dinner for which Baron Elie sent six vintages of pre-First World War Lafite, having been persuaded to this most generous gesture by Dr Otto Loeb. After six months' rest, the members of the West Riding Wine and Food Society and their guests, among whom I was fortunate to be numbered, sat down to the most memorable of memorable meals. The 1914 which came first was a pleasant light wine, the least remarkable of the six, and the only one to fade in the glass. The 1906 was in wonderful condition but lacked the graciousness and finesse of the older wines. The 1900 was an enormous, mellow, ripe wine of great quality which took some time to come out and show its paces. Of the 1899 I wrote, 'the finest claret I have ever tasted'. Although I have drunk many superb wines since, this must remain one of the giants. The bouquet was still superb, the wine perfectly balanced, the flavour wonderful, and there was no sign of decay at all. Finally, the 1896 was a really lovely wine still in perfect condition and only just beaten by the 1899. It is seldom that one gets an opportunity to compare old wines in this way, which is why it seemed worth while recording this occasion.

The 1920 is a giant among Lafites but, after this, the inter-war era was not a great one for Lafite. The 1928 had to be pasteurized, and I have always found the 1934 singularly lacking the usual Lafite charm and finesse. The 1924 was perhaps the most charming and typical wine of this era, the 1929 was unfortunately overshadowed by the fate of the 1928. The 1937, however, I would rate a very good wine for the year; although uncharacteristically firm, it has more charm than most. Of the wartime years, I found the 1944 the most enjoyable: although lighter than the 1943, it had more breed and charm.

Since the war, the 1945 is a very great wine, the best produced at Lafite for many a long year. This proved a good omen, for it was to be followed by the 1947, 1948 (an exceptionally elegant and fine wine for the year), 1949 (a very great wine), 1950 (one of the most successful Lafites in a light year), 1952, and 1953 (a great and classic Lafite). The 1955 is more attractive than many wines of this vintage; 1959 promised to be a great success but recent tastings have found it rather edgy; 1960 is a light wine of great charm but too light, not the equal of the 1950; 1961 is a very great wine but, while among the best of the year, has shown a distressing irregularity from bottle to bottle; 1962 is a very classic and powerful Lafite. For me, this was the last outstanding Lafite until 1970 and 1975. The 1963 should never have been given the Château label and the 1964 I find disappointing—it is light and lacks distinction—while the 1966, although a good wine and certainly superior to the 1964, lacks the richness and power of the 1962.

After disappointing wines in 1967 and even more so in 1969 (the 1968 is best forgotten), the 1970 is really fine. This was a vintage when nobody could produce a poor wine. The 1971, however, I find disappointing and already old, and the 1973 was a victim of the policy of only bottling after three years; even when tasted in cask in the summer of 1974 it was really too light and unsubstantial. The 1975, while not made by Jean Crété, was raised under his new régime. I was disappointed in the 1975 context when I first saw the wine just prior to bottling in 1977, but after it had settled down in bottle it gave the impression of being a great wine in the making. 1976 promises to be a delight, and both it and the charming 1977 will benefit from the scrapping of the old three-year bottling rule. The initial impression of 1978 is again of a great wine, while the 1979 is one of the outstanding wines of the vintage, with more power than usual.

As a postscript to this survey of vintages, it must be said that there have been in recent years far too many variations between bottlings of the same vintage. The 1953 and 1961 have been particularly instanced. While the 1953 was a large vintage and was apparently bottled over a long period, the same cannot be said of the 1961. It should be an axiom of château-bottling that the wine can be relied upon to be consistent. Now that so many tastings are written up, owners of fine vintages of Lafite have often found themselves disappointed by wines reported as being magnificent elsewhere. One trusts that this situation will now be put right. When such high prices are asked and paid today, the consumer has a right to expect that what he receives will be as good as that which goes into the private cellar at the château.

Something should be said here of the Carruades. The name comes from perhaps the finest stretch of vineyard on the property, but the wine came from young vines wherever they happen to be on the property. The general rule at Lafite is that only wine from vines of twelve years or older goes into Lafite, and that from seven to twelve years went into the Carruades; any younger wines are simply sold off with the generic appellation only. Thus the quantity of Carruades was always much smaller than that of Lafite, and it was a more quickly maturing wine, bottled before the Lafite itself. It was nevertheless true Lafite, was always château-bottled and was sometimes not far behind Lafite in excellence. The last Carruades to be made was the 1967. It was decided however, that this name was too close to Lafite itself and could cause confusion. Now the second wine is called *Moulin des Carruades*, and a completely different label is used.

The Lafite vineyards lie on slopes in a compact group at the northern end of Pauillac. One piece is even in St Estèphe, adjoining Lafon Rochet, but is allowed the Pauillac *appellation*. Its neighbour in St Estèphe is Cos d'Estournel, and in Pauillac, Lafite adjoins Mouton at many points. The château itself is a pleasing compendium of medieval turrets and seventeenth- and eighteenth-century buildings, standing among a group of trees on an eminence above the *route des Châteaux*. But most impressive of all are the *chais*. After the first year in the great *chais*, the wine is moved into a deeper, cooler one for slow maturation in cask prior to bottling, which at Lafite until recently invariably occurred in the third spring after the vintage, giving the wine on average some two-and-a-half years in cask. There is also a magnificent underground cellar for the storage of Lafite's unique collection of old wines, going back to the 1797 vintage. As at some other châteaux, the wines here are regularly recorked, on average approximately every twenty-five years.

Château Latour First Growth

The history of Latour is a good deal less complex than that of Lafite, but its origins are none the less ancient or aristocratic. In the Middle Ages, during the English period, an important fortress stood on this site, protecting the low-lying part of the river estuary from pirates and marauding Frenchmen alike. One of a number of forts guarding the river banks at this time, this fortress was destroyed by the forces of the King of France during the campaigns leading to the final expulsion of the English in 1452. The present tower is all that now remains to remind us of these martial beginnings, but dates from the first part of the seventeenth century (Louis XIII).

Perhaps the most remarkable fact about the ownership of Latour is that from 1670, when it was acquired by the de Charravas family, until 1963, it remained in the control of connected families, passing by marriage first to the Clauzels in about 1677, then to the Ségurs, then to four families of whom the de Beaumonts remained as the principal one down to 1963. The only occasion when the property was actually put up for sale was in 1842, when an auction was held so that the controlling families could determine the value of the property, and a Société Civile could be set up to facilitate the continuity of administration and pay out some of the smaller partners. The nature of this Société Civile was changed fundamentally in 1963, when interests controlled by Lord Cowdray acquired a majority holding, and Harvey's of Bristol a 25 per cent share. Members of the de Beaumont family have retained a minority interest. In practice, Mr David Pollock, until his retirement in 1978, and now Mr Clive Gibson representing Lord Cowdray's interest, are the final authority on all policy matters. Largely through the experience of Mr Harry Waugh, then of Harvey's, Mr Pollock was fortunate in obtaining the services of Monsieur Henri Martin, proprietor of Château Gloria, and Monsieur Jean-Paul Gardère, *courtier* of Pauillac, to manage and advise him on the new régime. I shall say more of this régime in the appropriate place.

Just as Lafite stands watch over the northern limits of Pauillac, so does Latour over its southern approaches. A small stream also marks the boundary between Latour and Léoville-Lascases in the same way as does another between Lafite and Cos d'Estournel. In this case, the stream is a good deal smaller and the two vineyards are much closer to each other. But the change of soil and the resulting change in the character of the wines are just as profound. The main vineyard of Latour lies between the road and the river, in the same way as at Léoville-Lascases, but it is not so easily seen from the road, because in the middle of the nineteenth century one of the de Beaumonts carved a piece out of the estate to permit the building of the château now known as Pichon-Lalande, the Comtesse de Lalande being the mistress of the Comte de Beaumont. Today the finest view of the vineyards of Latour is to be had from the terrace at Pichon-Lalande, which was constructed above the new *chais* in the mid 1960s. Another curiosity is that there is, strictly speaking, no château, the house which serves as such being a very modest affair, originally built in the last century for the *régisseur* and discreetly hidden among trees. The familiar landmark is, rather, the solitary tower and, near it, the *chais*, *cuvier* and cellars, built unusually and perhaps uniquely around a small courtyard planted with plane trees.

It was part of the *ancien régime* at Latour that nothing ever seemed to change and everything was done as it had always been. But the virtual change of ownership in 1963 heralded substantial innovations. The *cuvier* was completely rebuilt, only the walls of the original building remaining, and the great oak fermenting vats gave way to stainless steel ones, which can be thermostatically cooled by allowing water to run down the outside walls of the vats. The effect is hardly an aesthetic delight, and I am not personally convinced that a temperature control at least as effective cannot be obtained by the simpler system employed at La Mission Haut-Brion. Nevertheless, it must be admitted that since the oak vats had to be replaced, something of this sort was more or less inevitable. The space available for cask storage—important in a château where there are sometimes three crops in wood for at least part of the year—has been greatly augmented by a fine underground cellar. In the vineyard itself, some sections contained very old vines and many gaps, apart from an important unplanted area. Much replanting has been undertaken, but none of this wine from young vines will find its way into the *Grand Vin* until judged sufficiently mature. However, this has provided a useful addition as, with formerly only 45 hectares under vine against Lafite's 80 and Margaux's 66, Latour's production was the smallest of the first growths. But it now stands at 200 tonneaux, or 18,000 cases, the equal of Margaux, and greater than Haut-Brion.

Through the kindness of Jean Paul Gardère, I have been able to obtain a remarkable record of every vintage of Latour since 1918. These provide an interesting commentary on the low yields of the past, and the recovery under the new ownership.

In the 1920s the average *rendement* was 21·4 hl/ha. In the 1930s this fell to 15·9 and in the 1940s to 15·2. The 1950s brought a marked improvement to 27·45, which rose to 35·10 in the 1960s. In the 1970s this increased with the new plantations to a remarkable 51·9. By this time, however, only about 57·5 per cent of the total yield of the estate was now bottled as Latour. Between 35 and 40 per cent is now bottled as Les Forts and the rest sold as Pauillac, or declassified.

One of the major innovations since 1963 has been the creation of the new *marque* of Les Forts de Latour. This followed the decision to use only those vineyards which were shown on the plan of the Domaine of 1759 for the *Grand Vin* of Latour itself, and to replant certain vineyards owned by Latour and which were lying fallow. Thus the Les Forts de Latour comes from three parcels of vineyard called Les Forts de Latour, Petit Batailley and Comtesse de Lalande. The Les Forts vineyard adjoins the Grand Vignoble to the north-west, well placed near the Gironde, Petit Batailley is west of the village of St Lambert and adjoins Batailley, Léoville-Poyferré and Pichon-Lalande, while, as the name implies, Comtesse Lalande is a small parcel adjoining Pichon-Lalande. In addition the production of young vines from the Latour vineyard can be used if judged to be of sufficient quality. Thus it is not strictly accurate to call Les Forts de Latour the second wine of Latour, since it is based on different vineyards whose production, however good, would never be included in Latour itself.

Before the first vintages of Les Forts, the 1966 and 1967, were placed on the market in 1972, both were tasted blind against the leading second growths and acquitted themselves with distinction. So they are sold at second growth prices, at which level they offer excellent value. They have the Latour style but are lighter textured and so tend to mature more rapidly.

The style of Latour's great wine is famous, and it is easy to see

133

why its frank, outspoken qualities have for so long been particularly popular in England, so that Franck wrote that the greater part was consumed in that country, which bought it in nearly every good vintage. Until 1963, Latour was the most unashamedly traditional of Médocs in its style, that is to say, it always had great colour and took a long time to reach maturity. But this gruff and forbidding exterior, compounded of tannin and extract beyond what is usual today, gave way with time and patience to a marvellously rich and truly velvety texture. The incomparable bouquet, the most classic of Pauillac Cabernet aromas, was always evident from the wine's first year in cask; the flavour was always masculine and immensely characteristic, as recognizable as some familiar symphonic theme, at once noble yet often practically undrinkable it was so masked by hardness. This was the dilemma of Latour in the days of high interest rates and expensive storage; everyone admired the wines of great years but wondered when they would be ready to drink and if they would still be alive to enjoy them. It was therefore hardly surprising that the new proprietors decided that some concessions to the times were necessary, and they aim to produce wines which will be ready to drink rather earlier. These wines are certainly going to develop differently—so much is already clear. They do not bear quite the same unmistakable signature when in cask, but the fine character is evident in the flavour.

The oldest Latour I have ever tasted was the 1874. In 1967 I was fortunate to be present when a bottle from Lord Rosebery's remarkable cellar was opened at Christie's. Its fine, deep colour was only slightly tawny. The bouquet was clean and definite, quite distinctly conveying its Pauillac character across the years. The wine itself was full-flavoured, powerful and still rich in texture; there was only a suggestion of the fragility of great age, and the Latour character was unmistakable. This was a great and remarkable wine that had lived its life in England from the time it was first laid down in its infancy by the famous Liberal politician and racing enthusiast. Yet it was distinctly more vigorous than any of the 1875s I have drunk in Bordeaux. I mention all this in some detail because it shows the amazing longevity of the great clarets when properly stored and looked after. The wine, incidentally, had been recorked some thirty years before by Berry Brothers.

The Latour 1899 at its greatest was a wine to set beside the Lafite; how fascinating it would have been to have had the opportunity to do so. In 1960 I had a marvellous bottle, fresh and vigorous and such typical Latour that I even guessed the château. But only a year later, another bottle was only a shadow of the first, which shows that wines of this age must always be something of a gamble, and one poor bottle may not mean that any others still left will be the same.

One of Latour's outstanding characteristics has always been that it is magnificent in poor and moderate years. In the great years the palm may go to Lafite, but in lesser ones the list of Latour's success is formidable, and it is certainly one of the most consistently great wines in the Médoc today. Among these successes can be numbered 1936, 1940 and 1944—full-flavoured, fruity and delicious wine from light years—1951, 1954, 1958, and especially the 1960 which is quite outstanding—certainly the best wine of the year, in my opinion, and by some margin. In 1963, Latour made one of the very rare wines in that year which deserved to see the light of day, light but sound and charming. However, this admirable record for sound wines in lesser years stopped short with the 1965; even Latour's skills could make little of this poor year. The 1968 had always seemed a trifle stalky to me, and the lighter Les Forts preferable, but it has now come round very well, the 1969 is most disappointing, however, and I cannot believe that it will do anything now. In the 1970s, the 1972 was better than most, with distinct character, and the 1973 was stylish but solid, with charm, but the 1974 was dull, like most wine of this vintage. Surprisingly, the 1977 was disappointingly slight in a year when Latour might have been expected to do something more interesting.

Of Latour's great years, the 1929 is deservedly legendary. Its great fruit and perfect balance made it drinkable at an early age for Latour, but it has lasted much better than many good judges had expected. The 1928, if overshadowed by the 1929, nevertheless made a fine if not great bottle, full of character in old age. The 1934 is a fine wine—one of the great successes in a vintage when many fine growths and notably Margaux and Lafite, have disappointed. The 1937 is a man's claret—strong, firm and very much a wine of its year, but nevertheless very fine and long-lived. Of the post-war years, the greatest successes have been the 1945—

135

a timeless giant of a wine—and the 1961, more agreeable already and perhaps another 1929, only more solid. The 1949 is very fine, superior to the 1947, but perhaps just beaten in this vintage by Lafite and Mouton. On the other hand, the 1955 is, in my view, a really great Latour. It is finer than the 1959 or the 1962, and must be one of the best wines of a vintage which, while consistent, has conspicuously failed to reach the heights in most cases. The 1962 is a fine wine, the last of the *ancien régime*, masculine and aggressive and slow to develop, but perhaps not quite the peer of Mouton or Lafite in the long run. Latour's new masters have reason to be pleased with their 1964 as things have turned out, for it is probably the best wine in the Médoc, but the Latour character is not quite so aggressively asserted. On the other hand, the 1966 has turned out to be a classic Latour, of great power and vigour, yet drinkable at the age of thirteen, although with a long way to go still. Since then, the classic Latours have been 1970, 1971, 1975 and 1976, certainly to be followed by the 1978, which looks as though it will be outstanding, and then 1979, which has more substance than most wines of this year.

Château Mouton-Rothschild   Second Growth in 1855, First Growth in 1973

Mouton was curiously placed at the top of the second growths in 1855, but was universally regarded—and has been for many years—as a first growth. Baron Philippe de Rothschild's crusade for official recognition finally succeeded in 1973 when Mouton was declared a first growth by governmental decree. It has to be remembered that in the middle of the nineteenth century, there did not exist the enormous difference in price between first and second growths that is found today. Thus Charles Cocks recorded in 1846, a decade before the classification, that when the first growths sold for £96 a tonneau, the seconds sold for between £82 and £84 a tonneau. The other factor was that Mouton's fame was relatively recent, whereas the position of the first growths had been clearly consecrated by time.

Mouton only really begins to have a distinct history of its own in the eighteenth century. Most nineteenth-century books say airily that it had belonged to the Brane family for about a century, when it was sold in 1830, and Féret states (*Statistique Gen. Tome III 1er partie Biographie 1889*) that Joseph de Brane, who died in 1749, was Baron de Mouton. But the map showing the lands of the Marquis de Ségur shows clearly that Mouton was numbered among them. Monsieur Butel's researches seem to suggest that, by 1747 Mouton had passed to the Marquis de Ségur-Calon, who, as the Marquis de Ségur's son-in-law, was to be his principal heir. However, by the end of the century it was certainly the property of Hector de Branes (or Brane), father of the more famous Jacques-Maxime, the virtual creator first of Mouton, then of Gorce—later called Brane-Cantenac. For whereas frequent mention is to be found among eighteenth-century sources of Lafite, Latour and Margaux, nothing is heard of Mouton.

Maps and plans towards the end of the eighteenth century seem to show that it was only then that much of what is today the vineyard of Mouton was even planted with vines. It was probably only during the last decade of Baron de Brane's ownership that the fame and reputation of Mouton really spread, since he was only born in 1796 and the property was sold to Monsieur Thuret in 1830. As a result, the price was far superior to anything fetched at that time for any wine not a first growth—at 1,200,000 francs (£240,000).

Thuret did not prosper at Mouton in the way that Baron de Brane had done, and sold the property in 1853 to Baron Nathaniel de Rothschild, surprisingly taking a small loss on the transaction. It was, however, noted at the time that the price paid was well below the estate's real value. This cousin of the Rothschild who was later to buy the neighbouring Lafite had settled in England and adopted one of the national pastimes of his adopted country— fox-hunting. It was as a result of a fall while hunting, which had crippled him, that he decided to retire to France and bought Mouton. At this time the property was usually known as Brane-Mouton, and for many years after the Rothschild purchase, it was referred to simply as Mouton. It was only after some forty years of ownership, just before the turn of the century, that it became generally hyphenated with the Rothschild name.

As at Lafite, the presence of the Rothschilds at Mouton was at a rather remote level and they much depended on their *régisseurs*. Indeed, some of the labels of Mouton actually bear the name of the *régisseur*, raised to the even more exalted level of *gérant*, or manager—that is, until the arrival of Baron Philippe. It was in 1923 that, as a very young man, he arrived with full powers from his father to manage the estate; he was not to inherit it until several years later. When he arrived, he found the *gérant* burning the records in the courtyard, a spectacular end indeed to the old régime of absentee proprietors. Since that time, for over fifty years, Baron Philippe and Mouton have been synonymous. Only Henri Woltner at La Mission, among the contemporary proprietors of great Bordeaux châteaux, has combined over such a span of years a similar love and dedication to his wines which has, at the same time, been illumined with such civilization. While Baron Philippe is certainly a great connoisseur of wine, it will be as a publicist for Mouton and as a man of letters that he will be remembered. His knowledge, interest and taste in literature and the fine arts is unrivalled, and the wonderful museum he has created at Mouton is a permanent memorial to the breadth of his interest and taste. The splendid staging of this collection is mirrored in the whole layout of the great *chais* and in the presentation of Mouton's wines with its labels designed by famous contemporary artists, among whom have been numbered Jean Cocteau and Marc Chagall. It is this quality of showmanship pursued with such panache and success that has brought Baron Philippe criticism bordering on hostility over the years. One cannot fail to detect in this criticism both the innate conservatism of the Bordelais and an undercurrent of envy at the success such methods have brought. But surely, in an age when most publicity is brash and banal, we should be grateful when a fine product is publicized with a knowledge, taste and grandeur which so aptly suit it.

It is only in the case of Mouton Cadet that I personally would question the wisdom of Mouton's policy in the Baron Philippe era. It is easy to see how this position has grown up and how difficult it is now to decide on a change. The years 1930, 1931 and 1932 were all adjudged unworthy of Mouton's label and Baron Philippe, encouraged by his English agent, Teddy Hammond, hit upon the idea of blending the wines to be sold as a brand under the name of Mouton Cadet. The wine proved popular beyond their wildest dreams, so that what had begun as off-vintage Mouton, or vats not up to the highest standards from Mouton and Mouton d'Armailhacq, with the full Pauillac *appellation*, is now simply a branded claret with a simple Bordeaux *appellation*. It certainly can and does on occasion contain small quantities of Mouton

138

rejected from the final blend, and the majority of the blend is usually from the Médoc, but wines from the other side of the river are nowadays usually used to assist in making a supple, quick-maturing wine. All this is fine, and as a branded claret Mouton Cadet is a worthy example. The trouble is that a great many wine drinkers, including reasonably knowledgeable ones, believe that they are buying a second wine of Mouton comparable, say, to Les Forts de Latour. This intimate association between a great classified growth and an ordinary commercial brand cannot be regarded in the long run as anything but unfortunate, not least for Mouton itself.

As at Latour, the château at Mouton is hardly its crowning glory. It is a small, ugly and curiously suburban Victorian villa, situated in the centre of the open-sided courtyard formed by the *chais* and administration buildings of the property. The Baron has now almost completely succeeded in hiding it from view by allowing the surrounding trees and shrubs ample scope for unimpeded growth. The Baron himself, assisted by his late wife— a woman of unusual gifts and talents—caused another building to be converted into a most delightful flat where the Baron himself stays and entertains his guests.

The *chais* and cellars at Mouton are one of the showplaces of the Médoc. The great *chais* for the new wine is severely simple, yet the straight rows of casks with the arms of Mouton discreetly illuminated at the far end achieve a splendidly theatrical effect. The fine underground cellars where the wines mature in their second and third years in tranquil coolness are, on the other hand, classically traditional. The collection and range of bottled wines is also impressive, and is certainly one of the finest and most complete in the Médoc. It does not go back so far as the collection at Lafite, but from the 1850s onwards can have few rivals. Here again, wines are regularly recorked. I have one such treasured example in my possession; it says simply: 'Mouton Rothschild— 1926—rebouché au Château en 1957'.

It has always seemed curious to me that two such totally dissimilar wines as Lafite and Mouton could possibly adjoin one another. If Mouton's vineyards adjoined those of Latour, it would seem natural enough. It is perhaps this juxtaposition of the two great wines which has led to this long and at times overplayed rivalry. Cyril Ray (see Bibliography) has clearly shown that this rivalry is not one simply between rival branches of the Rothschild family; it goes back to the period in the 1840s when there were no Rothschilds at either château. Probably its origins lie in the fact that Lafite had, since the beginning of the eighteenth century, been undisputed master in the Pauillac vineyards north of the town; Latour seemed almost as distant, no doubt, as Margaux and was in any case a quite distinct wine. Then, in the early years of the nineteenth century, Baron de Brane had set out to build up Mouton right on Lafite's doorstep. The sight of this newcomer achieving such speedy success, the realization that these fine, adjoining slopes could, under expert management, produce a great wine—although a different one—no doubt caused uneasiness, even alarm, at Lafite. The aristocrats, as it were, felt threatened by the parvenu. Mouton in her turn was angry and indignant that her merits should not be given full face value, especially when customers were increasingly prepared to pay as much for their Mouton as for the first growths. Prejudice has certainly played its part; some partisans of Lafite and even of Latour affect to see no merit in Mouton, to urge that the 1855 classification was, indeed, correct and that for all her strivings and pretension, Mouton lacks the breed of a first growth. I must confess that I was not myself brought up to admire Mouton, but now that I have had the opportunity of drinking Moutons both old and new, I cannot but reject such judgements as biased and unobjective—though it is not always easy to be objective about such a subjective thing as wine! It seems to me that the very qualities for which, for example, Latour is often rightly praised, are accounted faults at Mouton.

There is no doubt that in the past, Mouton has often proved as hard and stubborn a wine as Latour. The very high percentage of Cabernet Sauvignon, much more pronounced than at Lafite, has much to do with this, as it has with the character of the wine. But there is no doubt that in recent years, Mouton has proved very successful in producing wines which, while maturing more quickly, seem to retain both their essential character and their keeping properties—a good omen, perhaps, for Latour. Nevertheless, it would be a mistake to suppose that the variations in *cépage* between Lafite and Mouton were the main cause of their differences—these merely serve to accentuate the existing differences in soil. It is these subtle but vital changes in soil throughout the great districts of Bordeaux which are the essential bases of the remarkable individuality of its great wines.

It is difficult to describe in words the difference in character between Mouton and Latour. Both have a very distinct Cabernet nose and flavour. Mouton tends to be rather lighter and softer in lesser years; in fine years it seems to have more vinosity and ripeness, with a distinct *cassis* nose and a beautiful harmony, so that while it is firm, it is not as hard as Latour—but some of these differences are certainly due to vinification. The basic difference is the very subtle difference of flavour in that there is, at the finish of a Mouton, some indefinable quality, almost a *goût de terroir*, which is absolutely characteristic. It is this quality which has led some critics of Mouton to assert that it lacks breed. Certainly it is different from Latour; some may prefer one, some the other, but this is a matter of taste and not basically, I would say, one of quality.

Like the other great Pauillacs, Mouton has great staying power, and those fortunate enough to have the chance to drink an old vintage which has been well kept will seldom be disappointed. The oldest good Mouton I have drunk is the 1869, one of the greatest surviving pre-phylloxera vintages of Mouton, which was still in wonderful form in 1969—certainly one of the greatest Moutons. The 1889 was one of the first successful years after the double scourge of phylloxera and mildew had subsided. The wine tasted clean and had a good flavour, aged but not infirm, when tasted in 1962. The 1900 was a very great wine—in its way one of the most perfect bottles of old claret that it has ever been my good fortune to drink. In 1960 it still had a most beautiful bouquet, the flavour was delicious, full-bodied and fruity, and the whole effect one of perfect balance and harmony. In the 1920s there were some very fine wines. Of those I have tasted, the 1921 was interesting because it had much more delicacy than is usual with this very hot year, when so many wines are burnt and a shade coarse. When I drank it in 1966, I felt it was just beginning to fade. The greatest Mouton of the decade for me is the 1926. In 1966 it seemed bigger than the 1945, but with such a wonderful combination of fruit and richness that it was delightful to drink. This is likely to be the wine which will outlive all its contemporaries. The 1928 was famous for its hardness, the 1929 for its charm, but it is now past its best. The 1933 was a magnificent wine, for many years much more enjoyable

141

than the 1934. This wine was for years a good example of what critics of Mouton most disliked. It was very hard and rich with little style or finesse. But by the mid-1960s, it was coming round better than had ever seemed possible—still a shade aggressive, but rich and well-rounded on the palate; an excellent wine.

Since the war, there have been many notable successes. The 1945 is typical of the year, with a slight tendency to dry up, but still very fine for all that. Both the 1947 and the 1949 are great wines, among the top examples of their respective vintages and superior to the 1945 in my view. They are beautifully balanced wines of great vinosity and attraction, and many claret lovers have, I suspect, preferred them in the end to the 1945. Unlike Lafite, at Mouton the 1960 was much more successful than the 1950. For me, the 1953 has certainly proved to be one of the most delightful examples of this charming year and has kept its freshness longer than most. The 1959 rates as a great success; it again kept its youthfulness for a long time and seems to lack the dryness of many 1959s. The 1961 I rated at the beginning as not outstanding for the year; how wrong I was! At Dr Taams' tasting in May 1978, it was clearly superior to Lafite and Margaux, and at least as fine as Latour, with some good judges just preferring the Mouton. It is a wine of great power and majesty with a long life ahead of it. The 1962 is very fine indeed, one of the best wines of the year along with Lafite. The 1963 was, with Latour, one of the few examples of this very poor vintage which was ever worth drinking. The 1964 was a great disappointment, an example of the late vintaging being caught out by the weather. The 1966 was most successful and is one of the best in the Médoc. As with so many wines of that year, the 1969 is something of a disappointment. However, the 1970 is a classic, although 1971 is no more than a pleasant lightweight, the 1973 ripe and showy, the 1975 a really top wine, the 1976 has great charm, the 1977 is disappointing, but the 1978 has the makings of a great wine with the 1979 not far behind. The average production is now 22,000 cases.

Château Pichon-Longueville   Second Growth

This growth is usually known as Pichon-Longueville-Baron, or simply as Pichon-Baron, to distinguish it from its twin across the road, but it is in fact perfectly correct to describe it simply as Pichon-Longueville. In the seventeenth century, the property belonged to Pierre de Masures de Rauzan, a member of the Bordeaux Parlement who, as we have already seen, was an important accumulator of estates at the end of the seventeenth and early eighteenth centuries. At this time, the property was called Batisse and it seems also, at an earlier time, to have gone under the name of Badère.

In 1694, Thérèse de Masures de Rauzan married Jacques-François de Pichon, Baron de Longueville, and her father gave this property as her marriage portion. The Pichon family was ancient, noble and distinguished. It can be traced back to the twelfth century, and from the fourteenth century, members of the family played a conspicuous part in affairs of state; thus Bernard, the father of Jacques-François, was a prominent and consistent supporter of the Crown during the troubled years of Louis XIV's minority, being at one time besieged in his house in Bordeaux and then forced to flee the city. In consideration of the support of Bernard de Pichon and his family, they were granted perpetual pensions by Louis XIV, and the King did Bernard de Pichon the honour of staying with him for some six weeks on his way to St Jean de Luz in 1659 for his marriage, though he passed only one night there on the return journey. After Bernard de Pichon, the Pichon inheritance split into two parts and remained separate until the middle of the nineteenth century. The elder son took Parempuyre, the second son, Jacques-François, Longueville. This was the son who acquired this property by marriage and so gave his name to the estate. It is interesting to note that there was a dispute shortly after the marriage as to the right of this branch of the Pichon family to nobility, and the judgement was only given in its favour by the Intendant of Bordeaux in 1698. The only other incident of note at this period was that the son of the King of Poland was received by Jacques-François de Pichon at the Château Longueville (not to be confused with the present château).

At the time of the Revolution, the head of the family was Joseph de Pichon Longueville. He was arrested and imprisoned, but escaped the guillotine. In 1816, he represented the city in congratulating Louis XVIII on the occasion of the Duc de Barry's marriage, and again, in 1820, at the birth of the Duc de Bordeaux. His son and heir, Raoul, also played a prominent part in the events leading up to the Restoration in 1814 and fought and was decorated for the Royalist cause. Like many others, he refused to play any part under the Orléanist régime after 1830. He showed his attachment to legitimist causes in a rather picturesque form by supporting Don Carlos, the founder of Carlism. He received Don Carlos at his house in Bordeaux in 1834, and conveyed him secretly from Bordeaux to Bayonne in his own carriage. He was afterwards decorated by Don Carlos, who was referred to by his supporters as Charles V.

It was during the administration of Raoul de Pichon Longueville that the château really acquired a reputation for its wines. As with so many properties in the eighteenth century, its proprietors were a good deal more famous than its wines, but during the first half of the nineteenth century, the wines became at least as distinguished as its noble proprietor. A sign of the growing reputation of the wines of Pichon is that in a classification of the 1820s and again in Charles Cocks's classification, only a decade before the Paris Exhibition, Pichon is placed among the third growths, but in 1855 it was placed among the seconds. This was a distinction which was only accorded to one other Pauillac, namely Mouton.

Raoul de Pichon Longueville had no children, but before he died in 1864, he adopted his cousin of the Parempuyre branch as his heir, thus reuniting the two branches, and this cousin, together with Raoul de Pichon Longueville's three sisters, inherited the estate. Curiously, though, the portion belonging to the Comtesse de Lalande, which amounted to three-fifths of the original estate, was separated from the rest of the property, although the other sisters and the new Baron continued together at the original Pichon-Longueville. The property now belongs to the Bouteiller family, who actually live at Château Lanessan. The château, one of the most striking in the Médoc, with its elegant, slender corner turrets, presents an almost fairy castle impression, but has been empty since the war. The former *hôtel* of the Pichon-Longuevilles, in the Cours de Chapeau Rouge, one of the finest eighteenth-century mansions, is now a bank.

The wines of Pichon-Baron are very classic Pauillacs, often rather aggressive at first, but acquiring a rich, velvety texture with maturity. The bouquet is particularly distinctive and fine. The 1928 was memorable as one of those that really repaid waiting for; in 1965 it was excellent and had probably reached its plateau of maturity. There have been some fine wines since the war, notably the 1947 and 1949, with the 1948 a very good example of the year. The 1950 was for a long time rather too hard for the year, but the 1953 and 1959 were worthy examples of those vintages. More recently, 1962 and 1966 have both produced good wines, but the 1964, while better than some 1964 Pauillacs, was not among the best. It is probably true to say that on the whole, Pichon-Baron produced rather better wines than Pichon-Lalande during the 1950s, but that in the 1960s the reverse was the case, and this tendency persisted through the 1970s. The 1979, however, is a wine of outstanding promise. The production, which is now around 8,000 cases, has been remarkably consistent, and this is a vineyard which has remained more or less unchanged since the 1855 classification.

Château Pichon-Longueville, Comtesse de Lalande
Second Growth

This is the full and correct name of this château, although it is sometimes referred to as Pichon-Longueville-Lalande. In the last few years, the proprietor has begun to label the wine simply as Pichon-Lalande, in order to try and make matters slightly less confusing for wine drinkers, and this certainly seems a welcome idea. This property, of course, shares with its neighbour the same history until the division. Then an attractive, if less theatrical, château was built, almost opposite the original Pichon-Longueville, in a small enclave of land entirely surrounded by the vineyards of Latour. This château is still used during the summer months. The *chais* was for many years scattered around the village of St Lambert, but now a fine, submerged cellar has been built behind the château, which has served an ingenious dual purpose. On the one hand, it has given Pichon-Lalande a superb new *chais*, on the other, a terrace from which there is an unrivalled panorama of the vineyards of Latour and the river.

In the new underground *chais* there are some fine, wrought-iron balustrades copied from those at the Hôtel Chapeau Rouge—a nice touch. Another interesting point for the visitor can be seen in the *chais*, where there are bunches of grapes preserved in glass jars, illustrating the principal red grape varieties used in the Médoc. This was, incidentally, one of the last properties where the *égrappage* was still performed by hand, an interesting spectacle at

145

vintage time. New stainless-steel fermentation *cuves* were installed just in time to receive the 1980 vintage.

One of the curiosities of Pichon is that it is the only classified growth whose vineyards straddle two *appellations* in any important way. Several leading growths in St Julien, as we have already seen, have small portions of their vineyards in other communes, and Lafite has a small vineyard in St Estèphe. But at Pichon-Lalande, as much as a third of the vineyard lies in St Julien. There was a period when the authorities insisted that the two parts be kept separate, and one had the confusing spectacle of some labels saying '*Appellation* Pauillac' and others '*Appellation* St Julien'. Eventually, the present proprietor won his fight for common sense against bureaucracy, insisting that Pichon was classified as a Pauillac and has always been regarded as such. But there is no doubt that this St Julien influence is to be seen in the wine and results in Pichon-Lalande's having a distinctly different style from its neighbour. There is not the frank, Pauillac character of the Baron, especially on the nose, but something more subtle, perhaps more feminine. In some vintages, the St Julien side of its personality seems more dominant than in others, but at its best this is always a wine of great breed.

Pichon Lalande came under its present ownership in 1926 when it was acquired by a Société Civile with Edouard F. Miailhe as administrator. The Miailhe family, who now control Pichon-Lalande, were for generations *courtiers* in Bordeaux and one of the few families to have been in business before the Revolution. Monsieur William-Alain Miailhe succeeded his father in the 1950s, and under his enthusiastic guidance great progress was made. By one of those coincidences which are so familiar in Bordeaux, his wife is a direct descendant of the Pichon-Longueville family. In the mid-1970s, a family row leading to protracted lawsuits ended Monsieur William-Alain Miailhe's administration of the property. First Monsieur Lahary of Chasse-Spleen and then Monsieur Delon of neighbouring Léoville-Lascases were called in to oversee the management of Pichon Lalande. Monsieur Delon installed Monsieur Gaudin as *maître de chais*, and this excellent choice stood the proprietors in good stead when Monsieur Delon parted company with them, and Monsieur Gaudin was appointed *régisseur*. One now has the impression that Pichon-Lalande is better run than at any time in recent years.

Monsieur Gaudin himself is one of a new breed of Bordeaux managers, who combine a solid, modern, technical training with an inbred aptitude. Today's proprietors, however enthusiastic, cannot effectively run large châteaux without a thorough technical and practical grounding, or without employing someone with these qualities.

As at Pichon Baron, the vineyard here has remained substantially the same since its partition a hundred years ago. The 49 hectares of vineyards, running on three sides with those of Latour, now produce in a good year about 20,000 cases, much the same as in the best years of the nineteenth century. In the search for improved quality, around 10 per cent of the vintage is usually disclassified and sold as Reserve de la Comtesse.

I was fortunate in 1968 to have the opportunity of comparing side by side at the château, the 1926, 1928 and 1929 vintages. It was interesting to find that the 1928 was seeing the 1929 out. It was attractive for a 1928, with much more life and vigour than the 1929. The 1929 itself was soft and fine flavoured, but beginning to fade. But the 1926 made a wonderful pair with the 1928 and in the end, to my way of thinking, it just had the edge over the 1928. The two wines were very comparable, but the 1926 had just a little more fruit and sweetness and so lasted and improved the better in the glass. In two capricious and uneven vintages, 1934 and 1937, Pichon-Lalande was very successful. Indeed the 1934, which I have been fortunate enough to drink on many occasions, is certainly one of the most successful Médocs of the year, with great fruit and charm allied to a well-defined, Pauillac character. This was a year when the Pauillac side was dominant. On the only occasion that I drank the 1937, I thought it nearly as good as the 1934, a high compliment indeed.

The 1950 took much longer than most 1950s to reach its best, but after eleven or twelve years, the original hardness fell away to reveal a very pleasant wine of this vintage. The 1952 was particularly successful here, with more fruit and fullness than many wines of this vintage, more successful perhaps than the 1953, which is charming but not outstanding for the vintage. The 1955 was also attractive, but the 1959 is not quite so outstanding as the Baron.

In the 1960s, Lalande really came into its own. The 1960 was very light and seemed to lack personality in the early years, but

147

was a wine which steadily improved. The 1961 is really an outstanding example of the year, a wine of great fruit and richness, so that it was extraordinarily supple at an early age, but it should certainly improve and last for many years. The 1962 has taken some time to develop, but seems to be more generous and elegant than the Baron. The 1964 is one of the most successful Pauillacs, or indeed Médocs, of this year of varied fortunes. In a vintage where St Julien in general took the palm, there were few better wines made outside it than here. The 1966 is a good example of the year, and in the more difficult 1967 vintage, the Lalande—one of the front-runners from the start—has aged more attractively than most. In the 1970s, the wine has gone from strength to strength. After a fine 1970 and good 1971, the 1975 is excellent, and 1976 and 1977 are among the best examples of these years. The 1978 looks like a great wine in the making, with the 1979 being one of the leading wines of the vintage.

Château Duhart-Milon Fourth Growth

It is remarkable that in the commune of Pauillac, after the heights of Lafite, Latour, Mouton and the two Pichons, there should be no third growths in the 1855 classification and but one fourth growth. Is it really true that such a gap exists? I believe that, although certain growths do today deserve a higher rating, there is in reality a significant difference in style and quality between the great first and second growths of the region and the rest.

Duhart-Milon, called simply Duhart in the 1855 classification, was a much more important growth in the nineteenth century than it has been in recent years. For most of this time it belonged to the Castéja family, who at one time were the hereditary notaries of Pauillac. Indeed, in Charles Cocks's list of 1846, the property is mentioned as Castéja, formerly Duhart. The family fortune was the work of Pierre Castéja, who was born in Pauillac in 1799, his father of the same name being mayor of Pauillac, and mentioned as being the proprietor of Duhart-Milon. Pierre Castéja had a very successful legal career, taking him from local councils in Lesparre and Pauillac on to that of Bordeaux and finally, in 1859, to be mayor of the city. In this role he was responsible for carrying out numerous improvements during a period of progress and prosperity in the city's history.

It is difficult to determine quite when Duhart-Milon's decline really set in. Certainly the 1929 was a very fine wine, but the 1949 was no more than passable, while wines of the 1950s were hard and tannic, with little grace, charm or breed. Part of the vineyard seems to have been sold off, and in the part that remained there was an excessive proportion of Petit-Verdot. Originally the vineyard had been in two parts, in the plateau of Carruades by Lafite and around the village of Milon.

In 1964, the Lafite-Rothschilds bought the property and reconstituted the vineyard, which obviously fits in very neatly with Lafite. Improving a really run-down property takes time, and it was hardly surprising that for some years after the Rothschild purchase, the wines, while certainly more attractive than hitherto, were hardly distinguished. But the new vineyard probably finally came of age with the 1978 vintage, which looked a really lovely wine in the spring of 1979, similar in elegance and weight to Haut-Batailley. At present, the former production of 140 tonneaux rising to over 200 in big years, has dropped to 80 tonneaux, or 6,000 cases. In a further effort to improve quality, it is the proprietor's intention in the near future, to introduce a second wine, Moulin de Duhart.

Château Pontet-Canet   Fifth Growth

The fifth group of the 1855 classification began with a string of five Pauillacs, headed by Pontet-Canet. In the classifications of the 1820s it is referred to simply as Canet, the property of de Pontet, and Charles Cocks called it Canet Pontet.

Pierre Bernard de Pontet, who was born in 1764, actually died in 1836, but his heir retained possession until 1865. Like so many proprietors of the age, Pontet was in politics, and was deputy for the Gironde as well as a member of the Conseil Général in the years immediately after the Restoration. But the real fame of Pontet-Canet began with its purchase by Herman Cruse in 1865. One of the new proprietor's first acts was to entrust the management of the property to Charles Skawinski, second son of the remarkable Pierre Skawinski of Giscours, although he was only twenty-three at the time. Under his management during Herman Cruse's lifetime and afterwards under his widow, Skawinski built up a great reputation for Pontet-Canet, so that it frequently fetched the price of a third or even a second growth. After Madame Cruse's death, the property was managed by the Cruse firm in

149

Bordeaux, until the great crisis in the firm's affairs led to its sale in 1975 to Monsieur Guy Tesseron, son-in-law of the late Emmanuel Cruse of Château d'Issan and himself already proprietor of Château Lafon-Rochet. A very fine new *chais* and *cuvier* were also built, and, for good measure, Pontet-Canet boasts one of the finest underground cellars in the Médoc, with ample space even for the large production of one of the largest vineyards.

Unfortunately, the reputation of this château does not stand as high as it once did. There was a feeling in the Bordeaux trade that Pontet-Canet was more of a brand than a classified growth, and the refusal to allow château-bottling lay at the heart of this distrust, together with the non-vintage wine sold on the French railways. The wine itself is also of variable and rather ordinary quality. One no longer sees the great vintages of the past which made Pontet-Canet famous. The last was the 1929, a very great example of this beautiful year which will long live in the memory of all who were fortunate enough to drink it. It lasted much better than most wines of this year, and when I last drank it in 1967, it was in superb condition at the height of its form, sweet and remarkably long, its flavour the epitome of great Pauillac, and wonderfully ripe. There is no doubt that with the wonderful position on the plateau of Pauillac, adjoining Mouton and Mouton Baron Philippe, Pontet-Canet has the potential to make fine wines.

In 1972, Pontet-Canet at last came into line with other classified growths and château bottled. After what has been achieved under Monsieur Tesseron's stewardship at Lafon-Rochet, the future for Pontet-Canet should be bright. All the ingredients are there, and so are the desire and capability to make great wines again. However, apart from a good 1975, the most recent vintages still seem to lack breed. The average production is 26,000 cases.

Château Lynch-Bages   Fifth Growth

This is one of several properties formerly belonging to the Lynch family. It does not appear in any of the classifications of the 1820s, but in Charles Cocks's 1846 list it is mentioned as Jurine à Bages. Monsieur Jurine was its proprietor at the time of the 1855 classification. Its present reputation, however, is largely due to the work of Monsieur J.-C. Cazes who managed the property for very many years. His son André, the mayor of Pauillac, has carried on the good work, aided by his son Jean-Michel. Recently, a fine, modern *cuvier* has much improved facilities here. The vineyard and château are very well situated at Bages, just to the south of Pauillac, on high ground to the west of the *route des châteaux*.

The relatively recent reputation of Lynch-Bages is emphasized by the fact that one seldom hears of, or finds, old vintages. In the 1950s, when the popularity of Lynch-Bages was soaring, it was often alleged by jealous neighbours that the special Lynch-Bages character, so beloved by wine-lovers, was in some dark and mysterious way a creation of Monsieur Cazes. However, when I tasted a bottle of the 1928 close to its fiftieth birthday—the only pre-Cazes Lynch-Bages ever to come my way—its character was completely consistent with more modern vintages. Furthermore, the wine was in superb condition, vigorous and rich, with no signs of excess tannin.

It is this balance which surely lies at the heart of Lynch-Bages's popular success. It always seems to produce easy-to-drink, fruity, ample wines, even in difficult years. Thus, one of the earliest examples I came across, the 1945—Bordeaux-bottled by Calvet— was extremely enjoyable to drink long before most 1945s could be approached. Looking at my tasting notes, I find myself frequently resorting to phrases such as 'typical Lynch-Bages', for this is a most individual wine. Its rich, plummy flavour and marked Pauillac bouquet remind one in some ways of Mouton—or rather of a young Mouton—before the youthful obviousness has given way to complexity and the breed has come through. Its great merits are its remarkable consistency and the ability to make its wines enjoyable in years like 1945, 1952 and 1957, at a time when most of its neighbours were still tough and ungrateful. This is almost certainly due to a skilful vinification on the part of Monsieur Cazes, by making very well-balanced wines with a lot of colour, extract and fruit, but never too much tannin.

Although this is deservedly a most successful growth, it would be wrong to suggest that it is quite in the top class. Certainly it lacks the breed and distinction of the best second growths such as the Pichons or the Léovilles, while being decidedly superior to its 1855 classification. The 1945, 1952, 1953, 1957, 1959, 1961, 1962, 1966 and 1967 were all very successful examples of their vintages, with the 1962 being really outstanding—among the best wines of the year. Only in 1964 did Monsieur Cazes's predilection for vintaging late get him into trouble, when Lynch-Bages was seriously affected by rain. More recently, the 1970, 1975, 1976, 1978 and 1979 have confirmed the reputation for quality, if not total consistency, with the 1975 and 1978 being outstanding. The average production is now around 22,000 cases.

Château Batailley   Fifth Growth

I have always had an affection for this growth, since it was one of the earliest I came to know well during my early visits to Bordeaux. The property lies a little way out of Pauillac on the road to St Laurent. The château is a pleasing example of the classic mid-nineteenth-century type, similar in scale and layout to Palmer but without the towers. The vineyard is well placed on the high plateau at the back of Pauillac, adjoining St Laurent.

The present management dates from 1942, when Monsieur Marcel Borie of Borie-Manoux, Bordeaux *négociants*, purchased it. The early reputation goes back to the period of Daniel Guestier of Barton & Guestier who bought it in 1818, his heirs selling it to Monsieur Constant Halphen in 1864. Interestingly, though, Daniel Guestier's régime did not succeed in getting his growth mentioned in a classification of 1827, but by 1846 Charles Cocks lists it together with the name of the proprietor. Since Monsieur Marcel Borie's death in 1961, the estate has been managed by his son-in-law, Monsieur Emile Castéja, himself from an old proprietorial family (see Lynch-Moussas).

The wines of Batailley are typical of the best sort of Pauillacs in the second rung of quality—solid and dependable, very consistent, but only occasionally really memorable. In its less successful moments such as 1955, for example, there is a tendency to be rather tough and mean, lacking flesh and fruit. Through the generosity of the proprietors, I have had the opportunity to drink several old vintages: the 1911, 1928 and 1934 were all successful wines of their years, and the 1911 even held up well when over fifty years old.

Since the war, the 1945 was fine but austere, the 1953 outstanding, the 1955 a trifle lean and austere, the 1959 generous, ripe and full-bodied, the 1961 a very good example of the year, the 1964 outstanding—certainly one of the best Pauillacs of this year of mixed fortunes—and the 1966 good without repeating the magic of the 1964. The average production is now around 8,000 cases.

Château Haut-Batailley   Fifth Growth

At the time that Batailley was acquired by the Borie family, the property was divided, this smaller portion going to the brother of Monsieur Marcel Borie, who at the same time bought Ducru-Beaucaillou. The property then passed to his widow and is administered by Monsieur Jean-Eugène Borie, the dedicated administrator of Ducru-Beaucaillou.

The château and *chais* having gone with the larger portion of the property, the wine of Haut-Batailley was for years vinified and kept in the *chais* at Beaucaillou, but since 1974 this has been moved to the new La Couronne *chais* in Pauillac. Because this part of the vineyard was completely reconstituted, the wines were for a long time lighter and not as powerful as those of Batailley; but as they achieved maturity, so the quality of the wine showed a marked improvement. The 1961 showed the full potential of the vineyard, and since then there has been a steady improvement, so that today its wines are a worthy rival to those of Batailley, although the style and emphasis are somewhat different. As now vinified by Jean-Eugène Borie, the wine has more elegance and less weight than most Pauillacs, and in this respect resembles recent vintages of Duhart-Milon. The 1966 is charming but at its peak by 1981. In recent years, 1970, 1971, 1975, 1976, 1978 and 1979 have all been marked successes. The average production is 7,000 cases.

Château Grand-Puy-Lacoste   Fifth Growth

The recorded history of this property goes back to the fifteenth century, when it belonged to a Monsieur de Guiraud, one of whose daughters married Monsieur de Jehan, a *conseiller* of the Bordeaux Parlement. It was a great-granddaughter of Jehan who married a Monsieur Saint-Guirous, whose name still appears on the label. He was a member of the *noblesse de robe*, and one of his daughters received a portion of the Grand Puy estate on marrying Monsieur Lacoste—hence Grand-Puy-Lacoste.

However, the present high reputation of this wine rightly reflects the efforts of Monsieur Raymond Dupin, the proprietor for many years. This energetic and delightful man was certainly one of the most universally loved in Bordeaux—one of the few men in this competitive business with no enemies. Although Monsieur Dupin did not restore his château, as many of his neighbours have, he did maintain essentials. His hospitality was proverbial, and the legendary Antoinette presided in the kitchen to the satisfaction of his many guests. In 1978, perhaps feeling the need to share his burden in advanced years, Monsieur Dupin sold a controlling interest to Jean-Eugène Borie of Ducru-Beaucaillou. In this new venture, it will be Xavier Borie, under his father's watchful eye, who has responsibility for managing the property, and he and his wife are now installed in a wing of the château which has been tastefully restored. He was fortunate in his first vintage—1978—and made the most of it. After the 1980 vintage had been vinified, Jean-Eugène Borie decided that the cuvier with its old, traditional wooden vats drastically needed renovation. After much soul-searching, it was eventually decided to make a clean sweep and install glass-lined steel tanks. They will not be as attractive as the old ones but should certainly make for easier maintenance and control of vinification. The whole installation will be ready for the 1981 vintage.

In style and quality Grand-Puy-Lacoste belongs to the same category as Batailley; it is full-bodied and typically Pauillac, perhaps a shade tough at first, but once the initial brusqueness has worn off, an attractive and rewarding wine. The big, immediate post-war vintages—1945, 1947 and 1949—are still full of life and interest; the 1953 at its best but not quite up to Ducasse by 1978; the 1955 was an attractive wine which came on early for a Pauillac; the 1960 was one of the successful wines of the vintage; 1961 and 1962 are typical of the years; 1964 was one of the wines picked before the rain, but was slow to develop and rather tough, while both 1966 and 1967 are very good examples of these two very different years, but the 1967 is now beginning to dry up. This consistency has been maintained in the 1970s, with big wines being made in 1970, 1975, 1978 and 1979, while 1977 was unusually full for the year. The average production is now around 10,000 cases.

Château Grand-Puy-Ducasse   Fifth Growth

This was a small vineyard of 10 hectares, rather fragmented for a

154

classified growth, consisting of three separate parcels. The château and *chais* are actually in the town of Pauillac and the château—a pleasing, neo-classical building on the quayside—has for some years acted as the Maison du Vin and headquarters of the Bontemps du Médoc. Like the other Grand Puy, Ducasse owes its name to an eighteenth-century member of the *noblesse de robe*. Curiously, though, its name in the 1855 classification appeared as Artique-Arnaud, although both the 1820s' classifications and Charles Cocks's in 1846 had called it Ducasse. For a number of years it was the property of the Bouteiller family, proprietors of Pichon-Baron and Lanessan, but was sold to a *syndicat* associated with the well-known *négociants* Mestrezat Preller in 1971. The new owners bought a further 10 hectares of old vines, and 10 hectares of fifteen-year-old vines, thus trebling the size of the vineyard.

The wine is not very well known in England, but whenever I have come across it, I have found it a very classic Pauillac in bouquet and flavour, with vigour and breed. The 1945 was still rather tough after twenty-two years, but the 1947 and 1949 were both outstandingly fine, as were the 1953—more vigorous than most—and 1955. The new régime seems to be maintaining quality with the larger vineyard. The 1975 is very rich and attractive with more fat and suppleness than many wines of this year, the 1976 has plenty of depth, the 1977 is fuller than most 1977s, and the 1978 has great promise. The average production is now 8,000 cases.

Château Mouton-Baronne-Philippe (formerly Mouton d'Armailhacq) Fifth Growth

Until the eighteenth century, this property formed part of Mouton, but then passed to the d'Armailhacq family. In the very year of the Revolution, Joseph Arnaud d'Armailhacq was born on the property, and under his direction the vineyard became renowned. In 1850 he published a work, *De la culture des Vignes, de la Vinification et des Vins dans le Médoc avec un Etat des Vignobles d'après leur réputation*. It was regarded as the most authoritative book on the subject at that time and went into a number of editions. Subsequently, the property passed to heirs of the Armailhacqs and was finally bought by Baron Philippe de Rothschild in 1933. In 1956 the name of the property was changed to incorporate the name of its present illustrious owner, and was then modified again in 1975 to 'Baronne Philippe' as a tribute to the memory of the Baron's gifted and greatly missed wife.

The château is something of a curiosity, its classical pediment being only half completed. This and the *chais* lie between Mouton and Pontet-Canet. Although Mouton-Baronne-Philippe's vineyards run side by side with those of its cousin and were once the same property, it is scrupulously run as an entirely separate property, but with all the same care as the great Mouton.

In style, the wines of the second Mouton are truly Pauillac, with the authentic blackcurrant aroma and the full-flavoured, assertive character, but softer and less massive than Mouton itself, and quicker to mature. Unfortunately, I have no experience of old vintages, save only a marvellously preserved and harmonious 1934, but currently the wines are consistent and have style and breed. The 1962 was particularly successful, the 1964 was picked too late, but the 1966 was back to form and a magnificent wine. Normally successful vintages follow those at Mouton. The average production has now risen to 18,000 cases.

Château Lynch-Moussas Fifth Growth

This is another property taking its name from the Lynch family. Moussas is the name of the minute hamlet in which it lies. The growth is not mentioned in any of the pre-1855 classifications. It is now the property of the Castéja family and is administered by Emile Castéja, head of the *négociants* Borie-Manoux (see Batailley p. 152). The Castéjas have the distinction of having owned a classified growth in Pauillac ever since the 1855 classification—they were then owners of Duhart-Milon (see Duhart-Milon p. 148).

This small vineyard has never reached any great heights but has mostly been a consistent and honourable fifth growth. The wine is on the light side and tends to mature fairly quickly. The only occasions when I have bought it—1959 and 1960—it developed into pleasing, easy-to-drink wine, especially the 1959. But whether it is really any better than a good *Bourgeois*, such as La Couronne, is another matter. It is certainly not in the same class as wines like the Grand Puys and Batailley. The average production is 1,500 cases.

156

Château Croizet-Bages   Fifth Growth

When I first visited the *chais* of Croizet-Bages (there is no château) in the early 1960s, it had a distinctly rustic appearance, and I remember thinking that this was how most *chais* must have appeared in the nineteenth century—with an earthen floor, a low, cobwebby roof and grimy casks in disorderly profusion.

The property lies on high ground behind Lynch-Bages, and was created out of the old domaine of Bages during the eighteenth century, by the brothers Croizet. Its best-known proprietor was Monsieur Julian Calvé, who bought the property in 1853 and whose name was sometimes found appended to the château title. It remained in the Calvé family until 1930, when Monsieur Paul Quié purchased it. Since his death it has been administered by his heirs.

Croizet-Bages produces good, robust, full-flavoured Pauillacs which mellow fairly early and can be put with the better Pauillac classified growths. After the 1945 which, while fruity, remained hard and tough for many years, came a number of most attractive and successful wines. The 1953 had all the ripeness and charm of the year and was at its peak when ten to fifteen years old; the 1955 was rather firm for some time but was more attractive than many wines of the vintage; the 1957 was a success, developing fruit and mellowness; the 1959 was attractive if not outstanding; the 1960 has been one of the most long-lived wines of the year and was still at its best after eleven years, when many others were fading; the 1961 is worthy of the year—an outstanding wine; the 1962 is easy and agreeable with a lot of fruit; the 1964, while not one of the best Pauillacs of the year, was more satisfactory than some; the 1966 repeated the success of the 1962; and the 1967 is a good example of the year.

To sum up, then, this is a growth which is producing very good, middle-of-the-road wines, fully worthy of its class. The average production is around 7,000 cases.

Château Pédesclaux   Fifth Growth

This is one of the obscurer classified growths. I can find no mention of it in any of the pre-1855 classifications. The name comes from a Bordeaux *courtier* who was proprietor at the time of the classification.

157

The *chais* is situated in the town of Pauillac. The vineyard lies to the northern extremity of the commune near Mouton. Since 1950, it has belonged to the Jugla family, and is now administered by Monsieur Bernard Jugla. The reputation of the growth does not stand very high today, and the wine is hardly of classified growth standing. On the few occasions I have tasted it, I have found the wine lacking in style and personality—rather commonplace. The average production is around 3,800 cases.

Château Clerc-Milon-Mondon   Fifth Growth

This property is situated in the small village of Milon. When driving from the village of Pouyalet north towards Lafite, one comes across it on a slope between the road and the river. Some of the vineyard lies on this side facing the road, some on the other side facing the river.

Monsieur Clerc was the proprietor at the time of the 1855 classification. Monsieur Mondon was a notary in Pauillac, and until recently the proprietors were his two grand-daughters, themselves the sisters of Monsieur Jacques Vialard, the present leading notary of Pauillac. In 1970 they sold to Baron Philippe de Rothschild. From 1947 until the sale, the exclusivity for the distribution of the wine was in the hands of Dourthe, *négociants* in Moulis and Bordeaux.

I have tasted the wine on a number of occasions and found it sometimes supple and attractive if rather light, sometimes a shade coarse and lacking in breed; it is not considered to be among the better Pauillac classified growths. However, with the excellent position of the vineyard, La Bergerie are confident that far better things can be achieved in the future. This will inevitably take time. I did not find the 1975 particularly impressive. The average production is 8,000 cases.

Château Haut-Bages-Libéral   Fifth Growth

This property lies on the high ground of Bages (hence the name) between the *route des châteaux* and the river, just to the south of Pauillac and near Latour; formerly there was another piece of vineyard north of Pauillac near Pontet-Canet, but when the Cruse and Peugeot families acquired it after the War, this part was added to Pontet-Canet. Libéral was the name of the proprietor at the time of the classification. After the Cruses took over the administration, the wine was made and stored at Pontet-Canet and was Bordeaux-bottled, not château-bottled until this became obligatory for classified growths in 1972. The *cuvier* and *chais* at Haut-Bages were no longer used, until the construction of a new *chais* recently.

The reputation of this property has not been very high for some years, and on the rare occasions that I have had the opportunity of tasting it, the wine has seemed unremarkable and rather commonplace. The average production is now 6,000 cases.

Château La Couronne

This growth was classified in 1932 as a *cru exceptionnel*. It was only created in 1874 by Monsieur Armand Lalande, the founder of the *négociant* A. Lalande & Cie., and owner of Léoville-Poyferré and Brane-Cantenac. Hence it was not classified in 1855, but has been granted the special status of a *cru exceptionnel*. The vineyards are very well sited in the southern part of Pauillac on the inland plateau.

Today the vineyard belongs to the Borie family and is administered by Monsieur Jean-Eugène Borie. Since the construction of a new *chais* and *cuvier* for 1974, the wine is made in Pauillac, and like all Monsieur Borie's wines, is most meticulously made. The style is very true Pauillac, sometimes a shade aggressive to start with, but developing good fruit and always harmonious and well balanced. A very good standard is being maintained, and the wine is as good as many fifth growth Pauillacs. The average production is 700 cases.

There are a number of good *Bourgeois* growths in Pauillac, and an important cooperative whose wines are sold under the name La Rose Pauillac. Founded in 1933, and for long administered by the legendary Monsieur J. C. Cazes of Lynch-Bages, its wines are consistent and typical Pauillacs and enjoy a good reputation. As many as 34,000 cases a year are made. There are also several good growths which vinify at the cooperative but are kept separately and can often be bought under their own label. Among the best of these are *Grand Cru les Carruades* and *Colombier Monpelou*, classified as a *Grand Cru Bourgeois*.

Among other important growths enjoying a good reputation and likely to be found in export markets are:

Château Rolland, classified as *Grand Cru Bourgeois*, belonging to Monsieur Maurice Gratadour, making 1,600 cases.

Château La Fleur Milon, classified as a *Grand Cru Bourgeois* and making 4,250 cases.

The others, classified as *Cru Bourgeois* are:

Château Haut-Bages-Monpelou, another property belonging to Borie-Manoux, averaging 4,250 cases.

Château Belle-Rose belongs to Monsieur Bernard Jugla, with an average of 3,000 cases.

Château Fonbadet, the largest of the *Cru Bourgeois* in Pauillac, belonging to Monsieur Gabriel Meffre of *Du Glana*, with an average of 8,500 cases.

Château Pibran the property of Monsieur Paul Billa, making 1,900 cases.

Château Duroc-Milon, making 1,275 cases.

Château Haut-Padarnac, making 850 cases.

ST ESTÈPHE

This is the most northerly of the great *appellations* of the Haut-Médoc, and produces more wine than any other. But it boasts fewer classified growths than Pauillac, Margaux or St Julien, and a very large number of *Bourgeois* growths of widely varying quality. It is the only one of the four great *appellations* of the Médoc, where the area of the *Crus Bourgeois* is greater than that of the classified growths.

In style, the wines have less body than those of Pauillac; at their best, they are very fruity, full-flavoured and quite rich, but, on the other hand, some lesser growths are tough and rather stringy with a certain *goût de terroir* and a certain dry meanness at the finish. So the range of quality is considerable; there are aristocrats worthy to take their place among the great wines of the Médoc, and plebeians which are on a quality level with the least in the backwoods of the Haut-Médoc.

St Estèphe itself lies near, but not on, the river, and there are other villages of some importance, notably Pez and Cadourne. Most of the vineyards lie on gravelly slopes which run from close to the river to some distance inland.

160

Château Cos d'Estournel   Second Growth

This strikingly placed property lies across marshy ground on a promontory above Lafite. Its pagoda-like façade is one of the most familiar landmarks in the Médoc, and it is rather a disappointment to discover that this is only a *chais* and not the château (there is none). Coming from St Estèphe, there is a formal entrance to part of the vineyard which now frames a horrific, science-fiction view of the enlarged Shell installation of Pauillac.

The property takes its name from Monsieur d'Estournel under whom the fame of the château was established. After he had bought back the property in 1821—his family having sold it in 1811—he enlarged the vineyard to approximately its present size and built the famous *chais*. At the time of the classification, the property actually belonged to an Englishman, a Mr Martyn, who owned it from 1853 to 1869. In 1919, it was bought by Monsieur Fernand Ginestet, and then for many years formed part of the domains owned, administered and distributed by the Ginestet family, firstly under Pierre Ginestet and, more recently, by his son Bernard. In 1971, when some of the Ginestet family holdings were divided up, Cos went to Pierre Ginestet's sister, Madame Prats. Her son, Bruno, has taken charge of the running of the property. At the same time, they decided to remove the distribution of Cos from the Ginestet firm and arrange this for themselves, which seems to have proved beneficial for the château. Curiously enough, Cos was placed as a third growth in early classifications, even as late as 1846. But there is no doubt that over the years it has consistently held its place as one of the leading second growths since 1855.

In my experience, Cos at its best is the finest of the St Estèphes, with more breed, delicacy and fruit than is achieved by other properties in the area. Certainly the finest bottles of St Estèphe that I have drunk come from Cos. Like most of the best Médocs, Cos generally requires some time for its various parts to harmonize. The constituents are a great vigour (which here is more than simple tannin), great fruit and charm which, with maturity, produce a mellow richness which is given life, character and verve by a firm backbone. Some lesser St Estèphes remind me of those drawings of Don Quixote, large in scale but very bony, so that one is more aware of the skeleton beneath than the flesh so

161

sparsely stretched upon it. With Cos, the skeleton is there but always in the background.

I have been fortunate in drinking some fine vintages of Cos. Outstanding among these was the 1869 which I had with Pierre and Bernard Ginestet on its ninety-sixth birthday. It had come from Madame Charmolüe's cellar, the Charmolües having been proprietors of Cos at the end of the last century. It was certainly one of the greatest bottles of claret I have ever had, the bouquet still fresh and lovely, the wine sweet and full-flavoured with great length—an apparently ageless beauty. In style it reminded me strongly of a 1900. After this, the 1909 was still wonderfully powerful and vigorous with a lovely ripeness when fifty-four years old. I noted that it seemed to show a combination of the virtues of Pauillac and St Julien. Among the great vintages of the 1920s, I would single out the 1926 and 1929 as very fine examples of these years which have lasted remarkably well. Since the war, the 1950s were an outstanding decade for Cos, but I was less enchanted with the 1960s, a period which coincided with a decline in the affairs of the Ginestets. The 1950 was attractive and lasted very well; the 1952 was less austere than some, but was slow to develop; the 1953 was a real beauty; the 1955 was fine and with more individuality than many; the 1957 was a success in an uneven year; the 1958 had the charm of the year and lasted well; the 1959 was a slow developer and was very rich; the 1960 was less attractive than the 1950; the 1961 promised great things from the beginning; the 1962 was very slow to come out and show its paces—rather tough and lacking ripeness; the 1964, while having more colour and body than some, lacked grace and breed.

The change of management has certainly seen a revitalization at Cos, which has been reflected in the wines. Fine wines were made in 1975 and 1976, while the 1977 was much better than most St Estèphes in that year. Both 1978 and 1979 are excellent in the context of their respective vintages.

A new departure is Maître d'Estournel. This is a branded wine with only a Bordeaux *appellation*, and is not a second wine of Cos. It seems a pity that such a name, which could cause confusion, should have been chosen. The average production is now put at 25,000 cases.

Château Montrose   Second Growth

This is the most modern of all the leading Médoc growths, although in most other respects it is the most traditional. The vineyard was created out of woodlands on the Calon estate only at the beginning of the nineteenth century. By 1846, when Charles Cocks wrote, it was placed with Cos as a third growth, although no mention of it was made in classifications of 1824 and 1827.

The large vineyard with its chalet-like château and *chais* lies on slopes bordering the Gironde near the town of St Estèphe, but well away from the main *route des châteaux*. This very well-run estate has belonged to the Charmolüe family since 1896; Madame Charmolüe still presides, but her son now administers. The *chais* is well ordered but traditional, with beautifully kept, wooden fermentation vats. Now that Latour has gone modern, this is probably the most traditionally-made wine among the classified growths, and the comparison with Latour does not end there. Here, there is also a high proportion of Cabernet Sauvignon; the wine is usually hard and tannic to start with and takes a long time to come round. Its qualities are usually very obvious at an early stage, then a dull period sets in. Off-vintages are sometimes very good, if they are not unbalanced, but good vintages do not always fulfil their early promise. Tasting the wine each year against other leading St Estèphes, I found Montrose was always impressive to begin with, but often failed to develop well, due to an imbalance of tannin.

The oldest vintages I have seen were the 1893 and 1899; both showed charm and breed but were fading. Undoubtedly the best bottle of an old Montrose I have had was the 1920 which was robust, but with great charm and vinosity, closely rivalled by the glorious 1929, which, while fading by the mid-1960s, still had a lovely bouquet and great charm.

In the 1950s, the 1953 was easily the best, but the 1952 and 1955 were rather tough and dull. But if Cos had the best of things in the 1950s, Montrose had the edge in the 1960s. The 1960 itself was one of the best in the Médoc, with a fine colour and plenty of body and flavour; the 1961 promised to be a classic but was most disappointing at the Taams tasting (see Chapter 12, pp. 366–7); the 1962 developed slowly but is very fine; the 1964 is a shade austere but is probably the best in St Estèphe; the 1966 is a very big wine;

the 1970 and 1976 are both very good, while 1978 and 1979 have outstanding promise in their different ways. This is a classic claret drinker's wine, not perhaps for beginners, but with its strong character and full-blooded qualities, a wine to appeal to English and, even more perhaps, to Scottish tastes. The average production is 18,000 cases.

Château Calon-Ségur   Third Growth

Of the three leading estates in St Estèphe, this is certainly the most ancient. Its origins can be traced back to the twelfth century when the lords of Lesparre gave it a bishop of Poitiers— Monseigneur de Calon. But the area was also referred to as de Calones after the boats that used to ferry timber across the Gironde. In the eighteenth century it belonged to the famous Marquis de Ségur, then the proprietor of Lafite and Latour. It was he who was supposed to have said that although he made his wine at Lafite, his heart was at Calon. This is the origin of the heart-shaped device seen on the label and at many places on the property. In the last century, it belonged to Pierre-Sevère de Lestapis, one of the most famed financiers of his time in France. Curiously, he received his training with Alexander Baring in London. In 1818, together with his two brothers, he established his own firm of Lestapis Frères in Bordeaux. This firm played a very important part in developing trade with India and South America. The property now belongs to the Gasqueton and Peyrelongue families, and has been administered by Philippe Gasqueton since the death of his uncle, Edouard, in 1962. It was Edouard Gasqueton who was responsible for building the modern reputation of Calon for reliability, between the wars and up to the time of his death.

The vineyard is beautifully situated, just to the north of St Estèphe, and is largely encircled by an old stone wall. It is the most northerly of the great St Estèphes and, indeed, of all the classified growths. The château itself is one of the finest in the region, with its distinctive, squat towers and cloister-like entrance by the *chais*. It dates from the seventeenth century.

Calon was accounted, with Cos, a third growth in the early classifications, but curiously failed to move up to the seconds with Cos and Montrose in 1855. In character the wine is fuller-bodied and more generous than Cos, softer and quicker to develop than

Montrose. If it is seldom the best of the three, it has the virtue of consistency, and this dependability has much to do with its popularity.

Calon is a wine which, nevertheless, lasts very well, and this has been brought home in the older vintages I have seen. Certainly one of the finest of all Calons was the magnum of 1924 that I was fortunate enough to drink with Madame Edouard Gasqueton and her nephew Philippe when it was forty years old. It had not faded as had most wines of that year by then, but combined power with finesse, and was full of vitality—a delicious wine. The 1926 was also a fine example of the year. Equally memorable is the 1934, certainly one of the most consistently enjoyable wines of that year that I know. Since the war, the 1945 is very fine, having sufficient richness to cope with the tannin—it has been very enjoyable for a number of years and there is plenty of life in it still; 1947 was successful and has lived well; the 1948 and 1950 were both outstandingly successful, the 1948 so much so that I have thought it superior to the 1949. In the next decade, the 1952 was unusually attractive for the year, although meatier than the 1953; the 1953, while fine, was not outstanding in this exceptional year; the 1954 was a most attractive wine which was still excellent when nearly fourteen years old; the 1955 was a good wine for the year; and the 1959 has developed well, being big and vigorous. The next decade did not begin so well: the 1960 was a disappointment—not in the class of the 1950 or even the 1954; the 1962 is a good, robust example of the year, but lost fruit rather quickly; the 1964 started badly with too much rain water in it—surprisingly, though, it has picked up and although light and of only average quality, has developed into an acceptable bottle; even more surprising was the 1965 which was one of the few drinkable wines in this very poor year; the 1966 was a return to form and has developed very well, as has the 1967. In the 1970s, Calon has maintained its reputation for reliability. When a blind tasting of leading growths of the Gironde was held in Nicolas's cellars in 1976 for the French gourmet magazine, *La Nouvelle Guide de Gault-Millau*, Calon came out with the highest average mark. The vintages tasted were 1966, 1970, 1971 and 1973. Good wines were also made in 1975 and 1976, but like most properties in the northern Médoc, Calon did less well in 1977. But 1978 and 1979 were both highly successful. The average production is 24,000 cases.

Château Lafon-Rochet   Fourth Growth

Although classified as a fourth growth in 1855, this was a little-known wine until very recently. The situation of the property is not unfavourable: it lies just past Cos d'Estournel (going towards St Estèphe) on the opposite (or inland) side of the *route des châteaux*.

In 1960, the property was bought by Monsieur Guy Tesseron, a *négociant* in Cognac who is married to Nicole, daughter of the late Emmanuel Cruse, of Château d'Issan. The wine was distributed by the firm of Cruse until the early 1970s. The château has now been completely reconstructed in the traditional *chartreuse* style. The vineyard has also been extensively replanted.

The reputation of this growth seems to have been unremarkable for some time, and *Bourgeois* growths such as de Pez and Phélan-Ségur were more widely thought of. When I first drank the wine, it seemed to have a pronounced *goût de terroir* and was rather undistinguished, certainly not of *Cru Classé* standing. But recently Monsieur Tesseron's labours seem to have borne fruit, and the wine has frequently come out well at blind tastings, elegant and stylish. Fine wines were made in 1975 and 1976. The wine still seems better-known in the United States than in England. The average production is now put at 15,000 cases.

Château Cos-Labory   Fifth Growth

The small, turreted château is immediately opposite its more famous neighbour, Cos d'Estournel. It is today one of the less well-known classified growths, but the wine is well made and attractive, if rather slight compared to the leading growths. Its reputation is quite serious, but no higher than some leading *Bourgeois* growths of the region. The average production is 4,000 cases.

Château Phélan-Ségur   *Cru Bourgeois Exceptionnel*

After the big three (Cos d'Estournel, Montrose and Calon), Phélan is certainly one of the most important properties in St Estèphe today, both in terms of production and quality.

The property itself is situated between the road and the river, and between Montrose and the town of St Estèphe. There is a château with a comfortable country house appearance, and the property is administered by Monsieur R. Delon, the uncle of the administrator of Léoville-Lascases. The domaine was actually founded at the beginning of the nineteenth century by Monsieur Phélan, partly from land which had belonged to the Marquis de Ségur.

The wine is not one I know at all well personally, but its reputation is one of consistent quality for some years. In style it is robust and typically St Estèphe, but with the extra weight and roundness which typifies the best growths. The average production is 17,000 cases.

Château de Pez

With Phélan-Ségur, de Pez is today the leading growth in St Estèphe after the big three. The property has ancient origins which can be traced back to the fifteenth century; in the seventeenth century it belonged to the Pontacs of Haut Brion, in the mid-eighteenth century to Pierre d'Aulède of Margaux, and just before the Revolution it belonged to Comte Joseph de Fumel, the commander of the province of Guyenne.

The vineyard and château with its two massive, squat towers, lie by the village of Pez, just to the west of St Estèphe, on a fine, gravelly plateau which has an ideal exposure. Since 1920 it has belonged to the Bernard family and in recent years Madame Bernard's nephew, Monsieur Dousson, has taken on the management.

The estate is very well run and the wine meticulously made. There is a high proportion of Cabernet Sauvignon. It is interesting that the Cabernet vines were largely replanted in 1950 and reached maturity in the 1970s. When I first tasted the wine in the 1950s, it seemed an admirable *Bourgeois* growth but no more; since the following decade, the wines have taken on an extra dimension, an extra richness, so that they can more and more be compared with the big three. Of recent vintages, the 1964 was one of the best in St Estèphe with a magnificent colour and great vinosity, while the 1966 has great richness and concentration of flavour. Even in poor years the Cabernet Sauvignon combined with careful selection has produced good results—the 1965 was far better than most wines of that year, and the 1968 was a most attractive wine. The 1970 is a classic for the year, and also witnessed a most interesting experiment. At the suggestion of

167

Martin Bamford, the head of Gilbey-Loudenne who buy and distribute the wine, a cask of each of the *cépages* represented in the vineyard was kept separately at the time of the *assemblage*. These were Cabernet Sauvignon, Cabernet Franc, Merlot and Petit-Verdot. Owing to the ideal conditions in 1970, even the Petit-Verdot reached perfect maturity. To taste these four wines and then the finished product is most instructive, for not only does one see the characteristics of each *cépage*, but the greatest lesson of all is how much better the *assemblage* is than any of its constituent parts. A most stylish 1971 was made, a tremendous 1975 and a fine 1976. The 1978 is really fine, and the 1979 is solid for the year. On current form, de Pez can certainly take its place alongside the leading classified growths of the *appellation*. The average production is 9,350 cases.

Château Meyney   *Cru Bourgeois Exceptionnel*

This large property lies between the road and the river south of St Estèphe, and the long, blank wall of the *chais* with its characteristic tower rising from the middle is just visible across undulating vineyards from the *route des châteaux*. In the seventeenth century it was the Prieuré des Couleys, and today its large courtyard gives it a somewhat monastic impression. Since just after the First World War it has belonged to the Cordier family.

The growth has a good reputation for sound, robust and consistent wines. They can, however, be somewhat on the coarse side and lack, for instance, the breed of de Pez. Perhaps because of these characteristics, I have usually found Meyney to be most enjoyable drunk young, when the youthful fruit blends pleasingly into the powerful, rich texture. Because of its weight, one feels that it should age well, but in fact it tends to become dull, the wine dries up and the *goût de terroir* dominates. This has happened, for instance, to the 1961. Of recent years, I have especially liked the 1970, very big but coming round well, a delicious 1971, a very attractive, forward 1973, a very big and fine 1975, and a promising 1976. The average production is 20,400 cases.

Château de Marbuzet   *Grand Bourgeois Exceptionnel*

This is one of several properties incorporating the name of Marbuzet. In 1966 it was classified by the Syndicat des Crus

168

Grands Bourgeois et Crus Bourgeois as a *Grand Bourgeois Exceptionnel* and this was confirmed in 1978. The property is well-situated close to the river and has an attractive château with an elegant, neo-classical portico. It is now the property of Bruno Prats of Cos d'Estournel. The wine enjoys a sound reputation and is carefully made. The average production is 4,250 cases.

Château Pomys

A wine which is often seen in England. It is a relatively small estate for St Estèphe, the property of the Arnaud family. The wine is attractive, well-balanced and reliable. The average production is 5,950 cases.

Château Beau-Site   *Grand Bourgeois Exceptionnel*

This property stands at the entrance to the village of St Corbian at the northern extremity of the St Estèphe *appellation*. An attractive courtyard in front of the *chais* is partly enclosed by wall and railings, marked by small pavilions at each corner. The vineyard runs from the road towards Calon-Ségur.

The vineyard has been classified since 1966 as a *Grand Bourgeois Exceptionnel*. The wine has been very consistent in recent years, full-bodied, and distinctive with a good deal of richness. It belongs to Borie-Manoux and is administered by Emile Castéja (see Batailley, p. 152). The average production is 11,475 cases.

Château Beausite Haut Vignoble

This is the property of Monsieur René Braguessac, whose *chais* is only a few yards down the road in St Corbian from Beau-Site. But the wine, although carefully made and very honourable, is not in the same class as Beau-Site. It has a tendency to be rather tough and unyielding and generally takes some time to come round. The lack of richness combined with a certain toughness is characteristic of many of the lesser growths of St Estèphe. The average production is 6,800 cases.

Château Tronquoy-Lalande   *Cru Grand Bourgeois*

This is an old property, formerly of more importance than it is today. Lalande is the name of the place, Tronquoy of the family who owned it early in the nineteenth century. It opened as a fourth growth in classifications of 1824 and 1827, but has failed to make

169

the grade since. The château boasts two distinctive towers at each end of a *chartreuse*-type building.

The wine has a very marked *goût de terroir*, which may not be to every taste, but it is undeniably a wine of some character and interest. With maturity the wine develops a pleasing harmony. The 1964 was delicious when sixteen years old. The château is now administered by Monsieur Jean-Philippe Castéje. The average production is 5,100 cases.

Château Haut-Marbuzet   *Grand Bourgeois Exceptionnel*

This is a wine well known in England where it is distributed by Bouchard Ainé. The property of Monsieur H. Duboscq, the wine was classified as a *Grand Bourgeois Exceptionnel* in 1966. It is situated near the village of the same name.

With a higher proportion of Merlot than is general, the wine is rather flattering and easy to drink for a St Estèphe, hence its popularity. The average production is 17,000 cases.

Château Capbern   *Cru Bourgeois Exceptionnel*

This is the subject of some confusion since the wine is sold under several different names. Officially Capbern is classified as a *Grand Bourgeois Exceptionnel*, and it is also sometimes known as Capbern-Gasqueton after the family who have now owned it for six generations. Part of the crop is also sold as a monopole by Dourthe Frères as Grand-Village Capbern, while for a number of years, Sichel & Co. had the monopole for the name La Rose Capbern.

The property itself adjoins Calon-Ségur and possesses an attractive château which could be taken for a Regency house were it not for the characteristically French roof-line. The property, which is owned by the Gasqueton family, is administered by Monsieur Philippe Gasqueton, the administrator of Calon-Ségur.

The wines have a good reputation for being solid and reliable, with some richness and style. The average production is 6,375 cases.

Château Les Ormes de Pez   *Cru Grand Bourgeois*

This is a well-known and well-regarded wine in England. The property is just outside the village of Pez and belongs to Monsieur

Cazes, the proprietor of Lynch-Bages, where the wines are actually kept. Although it lacks the breed of de Pez, it is an unusually supple and attractive wine for a St Estèphe. It is consistent, has a lot of fruit and richness and can usually be drunk with pleasure when fairly young. The average production is 6,800 cases.

Château Le Boscq   *Cru Bourgeois*

The property lies between the village of Cadourne and the river in the northern part of St Estèphe. It belongs to Monsieur Georges Bayé and has long enjoyed a good reputation; it was classified as *Grand Bourgeois Exceptionnel* in 1966 but was demoted to simple *Bourgeois* in 1978. I have fond memories of the 1953, but recent vintages have often been rather clumsy and a shade dry. The average production is 3,300 cases.

Also classified as *Grand Bourgeois Exceptionnel*, but not so well-known on export markets, are Andron Blanquet (6,375 cases) and Le Crock (8,250 cases).

Château Canteloup

A very good *Grand Bourgeois* in 1966 which has unaccountably been dropped. The property takes its name from Arnaud Canteloup, Archbishop of Bordeaux, who received it from Bertrand de Goth when he became Pope Clement V in 1305. It remained the property of the See of Bordeaux until the Revolution. The wine is rather lighter than most St Estèphes, but is very fruity and can be drunk early. The average production is 4,250 cases.

Also classified as *Grand Bourgeois* are Coutelin-Merville (3,800 cases), Mac-Carthy (1,000 cases) and Morin (3,800 cases).

There are also two growths classified simply as *Crus Bourgeois*. These are Chambert (1,000 cases) and Mac-Carthy-Moula (1,000 cases).

There are also two good châteaux, not members of the Syndicat des Crus Bourgeois, whose wines nevertheless deserve mention. They are Houissant (7,250 cases) and La Tour des Termes (1,100 cases).

There is a large cooperative in St Estèphe whose wines are sold under the *marque* of Marquis de St Estèphe. In total, some 127,500 cases are made on average. However, there are a number of

171

members whose wines are vinified separately and are sometimes sold under their own names:

Château Balangé	Clos du Moulin
Château La Tour de Pez	Château La Croix des Trois Soeurs
Château Haut Verdon	Château Ladouys
Château Violet	Château Gireaud
Château Palmier	Château Lartique
Château Valrose	Château de l'Hôpital
Château Le Roc	Château Faget
Château Les Pradines	Château Lille-Coutelin

Of these, Les Pradines has been consistently good in recent vintages, with more flesh than most *Bourgeois* growths of St Estèphe. It is distributed by Louis Dubroca, an important firm who have their cellars unusually at St Loubès in the Entre-Deux-Mers.

6

Moulis and Listrac:
Haut-Médoc and Bas-Médoc

MOULIS

In the introduction to the wines of the Haut-Médoc (see Chapter 4), I said that there were really two lines of vineyards, one lying close to the river, the other on a series of ridges and plateaux further inland. All the finest wines are produced from the vineyards near the river, but there are two groups of vineyards which produce wines of a quality superior to those generally made in the second line, and these have been given special recognition by being allowed their own *appellations*. They are Moulis and its neighbour, Listrac.

The vineyards of Moulis lie on a high plateau north-west of Margaux and almost directly west of Arcins. The wines have much more body and richness than those of Margaux, and also a tendency to firmness at first, but they do have more fruit and finesse than those of St Laurent to the north. When the wines are mature, they have a fineness about them which justifies their classification, and a fruitiness which is reminiscent of some Margaux. They also have the ability to age very well, when they develop characteristics which might be compared to some St Estèphes. The best growths cluster about the village of Grand Poujeaux to the east of Moulis itself. A number of them hyphenate their names with that of Grand Poujeaux, leading to a certain degree of confusion. Although no wines from Moulis were included in the 1855 classification, Chasse-Spleen is today recognized as of classified growth standing, and some of the others are certainly well ahead of the old classified growths in St Laurent.

173

Château Chasse-Spleen *Grand Bourgeois Exceptionnel*

This has for long been regarded as the leading growth of Moulis, and rightly so. In 1932, when an attempt was made to classify the *Cru Bourgeois*, this was one of six growths in the whole Médoc which was accorded the status of *Cru Exceptionnel*. Today it is certainly of *Cru Classé* standard. The vineyard lies between Arcins and Grand Poujeaux.

The property, for long owned by Monsieur Frank Lahary, was very carefully run along traditional lines by him. I have pleasant memories of seeing large numbers of eggs being broken here to prepare the fining (*collage*) in the traditional manner. The wine has the marked character of all Moulis wines; but while having a good deal of richness, it lacks the toughness which characterizes most of them, and has markedly more finesse and breed. It is this which sets Chasse-Spleen apart from its neighbours and justifies its special position in the district.

The wine matures easily, its attractive fruitiness making it drinkable fairly early, but at the same time it has fine keeping properties. I remember particularly the 1938, a wine of great charm still when nearly thirty years old. More recently, the wine has been consistently fine. I must own to being a little disappointed with the 1961 in its early stages—I have not seen it recently. 1962, 1964, 1966 and 1967 have all produced fine wines worthy of the year, with the 1966 likely to be the best. More recently, there have been major changes. Much modernization of the *chais* and *cuvier* was carried out, and then the property was sold to Monsieur Merlaud. Of recent vintages the 1975 is massive and will need a lot of time, and the 1978 is very promising. The average production now reaches 17,850 cases.

Château Poujeaux-Theil *Grand Bourgeois Exceptionnel*

The actual château is in the village of Poujeaux, and has ancient origins. Known then as La Salle de Poujeaux, it was mentioned in 1544 as a dependency of Château Latour. In the eighteenth century it belonged to Madame de Montmorin Saint-Harem, sister of the Marquis de Brassier, proprietor of Beychevelle. She sold in 1806 to Monsieur André Castaing, whose family were proprietors until 1920, when it passed into the hands of the present proprietors. Monsieur Jean Theil today runs the property. It is

174

well run and well situated on the gravelly plateau around the village. The wine is powerful and has a strong character. It keeps very well; I have drunk well-preserved and interesting bottles of the 1926 and 1928 vintages. I have not seen the wine very often in recent years, but it enjoys a good reputation as one of the leading growths on a par with Gressier and Dutruch. The average production is 10,600 cases.

Château Gressier-Grand-Poujeaux

This château has the distinction of having been in the hands of the same proprietors, the Saint-Affrique family, since 1724. The château and *chais* lie almost in the village of Poujeaux, and the vineyard lies between the village and Chasse-Spleen. This is a homely place, with a pleasantly intimate and traditional appearance about the *cuvier* and *chais*, and Monsieur de Saint-Affrique is very much in evidence. The château label is very distinctive, with the Saint-Affrique arms with its three negro heads as the main feature.

The wine is sometimes a shade stubborn at first, but with a tendency to be more fruity than some of its neighbours, with a little more finesse and elegance. It is very consistent: 1962, 1964 (with a small crop due to hail, but of fine quality), 1966 (particularly successful), and 1967, are all very good examples of their years. The wine generally matures fairly quickly but keeps well. The average production is 4,250 cases.

Château Dutruch-Grand-Poujeaux *Grand Bourgeois Exceptionnel*

Until recently this was the property of Monsieur Lambert, when the wine was sometimes known as Dutruch-Lambert. The house and *chais* lie in the village of Poujeaux, but the vineyard is between Poujeaux and Moulis. Under the régime of Monsieur Lambert, the property was run with great dedication and care. It has now been acquired by Monsieur François Cordonnier. In 1966 it was classified as a *Grand Bourgeois Exceptionnel*, confirmed in 1978.

The wines of Dutruch have more body and richness than Chasse-Spleen or Gressier, but less finesse and breed. The quality is very consistent, excellent wines being made in 1962, 1964 and 1966. The average production is 7,200 cases.

Château Maucaillou

This grandiose Victorian château lies a little outside the village of Poujeaux on the Arcins side, and has for long been the headquarters and pride of the Maison Dourthe. The name comes from the land on which the vineyard is situated.

The wine has the distinctive Moulis *goût de terroir* and is quite rich. It is never easy to judge the reputation of a growth which is exclusively marketed by a *négociant*, because when one tastes a range of Moulis wines, Maucaillou would tend to be missing as it is not on the general market. But I should say that the quality and style is somewhere near Dutruch and La Closerie. The average production is around 10,200 cases.

Château La Closerie-Grand-Poujeaux   *Bourgeois*

This vineyard was the creation of Monsieur Segonnes, a former *régisseur* of Chasse-Spleen. Since 1941 it has been in the possession of the Donat family, and for some years now the redoubtable Mademoiselle Marguerite Donat has continued her father's work. In 1966 it was classified as a *Grand Bourgeois Exceptionnel* but demoted to simple *Bourgeois* in 1978. The property is run on very traditional lines and Mademoiselle Donat is a businesswoman to be reckoned with.

The wine is very solid, often very fruity and powerful, and can last very well. I remember especially a remarkable bottle of 1947. The quality and style can be compared with Dutruch. The average production is put at 2,000 cases.

The six properties discussed above are certainly the leading ones of Moulis. The following are classified as *Grands Bourgeois*:

Duplessis-Hauchecorne, production 6,000 cases (the name Hauchecorne has now been dropped from the label); Moulin-a-Vent, production 7,650 cases; Brillette, a good property of similar quality and standing to Moulin-a-Vent, production amounts to 3,400 cases.

In addition there is one other *Cru Bourgeois*: Duplessis-Fabre, production 850 cases.

LISTRAC

If one drives from Bordeaux to the Pointe de Graves, and speed, rather than vinous scenery, is the order of the day, then one takes the D2 to Lesparre. Very few vines are to be seen from this road, and most of them are around the village of Listrac. This lies to the north and slightly to the west of Moulis.

As with Moulis, there were no classified growths in 1855, but today at least one growth would be in the running. The wines have a certain verve and style which gives them personality and interest. There is also a tendency to be tough and astringent, particularly at first. The wines tend to have less body and less fruit than those of Moulis, and can be compared to the lesser St Estèphes in some respects. Nevertheless, while not reaching the heights, they are very Médoc in style, and as such have many friends.

Château Fourcas-Hosten   *Grand Bourgeois Exceptionnel*

Certainly the best-known growth in England and the United States of America. For many years Fourcas was owned by Monsieur Saint-Affrique of Gressier. At this time the wine was made and kept at Gressier. Then, in 1972, it was acquired by a syndicate with a number of American members, and with Monsieur Bertrand de Rivoyre of Maison Diprovin & Louis Dubroca at the Bordeaux end, and his nephew, Monsieur Arnaud de Trabuc, in New York. The pretty little château has been tastefully renovated and the *chais* and *cuvier* reconstructed and enlarged, with stainless steel fermenting vats. Before the change of ownership, the wine was typical of Listrac in style, with a very strong, firm, frank flavour, but with more fruit than most of its neighbours. From my own experience, even in those days, this was the best of the Listrac growths. Good wines were made in 1959, 1962, 1964 and 1966. However, a serious defect of the Saint-Affrique régime was its cavalier attitude to the time of château-bottling. There was an unfortunate tendency to leave any wine not sold in cask, just in case a future purchaser might want to take the wine in bulk for his own bottling. So, when the new owners took possession in 1972, they found some of the 1966 crop still in wood and distinctly dried up, quite unrepresentative of what it had originally been. So pre-1970 vintages have to be treated with some caution.

177

The transformation from what was quite an acceptable *Bourgeois* growth into something to stand comparison with the best that Moulis can do, and challenging for classified growth status, has been remarkable. First, Professor Peynaud's advice was sought, then an experienced *régisseur*, Monsieur de Crevecoeur, was installed. He works under the general supervision of Monsieur Bertrand de Rivoyre. Monsieur de Crevecoeur is also responsible for Monsieur de Rivoyre's own property in the Côtes de Bourg, Château Guerry.

The first vintage for the new owners was 1972, hardly a propitious year to start, but the wine is one of the pleasantest Médocs of the year, far better than that of many more exalted growths. The 1973 was fruity and charming with a nice touch of fullness, but with 1974, the problems of the year were not solved, and the wine was mean; 1975 was a tremendous wine, very rich and powerful, with considerable weight; the 1976 had more elegance, but again good weight for a Listrac; 1977 was a success for the year; the 1978 promises great things, while 1979 has great charm. All in all, this is certainly a growth to watch in the future. The average production is 12,000 cases.

Château Fourcas-Dupré *Grand Bourgeois Exceptionnel*

Fourcas is the name of a small hamlet, just outside Listrac itself, which also lies on the D2. The *chais* of Dupré can be seen from the road. The property is managed by Monsieur Paul Delon, formerly the administrator of Léoville-Lascases. It was classified as a *Grand Bourgeois* in 1966 and promoted to *Exceptionnel* in 1978. Fourcas-Dupré is not as well known, for some reason, as Fourcas-Hosten, but the wine is probably on a par with it, or not far behind. The reputation is for well-made and consistent wines. The average production is 3,250 cases.

There is one other growth classified as *Grand Bourgeois*: Lafon, production 2,550 cases.

In addition there are five properties classified as *Bourgeois*:

La Becade, production 12,000 cases; Cap Léon Veyrin, production 2,000 cases; Fonreaud, one of the largest properties in the area, the château forms a notable landmark on the D2, production 15,300 cases; Lestage, the largest property in Listrac, production 15,300 cases; Saransot, lies in the hamlet of Fourcas, production 1,275 cases.

There is an important cooperative situated in the village of Listrac itself, producing on average 46,750 cases annually. Its wines are sold under the name of Grand Listrac and enjoy an excellent reputation, which is widespread on account of the wines having been available for many years on the French railways.

A member of the Syndicat de Crus Bourgeois, but unclassified is Château Clarke, recently purchased by Baron Edmond de Rothschild, and now being replanted.

OTHER WINES OF THE HAUT-MÉDOC

We have now dealt with the six major *appellations* of the Haut-Médoc covering, between them, nine communes. But there remain fifteen other wine-growing communes within the area, containing five growths classified in 1855. It is within this area that great changes are to be found. Compared with a hundred years ago, there was a marked decline in the area planted, a movement which gained its greatest impetus in the years between the wars. But in the 1970s there was a considerable revival, and the area under vine increased by over 48 per cent.

The view has been expressed, notably by Mr Ronald Barton (proprietor of Léoville-Barton and Langoa-Barton), that this decline is largely to be blamed on an *appellation* system which has singled out six areas for special treatment and left the remainder in the limbo of the Haut-Médoc *appellation*. But taking St Laurent as the most notable example, one cannot help feeling that wines of this type do not meet the modern taste, and are unlikely to do so unless methods of vinification are significantly changed. Also, this simple accusation does not explain why La Lagune and Cantemerle are as popular as at any time in their history, while Belgrave and even La Tour Carnet are rather hazy memories for most claret lovers. The recent revival of Camensac is a good example of what modern vinification can achieve in this area. Most of the back areas of the Médoc also suffer the considerable disability of being more subject to spring frosts, so that over the years, the double penalty of reduced harvests and declining popularity has been too heavy a burden for many proprietors to shoulder.

179

Of the fifteen communes concerned, eight lie adjacent to the Garonne or the Gironde, the remaining seven are inland. The riverside communes, going north from Bordeaux, are: Blanquefort, Parempuyre, Ludon, Macau, Arcins, Lamarque, Cussac and St Seurin-de-Cadourne. But of these, Blanquefort and Parempuyre in the south have rich, alluvial areas, which gave large quantities of wine in the eighteenth century, when soft wines for immediate drinking were required. These were the *vins de l'année* of their day. They have only small outcrops of the fine, gravelly soil on which the best Médocs are to be found.

Between Margaux and St Julien are three communes: Arcins, Lamarque and Cussac. This is a very poor, low-lying area; again, there are some good, gravelly outcrops—especially in Cussac—but they are not extensive. Of the remainder, Macau and Ludon in the south do produce some very fine wines, including two very successful growths classified in 1855, La Lagune and Cantemerle. Here there is a significant amount of soil analogous to that found in the communes of the Margaux *appellation*, and the wines have real finesse and breed. Then the most northerly commune of St Seurin-de-Cadourne has some excellent, gravelly ridges which are an extension of St Estèphe, and the wines here are comparable to the lesser St Estèphes; they are often more generous and less tough.

The second line of communes, again going northwards from Bordeaux consists of: Le Taillan, Le Pian-Médoc, Avensan, St Laurent de Médoc, St Sauveur, Cissac and Vertheuil. Of these, the most southerly, Le Taillan and Le Pian, are of little importance today. The few wines produced in Avensan adjoin Moulis and are very similar in character. St Laurent has three growths which were classified in 1855. The best vineyards are all to be found adjoining St Julien, but the strong-flavoured, rather coarse wines do not seem to be attuned to modern tastes. St Sauveur lies immediately behind Pauillac, and its best wines are similar to the lesser Pauillacs, having something of the same body and fullness of flavour. The two most northerly ones, Cissac and Vertheuil, lie immediately behind St Estèphe and, for the most part, their wines are rather light but tough and a shade coarse, like the poorer St Estèphes. Here are some notes on the most important individual growths.

Château d'Agassac (Ludon)   *Grand Bourgeois Exceptionnel*

This is the most important growth in Ludon after La Lagune, and since 1966 has been classified as a *Grand Bourgeois Exceptionnel*. It now belongs to a company and is run by Monsieur Philippe Gasqueton (see Calon-Ségur and Capbern) who, until recently, had his home there as well.

Agassac is one of the very few châteaux in the Médoc which actually has the appearance of a castle, and it has a moat as well! The fortress, one of the few to survive from the Middle Ages in the Médoc, dates from the beginning of the fourteenth century. The origins of the place go back even further, to Gaillard d'Agassac, who was *senéchal* of Guyenne in 1274. From 1580 until the Revolution, it belonged to the les Pomiès family, members of the Bordeaux *noblesse de robe*.

The wine is typical of the region, light in body but delicately perfumed and with an easy, attractive flavour. Good wine has been made for some years now and deserves to be more widely known. The average production is now 6,800 cases.

Château d'Arcins (Arcins)

This is the leading property in this small commune which adjoins Soussans, the most northerly of the Margaux communes. The wine still has some suggestion of Margaux about it, but it lacks the finesse of a Margaux or the vinosity of the neighbouring growths of Moulis. The château is today the property of the Costantini family and the wine is mostly sold in northern France. The average production is 1,500 cases.

Château Barreyres (Arcins)

This is another property of the Costantini family. The remarks on style under Château d'Arcins above apply equally here, but this growth is sometimes found in England. The average production is 25,500 cases.

Château Beau Rivage (Macau—Bordeaux Supérieur)

Strictly speaking, this growth should not be included here because, while it lies in the commune of Macau, it is not entitled to the Haut-Médoc *appellation*. This is because it lies in the *palus*.

181

However, it is more convenient to include it where it belongs geographically.

The property is interesting because careful viticulture and *élevage* by the Maison Borie-Manoux, who exclusively distribute this wine, have in recent years made this the only well-known wine from the Médoc *palus* sold in England. But in the days before Bordeaux wines were aged in bottle, these *palus* wines were more famous and widely known than many famous growths today. Changing techniques more than taste, perhaps, have changed this.

Beau Rivage, actually the property of Monsieur Barateau, produces a most consistent and agreeable wine, full-bodied but soft, with an attractive flavour. It can be drunk when only two or three years old, but will also keep for several years. The average production is put at 6,400 cases, but the wine is usually shipped in bulk or Bordeaux-bottled in Borie-Manoux's Bordeaux cellars.

Château Belgrave (St Laurent)   Fifth Growth in 1855

This is one of the more obscure classified growths in spite of its name which might be thought to be a help in English-speaking markets. It should not be confused with a little-known growth in the St Lambert parish of Pauillac, which is spelt Bellegrave and has an important-looking château near to Pichon-Lalande.

The extensive vineyards immediately adjoin St Julien and lie behind Lagrange. After rather frequent changes of ownership, Monsieur Gugès is now proprietor and administrator. Although the property was classified in 1855, it does not seem to have featured in earlier classifications. At the time of writing, it seems doubtful whether it would retain its 1855 status in any new list.

The wine itself is fairly full-bodied and pleasant, without any real distinction, nor has it been notable for its consistency in recent years. Its reputation seems to be that of a decent wine, but not much more. The average production is 8,000 cases.

Château Bel-Orme–Tronquoy-de-Lalande (St Seurin-de-Cadourne)   *Grand Bourgeois*

Not surprisingly, this is usually known as Bel-Orme for short, and is not to be confused with Tronquoy-Lalande, the growth in neighbouring St Estèphe. At one time the property also belonged to the Tronquoy family.

This is one of the best-known growths of St Seurin-de-Cadourne, and the vineyard is well placed on gravelly slopes between the *route des châteaux* and the river. The château itself is no more than a charming summer pavilion, flanked by a business-like *cuvier* and *chais*. It is the property of the heirs of Monsieur Paul Quié, of whose kindness and hospitality I have many happy memories. Since there are no châteaux at either Rauzan-Gassies or Croizet-Bages, the Quiés always use Bel-Orme for their visits to the Médoc.

Apart from a serious fall from grace in 1964, Bel-Orme has consistently produced good wines in recent years, and was classified as a *Grand Bourgeois* in 1966 and 1978. Monsieur Paul Quié kept a remarkable library of old vintages in the cellar here and in the early 1960s released some of them to some of his English friends. I myself have pleasant memories of the 1911, 1924, 1926, 1928 and 1929. They were most interesting in showing how wines in this part of the Médoc will develop and age. While they lack the fineness of bouquet of the great growths, they all developed a warmth and richness of texture which made them delicious and attractive wines with a surprising degree of delicacy and style. It is seldom that one sees *Bourgeois* growths of this age, and it is a revelation to see how such wines can develop, and emphasizes again the remarkable qualities of Médoc wines. More recently, good wines were made in 1961, 1962 and 1966. The average production is 11,050 cases.

Château du Breuil (Cissac) *Cru Bourgeois*

The château here is really more interesting than the wine, in that it is a medieval fortress which was of importance during the English period, especially in the Hundred Years' War. Although it is now no more than an imposing ruin, it is nevertheless well worth a visit. For the last hundred years, the château name has been spelt as above, but the Syndicat of Crus Bourgeois now refer to it as Le Breuilh.

The wine itself is not to be despised. It gained the classification of a *Grand Bourgeois* in 1966 but was demoted to simple *Bourgeois* in 1978, and has a good reputation. In style the wine resembles the lesser St Estèphes. The present proprietors are Messieurs Durand and Germain, and the average production amounts to 8,500 cases.

Château de Camensac (St Laurent)   Fifth Growth in 1855

If there were a contest for the least known of the classified growths, Camensac would, until very recently, been a very strong contender. It adjoins Belgrave and La Tour Carnet, lying behind Lagrange and close to St Julien. Before its classification in 1855, it does not seem to have featured in any of the previous classifications. Camensac's period of obscurity certainly seems to have been a long one, and I for one do not remember ever seeing a bottle before the new proprietors took over. The new proprietors, Messieurs Forner, father and son, are making considerable efforts both here and at Larose-Trintaudon, which they have also bought. Professor Peynaud has also played a large part in the revival. There has certainly been a considerable outlay in modernizing the *cuvier* and *chais*, and the results are promising. In spite of the French-sounding name, the Forners came from Rioja, where they also have vineyards.

The vinification methods now being used here are producing light-textured, fruity, harmonious wines, which are eminently drinkable and thus commercial—a far cry from the old style of St Laurent wines. The earliest vintage I have seen is the 1970, an attractive, forward wine. The 1972 was better than that of many better-known châteaux; there was a good 1973 and a promising 1975. While I do not think the wines are of classified growth quality, one must remember that they do not sell at classified growth prices either. But as attractive, easy-to-drink wines sold at a reasonable price, they are finding a ready market and deserve to do so. The average production has already risen to 18,000 cases.

Château Cantemerle (Macau)   Fifth Growth in 1855

A very ancient property with a history going back to the Middle Ages. From 1579 until 1892, it remained in the hands of a single family, Villeneuve. Then, for over fifty years, it was owned and run by Monsieur Pierre Dubos, one of the outstanding proprietors of his generation. I shall always have a strong affection for Cantemerle and for Pierre Dubos, since this was the first Bordeaux château I ever visited, and Pierre Dubos was the first proprietor I ever met. I shall also remember being shown the remarkable weather records he kept, and the notes he made on everything that had to be done during the harvesting and vinification. He illustrated the difference between vintages by showing me the records for 1920 and 1921. 1920 had been very straightforward, but 1921 had been full of headaches and the pages were covered in notes in red ink—indicating corrective measures. He remembered having to get up in the middle of the night to check the temperature in his fermentation vats and take appropriate action. We had drunk the 1921 at lunch and it was an eloquent tribute to the care that had accompanied its birth. Since Pierre Dubos' death, his son-in-law, Monsieur Henri Binaud, of the house of Beyerman, has lavished almost as much care on the wine and yields to none in his love of it. Cantemerle was sold to Cordier in 1980, so no doubt the investment in *chais* and vineyard which is badly needed will now be forthcoming.

The estate is the second of the classified growths to be seen on the *route des châteaux* as one leaves Bordeaux. The château itself is hidden in a heavily timbered park lying immediately to the left of the road. A turreted, nineteenth-century building replaced a medieval fortress, and there are fine and extensive *chais*. The vineyards are on fine, gravelly ridges going towards Ludon.

Holland was the historic market for Cantemerle, and it is said that this is the reason why it was only placed last of the fifth growths in the 1855 classification. Indeed, a look at the manuscript of the famous list shows Cantemerle added in, in small print, as something of an after-thought. It is said that the wine was hardly known in Bordeaux, and that this is the reason it was underrated, as it most certainly was. The general quality is certainly on a par with La Lagune, a third growth, and it often sells at second growth prices.

In style, Cantemerle has the lightness and elegance of a Margaux, but tends to be fatter, with less verve and sheer breed than a second growth Margaux. The charming bouquet and supple fruitiness of the wine naturally accounts for its great popularity, now especially marked in England, and for many years now this has been allied to remarkable consistency, due to the care with which the wine is made. I remember especially the excellence of the 1957 and 1958, but good vintages like 1952, 1953, 1955, 1959, 1961 and 1962 have all been highly successful. The 1964 was one of the outstanding wines in the Médoc in this very mixed year, although, like many 1964s, it has not lived up to its early promise. The 1970s was probably the most disappointing

185

decade for Cantemerle since the period before Pierre Dubos took charge. There have been many other decades which lacked the fine vintages of the 1970s, but probably none where Cantemerle failed to make the most of them. The decline was due to a slow, but nevertheless systematic, run-down of the property. There were many shareholders and nobody seemed prepared to make the investment necessary to renovate the *cuverie* and *chais* or maintain the rotation in the vineyard. Although it is sad to see an association which has lasted since 1892 finally severed, one can at least be sure that the Cordiers have the necessary finance and experience to restore Cantemerle to its legitimate position for quality and consistency. The average production has remained very constant over the years due to careful rotation in the vineyard, where a good proportion of old vines has always been kept, and is now put at 8,000 cases.

Château Caronne-Saint-Gemme (St Laurent) *Grand Bourgeois Exceptionnel*

The only growth in St Laurent to be classified as a *Grand Bourgeois Exceptionnel* in 1966, and again in 1978, it deserves to be more widely known. As with all the best St Laurent estates, it lies close to the border with St Julien and is a very extensive domaine, the property of La Veuve A. Nony-Borie. The label is unusual in being entirely devoted to a large array of ancient Medailles d'Or. It will be interesting to see what happens when they have to come into line with EEC regulations, which say that only awards for the vintage in the bottle may be mentioned.

When I had the opportunity recently of tasting a range of vintages, I was impressed with the finesse and breed of the wines, which seemed remarkably free of the coarseness so often found in St Laurent wines. On this form it must rank as one of the top wines in the commune today and is worth looking out for. The average production has recently risen to 15,300 cases.

Château Cissac (Cissac) *Grand Bourgeois Exceptionnel*

This is the property of Monsieur Louis Vialand, brother of the notary of Pauillac. Together with du Breuil, it is recognized as the best wine of the Cissac commune, but Cissac is certainly better known in England. It was classified as a *Grand Bourgeois* in 1966, but raised to *Exceptionnel* in 1978. Monsieur Vialard is an enthusiastic owner, and his wines enjoy some reputation. They are typical of the region and have a certain finesse and style, but also a certain asperity. The average production is 8,500 cases.

Château Citran (Avensan) *Grand Bourgeois Exceptionnel*

This is a property with a long history, and for six hundred years belonged to the noble family of Dounissan. In 1832 it was acquired by the Clauzel family who formed a company to carry out the administration in 1905. The actual administrator today is Monsieur Jean Miailhe, the proprietor of Coufran and cousin of Monsieur W. A. Burke Miailhe of Pichon-Lalande. It was classified as a *Grand Bourgeois Exceptionnel* in 1966, and this was confirmed in 1978. There is a handsome eighteenth-century château which replaced the medieval fortress of the thirteenth century, of which only traces remain.

My knowledge of Citran is not as intimate as that of its neighbour Villegeorge, but the reputation is good. The soil partly corresponds to that of Margaux and partly to that of Moulis, and the wine has individuality. The average production is now 11,050 cases.

Château Coufran (St Seurin-de-Cadourne) *Grand Bourgeois*

This is a château whose configuration is well known to me from my years at Loudenne. The vineyard lies on a large outcrop of gravelly soil close to the Gironde and overlooking Château Loudenne. It is the last vineyard in the Haut-Médoc, with a prominent look-out tower which serves as something of a landmark. The proprietor is Monsieur Louis Miailhe, cousin of the proprietor of Pichon-Lalande.

The wine is lighter than the neighbouring Bel-Orme and is also classified as a *Grand Bourgeois*. The style is fruity and attractive, but the wines seem to lack something in finish, perhaps due to rather heavy cropping. Nevertheless, this is a pleasing, consistent and easy wine, which matures quickly. The average production is 12,750 cases.

Château La Dame-Blanche (Le Taillan)

Again, strictly speaking, this name should not appear here, because the wine does not have the Haut-Médoc *appellation*, since it is one of the Médoc's rare white wines. In this region consecrated to red wines, no white wine may be called Médoc, but only Bordeaux Supérieur or Bordeaux.

In fact, this is thẹ white wine of Château de Taillan and it is amusing to see in Cocks & Féret (12th Édition) that a photograph of one side of the château is used under the Dame-Blanche entry, and the other side under the Taillan entry! It is owned and lived in by Monsieur Henri-François Cruse. The wine itself is dry and bears some resemblance to a Graves. The average production is 4,250 cases.

Château Dillon (Blanquefort)

This attractive property was bought by the Ecole Régionale d'Agriculture de Blanquefort in 1956. The château dates from the beginning of the eighteenth century and the property was once much more extensive than it is now. The name comes from General Robert Dillon who acquired the estate from the Comte de Marcellus in 1754. Although the name is Irish enough, he was certainly born in Bordeaux, presumably of *émigré* stock. The family remained proprietors until the Revolution. Curiously, for a wine made at what amounts to a wine school, the wines of Dillon have not been noted for their consistency. However, with recent improvements in the *cuvier*, better things can now be expected. At its best, Dillon is an elegant, attractive claret, on the light side but with finesse. The 1970 is excellent, as is the 1975, and the 1976, although rather light, is most attractive. The average production is 6,000 cases.

Château La Lagune (Ludon)   Third growth in 1855

The first classified growth or, indeed, château of any real importance to be found when coming from Bordeaux. The very extensive vineyard, which is in a single piece, can be seen on a ridge above the *route des châteaux* on the side towards the river. The château, a small but elegant pavilion on a single storey, is situated amid this, not far from the road, and adjacent to the vineyard.

La Lagune was originally planted as a vineyard in 1724, but its fame dates from the first part of the nineteenth century. Although the classifications of 1824 and 1827 make no mention of it, by the time Charles Cocks wrote in 1846, its position was assured. Later in the century, special mention was made of the wine's longevity.

From being one of the best-known and most sought-after third growths, the vineyard gradually declined in importance until, by the 1950s, only about 20 tonneaux were being made and great tracts of the vineyard lay fallow. Then, in 1957, the property was acquired by Monsieur Brunet, a man of energy and vision, from the south of France. The vineyard was replanted in the space of only two years, and the *chais* was transformed into one of the show-places of the Médoc. It is also a big farm. One interesting feature is that stainless steel pipes carry the new wine directly from the fermentation vats to the new casks in the *chais*, thus saving a great deal of handling. Unfortunately, the new proprietor did not stay to reap the benefit of his reconstruction. Like many other proprietors, he was tempted by the market conditions in the summer of 1961 to sell extensively *sur souche* (on the vine, that is, before the harvest), and found himself oversold when the vintage proved smaller than had been hoped for. He sold to Monsieur R. Chayoux, who came from Champagne, and whose heirs now own it.

In the last fifteen years, the reputation of La Lagune has climbed steadily, in spite of the youth of most of the vines. The wine is undoubtedly very well made and, although still rather light in colour and body, has a charming and most individual bouquet allied to great elegance and breed. I had only limited experience of the wine before its rebirth. The 1920 was unfortunately already well past its best by 1962, when I saw it, but the 1921 was a remarkable wine the following year. In England, the 1926 was sometimes seen and was, like the 1921, a big, strong wine. Just before the change, Allan Sichel shipped several vintages. I remember particularly the 1950 and the glorious 1953.

Since the reconstruction, the 1961 was a strange wine, typical neither of the year nor of La Lagune. The 1962 was too much of a light-weight, and the 1964 was the first undisputed success. Naturally the wine matured quickly and is soft and mellow. Nevertheless, there is great individuality, some depth, and a really fine flavour. The 1966 was really fine, the 1967 had great charm, while the 1968 was one of the more successful wines of the vintage. If the 1960s were years of steady improvement, then the 1970s saw the flowering of La Lagune, the fulfilment of work and investment begun by Monsieur Brunet in 1957. The decade began propitiously with the 1970 and the 1971, and after a beautifully balanced 1975, 1976 looked like one of the outstanding successes of the year. The 1977 was above average for the year, and the 1978 is very fine. 1979 is lighter, but has great charm.

The vineyard has truly come of age, and La Lagune is now one of the most consistently attractive and enjoyable of the leading classified growths in the Médoc. An unusual feature of La Lagune today is that it has a woman *régisseur*, Madame Boyrie, who is highly respected in the Médoc. The average production has now climbed to 20,000 cases.

Château de Lamarque (Lamarque) *Grand Bourgeois*

The name of Lamarque will probably be most familiar to many visitors to the region, as it is the Médoc end of the Blaye ferry. But the Château de Lamarque is of considerable interest as the best preserved of the medieval fortresses dating from the English period. Although the main defences and part of the chapel date from the eleventh and twelfth centuries, the main structure is fourteenth century and was built by Pons de Castillon. Both Henry V and the Duke of Gloucester stayed in the castle, and later it was used as the residence of the governors of Guyenne. In the seventeenth century, it belonged to the Duc d'Epernon (see under Beychevelle, pp. 110–13) who carried out extensive alterations. In 1841 the château became the property of the Comte de Fumel and passed, via his daughter, to the Marquis d'Evry in 1901. Now Marie-Louise Brunet d'Evry has married Roger Gromaud and they own the property today. As so often in Bordeaux, the names have changed but the families have not.

Before the First World War, the wines of Lamarque were sold to northern Germany. By the time that Monsieur Roger Gromaud took over the management of the estate in the early 1960s, the vineyard was much diminished and the wine almost forgotten. Now extensive replanting has been undertaken and under the supervision of Monsieur Peynaud, for many years the much respected oenologist of the Station Enologique in Bordeaux, a serious attempt is being made to re-establish the reputation of the wine. According to Charles Cocks, the wines of Lamarque are similar to those of Arcins but are more mellow, producing light, aromatic wines. A short while ago I had the opportunity of tasting several recent vintages of Lamarque and found the wines light and agreeable in the good vintages, but the vineyard will need to achieve more maturity before the wine can be fairly judged. It is now classified as a *Grand Bourgeois*. The average production is put at 17,000 cases.

Château Lanessan (Cussac)

This must surely be one of the best growths in the Médoc not to be classified in 1855. And the strange thing is that its excellence is no recent feature. Nineteenth-century editions of Cocks & Féret sing its praises and speak of its wines as above their class, and the old vintages of Lanessan that I have drunk have all been superb.

The property lies close to the border with St Julien and extends back almost to St Laurent. The château itself is an elaborate Victorian pile lying on high ground and is approached by a road going inland from the *route des châteaux*, just before one reaches Beychevelle. More interesting are the fine, extensive *chais* and the old stables which house a comprehensive and impressive collection of carriages and harnesses which may be viewed upon request. Since 1790 the property has effectively been in the same family and is today managed by Monsieur Bouteiller, who is also the proprietor of Pichon Baron, but whose home is at Lanessan.

Some of the old vintages of Lanessan are remarkable. I have had the 1916, the 1920, which was one of the best-preserved 1920s I have seen, the 1933, which is rather firmer than most wines of that year, and the 1934, which was outstanding and reminded me strongly of a St Julien of the Gruaud-Larose type. Since the war, the 1947 was outstandingly fine for the year, with a bouquet of great power and ripeness; the 1952 was beautifully balanced and has given much more pleasure than most wines of its year; the 1953 was surprisingly big and full for the year; the 1955 I found rather unsympathetic; the 1959 was fine; the 1960 was one of the most attractive and sound wines of the year; the 1961 was worthy of its year; the 1962 was fine and distinctive if a little on the dry side; and the 1964 was rather light and matured quickly, but was most attractive.

This is a wine, then, of strong individuality, having a very marked bouquet, great fruit and richness in some years, a tendency to firmness at first, with rich finesse and breed. When these are allied to considerable consistency, it is easy to see that Lanessan deserves its reputation in Bordeaux and ought, indeed, to be even better known. It was classified as a *Grand Bourgeois*

Exceptionnel in 1966. After frost damage in 1956, production has recovered and now averages 4,100 cases.

Château Larose–Trintaudon (St Laurent)   *Grand Bourgeois*

On my early visits to the Médoc I was always intrigued to see, when driving from St Laurent to Pauillac, this vast, nineteenth-century mansion standing in a completely derelict condition amidst ruined *chais* and fallow vineyards. The scene has now been transformed and desolation banished. The large plateau on either side of the road has been replanted, and the property incorporates the former vineyards of Larose-Perganson.

All this is the work of the enterprising Forner family, Spaniards who now also own Camensac. The object of the new owners has been to produce a very large quantity of quickly maturing, pleasant, easy-to-drink claret, and they certainly seem to be succeeding in this. I have tasted the 1972, unusually acceptable for the year, the 1973, typical of the merits of the vintage, and the 1976. All were well made, light-textured and attractively fruity. With reasonable prices, it is not surprising that they are finding a ready market in a number of countries. The average production is 63,750 cases.

Château Liversan (St Sauveur)   *Grand Bourgeois*

A new proprietor, Monsieur Louis Labeunie, acquired the property in 1955 and has reconstituted the vineyard. In my experience the wine is one of the best in these inland communes to the north of St Laurent, and in 1966 and 1978 was classified as a *Grand Bourgeois*. It is highly coloured, has a powerful, frank and very Médocain bouquet; the flavour is fine with some richness and a tendency to hardness at first, generally requiring some time to develop. The 1962 was particularly good. The average production is 11,050 cases.

Château Peyrabon (St Sauveur)   *Grand Bourgeois*

This château now has the largest production in St Sauveur. Under Monsieur René Babeau the wine enjoys a good reputation. I am not as familiar with its wines as with those of Liversan, but the quality should be comparable. The average production is 8,500 cases.

192

Château du Taillan (Le Taillan)   *Grand Bourgeois*

Physically this is the first château in the Médoc, only 12 kilometres from Bordeaux. The château itself dates from the early eighteenth century and has an attractive classical façade. It is classified as an historic monument. The estate has belonged to the Cruse family since 1806 when it was bought by Henri Cruse; today his grandson, Henri-François Cruse, is the owner. On the large estate of 150 hectares, more land is actually devoted to the breeding of fine horses than to the raising of wine.

The wine is light and supple. It is classified as a *Grand Bourgeois*. The average production is 850 cases.

Château La Tour Carnet (St Laurent)   Fourth Growth in 1855

This growth enjoyed a considerable reputation in the nineteenth century. It is mentioned in Cocks's classification of 1846, the only growth of St Laurent in his list. The property has a long history and takes its name from Jean Caranet or Carnet, who was one of the heirs of Jean de Foix when he died in 1485. It was Jean de Foix who seems to have built the actual tower which is now part of the name. In 1774 it was acquired by Henri de Luetkens, a Swede, and this family owned it at the time of the classification. After this it passed through a number of hands, including Fernand Ginestet in the 1920s, until by the 1950s it was an almost forgotten growth and production had fallen to a very low level. It was then acquired by Monsieur Lipschitz, who has reconstructed the vineyard and lavished much time and effort in re-establishing its reputation. In support of his efforts, he enlisted the house of Ginestet to market the wine exclusively in all countries.

The wine now being produced is highly coloured and has considerable individuality. Its vivid, extrovert character requires a certain amount of ageing. The 1962 was very good when I tasted it at an early stage. The average production has now recovered to 4,500 cases.

Château Villegeorge (Avensan)

This growth was classified as one of the six *Crus Exceptionnels* in 1932, and again, in 1966, it was placed with the *Grands Bourgeois Exceptionnels*. For many years it has been regarded as the leading growth of Avensan and should, in practice, be placed with the best growths of Moulis. In fact, part of the vineyard lies in Moulis and part in Soussans, and so is entitled to the Margaux *appellation*, but when the wines are put together, they can only bear the name of the lowest common denominator, Haut Médoc.

The production of Villegeorge has never been large. After going through a bad period in the late 1960s and early 1970s, the property was acquired by Monsieur Lucien Lurton of Brane-Cantenac. So there is the prospect of better things in the future. In character the wine is very full bodied and deep coloured with a strong personality. It has more bouquet than all but the best Moulis wines and can be very rich in the finest years. There is a good deal of tannin and the wine develops rather slowly. Recently, the 1959 was excellent, the 1961 outstanding, and the 1962, 1964 and 1966 all very good—the 1964 being above average for the year. The average production now reaches 3,400 cases.

Apart from the wines already mentioned in some detail, the following were also classified as *Grand Bourgeois* in 1978:

Château Ségur (Parempuyre)
Château Malleret (Pian)
Château Beaumont (Cussac)
Château La Tour du Haut-Moulin (Cussac)
Château Le Meynieu (Vertheuil)
Château Reysson (Vertheuil)
Château Fontesteau (St Sauveur)
Château Lamothe (Cissac)
Château Hanteillan (Cissac)
Château Sociando-Mallet and Pontoise-Cabarrus (St Seurin de-Cadourne)
Château Verdignan (St Seurin-de-Cadourne)

while the following are classified as *Bourgeois*:

Château Balac (St Laurent)
Château de Labat (St Laurent)
Château Fort de Vaubin (Cussac)
Château Moulin Rouge (Cussac)
Château Aney (Cussac)
Château Lamothe Bergeron (Cussac)
Château Ramage La Batisse (St Sauveur)

Château Fonpiqueyre (St Sauveur)
Château Hourtin-Ducasse (St Sauveur)
Château Le Landat (Cissac)
Château La Tour du Mirail (Cissac)
Château La Tour St-Joseph (Cissac)
Château Soudars (Avensan)
Château Bonneau (St Seurin-de-Cadourne)
Château Grand Moulin (St Seurin-de-Cadourne)
Château Lartigue de Brochon (St Seurin-de-Cadourne)
Château Plantey de la Croix (St Seurin-de-Cadourne)
Domaine de la Rose Maréchale (St Seurin-de-Cadourne)

There are a number of cooperatives in the Haut-Médoc. The most
important of these is that of St Seurin-de-Cadourne—La Paroisse
de St Seurin. Some 46,750 cases of very sound wine are made here.
There is a very large cooperative at Vertheuil, which now vinifies
most of the wine in this commune. It sells its wine under the name
of La Châtellenie, but most of it is bought by the *négociants* for
their blends. A smaller cooperative is to be found at Cissac, known
simply as Cissac Haut-Médoc. The cooperative at Saint Seurin
sells its wine under the name of Canterayne and in recent years has
been successful in winning awards. There is a small cooperative at
Arcins selling under the name of Chevalier d'Ars.

BAS-MÉDOC

This is the name traditionally given to the northern part of the
area. As far as the *appellation* is concerned, it is simply Médoc. But
it can be confusing to refer to this region as Médoc without
qualification, since the whole of the Haut-Médoc and Médoc
together are often loosely referred to as the Médoc. Geographically the area runs from St Yzans and St Germain d'Esteuil in the
south all the way up to Soulac, but in practice the vineyards stop
at Vensac, between Lesparre and St Vivien.

One has only to turn the pages of an old edition of Cocks's &
Féret to see how much the picture has changed. Now there are
fourteen wine-producing communes; in the 1870s and 1880s there
were as many as twenty. The population figures also make
interesting reading: a comparison of those published by Cocks's &
Féret in 1969 with those they published in 1883 shows that in most

195

villages there are hardly more than half the inhabitants that there once were—even the regional centre of Lesparre has 1,200 less. The countryside itself has a very different aspect from that of the Haut-Médoc; generally more low-lying, it is much more remotely rural, with vineyards far less in evidence among the trees and green fields. But the wines themselves are well worth attention. While they generally lack the bouquet and delicacy of the Haut-Médoc, they are robust, full-flavoured wines which keep extremely well and have plenty of character, like the men who make them. This is an area of cooperatives today; in the Médoc the cooperatives are larger and more important than in the Haut-Médoc (see Appendix), and there is a keen demand from the Bordeaux trade for these sound wines for the generic blends. By far the largest is at Bégadan, which also has members in the neighbouring communes of Valeyrac and Civrac. There are also important cooperatives at St Yzans (St Brice), Ordonnac and Potensac (Caves Bellevue) and at Prignac.

Although this has never been a region producing wines of the highest class—so that none of its wines were classified in 1855—it has always been an area for good *Bourgeois* growths. There is reliable evidence, both from the Gilbey diaries at Loudenne and from contemporary editions of Cocks's & Féret, that before the phylloxera, little or no distinction was made between the best Bas-Médoc *Bourgeois* growths and those in the neighbouring communes of the northern Haut-Médoc. I believe that this still accords with the facts. Indeed, the best growths of Bégadan, St Christoly, Ordonnac and Potensac, St Yzans, and St Germain d'Esteuil are often the equal of, and sometimes surpass, the wines from Cissac, Vertheuil and St Seurin-de-Cadourne.

While no properties were classified as *Grand Bourgeois Exceptionnels* in 1966 or 1978, there are nine *Grand Bourgeois*:

Château La Cardonne (Blaignan)

This is the most important growth of Blaignan. After belonging to the Crédit Foncier de France for over fifty years, it was acquired in 1953 by Monsieur Ludovic Cattan, who has now sold to the Lafite-Rothschilds. The vineyard is well placed on the central, gravelly plateau of the Médoc and enjoys a good reputation for robust, full-flavoured and well-coloured wines. In 1978 I had an opportunity of tasting the 1973 and 1975 vintages made under the new management, while on a visit to Lafite. In general, they were robust, well-coloured wines, but also pleasingly stylish and fruity—typical of what the area can do when care and patience are exerted. More depth will come as some of the vines get older. The average production is up to 25,500 cases.

Château Greysac (Bégadan)

In recent years much attention has been lavished on this property, so that it is now one of the leading properties of Bégadan. The wine is particularly well known in the United States of America. It enjoys an excellent reputation, is well vinified, and is typical of the robust attractive wines of the area, with a distinctive *goût de terroir*. The average production is 12,325 cases.

Château Laujac (Bégadan)

One of several well-known properties in Bégadan, Laujac is situated on the large, central plateau of the Médoc. Since 1852 it has belonged to the Cruse family, and as a result is very widely known and distributed. But the property is nothing like as important as it once was. In the last century, 300 to 400 tonneaux were made and even between the wars 150 were recorded; now the yield is reduced to around 20 tonneaux, or 1,700 cases. The reputation, objectively speaking, is not quite what it was. Although the wine is pleasant enough, it lacks the individuality and style of several other growths in Bégadan.

Château Loudenne (St Yzans)

I hope I shall be forgiven if I wax a shade eloquent on a property I know so intimately. Geologically Loudenne is a continuation of the gravelly ridges of St Seurin-de-Cadourne, and an illustration of the fact that communal boundaries do not always coincide exactly with natural formations of the soil. A curious feature of the property is that nowhere else in the Médoc or Haut-Médoc do these ridges approach the river so closely, and as a result Loudenne enjoys an unparalleled view over the Gironde, with hardly any intervening *palus*.

Loudenne is first recorded as belonging to the de Pons family in the fourteenth century, before it had any importance as a wine-growing estate. In 1482 it belonged to Odet Daydie, the seigneur of Lescun and admiral of Guyenne, in 1516 to Vicomtesse

Magdelaine de Lescun and eventually, in 1784, to the Verthamon family. In 1875 the owner was the Vicomtesse de Marcellus who was a Verthamon, and it was from her that Walter and Alfred Gilbey bought the property.

The château itself dates from the early part of the eighteenth century and is of the traditional *chartreuse* type, with a central, single storey linking two-storeyed buildings with turrets. It is situated on a narrow ridge of ground between the two main parts of the vineyard, and from the terrace in front commands an unrivalled view of the river, while on the landward side the ground again falls away sharply, offering a fine vista for some miles.

The history of Loudenne since its acquisition by the Gilbeys in 1875 provides a microcosm of the ebb and flow of fortunes in Bordeaux. First of all, the property was adapted to its new role as the centre of Gilbeys' Bordeaux operations. A large *cuvier* and *chais* were built near the river for the assembling of wine from the whole region prior to shipment for England, and a small port was constructed in front of the *chais*, from which wine was taken by barge to Bordeaux. (This port remained in use until after the Second World War.) Plans greatly to increase the production of Loudenne's own vineyards received a setback with the phylloxera, but by the end of the century, between 300 and 400 tonneaux were being made, including a certain quantity of white wine.

After the First World War, Loudenne rapidly declined in importance. Claret shipments fell to a fraction of what they had been before the war, and the Gilbeys themselves, much absorbed in building up their business in the Empire and Commonwealth, had less and less time for Loudenne. There was even talk of disposing of the property, and only the dogged persistence of Gordon Gilbey saved it for better days. At this period, the *régisseur*, Monsieur Gombaud, even made a dessert wine, Medullio, as a method of using up the unwanted surplus production. It was sold locally and is still remembered by many of the older generation in the Médoc.

After the Second World War, the property was in a very run-down condition. Under the German occupation, the vineyards in the *palus* had mostly been pulled up and the land turned over to cattle grazing, and production had shrunk to 30 or 40 tonneaux, half of it white wine. When I first visited Loudenne in May 1960, the reconstruction of the vineyard under Monsieur Bouilleau, the new *régisseur*, had recently begun, but the great *chais* was distressingly empty and the château extremely dilapidated, only habitable during the summer months.

Since that time, progress has been steady and at times spectacular. In 1963 the château was completely restored and modernized, and in 1970 a model estate of new houses for the families now living on the property was opened, to replace those originally built nearly one hundred years before. Extensive alterations have been made in the *cuvier* and *chais*, and the *chais* itself now positively bulges with wine in cask and in bottle, for large stocks of château-bottled wines from all the main Bordeaux districts are kept here. A happy renaissance indeed, and one which mirrors many others throughout the Bordeaux *vignoble*.

The white wine has been retained, but the quantity made has been reduced and the quality improved so that it would be hard to find its peer in the Médoc. It is made principally of Sauvignon with a small amount of Sémillon, and after a controlled fermentation in tank, is kept in stainless steel *cuves* until the bottling the following spring.

But while the white wine is a pleasing curiosity, the reputation of Loudenne rightly rests on its red wines. These are distinguished by a fine and individual bouquet, said by some to be reminiscent of chrysanthemums, while the wine soon develops a mellow and expansive flavour and keeps extremely well. It is interesting to compare Loudenne with the neighbouring Coufran, which is in the Haut-Médoc. There is a marked similarity of style, but the Loudenne loses nothing by the comparison. The colour is not as deep as some of its neighbours' at first, but fills out with maturity. Some of the old vintages are remarkable and provide yet another demonstration of the quality attainable by the best-known *Bourgeois* growths in this part of the Médoc.

The oldest bottle of Loudenne that I have tasted was the 1896, still wonderfully fresh and pleasant to drink when sixty-seven years old. The 1926 and 1928 were outstanding, the 1934 and 1937 had some of the shortcomings of their vintages, but many of the lesser years are delicious, particularly the 1923 and the 1938. More recently, the 1961 was quite outstanding—the best wine made since the war, remarkably concentrated and generous. Since then, the 1962 was classic and lasted well, the 1964 rather full-blown and an early developer, the 1966 very fine indeed, with more body than

199

the 1964 and more fruit and vinosity than the 1962, while the 1967 was light but charming. The poor years of 1963, 1965 and 1968 were not sold under the château name. During the 1970s, excellent wines were made in 1970, 1975 and 1976, while the 1971 was charming if rather light. It was perhaps a sign of increasing commercial pressures that the 1972 was bottled under the château label.

No mention of this period of renaissance for Loudenne would be complete without a tribute to the work of Mr Martin Bamford. Since 1968 he has been generally based at Loudenne, and nothing has happened there that has not come under his critical scrutiny. He is a true perfectionist who is also a man of taste, so that everything that has been done has been meticulously and energetically pursued.

As the reconstituted vineyard matures, so production increases; from 50 to 60 tonneaux of red wine and 20 to 25 of white in the early 1970s up to 150 tonneaux now the replanting is nearly complete (the equal of 12,750 cases of red wine). Whereas until recently the wines of Loudenne were to be found almost exclusively in the UK and Ireland, they are now exported to the USA and many other markets.

Château Les Ormes Sorbet (Couquèques)

The small and obscure commune of Couquèques lies inland from the Gironde between St Yzans and St Christoly. The name itself is derived from the fossilized sea-shells which are richly deposited on this particular outcrop of gravelly ridges which provide the soil for this excellent growth. The reputation of the wine has increased of late, and this was recognized when the 1978 classification raised Les Ormes Sorbet to a *Grand Bourgeois*. In 1966 it had only been given the status of a simple *Bourgeois*. The average production is 6,800 cases.

Château Patache d'Aux (Bégadan)

This growth first made its appearance in the 1886 edition of Cocks & Féret as Cru Patachon, and until quite recently was called a simple *cru* and not a château. But the property has survived and prospered while many others have disappeared, and today it is one of the most important wines of Bégadan. The d'Aux which is now

200

affixed refers to the family d'Aux, descendants of the Comtes d'Armagnac, who owned the property before the Revolution. The family was long associated with the running of the diligences which in those days provided the only alternative to the river as a means of reaching Bordeaux. The connection is attractively commemorated on the label.

The property—now formed into a company—has for many years belonged to the Delon family (see Léoville-Lascases and Phélan-Ségur. It enjoys a good reputation and consistently makes a robust, full-flavoured wine which needs time to mature. The average production is now 17,000 cases.

Château Potensac (Ordonnac et Potensac)

Several good wines are made on the gravelly outcrop of Potensac which lies between St Yzans and St Germain d'Esteuil, and Château Potensac is the best known of these. For long the property of the Liquard family, it now belongs to the wife of Monsieur Paul Delon of Léoville-Lascases, who is herself a Liquard, and it is administered by Monsieur Paul Delon.

The wine is very consistent and carefully made. In style it is full-bodied and quite fruity, with a tendency to harshness at first and developing a markedly strong flavour or *goût de terroir*. Potensac always fetches one of the top prices in the Médoc. The average production is 17,500 cases.

Château Sigognac (St Yzans)

Although the vineyard here is not quite so favourably placed as those of neighbouring Loudenne, these are good slopes further away from the river. The vineyard has recently been extensively replanted and the property modernized. The wine, which used to enjoy a good reputation, is now very good again and well merits its new position in the 1978 classification. The average production is now 15,300 cases.

Château La Tour de By (Bégadan)

This is probably the most important growth in Bégadan today. It is beautifully situated on a series of gravelly ridges near to the Gironde, and there is a tower (not unlike the one at Haut-Batailley) on one of the highest points of the vineyard. The château itself is charming, although the setting is notably rustic. The wine is most distinctive. It is highly coloured and has a powerful bouquet with a very characteristic perfume. The wine is full-bodied and has a very strong character with, perhaps, a certain *goût de terroir*. But the whole character is highly Médocain with its rugged individuality of style.

The property came into the hands of three partners, Messieurs Cailloux, Lapalu and Pages in the 1960s, and is now very carefully run, with the wine well-made and consistent. This is today one of the best wines of the Médoc and fetches one of the top prices. 1962, 1964, 1966 and 1967 were all very successful. The production has now risen to around 25,500 cases.

Apart from these *Grands Bourgeois*, there are twenty properties simply classified as *Bourgeois*, of which no fewer than seven are in Bégadan. The wines of St Christoly have long enjoyed an excellent reputation for their fine flavour and attractive bouquet. They have more finesse than the wines further inland. There was a time when some English wine merchants sold a wine under the commune name of St Christoly, but this practice has now lapsed.

The actual list of *Bourgeois* growths is as follows:

At St Germain d'Esteuil: Château du Castera
At Potensac: Château Gallais-Bellevue
    Château Lassalle
At Blaignan: Château La France
    Château Pontet
    Château La Tour Haut-Caussan
    Château Les Tourelles
At Couquèques: Château Haut Canteloup
At St Christoly: Château St Bonnet
    Château La Tour Blanche
    Château La Tour St Bonnet
At Bégadan: Château de By
    Château La Clare
    Château Haut-Garin
    Château Landon
    Château Monthril
    Château La Roque de By
    Château Vieux Robin

At Valeyrac: Château Bellevue
At Queyrac: Château Carcannieux

The two growths at Potensac, Gallais-Bellevue and Lassalle, belong to Monsieur Paul Delon of Château Potensac and are run jointly with it. The wines are, in fact, very similar and all enjoy an excellent reputation, which is well deserved from my experience. They make 3,400 and 2,550 cases respectively.

The most important property in St Christoly is La Tour St Bonnet. Here, Monsieur André Lafon has now put together three properties: La Fuie St Bonnet making 50 tonneaux, La Tour St Bonnet making 150 tonneaux and La Croix St Bonnet making 20 tonneaux, to produce one wine. The resulting 18,300 cases make this one of the largest *Bourgeois* growths in the Médoc. The reputation of the wine is good, the style typical of the warm, fruity wines of St Christoly.

La Tour Blanche, the property of Monsieur Louis Merlet, also makes very pleasant wine and enjoys a deserved reputation. It has a production of around 12,750 cases. Another good wine is made at St Bonnet, the property of Monsieur Solivares. I have found this wine particularly fruity and agreeable. The average production here is 12,750 cases.

Château du Castera (St Germain d'Esteuil)

One of the important growths in St Germain d'Esteuil, Castera lies on a series of high, gravelly ridges which are a continuation of the outcrops found in Vertheuil to the south. The property has a very long history, the original château having been besieged by the Black Prince. The de Verthamon family, once proprietors also of Loudenne, owned it for some 200 years until 1901. Today, the property is a company with Monsieur Deschodt as administrator. In spite of its size and the good reputation of the wines of St Germain d'Esteuil, Castera is not very well known today. The average production is 12,350 cases.

Before completing the survey of the Bas-Médoc, there is one other property which does not feature in the 1978 *Bourgeois* classification, but which should be mentioned. This is Livran at St Germain d'Esteuil. This property, of impressive appearance, was from 1889 until 1962 the proud possession of an English company,

James L. Denman. Unfortunately, like so many old family businesses, it has now ceased to exist, and the wine, once well known in England, is little seen. The proprietor is now Monsieur Robert Godfrin who once ran it for Denman's, and the average production is 17,000 cases.

7

Graves: both red and white

The Graves is an ancient and singular region: ancient, because its vineyards are amongst the oldest in Bordeaux and its wines amongst the first to be recorded; singular, because it is the only region in Bordeaux where almost every property produces both red and white wines, and they both have an almost equal importance. If one were to mention the name of Graves to the casual wine drinker, it is probable that his first reaction would be to think of a white wine—and, indeed, Graves used to produce much more white than red wine. But in the last decade red wine has finally overtaken white wine production. Most of the white wine is fairly ordinary, and varies from dry to slightly sweet. The finest wines are the red, grown in a few communes just outside the city of Bordeaux, while more ordinary reds are made throughout the rest of the area. In this same area close to Bordeaux, a much smaller quantity of very fine, dry, white wine is also made.

A glance at the map will show that this is a very large area, stretching some 35 miles (50 kms) from the southern limits of the Médoc, round the west and southern outskirts of Bordeaux, past Langon, and almost to the limits of the Bordeaux region along the western bank of the Garonne to a depth of 10 to 15 miles (15 to 20 kms). Inserted in its midst is the district of Sauternes-Barsac and Cérons, and the white wines produced in the part of Graves adjoining Sauternes are nearer that region in style than Graves. Indeed, many properties in Cérons, Illats and Podensac have the right to call their white wines 'Graves' or 'Cérons', according to the style of the wine produced. Old maps of the Bordeaux region show that the name of Graves was used originally to embrace the whole area of the left bank of the Garonne and Gironde, including the Médoc. It was, understandably, those vineyards lying just

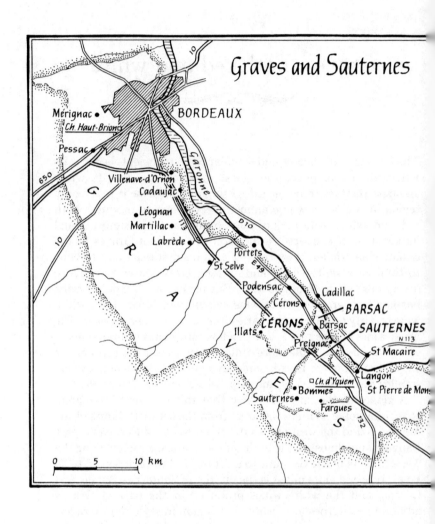

outside the city limits which first became known, and Haut-Brion is the first growth to be mentioned in English literature, by the indefatigable Pepys in 1663, although his spelling, Ho Bryen, might not be immediately recognizable to today's wine drinkers.

The finest red wines of the Graves are, not surprisingly, nearest in style to those of the Médoc, the gravelly soil and the *encépagement* closely resembling those of its northern neighbour. But, just as there are discernible differences between the various major communes of the Médoc, so the red Graves have their own character—a very marked and powerful bouquet almost with a hint of tobacco, frank and open, but not perhaps as subtle as the Médoc, while the flavour is very clean and almost crisp, pleasantly fruity, but with a firm, often rather tannic background. These are very individual wines, but it should be remembered that there is only a very tiny group of really top-class properties, and that most red Graves are decent, but no more than ordinary, small wines. These lesser red wines tend to be light in colour and body, distinctive in bouquet and flavour, usually with a certain *goût de terroir* typical of Graves, and delicious when drunk young.

The INAO produced a classification of both red and white Graves in 1953, which was revised in 1959. It lists only thirteen red wines and eight white wines, but without any distinction between them. Haut-Brion was, of course, the only growth of Graves to be included in the 1855 classification, and belongs in the category of the great first growths of the Gironde. La Mission Haut-Brion now holds a position similar to that of Mouton in the mid-nineteenth century, in between the first and second growths—not quite accepted as a first growth, but nearly there. Then come Domaine de Chevalier, Haut-Bailly and Pape-Clément, which by both price and merit belong with the best second growths of the Médoc. The remainder belong further down the scale, so that the Graves contribution to the great growths of the Gironde is small in number but memorable in quality.

The white wines are equally varied. There is a tiny number of wines which are the best dry white wines of Bordeaux, and also among the best in France, and there is a great quantity of other wines which vary from stylish, dry and fruity, to mawkish, over-sulphured and semi-sweet—the whole gamut of quality. The traditional style of white Graves was full-bodied with a marvellously honeyed bouquet, a wine with a good deal of alcohol and

GRAVES: 1959 OFFICIAL CLASSIFICATION

The vineyards of the Graves district were officially classified in 1953 and in 1959. Château Haut-Brion, is also officially classified with the great Médocs.

	COMMUNE	TONNEAUX
Classified red wines of Graves		
Château Haut-Brion	*Pessac*	150
Château Bouscaut	*Cadaujac*	120
Château Carbonnieux	*Léognan*	90
Domaine de Chevalier	*Léognan*	40
Château Fieuzal	*Léognan*	60
Château Haut-Bailly	*Léognan*	55
Château La Mission-Haut-Brion	*Pessac*	70
Château La Tour-Haut-Brion	*Talence*	18
Château La Tour-Martillac		
(Kressmann La Tour)	*Martillac*	50
Château Malartic-Lagravière	*Léognan*	45
Château Olivier	*Léognan*	10
Château Pape-Clément	*Pessac*	100
Château Smith-Haut-Lafitte	*Martillac*	140
Classified white wines of Graves		
Château Bouscaut	*Cadaujac*	18
Château Carbonnieux	*Léognan*	150
Domaine de Chevalier	*Léognan*	10
Château Couhins	*Villenave-d'Ornon*	40
Château La Tour-Martillac		
(Kressmann La Tour)	*Martillac*	6
Château Laville-Haut-Brion	*Talence*	20
Château Malartic-Lagravière	*Léognan*	6
Château Olivier	*Léognan*	80
Château Haut-Brion*	*Pessac*	16

* Added to the list in 1960.

some richness, which required up to ten years' maturation to give of its best, and could live for many years more. But the poor and cheap imitations of this style were detestable, and helped to give Graves the bad name which still hangs over it. Today, the fashion is to make much lighter, crisper wines which can be bottled and drunk young, in line with dry white wines produced in other regions of France. Such wines are excellent and will, I am sure, win back much of Bordeaux's lost white wine trade.

The best Graves, both red and white, are produced in six communes which lie close to Bordeaux, out of the thirty-seven which today make wines with the *appellation* Graves. I will deal with these six individually.

PESSAC AND TALENCE

These are two communes so interdependent that it seems sensible to deal with them together. They produce the greatest red wines of the Graves and, in tiny quantities, some of the greatest white wines as well. Unfortunately, for many years now the suburbs of Bordeaux have steadily encroached on the vineyards of Graves, so that today much fine, gravelly soil lies beneath rows of houses, and suburban gardens now flourish where the vine used to grow. I once had the experience of drinking a bottle of one of these casualties of progress with Ronald Barton; it was Château Laburthe-Brivazac 1929, which he had bought when the property was sold up, and very good it was.

Château Haut-Brion   First Growth

This was the only Graves to be included in the 1855 classification, where it was placed as a first growth. It had long been regarded as being on a par with the leading growths of the Médoc. The origin of the name is obscure, but it can safely be said that Maurice Healy's fond wish to find an Irish connection as a corruption of O'Brien has no foundation in fact. It is said that the name comes from the *seigneurie* of Brion, and that over the years it became transformed to D'Obrion or Daubrion, to Hault-Brion, and finally to its present form. The fame of the place seems to date from its acquisition in 1529, when a de Pontac married Jeanne de Bellon, daughter of Pierre de Bellon, then mayor of Libourne and *seigneur* of Hault-Brion. From then until just before the Revolution, Haut-Brion remained in the hands of the Pontac family, and was often sold under the name of Pontac. Unfortunately, the Pontacs were such large proprietors of vineyards in the area that it is not always possible to tell if wine sold during their régime actually came from Haut-Brion or from their other properties as well. Before the Revolution, the property passed by marriage to the de Fumel family, at that time also owners of Margaux.

The Revolution began a confused period in Haut-Brion's history. The Comte de Fumel was an *émigré*, and so the property was seized by the State. From then onwards it passed through many hands; for three years it belonged to Talleyrand, and at another time to one of the Beyermans from the old firm of Dutch *négociants*. Eventually, it was bought by Joseph-Eugène Larrieu in 1836, whose family owned it until 1923. Then there was an unhappy period of decline in the château's fortunes until Mr Clarence Dillon, the American banker, bought the property in 1835. Since then it has gone from strength to strength under the supervision of the devoted Seymour Weller, and the *régisseur*, Jean Delmas, who still manages it. It was, perhaps, appropriate that a wine which had been much loved and praised by Thomas Jefferson during his stay in France, should later become the property of another distinguished American. Since Clarence Dillon's death in 1979, his grand-daughter, the Duchesse de Monchy, has been head of the company.

The château itself is a charming, turreted affair, parts of which go back to the sixteenth century, and it is well depicted on the label. Part of the vineyard adjoins the château and part lies across the road adjoining that of La Mission Haut-Brion. These two now form an oasis of vineyards surrounded by housing. Haut-Brion went modern in 1960, when stainless steel vats were installed for the vinification. Apart from this, the *chais* is well kept and workmanlike, not as showy as some of the Médoc châteaux.

The wines of Haut-Brion have known their ups and downs. Before Larrieu bought the property in 1836, its reputation lagged behind that of the first growths of the Médoc, but by the late nineteenth century it stood very high indeed. Both 1899 and 1900 enjoyed a great reputation, and actually sold at a higher price than either Lafite or Margaux. The 1906 was also one of the successes of that year. The earliest Haut-Brion I have seen was the 1921 which, when I drank it in 1963, was still very dark in colour with a most distinctive, 'roasted' nose. The wine was still very big, hard and unyielding, and quite without any of the charm of age. This was, I believe, in part the then Haut-Brion style, but also in good part, at least, the character of the 1921 vintage. When tasted again in 1979, sixteen years later, the wine was quite transformed, now elegant with a sweet fruitiness, delicacy and finesse, and a lovely finish. But the finest of the vintages of this decade was probably the 1926. As at Mouton, it has the power of a 1928 but the sweetness of a 1929. In a pre-sale tasting of the late Clarence Dillon's cellar held at Christie's in 1979, the 1926 was comfortably the best of a range of the main vintages between 1921 and 1937. It had a really lovely flavour and was completely harmonious, sweet and rich: altogether a great classic claret in the heroic mould.

The 1928, which I drank against the Latour of the same year in 1957, was a good deal harder than the Latour and very aggressive, with a most distinctive, but not altogether agreeable, character. When I had another bottle of the same wine some years later, it had disintegrated. My impression of the oddness of the 1928 was borne out by the sample from the Dillon private cellar in 1979. I noted that it was still an enormous wine, but quite unbalanced, with a very strange, rather medicinal after-taste. The 1929 had something of the same stamp about it, with an almost port-like character. One classic vintage of the 1920s I have not mentioned is the 1924. This was a wine of considerable breed and elegance, but without the staying power of the 1926 or the 1921, and the sample from the Dillon cellar was clearly past its best.

The 1930s produced nothing to match the 1926, nor did they repeat the freaks of 1928 and 1929. The 1934 was still very rich in 1979, with a touch of that port-like style noted in the 1929, but with a very dry finish, yet with more fruit than the 1937. It was clearly the superior wine. When I first tasted the 1937 in 1971, I had quite liked it, noting the distinction of flavour and great richness, and finding it not unduly hard—like most 1937s. Yet by 1979, the sample from the Dillon cellar, while retaining the classic flavour, had a very dry, tannic finish which made the wine short and unharmonious.

Since the Second World War, Haut-Brion seems to have undergone a gradual but steady change of style. Gone are the black-strap wines of old, with their very special character; instead, we have much lighter, more elegant wines which develop much more quickly. In some recent vintages, the wines have almost seemed to lack weight and staying power, especially in off-vintages. But in the fine years, wines of great breed and distinction have consistently been made. During the war, the 1940 and 1944 were both delightful, light wines. The 1940 has stayed remarkably well—it still showed well at the Dillon tasting in 1979—but the 1944 was going down-hill rapidly. After this, the 1945 was very successful and developed more quickly than most of the first growths, the 1953 was outstanding, the 1955 a good example of the year, the 1959 again one of the best of the year, the 1961 outstandingly attractive but forward from the start, the 1962 most attractive and fine, and the 1964 again most successful, as was the 1966. However, years like 1958 and 1960 tended to fade rather quickly and, as with many other châteaux, it was a mistake to offer the 1963 and 1965.

The 1970s have followed a rather similar pattern, with wines of great style and breed in the great years like 1970, 1975, 1976 and 1978, but terribly light, insubstantial offerings in 1973 and 1977. At a tasting held in 1979 to take a first look at the 1975s after they had settled down in bottle, the Haut-Brion was extremely attractive but, in startling contrast to the other first growths, seemed already drinkable. Should a first growth be producing instant claret? In line with my own notion of a hedonistic scale to chart the excellence of any wine, my answer would be that this was a great break-through if the wine lasted, because then it would be drinkable and enjoyable for much longer than its rivals. But it remains to be seen if such wines will indeed last.

There is a second wine, Bahans-Haut-Brion, which is nowadays sold only as a non-vintage. Production is limited to around 1,800 cases and the wine is mostly sold in France.

Due to its American connection, Haut-Brion has a great following in the USA and is not, perhaps, seen as often in England as it used to be. The average production is 12,000 cases.

Haut-Brion also makes a very small quantity of white wine. Curiously enough, its very existence has been stolidly denied in both the 11th (1949) and 12th (1969) editions of Cocks & Féret, but exist it certainly does. Unfortunately the quantity is so small—seldom much more than 1,500 cases—that the demand from the USA means that one seldom finds any in England now. The first vintage I had was the 1949, a superb wine with the

212

typical honeyed nose of the classic Graves. I had not seen the wine
for many years, until recently I saw the 1962, which unfortunately
seemed to have too much sulphur. I daresay that this was no more
than a momentary lapse. But, regrettably, notes on Haut-Brion-
Blanc now have little more than academic interest.

Château La Mission Haut-Brion

Almost opposite Haut-Brion, a fine pair of wrought-iron gates
gives a glimpse of a vineyard as neat as a garden, and a drive
leading to a low-built château of modest proportions standing in
its midst. This is La Mission Haut-Brion, the pride of its late
owner, Monsieur Henri Woltner, surely the greatest proprietor of
his generation who, by his enquiring mind and meticulous
attention to detail, raised the reputation of this property so that it
can now stand comparison with the finest in Bordeaux. The
ownership has now passed to Monsieur Fernand Woltner's
daughter and son-in-law, Monsieur and Madame Francis Dewavrin, who are jealously guarding the standard and reputation of
the wine.

The lineage of La Mission is long and interesting. Until the
seventeenth century, it formed a part of the Haut-Brion estate.
Then, in 1630, Olive de Lestonnac, widow of Antoine de Gourgue,
first president of the Parlement of Guyenne, bequeathed it to a
congregation of priests known as the Lazarites, which had been
founded by St Vincent de Paul. It was described in the deed as
'Ixelle Metaire d'Haubrion, située ez la paroisse de Talence, et une
chambre basse à loger des vallets au fond et en suitte un grand
chay cuvier garni d'une fauloire en pierre de taille et vingt deux
journaux de vignes'. In 1698, a chapel was built and consecrated
under the name of Notre Dame de la Mission. Meanwhile, the
wine produced by the Lazarites gained a considerable reputation.

With the coming of the Revolution, the estate—like all Church
property—was confiscated and sold in 1792 to Martial Victor
Vaillant for 302,000 *livres* in paper money, the equivalent of
100,000 silver *livres*, a great sum for that time. Then, for nearly a
hundred years, it belonged to the Chiapelle family. The first
member of this family, Célestin Chiapelle, had a great reputation
as a viticultural enthusiast, and it is interesting to note that in
Cocks's classification of 1846, La Mission is included among the
fourth and fifth growths of the Médoc. Evidently, later gen-

213

erations of the family did not continue with his skill and enthusiasm. Henri Woltner's father acquired La Mission in 1918, but in 1921 Henri Woltner assumed the management of the property which, together with his brother Fernand, lasted for fifty years. Under the Dewavrins there is the same *régisseur*, Monsieur Henri Lagardère, to help assure continuity; his son Michel, now assists his father and is a qualified oenologist.

The château itself deserves a note. Its charming interior, of comfortably domestic proportions, contains a marvellous collection of *objets d'art*. The staircase displays a remarkable selection of porcelain: holy water stoops, as well as a fine eighteenth-century altar piece. Then, in the chapel, there is some attractive sixteenth-century stained glass and some fine church furniture.

The soil of La Mission is remarkable for its stoniness. When an extension had to be made to the cellar, it was found that there was solid gravel to a depth of 18 feet, and Monsieur Woltner estimated that at least two-thirds of the soil was stones. It is noticeable that a high proportion of old vines are maintained. At present, the vineyard is planted in the proportion of 65 per cent Cabernet Sauvignon, 10 per cent Cabernet Franc and 25 per cent Merlot. The average production is now 6,000 cases. Unfortunately, the size of the vineyard was reduced by the construction of the Bordeaux-Toulouse autoroute. This happened in spite of many representations, proving that even in Bordeaux such things are no longer sacred.

Over the years, Henri Woltner concentrated his attention both on perfecting his vineyard and on his wine-making. He used to observe that there comes a moment when the maturation of the grapes ceases, even though in some years they have not attained perfect maturity. When this point has been reached, picking should proceed as speedily as possible, since nothing is to be gained by further waiting. Then, in the most favourable years, the falling acidity must be watched as closely as the rising sugar level, and when they have reached equilibrium, picking should begin if a properly balanced wine is to be made. Henri Woltner believed that some properties today make the mistake of picking too late, thus either endangering their crop without the prospect of making any better wine, or making a wine where there is too much sugar and not enough acidity (essential for a wine to keep well).

Henri Woltner was also a pioneer in vinification techniques. As early as 1926, he installed the first glass-lined, steel vat. After years of experiment, when he was confident that better results could be obtained by using this method, he went over completely to this system in 1951. He called his system *fermentation froide*, by which is meant a controlled fermentation at a steady, mean temperature. The *maître de chais* has told me that since these vats have been used, the temperature has never risen above 30°C—an average of 27°–28°C is usual—and they seldom have to resort to special cooling techniques. For some reason, no one else has adopted exactly the same system although, of course, Latour and others control the temperature by spraying water over the outside of its stainless steel vats when the temperature reaches a certain level, thus achieving the same object. But the smaller, discreet, white vats at La Mission are certainly more aesthetically pleasing, and are said to be cheaper to install.

I have seen no wines of the pre-Woltner era. Maxwell Campbell in the *Wayward Tendrils of the Vine* mentions the 1905 La Mission as the outstanding wine of that year, and shows that even at that time, La Mission often rivalled its more famous neighbour. The 1920 was still wonderfully preserved when I saw it on its forty-sixth birthday. At the great retrospective tasting of La Mission vintages held at Christie's in December 1978, it was still a lovely, almost ethereal wine, old but still there. The classic vintages of 1924, 1926, 1928, 1929 and 1934 were all highly successful. A very elegant 1933 is worth noting, but the most surprising item was a delightful 1936, while the delicious and well-preserved 1940 must not be forgotten.

Since the war, the greatest years have been 1945, 1947, 1948, 1949, 1950 (one of the outstanding wines of the vintage), 1952, 1953, 1955 (again one of the most attractive wines of the year), 1957 (a triumph in this usually ungrateful year), 1959, 1961, 1962, 1964 and 1966. The 1958 and 1960, tasted again in October 1978, were both very successful wines and have lasted better than most wines from these vintages. In those two terrible years, 1963 and 1965, surprisingly drinkable wines were made. The 1967 was at its best by the time of the 1978 tasting, with that dry finish that marks so many examples of this year. The 1968 was honourable without achieving the success of 1960, but the 1969 was one of the few wines that I do not care for. In the next decade, 1970, 1971, 1975, and 1976 have all produced classic examples of these years, the lighter styles of 1971 and 1976 contrasting with the massive wines made in the other years. The 1973 is a disappointment—the vintage was irreparably damaged by a hail-storm just a few days before the picking. The 1974 deserves mention as above average for the year. The 1977 is a fine example of this variable year, and should be good for early drinking. First impressions of the 1978 promise a magnificent wine, and the 1979 while less powerful is rich and well structured.

Thus La Mission is today one of the most consistent of all Bordeaux growths. The wine is distinctly different in style from its neighbour, Haut-Brion, whether one compares it with the old or new style. Always deep in colour, the wine is rich and concentrated in flavour, and although it never seems to be too tannic, it undeniably requires more time to show of its best today than does Haut-Brion. It also lasts very well. Even so, Henri Woltner always considered that even in big years his wines should be capable of being drunk with pleasure at ten years, although they will usually be drinkable well before this. In some ways, the stylistic difference between Haut-Brion and La Mission may be equated to the difference between Lafite on the one hand, and Mouton on the other, allowing of course, for the difference between Pauillac and Graves. Curiously enough, the situation between La Mission and its illustrious neighbour is in other ways reminiscent of that between Lafite and Mouton in the mid-nineteenth century: La Mission is striving to gain recognition as a first growth, while Haut-Brion deeply resents any suggestion that its neighbour should have any sort of parity.

There were several other proprietors of Henri Woltner's generation who were every bit as enthusiastic as he, but none who combined this with such a thorough technical knowledge. This is why such progress was made in the quality and consistency of his wines—a legacy much prized by his successors. Certainly it would be a fitting culmination to half a century's work, and a memorial to Henri Woltner as a pioneer in Bordeaux, should La Mission be accepted one day as a first growth by its peers.

Château Pape-Clément

After Haut-Brion and La Mission, this is the most important vineyard in Pessac-Talence. It has the proud claim of being the oldest clearly identifiable vineyard in the entire region. It was planted in 1300 by Bertrand de Goth, then Archbishop of Bordeaux. When, in 1306, he was elected Pope as Clément V, he gave the vineyard to Cardinal Arnaud de Canteloup, the new Archbishop of Bordeaux, for his benefit and that of his successors.

Pape-Clément remained the property of the Church until the Revolution. During the last century it enjoyed a good reputation, and in the 1920s some fine wines were made, notably the 1920, 1924 and 1929. Then disaster struck—a hail storm on 8 June 1937 virtually destroyed the vineyard. This was a bad time commercially for Bordeaux, and the proprietor was in no position to face such a loss. He was compelled to sell, and the property was acquired by developers: it seemed possible that this great vineyard, which had continuously produced wine for over 600 years, might end up as a housing estate.

Fortunately, the property was bought in 1939 by Monsieur Montagne. The vineyard had to be reconstituted from scratch, and it was not until the 1949 vintage that it was to give any hint of its former glory. The château itself rates the 1955 as the first really worthy example—the wine was very fine and typical of the best Graves style, but still distinctly light. The 1959 was really fine, a wine of richness and balance, while the 1961 was truly among the best of this great year. The 1962 was oustandingly successful, the 1964 full and well balanced—very successful, as were most Graves in this year—and the 1966 a very good example of this fine vintage.

So this ancient and famous growth has been successfully resurrected, thanks to the dedication of Monsieur Montagne. It is yet another instance of the fact that, were it not for rich enthusiasts being prepared to make investments which cannot yield a return for many years, some great and famous vineyards would not still be delighting wine lovers. Today, the vineyard of about 25 hectares produces on average 9,000 cases.

Château La Tour Haut-Brion

This is a small property adjoining La Mission, which was acquired by the Woltner brothers in 1933. It is yet another illustration of the fact that even small differences of soil make for important differences in quality. The wines of La Tour Haut-Brion are very fine, but they just miss the finesse and breed of La Mission. Henri Woltner's experience over the years was similar to Ronald

Barton's with Léoville-Barton and Langoa-Barton. Nevertheless, La Tour Haut-Brion is a very fine wine and fully justifies its classification as a *Grand Cru Classé* of Graves. The wine is just as meticulously made as those of La Mission—full-bodied, but perhaps a shade less generous than La Mission. Unfortunately the vineyard is very small, and on average only about 1,500 cases are made, so that the wine is not as widely known, at least in Great Britain, as its quality deserves.

The vintages of La Tour Haut-Brion closely followed those of La Mission. Normally the La Tour is more precocious and so the 1975 will be drinkable earlier. But in some years, such as 1976, I detect a lack of that fat and richness that La Mission has to counterbalance the tannin. The 1971 is particularly attractive, and while the 1966 is noticeably lighter in texture than the La Mission, the 1969 La Tour seems fuller.

Château Laville-Haut-Brion

This might almost be called the white La Mission but, in fact, it has always been run as a separate property producing only white wines. It was acquired by the Woltner brothers in 1928. It is today the outstanding example of a classic white Graves made in the traditional style. It is full-bodied and takes some time to reach its best. Henri Woltner used to say it could be drunk when five years old, but it is seldom at its best before ten years—in marked contrast to the new style of instant white wines. As with some of the best white Burgundies, the complex flavour and character only gradually develop until, when mature, it has a marvellous, honeyed nose, a pale golden colour and a very complex flavour—dry, yet full in the mouth, with that sort of richness compounded of alcohol and natural glycerine which is found in a fine Montrachet. The production is very small—now only some 1,800 cases on average—so that even though white Graves tends to be out of fashion today, there is not too much around for a world demand. Unfortunately, some 3 hectares of vineyard were lost when the main Bordeaux-Bayonne railway line was re-routed some years ago, a sad hostage to 'progress'. It is a wine worth searching and saving for.

The soil of the Laville vineyard is richer and less stony than that of La Mission or La Tour. The *encépagement* is 50 per cent each of Sauvignon and Sémillon, but the proportion of Sémillon, contrary to fashion, is being increased. It is interesting to note that this wine is fermented in individual barrels and not in *cuve*, but the temperature of the small *chais* can be controlled. Since 1961, the wines have been bottled in the late spring to early summer after the vintage, and with only the lightest of filtrations. As with many white wines, the best years are not necessarily the same as for the reds, because in the greatest years, the whites are often too alcoholic and lack finesse. Thus I personally prefer the 1962 to the 1961, the 1971 to the 1970, and the 1976 to the 1975. The 1978 looks likely to follow in the footsteps of the 1976.

Château Les Carmes-Haut-Brion

This is a small property which takes its name from the Carmelites who owned it from 1584 until the Revolution—yet another example of the Church property so widely found in this area. Today the property of Madame Robert Chantecaille, Les Carmes produces on average around 700 cases of red wine. I have only once or twice had the opportunity of drinking it. It was rather light, although pleasant and easy to drink, but not in the same class as the preceding wines of this area.

There are very few other growths left in these two communes: the most recent casualty to development was Cordier's property of Fanning-Lafontaine, which enjoyed a reputation as a good *Bourgeois* growth.

Other small growths still producing are:

	Red	White
Château Rostang-Haut-Carré	500 cases	180 cases
Château Madran	350 cases	—
Château Saige-Fort-Manoir	950 cases	—

LÉOGNAN

This important commune lies to the south-east of Pessac, only 14 kms south of the centre of Bordeaux. Even so, its appearance is a great deal more rural, and there is much wooded land, amongst which many of the vineyards seem almost hidden away.

A larger quantity of the finest red and white Graves is produced in Léognan than in any other commune. The red wines have great distinction, the most typical, pronounced Graves bouquet, with a clean flavour and great finesse, second only to the great wines of Pessac. The white wines are very fine and delicate, yet with a fine persistence of flavour.

Domaine de Chevalier

One of the few leading properties in Bordeaux which still does not call itself a château, Chevalier is a small vineyard surrounded by woods, so that when one discovers it by a quiet, country road, it seems like a clearing in the woods, with only a few modest farm buildings at the end of the vineyard.

Chevalier has consistently made both one of the finest red and one of the finest white wines in the Graves over a considerable period, but due to the small production (3,800 cases red, 950 cases white), has not become as widely known as other leading wines. It was, incidentally, one of André Simon's favourites. Its fame began towards the end of the nineteenth century when it belonged to the grandfather of the present proprietor, Jean Ricard. Then, from 1900 to 1942, it belonged to Gabriel Beaumartin, a relation of the Ricards, who had a deserved reputation as a great wine-maker. Unfortunately, the vineyard was badly frosted in 1945 and, following partial replanting, did not begin to return to its old form until the 1953 vintage.

In style, the red Chevalier is rather lighter in both colour and body than the other leading Graves, with the exception now of Haut-Brion, but has greater delicacy and breed, a lovely bouquet and a more refined flavour than most Graves—a very individual wine. The white Chevalier is lighter and more steely in character than the Laville-Haut-Brion, but also takes several years to develop fully its fine bouquet and distinguished flavour. It is probably true to say that this and the Laville are in their different ways the best white Graves today in most vintages. The white vineyard is planted with 70 per cent Sauvignon and 30 per cent Sémillon, which in terms of juice means that the wine contains about 60 per cent Sauvignon and 40 per cent Sémillon. The wine is always bottled after the second winter in about March and is fermented entirely in individual barrels.

I have no personal experience of the old vintages of the red Chevalier, but André Simon (see Bibliography) placed the 1899 among the best wines of that famous year, and the 1907 and 1909 as highly successful in rather average years. Edmund Penning-

Rowsell (see Bibliography) records that the 1923, 1924, 1928, 1929, 1934 and 1937 were all good, while useful wines were made in the otherwise poor years of 1931 and 1936. Since 1953, good wines have been made in 1955, 1959, 1961, 1962, 1964 and 1966, while the tradition of making good off-vintage wines was maintained in 1963 and 1968. More recently, the 1978 was outstanding, while 1970, 1975, 1976 and 1979 have produced classic examples of these vintages.

Of the white Chevalier, the 1937 and 1947 both had fine reputations, and I have memories of the 1957 being outstandingly attractive. Later, the 1960, 1962 and 1966 were good, but I found the 1964 somewhat disappointing. As at Laville, the 1976 is magnificent, as is the 1979.

After Haut-Brion and La Mission, Chevalier is always among the top two or three red Graves, and in off-vintages sometimes higher up the scale than that. As the white wine is always in the top two or three, this places Chevalier among the outstanding growths of Bordeaux, with the best of the second growths of the Médoc, if one is to make that sort of comparison.

Château Haut-Bailly

The fame of Haut-Bailly dates from its acquisition in 1872 by a famous viticulturist of the period, Bellot des Miniéres. The vineyard is situated on one of the highest ridges of fine, gravelly soil in the region, and is dedicated solely to the production of red wine. The château is a simple, four-square, nineteenth-century house, which stands next to the *cuvier* and *chais*.

The story of Haut-Bailly is that, after a period of fame under Bellot des Minières (the 1878 was judged one of the outstanding wines of that vintage) the property passed through a period of decline. It was even said at one time that the wine was pasteurized, a story repeated in Morton Shand's classic on the wines of France. In 1955, the property was bought by a Belgian wine merchant, Daniel Sanders, and since then, he and his son have worked hard to restore its great reputation.

I shall always remember the first occasion that I ever tasted Haut-Bailly. I was looking at samples of the great 1961s at Loudenne when a sample of the Haut-Bailly appeared. We had never been offered the wine before, and I had never even tasted a bottle of it. The sample was so outstanding that, although the

221

price was very high—even for a 1961—and the château virtually forgotten then in England, I bought what was offered and never regretted it. Since then, I have grown to love and increasingly admire the wines of Haut-Bailly although, some of the vintages of the seventies do not quite live up to the château's potential. In style, it is probably closer to the wines of Pessac than any other wine of Léognan. It is somewhere between La Mission and Pape-Clément, perhaps, having something of the great vinosity and richness of La Mission, but it is slightly lighter in texture and develops more quickly. The bouquet is often strikingly similar to that of Pape-Clément, but tends to have more definition and style. Above all, this is a wonderfully harmonious wine, never too tannic, never too soft-centred.

The only pre-war wine I have seen was the 1937, which I have drunk on a number of occasions. It is certainly one of the most enjoyable wines I know of from that vintage. The 1928 also had a good reputation. Since the Sanders era began, the 1957 was a great success, with much more vinosity and charm than most wines of that year, not far behind La Mission. In 1959 and 1960, frost struck disastrously, only 10 tonneaux being produced in 1959 and 6 hogsheads in 1960. The 1961 was a great wine which has steadily developed its considerable potential, and this has been followed by a succession of wonderfully consistent and fine years: 1962, 1964 (an outstanding wine in this mixed year), 1966, 1967 and 1970. During the 1970s, Daniel Sanders was growing old and less and less able to exercise the meticulous control which had been responsible for the revival of Haut-Bailly's fortunes. Nor, unfortunately, would he entrust the task to his son, Jean. The result was a series of disappointing wines, judged by the highest standards. Monsieur Jean Sanders took over the running of the Château after the death of his father in 1980, and made the 1979. The result is that the 1978 vintage is fine, but lacks the intensity of the best 1978s, while the 1979 has a wonderfully rich, perfumed bouquet and a fine, opulent, supple flavour, very reminiscent of the good vintages of the 1960s. To achieve this one third of the crop was eliminated. I would not be surprised to see the 1979 turn out better than the 1978, and it is encouraging to know that Haut-Bailly is back on the right path. The average production is 5,000 cases. It is good to see this fine growth restored to its rightful place and once more being enjoyed in both Great Britain and the USA.

Château Malartic-Lagravière

This is another property producing both red and white wines. The vineyard occupies a well-exposed position on quite a high plateau of typically gravelly soil. It has passed through the same families for several hundred years, the present proprietor, Monsieur Jacques Marly-Ridoret, being descended from the Malartic family who gave it their name. This is a very well-run estate; the *chais* has been well modernized and is well kept. The label is rather distinctive, and, in 1962, it appeared that the proprietor had decided to write the château name in the Russian alphabet, until one discovered that if the bottle were held upside down and the label reflected in a mirror, the name could be read. As one does not normally expect to see a bottle of claret in a bar optic, I always felt that this was a rather eccentric piece of labelling!

The red wines of Malartic have a very strong and distinct Graves flavour, but tend to lack richness, so that the robust, slightly earthy flavour is not covered with enough fruit or fat in some years, and the wines can be lean. My general criticism of these wines is that they tend to be light, but hard and tannic.

I think the first Malartic that I drank must have been a 1943 which my father had as a concession wine after the war. It was rather tough and not one of my early favourites. Since then, I have had the opportunity of tasting a number of vintages. The 1953 was still surprisingly firm for that year when nine years old, and lacked the usual charm of the year. The 1955 was more successful in the context of that year, a well-balanced wine; the 1957 was all too typical of that year; the 1961 was very big and tough and is a slow developer; the 1962 was light but surprisingly slow to develop, with a hard background; the 1964 was rather light-weight but attractive, and the 1966 was a full, generous wine. More recently, the 1975 was particularly good, with more body and fruit than usual, while both the 1976 and 1978 were very successful, suggesting less lean, more attractive wines than hitherto. This has been followed by a most attractive 1979 with a lot of fruit and character.

The white Malartic can be one of the most attractive of white Graves, but unfortunately the production is very small (only 500 cases on average, compared with 4,000 cases of the red wine). I have not often had the opportunity of seeing this wine, but have always been struck by its outstanding bouquet and charmingly individual character. It is a wine of great breed, very carefully made, in some years rather full and rich like Laville but developing more quickly, in others very dry and delicate with a very grapey and beguiling aroma. Undoubtedly, the reputation and standing of the white Malartic would be much higher than it is, were the production not so small.

Château Carbonnieux

This is an extremely old property, second only to Pape-Clément in its long and continuous history of wine-making. It is the largest producer of white wine among the classified Graves, with 14,000 cases, and 8,000 cases of red wine are also made in the very large vineyard, which is the biggest of the classified Graves. The turreted château dates from the end of the fourteenth century and, after belonging to the Hospices de Bordeaux, who had it as a gift from the du Ferron family—members of the Parlement de Guyenne for over two hundred years—it passed into the hands of the Benedictine monks from the abbey of Sainte Croix de Bordeaux in 1741. Up until that time, the Graves region around Bordeaux had produced almost exclusively red wines. The monks were the first to produce white wine on a large scale, and so gave rise to the famous story about Carbonnieux. During the eighteenth century, the wines of Carbonnieux were apparently well known in most parts of Europe and were even sent to Constantinople where, to avoid the strictures of the Koran—which forbids Moslems to touch alcohol—the Benedictines labelled their white wine 'Eau minérale de Carbonnieux'. The property now belongs to Monsieur Mark Perrin, who came over from Algeria in the 1950s.

Recently, great efforts have been made to improve the quality of Carbonnieux. In 1973, stainless steel *cuves* were installed to control the vinification of the white wines, and they are now bottled in the spring following the vintage. Undoubtedly this has greatly improved their quality, but I have noticed that while a young, white Carbonnieux of only one or two years old is quite delicious, a year later it can seem rather dull. The red wines are still decidedly rustic, and are not among the top classified Graves. Certainly the white wines at present have the higher standing.

224

Château d'Olivier

The château at Olivier must be the most attractive and splendid of the Graves. Classified as a *monument historique*, the oldest parts date from the eleventh century, and the latest additions from the sixteenth century—ranging from a grim, medieval fortress to an elegant, Renaissance château. At one time, it was a hunting lodge of the Black Prince. The property actually belongs to the Bethmann family, once part-owners of Gruaud-Larose, but the estate has for over seventy years been run by the Bordeaux *négociants*, Eschenauer, who have the monopoly of the production.

While 10,000 cases of the white wine are produced on average, the less well-known red wine production is growing—now averaging 6,500 cases—and, indeed, I have never come across it although, like the white, it is among the small band of classified Graves. On the other hand, the white is widely distributed and well known. It is not usually reckoned to be among the top white Graves, but the quality is consistent and the wine carefully made.

Château de Fieuzal

This is a small property, producing both red and white wines, of which the red is classified but the white is not. The estate is an old one, and once belonged to the family de la Rochefoucauld. The present, excellent reputation was acquired under Erik Bocké, Swedish in origin but Bordelais by adoption, who lavished both money and love on the estate in the past few years, and the *chais* and *cuvier* is a show-place of cleanliness and order. In 1973, it was bought by Monsieur Négrevergne, a Bordeaux pharmaceutical manufacturer, who has continued the good work.

I had the opportunity of tasting several vintages a few years ago, and found the red wine extremely well made, on the light side, but very elegant, fruity and pleasing to drink, well balanced without too strong a Graves character—indeed, some vintages were quite Médocain in style. The 1953 was pleasing without being special, the 1960 highly successful for the year, and the 1962 very well balanced. They were the sort of wines which could take a worthy place with the fourth or fifth growths of the Médoc. The white Fieuzal is a comparatively recent innovation, introduced by Monsieur Bocké. When I saw it, it was light and well made, of the

225

modern type of Graves, meant for early bottling and drinking. 400 cases of this are now made, compared with 5,500 cases of red.

Château Larrivet-Haut-Brion

Formerly known as Haut-Brion-Larrivet, the property is well placed, adjoining Haut-Bailly. Since 1941, it has belonged to Monsieur Guillemaud, who has done much to improve both *chais* and vineyard. For some years, he granted the *exclusivité* for the distribution of his wines to the Maison Ginestet. Originally, only red wine was made on the estate, but a small quantity of white is now also produced. These are wines that I have seldom tasted. The 1966 red is light and was still surprisingly youthful and fresh when thirteen years old. The wines of Larrivet enjoy a good reputation in their class. The average production of the red wine is 1,200 cases.

Château La Louvière

This very large property, larger even than Carbonnieux, has known fame and neglect. Today, fortunately, it seems to be firmly on an upward path. The estate borders Carbonnieux and Haut-Bailly, and consists of 62 hectares, of which 50 are at present under vine. At the heart of the property lies the magnificent château, one of the largest and finest mansions to be found in the Bordeaux region. It was built at the end of the eighteenth century by the architect Louis, who was also responsible for the theatre in Bordeaux, one of the city's finest ornaments. This was at a time when the property belonged to Monsieur J. B. Mareilhac, mayor of Bordeaux and a leading merchant of the period. Earlier, it had belonged to Jean de Guilloche, a *conseiller* of the Parlement, who in 1550 gave it to his daughter Joanne, who was mistress of both Roquetaillade and La Louvière. In the seventeenth century, it belonged to the Carthusian monks and remained their property until the Revolution. The Mareilhac family owned La Louvière until 1911, when it was bought by a company headed by Monsieur Bertrand-Tacquet, the then mayor of Léognan. Monsieur André Lurton, a member of the well-known family which owns, among other properties, Brane-Cantenac and Durfort-Vivens, was appointed administrator in the 1960s, and undertook the formidable task of reconstituting the vineyard and restoring its former reputation.

226

Now a large section of the vineyard has been planted to produce white wines, and in 1970 and 1971, wines of outstanding finesse, delicacy and fruit, light and charmingly fresh, were made as a herald of the new order. Recently, 1975 and 1978 have been outstanding. The wine is made in the modern style, intended for early drinking, and is a fine example of this; 4,000 cases of white wine are now being made. The red wine is also now well made, light and fruity, an agreeable wine which develops fairly quickly except in big years like 1970 and 1975, when the wines are rich and tannic. 1,600 cases of the red wine are made on average. Certainly this is a name to watch for the future.

Apart from the wine sold under the La Louvière label, various other names are used in conjunction with the château name; they are mostly *exclusivités* of various *négociants*. The names are: Le Vieux-Moulin, Clos-du-Roy, La Haute-Marnière, La Tourette, Le Pin-Franc, La Haute-Gravière, Coucheroy, Les Agunelles, and Les Lions.

Château Le Pape

This is one of the better-known, unclassified wines of Léognan, although the vineyard is relatively small. The château itself is particularly pleasing, built on the *chartreuse* plan, but in a very simple and classic First Empire style. The present proprietor, Monsieur Monjanel, also owns vineyards in Margaux and St Emilion. He has recently planted a portion of the vineyard with Sémillon and Sauvignon, whereas previously only red wines were made. Production is now divided between 200 cases of red wine and 300 cases of white. The red wine has a good reputation. I have not yet seen the white.

Château-Neuf

This handsome property belongs to the Caisse Primaire d'Assurance-Maladie, but Monsieur André Lurton, administrator of La Louvière, was appointed administrator in the 1960s so that the wines of Château-Neuf should be worth watching. The château itself is a handsome building in what we would call the Regency style. It has more the air of a villa in Biarritz or the Côte d'Azur than of a Bordeaux château and was obviously designed for the summer. The average production is now 350 cases each of red and white wine.

Unfortunately, the developer's hand has stretched to Léognan as well as Pessac. Among the properties to disappear, I particularly mourn Château Brown, formerly one of the largest properties of the district. The 1928 was a delectable wine which was introduced to my father by Allan Sichel around 1950. It had great vinosity and a really beautiful flavour.

Others still making wine in Léognan are:

	Red	*White*
Château de France	800 cases	550 cases
Château La Tour-Léognan	180 cases	800 cases
Domaine de Grandmaison	450 cases	450 cases
Château Haut-Bergey	500 cases	180 cases
Château Gazin	850 cases	100 cases

MARTILLAC

This is an important commune lying to the west of Léognan. Red wines are again more important than whites. Good second-rank wines are made, but they cannot be compared with the best wines of Léognan.

Château Smith-Haut-Lafitte

The most important vineyard in the commune, it belongs to the firm of Louis Eschenauer. After holding the monopoly for the vineyard for more than forty years, they finally acquired it in 1958. Until 1968, only red wine was produced, but now some 2,500 cases of white (entirely Sauvignon) are made in addition to the 17,000 cases of red wine. The production has been considerably increased and many other improvements have been made since Eschenauer bought the property outright. In 1960 less than 6 hectares were planted, by 1980 this had risen to 51 hectares.

The red wine has a good reputation as a steady, reliable wine of the second rank, comparable to a fifth growth Médoc. I have found it to be of medium weight with a characteristic bouquet and pleasant fruit, but a tendency sometimes to be rather hard at the finish—the 1961, for instance, took longer than most wines of that year to develop. This touch of austerity can sometimes make one think one is drinking a Médoc. I have not yet had an opportunity to taste the white wine. The red wine was classified in 1953.

228

Château La Tour-Martillac

This is the property of Jean Kressmann, head of the Bordeaux firm of that name, who is a great enthusiast and a most cultivated man; his property boasts probably the oldest vines still producing in Bordeaux, for part of the vineyard dates back to 1884. The average age throughout the vineyard is high and, indeed, the first wine of the property comes entirely from vines of twenty-five years or older, the production from the younger vines being reserved for the non-vintage wine—a practice which has been followed since the time of Jean Kressmann's grandfather. A part of the vineyard once belonged to Jeanne de Lartigue, the wife of the great historian and philosopher, Montesquieu, whose home was at nearby La Brède. A tower marks this part of the vineyard; dating from the Middle Ages, it is thought to have once formed part of the outer defences of the original, twelfth-century château of La Brède.

With so many old vines, the production is, of course, not large: 4,500 cases of red wine and 500 cases of white. The red wine is fine and distinctive and ages well. The white wine is most individual, very full-flavoured with a rather special character. Both appear in the Graves classification.

Château La Garde

This is another good-sized property belonging to the firm of Louis Eschenauer. It now has 46 hectares in production, compared with 15 a few years ago. Again, until recently only red wine was made, but a start has now been made in the production of white wine. La Garde is one of the better-known, unclassified wines. I have found it soft and full-flavoured on the occasions I have tasted it, and in character easily mistaken for a St Emilion. I have not seen the new white wine. 3,500 cases of red and 500 cases of white wine are made on average.

A number of other small growths exist in Martillac, but none produces more than about 20 tonneaux; most make red and white wines. The only name which is likely to appear in either Great Britain or the USA is that of Château Ferran for which the Maison Dourthe have the exclusive selling rights. It produces on average 1,000 cases of white and 100 cases of red wine.

VILLENAVE D'ORNON

This commune borders the Garonne only 9 kilometres south of Bordeaux, and touches Léognan to the south and Talence to the west. It is more famous for its white than its red wines—the only one of the important northern communes of Graves where this is the case. The white wines have real distinction and finesse.

Château Couhins

Apart from Laville-Haut-Brion, this is the only classified Graves devoted exclusively to the production of white wines—although a part of the property does make an excellent rosé, but this, of course, is not entitled to the Graves *appellation*, nor is it sold under the château name. For many years, this was the property of the Gasqueton and Hanappier families, and was then acquired by the Institut National de la Recherche Agronomique and came under the Ministry of Agriculture. In 1967, they appointed Monsieur André Lurton, who also runs La Louvière and Château-Neuf, to manage the estate. Subsequently Monsieur André Lurton purchased the property. In the days when the Gasquetons and Hanappiers ran the estate, the wine was vinified and raised in the traditional manner, and had a good deal of body, but developed in three to four years. It was a wine of breed, with an elegant bouquet and plenty of flavour. Now it enjoys a good reputation as a light wine of charm and character, very consistently made—as one would expect of Monsieur Lurton. The 1979 was typical of many new style Graves, fresh and light yet lacking the complexity of old and finally rather dull.

The château has a subsidiary name, Cantebau-Couhins, which is a monopoly of the Maison Dourthe. The wine comes from selected *cuvées* from the same vineyard; 3,000 cases of Couhins and 800 of Cantebau-Couhins are produced.

Château Baret

This is a property in the part of the commune adjoining Léognan. The vineyard dates at least from the eighteenth century, and produces 800 cases of red and 1,550 cases of white wine. The present proprietors are the Ballande family. The wine enjoys a good reputation, and on the few occasions I have come across it I

230

found the white wine, in particular, well made and really fine and attractive. The red wine is light and pleasantly fruity.

Château Pontac-Monplaisir

This is an attractive property situated in wooded country and which, during the seventeenth and eighteenth centuries, belonged to the Pontac family, when the wine was sold as Pontac-Haut-Brion. The present proprietor, Jean Maufras, runs the estate with great care, and the wines are well made and of good repute. Some 1,300 cases of red wine are made, this being of medium weight and typical of the district, but the white wine (1,800 cases) has real distinction, finesse and delicacy, yet ages well. I have particularly good memories of the 1962, which was a classic white Graves in its way.

The only other property of note in Villenave d'Ornon is Château Limbourg, also belonging to Jean Maufras and producing some 450 cases of white wine, and 500 of red.

CADAUJAC

This commune, bordering the Garonne, lies immediately to the south of Villenave-d'Ornon, with Léognan and Martillac to the west. Its fame rests on its one outstanding estate, Bouscaut. Apart from this, its wines are neither well known nor very plentiful; Château Valoux, which belongs to the proprietors of Bouscaut, makes 1,500 cases of red wine, but there are no other properties of importance in the commune.

Château Bouscaut

An impressive and beautifully kept property which lies on the main road from Bordeaux to Sauternes. Its reputation seems to have been firmly established just before and after the First World War. It produced several vintages of note in this period, especially the 1928. Then, in 1968, an American syndicate purchased it from Monsieur Victor Place, the proprietor, and Domaine Wohlstetter-Sloan became the owners. Although the estate had been well cared for, the new owners spared no effort to ensure that Bouscaut became a model property. In 1980 they sold to Monsieur Lucien Lurton, the proprietor of Brane-Cantenac.

The reputation of Bouscaut rests principally on its red wine, of which around 10,000 cases are made. The wine is not well known in England (being widely distributed in the USA), but has a good reputation as one of the better wines of the second rank of red Graves—comparable to a fourth or fifth growth Médoc. The white, of which some 1,500 cases are now made, has also been deemed worthy of classification. It is a wine in the modern style, to be drunk fresh and young.

Few of the remaining communes of Graves are of any outstanding importance by themselves, and only a handful of properties within them actually sell their wines under their château names on a regular basis. Most of the white wine is, of course, blended to produce the generic Graves and Graves Supérieur sold by every Bordeaux *négociant*. However, there are a few communes and properties which do call for some special mention.

PORTETS

Although well to the south of the Graves region and only 8 kilometres from Podensac in Cérons, this is an important commune for red as well as white wines. The red wines tend to be light, fruity and easy to drink, developing fairly quickly. They are in the category of the *Crus Bourgeois* of St Emilion.

The following growths are worth mentioning as among the best of the communes which are sometimes to be found offered under their own labels:

	Red	*White*
Château de Portets	3,250 cases	1,650 cases
Château La Tour-Bicheau	1,450 cases	800 cases
Château Doms	1,000 cases	2,600 cases
Château Millet	1,700 cases	1,550 cases
Château du Mirail	1,200 cases	1,450 cases
Château La Vieille-France	600 cases	1,450 cases
Château Bernard Raymond	950 cases	1,200 cases
Château Jean-Gervais	250 cases	3,500 cases
Château des Graves	350 cases	550 cases
Château Rahoul	2,200 cases	450 cases

PUJOLS-SUR-CIRON

This is an important commune of white wines just inland from Sauternes. These wines tend to be fairly full-bodied in style, with a notable bouquet.

The most important property is Clos Saint-Robert, which makes some 4,900 cases of white wine, and 700 of red.

SAINT-PIERRE-DE-MONS

The most important commune in that part of Graves lying to the south and east of Sauternes. It borders on the Garonne, and is only 2 kilometres from the important centre of Langon. There are some useful red wines, but the whites can be really fine. One I tasted recently, the Château des Queyrats, is one of the finest examples of the modern vinification of white Graves I have seen—finely perfumed, fresh, light and fruity. Another outstanding white is Château Magence, a very Sauvignon wine. The leading properties are as follows:

	White
Château Magence	2,450 cases
Château St Pierre ⎫	
Clos d'Uza ⎬	7,000 cases
Château Queyrats ⎭	
Château des Jaubertes	1,350 cases

Other wine-producing communes of the Graves are as follows, from north to south:

Mérignac

What with the airport and the Bordeaux suburbs, not much is left of the vineyards of this once fairly important commune.

Bègles

A very small production of red wines.

Gradignan

A very small production of red and white wines.

Isle-Saint-Georges

Red wines only are produced on alluvial soil.

233

Saint-Médard-d'Eyrans

A small production of red and white wines.

Ayguemorte-les-Graves

A moderate production of both red and white wines.

Beautiran

A fair quantity of red and white wines, but some on *palus*.

Castres

A fair quantity of red and white wines.

La Brède

Chiefly noted for its château (now visible from the autoroute), once the home of Montesquieu, the seventeenth-century French philosopher and historian. White wines are more important than the reds, and there are a number of small properties.

Arbanats

Moderate wines, a fair number of small properties making red and white wines.

Saint-Selve

A small production of red and white wines, but more white than red.

Virelade

A good quantity of both red and white wines is made.

Saucats

A very small quantity of mostly red wine is made.

Saint-Morillon

A good quantity of white wine and some red is produced.

Saint-Michel-de-Rieufret

A small quantity of red and a few white wines, all of rather ordinary quality, is made.

234

Cabanac-et-Villagrains

A moderate quantity of red and white wines, with the whites just predominating.

Landiras

A large number of small properties producing a good quantity of red and white wines, but there are more whites than reds.

Saint-Pardon-de-Conques

A small number of good wines is made, rather more red than white.

Toulenne

A fair quantity of wine is made, the reds are pleasant, ordinary wines, the whites are fine and predominate.

Langon

This is quite an important commune, for some years the scene of research work both on the selection of American root-stocks for the Cabernet Sauvignon and Merlot, and on the selection of these varieties themselves. There is a good number of fair properties, and although white wines are the most important, a fair amount of pleasant and good-quality red wines is also made.

Budos

A good quantity of red as well as white wines is produced.

Léogeats

A small quantity of red and white wines is produced—the whites have some similarity to Sauternes.

Roaillan

A moderate quantity of white and red wines is produced—the whites tend to be rather liquorous, with some similarity to Sauternes.

Mazères

Red wines of good quality and fine white wines are produced. Château de Roquetaillade is a fine medieval fortress which produces a particularly pleasant red wine.

Auros

Only a small production of full-bodied reds and whites, inclined to be liquorous.

Finally, this seems the right place to mention some of the wines made in the communes of Cérons, Illats and Podensac. While all the properties in these three communes can make a sweet white wine entitled to the Cérons *appellation*, they have the option of making Graves or Graves Supérieur for their whites, if vinified in the normal manner. Their red wines are, of course, also entitled to the Graves *appellation*. Actually, this rather odd situation in Cérons does contain a glimmer of common sense which, if more widely applied, could do much to assist Sauternes-Barsac growers with some of their present problems. Thus the growers of Cérons have a choice: if conditions are favourable, they can select grapes infected by noble rot and make a wine in exactly the same way as in Sauternes. A good Cérons is very similar to a Barsac. Or they can pick when the grapes are just ripe, and make a Graves without any financial sacrifice. But the poor Sauternes grower must make either Sauternes or Bordeaux Blanc—a much cheaper wine. There is no logical reason why he too should not have the right to call his dry wine Graves, or why a Cérons should not benefit from the Sauternes *appellation*.

While many of these wines find their way into generic blends, there are several good growths which have found their way on to export markets.

CÉRONS

Château de Calvimont

The proprietor, Monsieur Jean Perromat, has for many years been the president of the INAO. The average production is 3,600 cases.

Château Lamouroux

The average production is 2,000 cases.

Château du Peyrat

The average production is 1,900 cases.

ILLATS

Château Archambeau

The proprietor is Docteur Jean Dubourdieu, a member of the well-known Barsac family, who nevertheless here makes an excellent, dry Graves. A very good second wine is sold under the name of Château Mowrlet. The average production is 3,000 cases.

PODENSAC

Clos Chantegrive and Château le Bon-Dieu-des-Vignes

The proprietor, Monsieur Lévêque, is a well-known local *courtier*. The average production is 4,500 cases of white wine, and 2,150 of red.

St Emilion, Pomerol, Fronsac, Bourg and Blaye

8

St Emilion

Although the history of the St Emilion vineyards is an ancient and honourable one, it is only in recent years that they have come to receive their just due. The reasons for the late development of their estates and the prejudice against their wines in the Bordeaux trade are long and complex, and deserve a separate study of their own. The main lines, however, seem fairly clear.

In the Middle Ages, the region was important largely because Libourne had some standing both as a port and as an English outpost. In 1199, the original Jurade of St Emilion received its charter from King John, but Libourne's development did not keep pace with that of Bordeaux, and it was in any case much more exposed to sorties from the French. By the eighteenth century, the city of Bordeaux was clearly established as the commerical as well as the administrative centre of the whole region. What merchants there were in Libourne were of strictly local importance. When the *noblesse de robe*, the provincial establishment of the *ancien régime*, looked for estates, they turned naturally to the Médoc and Graves. St Emilion was too far away and many vineyards, in any case, belonged to the Church. In the early and formative years of the nineteenth century, when wealthy Bordeaux merchants were developing the Médoc, St Emilion seemed a remote rural back-water with its many small properties and farms, as compared with the Médoc grand estates. So it was, not surprisingly, neglected at this period, failing to benefit from this time of rapid growth in the promotion of the Médoc. When the wines to represent Bordeaux at the 1855 Exhibition were chosen, St Emilion was excluded; no one in Bordeaux would then have thought of these humble country cousins as the equals of the aristocrats of the Médoc. In addition, the *courtiers* who made up the list were, of course,

Médoc-orientated. Even today you will not find a Médoc *courtier* who deals with St Emilion wines. St Emilion and Pomerol have their own *courtiers* for their own wines.

The recognition of St Emilion wines has not come rapidly or easily. In 1867, a selection of leading growths represented the region at the Paris Exhibition, as a counterblast to their total omission in 1855, and collectively they won a gold medal. But it was not until this century that anyone began to think of Ausone in terms of the first growths of the Médoc, and not until the famous 1921 that Cheval Blanc was thought capable of joining it. Even then their prices remained well below those of the Médoc until the claret revival of the 1950s.

When I first went to Bordeaux in the early 1950s, the leading Bordeaux merchants still tended to be rather patronizing when speaking of St Emilion, and there was surprise amounting almost to indignation if any St Emilion proprietor suggested that his wine should merit the same price as a leading classified growth Médoc. The attitude of Médoc proprietors themselves was quite simply that, since St Emilions could not be compared to Médocs and were certainly never as fine, it was an imposition to be asked to pay high prices for such wines. This attitude has died hard, and while wine drinkers in France, and especially in Belgium, have for many years eagerly sought out and paid high prices for the leading St Emilions, some English merchants have continued to reflect the traditional Bordeaux-Médoc view, and this is still apparent from many wine lists—especially in hotels and restaurants.

The physical aspects of the region are in marked contrast to the Médoc in almost every way. In area, it is small and compact, but very intensely cultivated, so that its production often rivals that of the Médoc (see Appendix VI). It is also hilly and rocky, with many remains from the Gallo-Roman period. With its numerous small properties, mostly run by working resident proprietors, it is no easy matter for the uninitiated to find their way about, and I have known more people get lost in St Emilion and Pomerol than in any other part of Bordeaux.

The town of St Emilion itself is certainly the most attractive regional centre in the Gironde. The ancient city ramparts are still preserved in part; there is the Monolithic Church dating from the ninth century, with its bell tower rising up surprisingly in one corner of the main square, as well as the fine medieval collegiate church. The main square is the best vantage point from which to see the small, cramped, medieval town. It boasts both the Plaisance, the principal restaurant, with a fine terrace overlooking the town, and the more modest but more homely Chez Germaine. From the terrace of the Plaisance one can see the entrance to the Monolithic Church below, as well as the tiny chapel built above the cave or hermitage of St Emilion, the hermit who gave the town his name. Further off, across steep roofs of ancient, mellowed tiles is the Château du Roi, a narrow medieval keep, and then the vineyards seem to spring out of the town on every side.

One of the features of the district is the magnificent caves which are frequently used instead of a *chais*. Originally constructed when quarrying stone for building, some are extremely ancient. Among the finest are those at Clos Fourtet, Ausone and Belair, close to the town, and at Pavie, only a little further off. They are, of course, much cooler than the *chais* of the Médoc, and the damp usually makes it impossible to keep the casks free of mould, so that some extra vigilance is required to ensure that the wine remains untainted. On the other hand, the lower temperature safeguards the wine, especially in hot summers. This limestone is also of prime importance to the vineyards, because in winter it soaks up water like a sponge, providing moisture for the vines during dry summer spells. This is why the best St Emilion growths of the Côtes do so well in dry years compared to the Médoc.

A most important feature of the district is its distinctive *encépagement*. Whereas in the Médoc and Graves the Cabernet Sauvignon is recognized as the most important variety, here it is the Cabernet Franc (called the Bouchet locally) and the Merlot. The disastrous frost of February 1956 did far more serious damage here than elsewhere, and after this much more Merlot was planted. It now seems to be recognized, however, that this movement has gone far enough, and there is a tendency to balance the Merlot with Cabernet Franc in new plantings. It was also as a result of the rot problems of the Merlot that the INAO actively encouraged growers in the 1960s to plant Cabernet Sauvignon. The experiment has not been very successful as this vine has proved less suited to the cooler soils of St Emilion, with its limestone substrata, and even less so to those of Pomerol with its higher clay content. The Merlot weakness to rot in damp weather caused 1963, 1965 and 1968 to be even more disastrous in St

Emilion and Pomerol than elsewhere. This problem has now largely been overcome by new sprays. The Malbec (here called the Pressac) is also more widely found than in the Médoc.

The wines of St Emilion are generally characterized by their marked richness and suppleness. They are naturally richer in alcohol than other Bordeaux wines, usually between 12 and 14 per cent, so that although they have less tannin than Médocs, their marked vinosity and balance, combined with their natural alcoholic strength, enables them to develop early and then to live and flourish for thirty or even forty years. Often in the past, when Médocs have been spoiled by excessive tannin, St Emilions have continued to be fresh and delicious when their cousins have become mean and leathery—1928 and 1945 were good examples of this.

St Emilion wines are often said to lack finesse, yet their flavour is complex and varied. It is true that they have an immediate appeal which makes them the most readily appreciated among Bordeaux wines. They are sometimes compared to Burgundy and certainly have a similar warmth and vinosity. All these excellent qualities are often quoted to praise and yet disparage. Yet I have often been struck by their consistency compared to Médocs. They seem to stay on form with reassuring regularity, while one is often dismayed to find that a fine Médoc growth, which was tasting beautifully six months before, is edgy and disappointing when wheeled out for some important occasion. Such flights of temperament seem foreign to St Emilion.

The most positive qualities of the St Emilion wines, to my way of thinking, are their superb fruit on both nose and palate, that certain hint of the exotic on the nose of many of the finest growths, an outstanding vinosity, sometimes almost approaching unctuousness, and a ripeness and mellowness of flavour which warms the heart on dull days, yet seems fresh and cool on a summer day. How elusive are such flavours to the pedestrian pen; it is easy to see why those who write in praise of wine are often accused of whimsy. It would need a poet's pen to recall such sensations.

A key word in the description of St Emilion, as of all great wines, is balance. The fruit and vinosity are devoid of any hint of the soft-centred or flabby. There is just enough tannin and acidity, yet it is one of the pleasures of St Emilion that one is rarely aware of their presence. It is for this reason that the wines develop more rapidly than Médoc or Graves, usually being ready to drink in anything from two (for a *Bourgeois* growth) to four years (for a classified growth) earlier than similar wines across the river. Yet their keeping qualities, as has already been said, are excellent.

St Emilion is subdivided into a number of areas producing differing styles and qualities. Firstly, there is the area of the St Emilion *appellation*. This was defined in 1936 and exactly corresponds to the traditional area administered by the Jurade in the Middle Ages, consisting of eight communes: St Emilion, St Christophe des Gardes, St Etienne de Lisse, St Hippolyte, St Laurent des Combes, St Pey d'Armens, St Sulpice de Faleyrens, and Vignoiret. Then there are the so-called St Emilion satellites, originally six in number: Sables, Lussac, Montagne, St Georges, Puisseguin and Parsac, each of which hyphenates its name with that of St Emilion—thus, for example, St Georges-St Emilion. These six parishes all sold their wines as St Emilion prior to the delineation of the *appellation* in 1936, when they were each granted their own *appellation*, retained their right to use the name of St Emilion, but were obliged to hyphenate it with their own parish names. In 1973, the growers of Parsac were given the option of declaring their wines as Puisseguin. A few loyalists lingered on, but the declarations in 1973 and 1974 fell to a few hundred hectolitres, and in 1975 the *appellation* disappeared. The even smaller *appellation* of Sables disappeared at a single sweep of the pen, the last declarations being those of the 1973 vintage.

In practice, this division of the region owes more to tradition and parish boundaries than it does to logic and differing qualities and styles. Within the St Emilion *appellation* proper, nearly all the best wines are produced within the commune of St Emilion itself. Thus, when the INAO classification was first drawn up in 1955, only one of the sixty-three *Grands Crus Classés* came from outside the commune of St Emilion itself, namely Château Larcis-Ducasse in St Laurent des Combes. For the most part, these other seven communes within the St Emilion *appellation* produce wines which are nearer in quality to the wines produced by the six St Emilion satellites than to those produced in the commune of St Emilion itself. The *appellation* thus unduly favours these wines, while placing the satellites at a disadvantage. From a marketing and selling point of view, it is a disadvantage to divide the satellites into four different *appellations* with no opportunity of

243

GRANDS CRUS CLASSÉS
DE ST EMILION

Premiers Grands Crus Classés

Ausone	H. Dubois-Challon - H[tiers] Vauthier
Cheval-Blanc	Fourcaud-Laussac
Beauséjour	Bécot
Beauséjour	Duffau Lagarrosse
Belair	Dubois-Challon
Canon	Fournier
Clos Fourtet	Lurton
Figeac	Manoncourt
La Gaffelière	De Malet-Roquefort
Magdelaine	J. P. Moueix
Pavie	Valette
Trottevieille	Borie Manoux

Grands Crus Classés

L'Angélus	De Bouard
L'Arrosée	Rodhain
Balestard la Tonnelle	J. Capdemourlin
Bellevue	Société Civile
Bergat	J. Bertin
Cadet-Bon	Gratadour
Cadet-Piola	Jabiol
Canon-la-Gaffelière	De Neipperg
Cap de Mourlin	J. Capdemourlin
Cap de Mourlin	J. Capdemourlin
Chapelle-Madeleine	H. Dubois-Challon - H[tiers] Vauthier
Chauvin	Ondet
Corbin	Giraud
Corbin-Michotte	Boidron
Côte Baleau	Société Civile
Coutet	David-Beaulieu
Couvent des Jacobins	Joinaud Borde
Croque-Michotte	Géoffrion-Rigal
Curé-Bon	Landé
Dassault	Dassault
Faurie-de-Souchard	Jabiol
Fonplegade	Moueix
Fonroque	Moueix
Franc-Mayne	Theillassoubre
Gd-Barrail-Lamarzelle-Figeac	Carrère
Gd-Corbin-Despagne	Despagne
Grand-Corbin	Giraud

Grands Crus Classés

Grand-Mayne	Nony
Grand-Pontet	Barton-Guestier
Grandes-Murailles	Société Civile
Guadet-St-Julien	R. Lignac
Haut-Corbin	Guinaudie
Haut-Sarpe	Janoueix
Jean-Faure	M. Amart
Clos des Jacobins	Cordier
Clos la Madeleine	H. Pistouley
Clos St-Martin	Société Civile
La Carte	Bécot-Berjal
La Clotte	Chaillot
La Clusière	Valette
La Couspaude	E. Aubert
La Dominique	Fayat
Laniote	Freymont Roujat
Larcis-Ducasse	H. Gratiot
Lamarzelle	Carrère
Larmande	Meneret
Laroze	Melin-Gurchy
La Serre	L. d'Arfeuille
La Tour-du-Pin-Figeac	Giraud-Bélivier
La Tour-du-Pin-Figeac	Moueix
La Tour Figeac	Société Civile
Le Chatelet	Berjal
Le Couvent	Galhaud
Le Prieuré	Guichard
Matras	Bernard-Lefèbvre
Mauvezin	P. Cassat
Moulin-du-Cadet	Fagouet-Moueix
L'oratoire	Société Civile
Pavie-Decesse	Valette
Pavie-Macquin	F. Corre
Pavillon-Cadet	Le Morvan
Pᵗ-Faurie-de-Soutard	Capdemourlin-Aberlen
Ripeau	M. Janoueix
Sansonnet	Robin
St-Georges-Côte-Pavie	Masson-Charoulet
Soutard	De Ligneris
Tertre-Daugay	De Malet-Roquefort
Trimoulet	P. Jean
Trois-Moulins	Gauthier
Troplong-Mondot	Valette
Villemaurine	Giraud
Yon-Figeac	Lussiez

putting neighbouring wines of similar quality and style together. It would certainly be preferable to group the four together under a general *appellation* such as St Emilion Villages. Some recognition of this viewpoint was shown when the wines of Parsac were given permission to be grouped with those of Puisseguin. It is interesting to note that in neighbouring Pomerol, since permission was given to sell the wines of Néac as Lalande-de-Pomerol, the latter *appellation* is almost universally used and preferred by the growers of this Pomerol satellite.

On the other hand, within the commune of St Emilion itself, there is a useful distinction to be drawn between the wines of the Côtes and of the Graves. The Côtes are the hillsides, often steep, with outcrops of rock, which surround the town of St Emilion. The Graves is a sandy, gravelly plateau which adjoins the plateau of Pomerol and closely resembles it. The finest wines of the Côtes, typified by Ausone, Canon, Magdelaine and Belair, have great breed and a delicacy which quickly develops. In all but the greatest years, they are lighter in body as well as in colour than lesser St Emilions and develop an extremely characteristic perfumed bouquet and a long, lingering flavour, powerful yet delicate, very harmonious and original, and essentially very attractive. In contrast, the wines of the Graves, typified by Cheval Blanc and Figeac, are richer and more unctuous, almost overpowering in bouquet and flavour when young, distinctly fleshy in texture, and only developing finesse after some ageing. But with these wines it is the voluptuous exaggeration of youth which is perhaps their most characteristic and appealing trait, the sheer animal vigour and confident swagger which demands that they be judged on their own terms. Again, it is soil that singles out Cheval Blanc and Figeac. They have a high proportion of gravel in their vineyards, in contrast to the sandier soils elsewhere in the district. It should be remarked that among the wines classified as Côtes are a number of growths, including some *Grand Crus Classés*, which lie on flatter, richer, sandier soil and produce heavier and sometimes firmer, denser wines of markedly less finesse and breed than the leading growths of the Côtes.

I have dealt with the St Emilion classification in some detail separately (see Chapter 3). It will suffice to say here that while there is some inequality among the top twelve wines classified as *Premiers Grands Crus Classés*, so that some consistently command higher prices than others, all are none the less indisputably wines of breed and class, worthy standard-bearers for all that is best in St Emilion. The sixty-three (subsequently increased to seventy) *Grands Crus Classés*, however, include wines of widely different qualities, some approaching or rivalling the *Premiers Grands Crus* in finesse and breed or power and beauty, while others are distinctly coarser and more rustic. But where questions of taste (in both senses of the word) are concerned, a unanimous or consistent point of view is hardly to be expected.

ST EMILION—CÔTES

PREMIERS GRAND CRUS CLASSÉS

It should be noted that these wines are not entitled to this classification without a tasting. This means that if the tasting commission deems a wine not to be worthy of the *appellation Premier Grand Cru* in a particular year, this cannot appear on the label, so that instances may be found where one of these wines is only described as *Grand Cru Classé*.

Château Ausone

This is one of the oldest and most famous properties in Bordeaux, in spite of its very small production. The small steep-roofed château is only nineteenth-century, but according to tradition it stands on the site of the villa of the Roman poet Ausonius, just outside the town of St Emilion. The greatness of Ausone is due to a combination of soil and exposure. The soil is a mixture of clay and sand on limestone that is unique in the district, planted with old vines. No replanting took place between 1950 and 1976. The vines are almost equally divided between Merlot and Cabernet Franc. The situation of the vineyard is ideal, with steep slopes arranged like an amphitheatre, facing south-east, and so providing a perfect exposure and the maximum protection from adverse winds. The ownership of the property has rested in the same family since the Revolution, from Monsieur Cantenac to Madame Lafargue, and through her nephews to the Dubois-Challon and Vauthier families. Ausone shared its *chais* with Belair until 1976. It is a cave cut into the hillside close by the château, under a cemetery, and reminds one more of Vouvray and Touraine than Bordeaux.

Ausone only moved ahead of other St Emilions in general estimation during the last decade of the nineteenth century, and there is a note in the 6th edition of Cocks and Féret (1898) explaining that Ausone had for the first time been placed above Belair because of the superior prices it had been obtaining, but that this did not indicate that there had been any decline in the fortune of Belair. This position was well consolidated by the 1920s, by which time Ausone's special position had penetrated even the British consciousness with its Médoc bias. Colonel Campbell recalls the excellence of the 1904 and 1905, the earliest Ausones he tasted—he never saw the wine during his stay in Bordeaux in the early 1890s!

It has to be confessed that of all the first growths today, Ausone has passed through the most disappointing period between 1945 and 1974. Yet anyone fortunate enough to have drunk any of the great pre-war vintages will know that Ausone is potentially one of the finest of all the great clarets. I have enjoyed and marvelled at the seemingly timeless beauty of the 1928, and the vigour of the 1934 and 1937, but Madame Dubois-Challon has in her cellars vintages from well back into the last century, which are said to be in marvellous condition. What then went awry?

All one can say for certain is that the wine for many years seemed too light and lacking in vigour. The colour was very light from the start and quickly went brown, the bouquet was certainly perfumed and had great finesse, but the wine developed very rapidly and seemed to lack the power of other leading St Emilions. What the reason for this was, is hard to say. One always suspected that it came down to management, and this seems to have been confirmed by recent events. The firm of J. P. Moueix have long had an association with Ausone in the sense that they purchase half the crop. So when a new *régisseur* was required, it was natural that they should offer assistance. It was Monsieur Christian Moueix, with his very recent, first-hand experience of running their own estates—including Pétrus—who seems to have found just the right man, in Pascal Delbeck. The result has been immediate and startling. The 1975 is a remarkable wine which promises to take one straight back to the glory of the pre-war vintages. Certainly it is a serious rival to Cheval Blanc and Pétrus itself. This has been followed by very fine wines in 1976, 1978, and a great 1979. Around 2,800 cases are now produced in a normal year.

Of post-war vintages, the 1953 was very attractive but very lightweight, the 1962 was one of the most successful and promises a longer development than most (the first occasion when Ausone was clearly superior to Cheval Blanc since the war); the 1964 and 1971 were also good.

Château Belair

This is a close neighbour of Ausone and hardly less ancient in origin or less famous for the excellence of its wines. Like Ausone, the property is said to have belonged to Ausonius, but its real history begins during the period of English rule. In the fourteenth century it belonged to Robert de Knolles, who was grand seneschal and governor of Guyenne. When the region was finally reconquered by Charles VII, the descendants of Robert de Knolles returned, their name changed to Canolle, and the property remained in the family until the Revolution, after which it was again restored to them. In 1916, it was acquired by the Dubois-Challon family, the owners of Ausone. The wines of Belair are now once more kept in their own ancient caves. The vineyard comprises 13 hectares, half on the Côtes and half on a plateau above the château, and adjoins Ausone, sharing its fine exposure and producing around 4,000 cases in a good vintage. It is this portion of the vineyard, on the plateau adjoining Canon, which is responsible for the difference in emphasis between Belair and Ausone. Merlot accounts for 60 to 65 per cent of the vineyard, the rest being Cabernet Franc. At present (1980) the average yield is only 22 hectos per hectare, due to old vines, and it will take some years to restore a proper rotation to the vineyard.

The reputation of Belair has always been high. Indeed, at one time in the nineteenth century it was more highly esteemed among the wines of the St Emilion Côtes than Ausone. Today, it deserves its place as one of the leading growths of the region. Its wines have more richness than Ausone, combined with great finesse, in some years a touch of hardness, but are usually suave and supple. The 1945 was a great success, being vigorous and powerful, and I have especially good memories of the 1955. The 1961 is enormous and magnificent, the 1962 and 1966 are supple and fine. Recently the 1975 appears too tannic, the 1976 attractive but soft and forward, the 1978 really fine and concentrated, the 1979 exceptional. Now it is sharing in the renaissance experienced at Ausone. As soon as the 1980 vintage was safely made, the old fermentation vats were removed and a battery of stainless steel vats, of varying sizes to fit into the cramped corners of the caves which house them, were installed. In 1981, in a new departure for Belair, a new marque, 'Roc-Blanquant', was bottled for the first time. It is a blend of vintages of wines that have been excluded from the *grand vin*. The wine has been bottled only in magnums and will not pass through the normal channels of distribution but rather will be sold direct by the Château.

Château Beauséjour (Daffau-Lagarrosse)

Like most of the *Premiers Grands Crus* of the Côtes, Beauséjour is situated just outside the old ramparts of St Emilion. The growth of Beauséjour was a single property until 1869, when the proprietor, Monsieur Ducarpe, divided it between his two children. His daughter married Docteur Duffau-Lagarrosse, a medical practitioner of St Emilion, and the property now belongs to their heirs. Much of the wine is sold direct to private customers.

The wine has breed, delicacy and charm; it is light and perfumed, with a tendency to firmness, but was perhaps somewhat fortunate to be classified as a *Premier Grand Cru* in 1955. This owed as much, perhaps, to the situation of its vineyard as to the wine, which is fine but not outstanding. There are several wines classified as *Grand Crus* which are just as good. The average production is 2,000 cases from only 7 hectares of vineyard. The 1955 was particularly good, while 1978 and 1979 are good examples of these years.

Château Beau Séjour (Bécot—formerly Fagouet)

The property now of Monsieur Michel Bécot, assisted by his sons Gerard and Dominique, the history of which is to be found above under Beauséjour (Duffau-Lagarosse). This part of the property consists of 16 hectares, mostly on steep slopes, producing on average 7,000 cases. The vineyard is planted with 70 per cent Merlot, the rest divided between Carbernet Franc and some Carbernet Sauvignon. The style of the wine is now in marked contrast to the other Beauséjour, being fuller bodied, less tannic and almost plummy. A fine 1928 has lasted well, the 1945 is ripe and powerful, not too tannic. More recently, the 1973 is delicious, marked by *surmaturité*, 1976 attractive if lightweight, 1978 perfumed, rich and concentrated, 1979 again most successful.

Château Canon

The château is situated just outside the old town. It has more the appearance and air of a château than most of its neighbours, with an impressive entrance and castellated towers. There is a vineyard of 20 hectares, all on the plateau above the Côtes, producing around 9,000 cases. There are 53 per cent Merlot and 45 per cent Cabernet Franc, the rest Cabernet Sauvignon. For some years the château has prospered, first under the meticulous management of Madame Fournier, now under her grandson Eric.

The wine has long enjoyed a high reputation and deservedly so. The 1929 won great fame as the best wine on the Right Bank, and was still superlative in 1980. When I had the opportunity of trying a bottle of 1933 when it was nearly forty years old, it was still fresh and delicious, although of course light. More recently, the 1947 was magnificent, the 1953 delicate—just beginning to fade in 1980, the 1959 big and powerful if a little dry, and 1964 was rich and supple, the 1966 really fine, a lovely 1976, and exceptional wines in 1978 and 1979 which really show the great breed of this growth. The wines of Canon are sometimes a little hard to begin with, but this cloak of tannin soon drops to reveal a wine which is supple and powerful, of exceptional quality, certainly one of the top growths of the Côtes.

Clos Fourtet

This famous property is situated immediately opposite the main entrance to the old town of St Emilion, just in front of the parish church of St Martin. The actual château is no more than a rather modest stone house with some fine eighteenth-century features, but the cellars are among the finest to be seen in the region, extending in long galleries for a considerable distance under the vineyard, which itself surrounds the château. The wine has for some time been one of the best-known St Emilions, perhaps assisted by the fact that it belonged to the Ginestet family until just after the war, so that the wine was more on the general Bordeaux market than many other St Emilions. The Ginestets then sold it to Monsieur François Lurton at the time when they bought control of Château Margaux. Dominique Lurton is the member of the family currently in charge.

The vineyard is interesting in that it has a much higher percentage of Cabernet Sauvignon and Franc ('Bouchet' here in St Emilion) than is usual, 25 per cent of each, the other 50 per cent being Merlot. This makes the wine much firmer and slower to develop than most St Emilions, but when mature, it has great depth and suppleness, and is very long-lived. I had a bottle of 1917 when it was fifty years old, and the wine was fresh and well-preserved, charming and supple. The 1923 was one of the loveliest examples of this year that I have ever tasted, silky and sweet at the finish, and still fresh when over forty years old and when most 1923s were over the top. But my first memory of Clos Fourtet is of the 1940 which my father had as a 'concession wine' after the war. When around ten years old, it was quite delicious and, to my surprise, when another bottle came my way twenty years later, it was still in excellent form and had not faded, although it had lost some punch. In the 1950s and early 1960s, the château went through a disappointing phase; the wines seemed green and mean, lacking fruit and flesh, but the 1961 heralded a return to its old form, and after a stubborn 1962, the 1964 is really fine, and the 1966 followed up the good work. Improvements to the *cuvier* in the early 1970s have resulted in further progress. The 1979 is exceptionally attractive for the year. 1976 is rather overblown, but both 1978 and 1979 have real breed and suppleness. The average production is around 6,700 cases from 18 hectares.

Château la Gaffelière

The actual château buildings at Gaffelière are older and more interesting than those of most of its neighbours. The oldest part goes back to the eleventh-century, there is an eighteenth-century wing, the whole encased in a nineteenth-century copy of the marvellous *logis de Malet-Roquefort*, still to be found in the walls of St Emilion. It has belonged to the family of the Comtes de Malet-Roquefort for over three centuries, a record unique in St Emilion. The building stands on the site of a medieval leper house, and it is from this that the name of Gaffelière derives. Curiously, however, the growth was entered as Puygenestou-Naudes in early editions of Cocks & Féret, and it was not until 1898 that it was to appear under its more familiar name. One point should be cleared up right away. This growth was known as la Gaffelière-Naudes, which name appeared on all its labels until the 1964 vintage, when the Naudes was dropped in the interests of simplicity and clarity.

The château and *chais*, which is of the conventional type, lie in a small valley a little way outside St Emilion, with the vineyard on the lower hillsides of the Côtes each side of the valley. After Pavie, it is the largest of the *Premiers Grands Crus* in the Côtes, with 21 hectares planted with 65 per cent Merlot, 25 per cent Cabernet Franc and 10 per cent Cabernet Sauvignon, and an average production of around 9,400 cases. Like other St Emilion properties, the experience with Cabernet Sauvignon has not been a happy one, and it is gradually being replaced. It is probably in the last twenty years or so that the wines of Gaffelière have come to be as well known and appreciated as they deserve to be in England. They are fuller and more fleshy than most other wines of the Côtes, without quite the breed of the top growths perhaps, but with a most distinctive savour, a deep colour and generous bouquet, which quickly develops a flavour of great charm, powerful yet subtle and complex. In 1974, stainless-steel vats were installed in the cuvier, and this has improved the control of the vinification. Gaffelière made one of the great 1945s, still superb in 1980, but it was the 1953 which was probably the first vintage to win this growth a real reputation among the English trade, and this has been followed by many other fine vintages, among which the 1966, 1970, 1971 and 1976 are especially typical. Recently, the 1978 is rather light, but the 1979 has real promise.

Château Magdelaine

For over two hundred years, the property belonged to the Chatonnet family, until acquired in 1953 by Monsieur Jean-Pierre Moueix. It is situated close to the town of St Emilion and adjoins Belair on one side. Here, the hillside gives way to a small plateau above the Dordogne, and 5 hectares are on the Côtes, 6 on the plateau above. Unusually, as much as 80 per cent is planted with Merlot, the rest with Cabernet Franc. The average age of the vines is thirty years. Due to its small production—on average not more than 3,700 cases are made from 11 hectares of vineyards—this fine growth is not as well known as it deserves to be. But under the loving care of Monsieur Moueix, who has done so much to spread the fame of St Emilion and Pomerol through England and the USA, the reputation of the wine has spread further afield. It is clear, however, that Magdelaine has long enjoyed a reputation as one of the finest St Emilions. The 7th edition of Cocks & Féret (1898) speaks in glowing terms of the wine, 'brilliant and velvety, strong but incomparably delicate, with an exquisite bouquet'. It was already famed for its keeping qualities, the 1865 and 'even the 1858' were still preserved at the château, still full of freshness and vigour.

Since 1962 I have seen the wine in every vintage, and only in the disastrous years of 1963, 1965 and 1968 or the mediocre ones of 1969, 1972 and 1974 did it fail to produce with wonderful consistency wines of great breed and distinction. The bouquet, which develops quickly, has great finesse and breed and is delicately perfumed. The colour is brilliant, never very deep, but not too light, as Ausone and Belair are on occasion. The flavour is unfailingly flattering and charming, always the aristocrat, well-balanced, with just enough generosity but great delicacy and length on the palate. The years 1962, 1964, 1966, 1967, 1970, 1971, 1973, 1975, 1976, 1977, 1978 and 1979 are all worthy examples of their vintages and of the best of St Emilion. In the more difficult years of 1969, 1972 and 1974, honourable wines, above the general level of the year, were made, but they lack the personality and breed of a really good Magdelaine. Unfortunately production is so small that the circle of friends that Magdelaine has already won must of necessity remain strictly limited.

Château Pavie

This property as it now exists owes much to the labours of Monsieur François Bouffard; it now belongs to the Vallette family, and Jean-Paul Vallette is the man in charge. With its production of around 16,200 cases, Pavie is easily the largest of the *Premiers Grands Crus* as well as being rather larger than any of the *Grand Crus Classés*. It lies a little beyond the other *Premiers Grands Crus* on a long, gently sloping hillside, capped with a rocky outcrop. Into the cliff face of this hilltop are tunnelled out the extensive caves where the wines of Pavie are kept. There are 22 hectares of vines on this coteau facing due south, 7 hectares at the foot of the coteau, and 8 hectares on the more sandy plain. It is for this reason that Pavie, for all its charm, is not among the top wines of the Côtes.

254

Because of its large production, Pavie was frequently in the past shipped to England in bulk for UK bottling, and so the wine was taken out of the Pavie caves to be stored in the *négociants'* cellars for *élevage* prior to shipment. On several occasions I had the opportunity to observe the difference in the development of such wines stored in a normal Bordeaux *chais* as against those kept in the caves of Pavie, and it was interesting to see how the cooler temperature in the caves slowed down the development and seemed to keep the wine fresher. I have also noticed, however, that this advantage was sometimes dissipated by the château's bottling too late so that when the château-bottled and English-bottled wines of the same vintage were subsequently compared, the château-bottled example seemed parched and lacking fruit compared with the wine bottled in England; which shows that the timing of the bottling can be just as critical as its *élevage*.

Pavie has long enjoyed a reputation in England, though this is not as high, it should be said, as some of the other *Premiers Grands Crus*. At its best, the wine is very supple, elegant and charming, usually quick to develop. However, in some years it can be rather hard, and too much alcohol seems to rob it of its customary finesse and charm. It must be confessed that the wine has not been as consistent in recent years as it should be. The 1961 was attractive but quick developing, a fine 1970 was made, while 1971 was dense and rich, but the 1975 seems to lack the power of that year. The 1976 is charming but very forward, 1978 is finer, and 1979 promises even better things. Professor Peynaud is now advising here.

Château Trottevieille

This growth lies on a small hillside somewhat away from the other *Premiers Grands Crus*, just to the east of the town. What the wine lacks in delicacy is compensated for in generosity and vigour. Although the situation of the property differs from the other growths, there is no doubting the quality of the wines produced. The property was acquired in 1949 by Monsieur Marcel Borie, then head of the firm Borie-Manoux, and I first came across the wine, as did many Englishmen, I suspect, during the late 1950s when Monsieur Borie first began selling his wines in England on a direct basis.

The wine has something of the roundness and body of the wines of the Graves, but with a bouquet and finesse reminiscent of the Côtes. It is fleshy in the same way as Gaffelière, yet the style is distinctly different. I once tasted the 1943 in Bordeaux and it was very fine and most distinguished. After that, the 1952, 1955, 1959, 1961, 1962, 1964 and 1966 were all very successful and often outstanding examples of their vintage. Recently I have found 1970 powerful and forward, 1976 and 1978 rather lightweight, and 1979 big and strong flavoured. The property, which produces 4,000 cases on average, is now administered by Monsieur Emile Castéja on behalf of the firm of Borie-Monoux. It is worth mentioning that the label is in the traditional black and gold, once very popular in Bordeaux.

GRANDS CRUS CLASSÉS

It does not seem practical to write in detail on all seventy of these wines. Some have a very small production, and many have specialized markets and are hardly seen outside France and Belgium. I have certainly not been able to visit or taste them all. I am, however, listing all the wines in the classification in alphabetical order, as they appear in the classification.

As with the *Premiers Grands Crus Classés*, these growths have to be confirmed by tasting in every vintage, and this did much to dissuade proprietors from following the example of some Médoc proprietors in offering unworthy wines in years such as 1963, 1965 and 1968.

Château l'Angélus

This is one of the largest and most important growths of the Côtes, with an average production of around 12,750 cases. The proprietors, the de Bouard de Laforest family, acquired the property in 1924 and are responsible for enlarging the vineyard to its present size by judicious acquisition. Helped by the size of its production and its distinctive name, it has become well known on export markets. The wine is typically St Emilion, full and generous.

Château l'Arrosée

This is the property of the Rodhain family, with an average production of 12,750 cases. It is an old, established growth, being one of the twenty-nine growths mentioned in the list of 1859 at the St Emilion Maire, but it is not widely known on export markets.

Château Baleau

This is one of the eight growths added to the list of *Grands Crus* in 1969. The production is 6,800 cases and the growth is under the same ownership as Grandes-Murailles, a very small *Grand Cru*. It is not a wine I have ever come across.

Château Balestard—La Tonnelle

This is one of the most ancient growths of St Emilion, owned by one of the oldest families of wine growers. The wine has the unusual distinction of being mentioned in a poem of the fifteenth century by François Villon (1421–85), where the poet speaks of: 'ce divin nectar, qui porte nom de Balestard'. The proprietors, the Capdemourlin family, have been wine growers in St Emilion for no less than five centuries—a remarkable record. The curious name owes its origin to the insignia of the *chapitre* of St Emilion (Balestard), while Tonnelle refers to an old tower which has always stood in the vineyard.

This is the big, strong, full-bodied, uncomplicated style of St Emilion, not outstanding for finesse or breed, but consistent and robust—a very much sought-after style. The 1947 was still superb when tasted in 1980. The average production is around 3,400 cases.

Château Bellevue

This has the misfortune of bearing one of the commonest names in the Gironde. The 12th edition of Cocks & Féret reveals no fewer than twenty-three properties at present using this name, and several of these are in the St Emilion region. This property, formerly known as Fief de Bellevue, belonged to the Lacaze family from 1642 to 1938, when it passed to cousins, one of whom, Louis Horeau, is now the administrator. Gaston Lacaze was well known as a leading Girondin during the French Revolution, and sought refuge here when the Girondins were proscribed by the Jacobins. The average production is around 3,000 cases.

Château Bergat

The property of Colonel Bertin, this is one of the smallest *Grands*

Crus, producing only 1,700 cases. The management and distribution are in the hands of the Bordeaux firm of Borie-Manoux.

Château Cadet-Bon

The average production is only 850 cases. The vineyard is adorned by the tower of a fifteenth-century windmill. The proprietor is Monsieur Gratadour.

Château Cadet-Piola

This is a wine which is graced by one of the most charming, if unusual, of claret labels. The property produces 6,400 cases, and the proprietor is Monsieur Jabiol. The *caves* quarried into the rock act as a *chais*. The first vintage I came across was the 1959, which began by being rather firm, and then unaccountably went to pieces. However, the 1964 was much better, concentrated if rather lean. Because of the position of its vineyard, this is a growth of real potential.

Château Canon-la-Gaffelière

An important growth in terms of size, quality and reputation. The production, from some 22 hectares, is up to 10,650 cases and the wine has for some years been well known and liked in England. The proprietor is now the Comte de Neipperg. The history of the property goes back some five hundred years, when it belonged to the family of Boitard de la Poterie and was known as Canon-Boitard.

The wine is supple, generous and attractive, on the light side, typically St Emilion. While not among the very top growths of the *Grands Crus* on all occasions, it often produces charming wines and has a good following.

Château Cap-de-Mourlin

The property has belonged for nearly five hundred years to the Capdemourlin family—surely one of the oldest associations between a family and a property in Bordeaux. The 17 hectares produce an average of 7,650 cases, and the wine is robust and generous, if lacking in real distinction.

Château Chapelle-Madeleine

This belongs to the Dubois-Challon family who are proprietors of Ausone and Belair. Production is now only a token 100 cases. There is, as might be expected, a small chapel in the vineyard.

Château Coutet

Some 12 hectares produce 3,000 cases on average. In spite of, or because of, the confusion in name with the famous Barsac château, this wine does not seem to have found favour on export markets.

Couvent des Jacobins

This growth was added to the classification in 1969. As the name implies, it was a religious foundation belonging to the Frères Prêcheurs Jacobins. The foundation is an ancient one, resulting from a gift to the Brothers confirmed in 1289 by the Duke of Lancaster, son of Henry III and Lieutenant-General of Guyenne at the time. The building itself, situated in the heart of the old town of St Emilion, is of thirteenth-century origin, and the vineyard adjoins the old ramparts. According to tradition, the wines of the Couvent des Jacobins not only found favour at the tables of the governors of Guyenne during the fourteenth and fifteenth centuries, but were also shipped to London to be served at coronations and at royal banquets. The Jacobins left their house in the eighteenth century, since when it has belonged to a succession of proprietors. For some time now, the Joinaud family have been owners. Some 3,400 cases are produced and the wines have a fruity, unctuous quality that is very St Emilion. The quality is good average.

Château Curé-Bon

The classification lists this growth as Curé-Bon, but the label says Curé-Bon-la-Madeleine. The property owes its name to a priest, Curé Bon, who planted this vineyard (which had actually been in his family since the seventeenth century) early in the last century. When the vineyard passed to his nephew, Camille Lapelletrie, the latter named it after his uncle and added the suffix 'la Madeleine', indicating that the vineyard is situated on the plateau of la Madeleine between Ausone, Belair and Canon. The present proprietor is Monsieur Maurice Lande, and some 1,700 cases are made. The wine is of good average quality, inclined to be a little firm and lacking fat in some years, but generous and fleshy with a fine and distinctive bouquet in good years such as 1964. The general style leans towards finesse rather than body, with real breed.

Château Dassault

This is one of the eight growths elevated to *Grand Cru Classé* status in 1969. Much time and trouble has gone into the reconstruction of both *cuvier* and vineyard in recent years by the present proprietor, who is the head of Sud-Aviation, makers of Concorde and Mirage. The label seems to be inspired by Lafite, and the wine—though more modest than this—is good, having charm with some breed and delicacy, the lighter style of St Emilion. Around 6,000 cases are produced.

Château Fonplégade

A fine property with a nineteenth-century, turreted château more in the style of those found in the Médoc. It belongs to the family of A. Moueix, important proprietors and merchants in both St Emilion and Pomerol, related to—but not to be confused with—their cousin Monsieur Jean-Pierre Moueix, who is the leading proprietor and merchant in the region.

The vineyard is very well placed just below Magdelaine and produces wines of style and finesse, with a touch of firmness which takes some time to mature. This is not one of the fat, fleshy St Emilions, but a wine of some class nevertheless. In recent years, the wines have proved very consistent. The average production is around 3,850 cases.

Château Fonroque

A wine of marked individuality. Very full in colour, it has more firmness than most St Emilions and takes rather longer to reach maturity. When it does so, the flavour is rich and powerful. I remember particularly the 1959, not a vintage which was always outstanding in the region, when the effects of the 1956 frost were still being felt.

The château belongs to the Moueix family and is distributed by the firm, J.-P. Mouiex. The vineyard is of about 18 hectares and produces some 5,100 cases on average.

Château Franc-Mayne

This château produces around 3,000 cases of the full-bodied type of St Emilion. It is not well known in England. The proprietor is Monsieur Theillassoubre.

Château Grand Mayne

This was enlarged in 1928 by the addition of the neighbouring property of Beau-Mazarat. The château is relatively imposing for the region. The production is around 6,000 cases and the proprietor is Monsieur Nony.

Château Grand Pontet

This was acquired by the firm of Barton et Guestier in the 1960s. The vineyard consists of 14 hectares and overlooks the St Emilion-Libourne road. It is a solid, meaty wine, not among the best of the *Grand Crus*, but good and dependable. The production averages 5,100 cases.

Château Grandes Murailles

This is one of the smallest of the *Grands Crus*, producing only 700 cases.

Château Guadet-St Julien

This produces up to 2,100 cases and is the property of the Lignac family.

Château la Carte and le Châtelet

This property occupies a very ancient site not far from the town ramparts. It is said that legionaries of the Emperor Probus (276–282) first planted vines here, and were also responsible for carving the rectangular patterns in the rock which are still to be seen. Today it produces some 2,100 cases and the joint proprietors are the Bécot and Berjal families. Although not widely known, the wine is of some distinction.

Château la Clotte

This small property would doubtless be more famous were its production not so limited. Only 2,100 cases are produced on average. But the vineyard is perfectly situated on the best slopes below the ramparts of the town and similarly placed to adjoining *Premiers Grands Crus*. For many years it has been lovingly tended by Monsieur Chailleau, a leading member of the Jurade. Until 1904, the vineyard was even smaller, but at that time, the Clos Bergat-Bosson-Pegasse was joined to la Clotte to make a single property. The wines are kept in small but very ancient *caves* at the top of the vineyard which are said to date from the days of English rule.

I have been fortunate in being able to follow the wines for some years, and they have been marvellously consistent. Normally the wine is among the lighter style of St Emilion, typical of the finest wines of the Côtes, with great finesse and delicacy, fresh and very supple, having an exquisite bouquet: 1959, 1962, 1967, 1969, 1971, 1976 and 1978 were wines like this. But in the best years, the wine can acquire a remarkable body and fleshiness, as was the case in 1964 and 1970 and, to a lesser extent, in 1966. This is a wine which should certainly rank with the best *Grands Crus*. Visitors to St Emilion can always find a range of la Clotte vintages at the small, vine-covered restaurant, le Logis de la Cadène, owned by the Chailleau family.

Château la Cluzière

This is a very small property near to Pavie, to whose proprietor it belongs. It produces 1,000 cases of a wine of good repute.

Château la Couspaude

This property produces 1,700 cases. The proprietor is Monsieur Aubert.

Clos la Madeleine

This is a very small property situated on the plateau of la Madeleine. The proprietor is Monsieur Pistouley, and only about 350 cases are made.

Château Larmande

This is owned by Monsieur Meneret and produces 4,250 cases.

Château Laniote

This is one of the new wines classified in 1969. The vineyard lies not far outside the walls of St Emilion and has belonged to the

Freymond-Rouja family for several centuries. Some 2,100 cases of wine are produced.

Château Laroze

A large property of 30 hectares, producing as much as 8,500 cases, the vineyard lies near the limit of the St Emilion Côtes and near to the Graves. Perhaps for this reason, the wine has a certain fullness of body coupled with some firmness. Wines are of good average quality and recent successes are 1971, 1976, 1978 and 1979. The château belongs to the heirs of Meslin-Gurchy.

Château Laserre

At the end of the last century, the vineyard of la Serre belonged to Monsieur Macquin and formed part of a large vineyard of 26 hectares, including part of Pavie as well as de Peygenestou. Some years ago, the 7 hectares of la Serre were detached and the property now belongs to the d'Arfuille family, who also own la Pointe in Pomerol. The reputation is for good dependable wines on the light side. Although listed as one word in the classification, the label says la Serre. The average production is 3,400 cases.

Château le Couvent

Easily the smallest of the classified growths of the region, producing only about 250 cases, the vineyard is actually within the ramparts of St Emilion, near the Château du Roi. It once belonged to the Couvent des Ursulines, which was originally responsible for producing the macaroons for which St Emilion is now famous (after its wines, of course!). The property now belongs to the Galhaud family, who are also merchants in St Emilion and owners of the well-known growth, Tertre-Daugay.

Château le Prieuré

This small vineyard, producing about 2,100 cases, was once Church property, being part of the important vineyard of the Cordeliers. It lies between Trottevieille and Troplong-Mondot on one side, and la Serre and Villemaurine on the other. The proprietor is Baronne Guichard who inherited it from her father, Monsieur Brisson, in 1942. She is also the proprietor of la Vraye-Croix-de-Gay in Pomerol and Siaurac in Néac.

263

Château Matras

This was first classified in 1969. The name has an interesting origin, as Matras means a cross-bowman. At the time of the Hundred Years' War, it may be remembered, the French had gone over to the cross-bow which fired a heavier and more deadly bolt than the arrow from the traditional long-bow favoured by the English. But the long-bowman could discharge a number of arrows for every bolt fired by the cross-bow because of the time it took to wind back the bow. It was this that gave the small English armies under Edward III and Henry V their superiority over the much larger French armies they encountered at Crécy and at Agincourt. Supposedly the property must once have belonged to some retired warrior of that time.

The vineyard is well placed, near to Canon and l'Angélus, and the 9 hectares produce some 3,000 cases. There is a good proportion of really old vines in the vineyard. Once the property of the Comte de Carles, it now belongs to Monsieur J.-B. Lefebvre.

Château Mauvezin

This is the property of Monsieur Bertin-Morel, producing 850 cases.

Château Moulin du Cadet

The property of Madame Fagouet-Moueix, producing 2,550 cases, it grows a firm, solid yet stylish wine of good quality which is distributed by the firm of J.-P. Moueix.

Clos de l'Oratoire

A growth newly classified in 1969, some 3,000 cases are produced, and the vineyard is run jointly with that of Château Peyreau. On the occasions I have tasted the wine, I found it possessed a rather marked *goût de terroir* which is sometimes found in the lower-lying vineyards of the commune. The wine is full-bodied and fleshy, of average quality.

Château Pavie-Décesse

This is one of two vineyards (Pavie-Macquin being the other) which occupy good secondary positions on the slopes of Pavie, the best part of which belongs, of course, to the property of that name.

Monsieur Blegnie is the administrator and some 3,400 cases are made.

Château Pavie-Macquin

This second Pavie 'satellite' owes its name to Monsieur Albert Macquin, who was one of the pioneers of grafting European vines on to American root-stocks, and so played an important part in the reconstruction of the Bordeaux vineyards after the phylloxera. He also owned a vineyard in St Georges-St Emilion, which carries his name, and both are now owned by Monsieur François Corre. The average production is around 4,250 cases and a pleasant, elegant wine of good average quality is produced.

Château Pavillon-Cadet

This is a property which produces 1,300 cases and belongs to Monsieur le Morvan.

Château Petit-Faurie de Souchard

It is very confusing to find two such similar names as Petit-Faurie de Souchard and Petit-Faurie de Soutard. It certainly makes it hard to remember which of the two wines one has drunk! I had supposed that they once formed one property, but this seems not to have been the case. This was formerly known as the Domaine de Petit-Faurie de Souchard. The Souchard family owned it as far back as memory or records go, but it now belongs to Monsieur Jabiol who is also owner of Cadet-Piola, as well as two lesser growths.

The property was formerly as large as 25 hectares, but a vineyard at Aigrières was sold off in 1933. However, it is still of a considerable size and produces up to 3,800 cases.

Château Petit-Faurie de Soutard

Until 1850 this property formed part of Soutard. The proprietor is Monsieur Aberlon, and about 4,250 cases are made.

Château Sansonnet

This is the property of Monsieur Robin and the average yield is some 2,550 cases.

Château St Georges-Côte Pavie

The proprietor is Monsieur Masson-Charoulet and some 1,800 cases are made.

Château Clos St Martin

This is a small property, producing no more than 850 cases, which is under the same ownership as Grandes-Murailles. The only vintage I have tasted, the 1970, was most impressive, combining a lovely flavour and suppleness with plenty of body—typical of very good St Emilions.

Château Soutard

This is one of the most beautiful châteaux as well as one of the most distinguished wines. The château itself is a gem of the second half of the eighteenth century, pleasantly domestic in scale with all the elegance and perfect proportion of the period. Since 1785, it has belonged to the Comtes des Ligneris, and the present member of the family takes the greatest care and pride in his inheritance. Unfortunately the domaine was split up in 1850; the other portion is now known as Petit-Faurie de Soutard. The vineyard now consists of 18 hectares which yield up to 6,000 cases.

The wines of Soutard have an unmistakable elegance and savour, and are consistently among the most distinguished of the *Grands Crus Classés*, those of 1962, 1964, 1966, 1967 and 1970 being all highly successful examples of their vintages.

Château Tertre-Daugay

The château is very well situated, with a fine view over the Dordogne. This is one of the old established growths of St Emilion and belonged to the Galhaud family until 1978 when it was bought by Comte Lio de Malet Roquefort of La Laffuliere. It has a good reputation for producing consistent wines of rather above average quality, which have been seen in England for a number of years. The production averages about 5,500 cases.

Château Trimoulet

An important property producing some 6,000 cases, it is not as well known in England as it should be. The wine has an excellent reputation and is well distributed in France, Belgium and

266

Switzerland. On the few occasions I have drunk it in France, I have always found it attractive and of some breed. The records of the property go back to 1773 and the present owners, the Jean family, have had it for several generations.

Château Trois Moulins

A very small growth, well situated near the town of St Emilion it produces only about 2,100 cases. The wines seem to have been widely exhibited and to have obtained many awards around the turn of the century, but the château is not much seen today, at any rate in England.

Château Troplong-Mondot

One of the leading properties in St Emilion, the 25 hectares produce some 12,750 cases. The name Troplong comes from a former proprietor who was a leading lawyer and president of the Senate during the Second Empire. It was his son, Monsieur Edouard Troplong, who was subsequently responsible for much of the development of the property. Its situation is remarkable, the château standing at the top of the vineyard with woods finally crowning the summit of the hill, which commands unique views towards Bordeaux, down the Dordogne towards Fronsac, and away towards Castillon.

Of all the vintages of Troplong-Mondot, I shall always remember the 1928, rich and velvety in texture with a lovely bouquet, a perfectly harmonious wine, unlike so many of that year. In recent years, some good wines have been made, developing considerable breed and elegance. The present proprietors are Messieurs Claude and Alain Valette.

Château Villemaurine

This growth, situated near the ramparts of St Emilion, seems to have been more important in the past than it is now. Monsieur Raoul Passemard was responsible for enlarging the vineyard to its present size in 1893. The present proprietor is Monsieur Robert Giraud, and the wines are now made to a high standard. The average production is 3,000 cases.

Clos des Jacobins

Cocks & Féret (12th edition) has the curious suggestion that the origin of this name comes from the Revolutionary era. This seems most unlikely. The Jacobins of the French Revolution acquired their name solely because they held their meetings in a convent which had belonged to the Jacobin Brothers, a religious order widely found in pre-Revolutionary France. It seems most likely, therefore, that this vineyard once belonged to the Couvent des Jacobins, which was established in St Emilion in the thirteenth century and part of whose vineyard still goes under this name.

The property now belongs to Cordier, the important vineyard proprietors and Bordeaux *négociants*, and is under their customary care and proficiency. The wine is rich and full-flavoured, but rather soft-centred. It develops quickly. Some 3,800 cases is an average production.

ST EMILION—GRAVES

PREMIERS GRANDS CRUS CLASSÉS

Only two growths enjoy this classification in the Graves, but they are among the glories of the whole region. Exactly the same rules as to yearly tastings apply here as have already been mentioned for the St Emilion Côtes.

Château Cheval Blanc

If you were to ask any wine lover what the finest St Emilion is today, he would be most likely to reply, 'Cheval Blanc'. This was not always the case. Once Ausone had a greater reputation—and perhaps will have again—while Figeac was placed first among the growths of the St Emilion Graves. Cheval Blanc's reputation in England was certainly made by the 1921 vintage, and from that time onwards it was spoken of in the same terms as the first growths of the 1855 classification, although it did not achieve equality of price until after the Second World War. When the first official classification of St Emilion was made by the INAO in 1954, it was only just that Cheval Blanc, together with Ausone, should be marked out among the *Premiers Grands Crus Classés* by means of an 'A' category.

Here on the open plateau of the Graves St Emilion, the

properties tend to be larger than those that crowd the cramped hillsides around the ramparts of St Emilion, and Cheval Blanc is no exception to this. The large vineyard of 34 hectares immediately adjoining Pomerol produces as much as 14,000 cases annually. It is one of the curiosities of Cheval Blanc that the soil and sub-soil contain almost every variation to be found in the region, and this, no doubt, contributes to the unique style of the wine. With Figeac, Cheval Blanc has the lion's share of the gravelly outcrops that give this district its name. In addition, a proportion of ungrafted vines have been maintained in the vineyard, and the proprietors believe this to be an important factor in preserving quality.

The property formed part of Figeac until the nineteenth century, when it was sold off. It has now been owned for many generations by the Fourcaud Laussac family, who have made it more famous than the property from which it sprang. The heiress of the family is married to Jacques Hebrard, the present administrator. The château itself is a modest but charming house with small turrets and pleasing proportions which, together with its white paint, give the appearance of a summer villa. But this is now completely overshadowed by the palatial new *chais* which more truly reflects the present prestige of Cheval Blanc. For many years, the wines in their second year in cask had to be moved to a cellar in Libourne where the château bottling was allowed to take place, the *chais* at Cheval Blanc being too small to accommodate all the wine, once sales of wine in cask ceased after 1952. Quite a number of English merchants shipped out and bottled the plentiful 1950 vintage, while Christopher's enterprisingly shipped the despised 1951 as 'St Emilion', only to find it turned out remarkably well. Now the new *chais* allows ample room for storage and bottling in ideal conditions.

The wine of Cheval Blanc typifies the difference between the Graves and the Côtes in St Emilion. It usually has a big colour, a very powerful, enveloping bouquet which is rich and sometimes almost spicy; a very full, mellow, almost unctuous flavour which is very concentrated and takes time to unfurl. In good years, the wine can have as much as 14° of alcohol. It is indeed a stunning wine, not subtle, but winning admiration by its sheer beauty and animal vigour; it assails the palate in the way some of the French Impressionists assail the eye with the brilliance of their colours. It is a quality only matched in Bordeaux by Pétrus, not far away in Pomerol.

The oldest vintage of Cheval Blanc I have come across is the 1911. We found a number of forgotten cases of it some years ago at Loudenne, but that was before old wines were so prized! The first bottle I tried was a disappointment, and I wrote it off as well past it. Subsequently, however, I have drunk some remarkably good bottles of this vintage. Unfortunately, I have never seen a bottle of the famous 1921, but from descriptions of it, the wine must have resembled the 1947. The 1928, 1929 and 1934 were all very fine wines which, however, have not lasted quite as well as some of the first growth Médocs of those years, or Ausone for that matter, although the 1934 was a more attractive wine than any of its Médocain cousins.

The great age of Cheval Blanc came after the war. It began badly, because half the 1945 crop, already much reduced in size, had to be pasteurized, due to volatile acidity. But then came a wonderful run of vintages: 1947, one of the most celebrated clarets made since the war, which soon commanded record prices because everyone in Bordeaux wanted to have it in their cellars—it was already being drunk in the early 1950s; the 1948, overshadowed, of course, but robust and fine; 1949 was only a little behind the 1947, a great wine instead of a masterpiece; 1950 was excellent but did not last; 1952 was big and powerful; 1953 was light, elegant and slightly atypical; 1955 was big and mellow. Even the off-vintages, 1951 and 1954, were charming and gave a number of years of inexpensive pleasure to those with the enterprise to buy them.

Then came the disaster of 1956, 1957 and 1958 which produced hardly anything, and 1959, an almost unnaturally plummy wine which turned out better than expected. The 1960 was very light but pleasing, somewhat like 1954; 1961 was very big but did not repeat the success of 1947; 1962 was, frankly, disappointing in a year when most St Emilions were back to their best; but with 1964 and 1966, the wine was really back to its pre-frost form. Since then, outstanding wines have been produced in 1970, 1975, 1976, 1978 and 1979. The 1971, which promised so much, already seemed unbalanced and tired by 1980.

270

Château Figeac

This fine property adjoins Cheval Blanc which once formed a part of its estate. The château itself is elegant and rather grand for St Emilion, the *chais* spacious and recently superbly modernized and enlarged, with an impressive battery of stainless-steel *cuves* for the fermentation. The Manoncourt family have owned Figeac for many generations, but none has been as jealous of its quality and reputation as the present proprietor, Thierry Manoncourt, who took over its management in 1947. He has told how in the nineteenth century, Figeac was regarded as the first wine in the St Emilion Graves, but that while his forebears spent most of their time in Paris and left the running of Figeac to managers, the Fourcaud Laussac family at neighbouring Cheval Blanc were busy building up the reputation of their property until it successfully assumed its present, unrivalled place. Monsieur Manoncourt has for some years now been steadily rebuilding the reputation of Figeac, and one day, who knows, it may take its place beside Cheval Blanc in the eyes of the world.

Trying to be as objective as possible, I would say that today Figeac often comes close to Cheval Blanc in quality, and even in style, but it seldom achieves the sheer weight of Cheval Blanc. In body it is slightly lighter, with a touch of elegance, yet with that same Graves power and richness. Certainly, in many vintages it is the second best wine in the whole St Emilion region, and occasionally it is first. An early assessment of the 1978 promises a great success, and the 1979 is on the same high level.

The vineyard itself is a very large one, with 34 hectares under vine, producing some 15,000 cases on average. It is planted with 35 per cent each of Cabernet Sauvignon and Cabernet Franc, and 30 per cent Merlot. Because of its soil, the Cabernet Sauvignon is successful here, and this helps to give Figeac its distinctive character. Since the war, Figeac has produced some splendid wines. A well-balanced 1950 was still very fine after thirty years. The 1953 and 1955 were particularly outstanding, probably the best wines, of these years in this region. Then, most surprisingly, the 1958 was magnificent and lasted very well—the only really good wine of this vintage from St Emilion that I have come across, in a year still under the shadow of the 1956 frost. Since then, 1959, 1961 especially, 1962—lighter than usual and a trifle atypical—

1964,1966,1967,1970 and 1971—a rival here to Cheval Blanc, if a shade too full-blown—tell a tale of consistent achievement. The 1974 is unusually attractive for the year, and 1975, 1976, 1978 and 1979 are all fine wines.

GRANDS CRUS CLASSÉS

This is a much smaller group than in the Côtes, but the properties are rather larger and, on average, in my experience rather more homogeneous in quality. The tasting rules, of course, apply to the *appellation* as in the Côtes.

Château Chauvin

A wine very much of the Cheval Blanc type—very rich and powerful, but with just a touch of coarseness in its make-up. At its best, this is a very fine wine, very unctuous and mellow, but unfortunately the wine is not quite as consistent as could be wished. The 1966 was excellent, for instance, but the 1967 a disappointment, whereas generally the 1967s in St Emilion were at least as good as the 1966s and sometimes better.

Chauvin belongs to Monsieur Henri Ondet and produces 3,000 cases on average.

Château Corbin (Giraud)

The duplication of names is one of the curses of St Emilion, and this is a bad case. There are no fewer than five growths in the St Emilion Graves, all *Grands Crus Classés*, which incorporate Corbin in their names, to say nothing of lesser growths in the Graves and in Montagne-St Emilion. Corbin is especially confusing because it belongs to the Giraud family, another member of which owns Grand Corbin. The property has interesting origins in that it formed part of a much larger domaine in the Middle Ages belonging to the Black Prince. Only traces of the fourteenth-century castle remain, and the present château is a very modest affair.

The vineyard is extensive, producing 8,500 cases on average, but some of the wine is commercialized under the subsidiary names of La Tour Corbin and Corbin Vieille Tour. The wine is best known in northern France, Belgium and Holland, and enjoys a good reputation. The Domaines Giraud, the proprietors, also own Certan-Giraud, a leading growth of Pomerol.

Château Corbin Michotte

An average of 4,250 cases is produced. The proprietor is Monsieur J.-N. Bordon. This is not to be confused with Croque-Michotte.

Château Croque-Michotte

This château lies behind Cheval Blanc. Some 4,250 cases of a generous wine are produced. I particularly remember the 1950, which was an enormous, dark wine which threw something resembling a port crust in bottle. The 1970 faded rather quickly. Madame Geoffrion-Rigal is proprietor.

Château Grand-Barrail-Lamarzelle-Figeac

This certainly holds the record for the longest name among all the classified growths, and perhaps for any Bordeaux growth! The vineyard is a large and important one, producing 12,750 cases on average. The wine is generous, easy, attractive and well-balanced. It is somewhat lighter, perhaps, than some of the Graves wines, but one of the most consistent, and it has the reputation for making above average wines.

Château Grand-Corbin-Despagne

This is another large property, producing some 13,600 cases. It suffered badly from the 1956 frost, and has taken time to recover. The wine has a good reputation, but I must confess I seem to have been unlucky when I have tasted it, as it has never quite come up to expectation. The proprietor is Monsieur Paul Despagne.

Château Grand Corbin Pécresse

This is how this growth is described in the classification, but the proprietor, Monsieur Alain Giraud, calls it Grand Corbin Giraud. It once formed part of the same domaine as Corbin. Some 5,500 cases is the average yield.

Château Haut-Corbin

The only growth in the Graves to be upgraded when the INAO revised the classification in 1969. It is a small property for the area, producing only about 1,275 cases. The proprietor, Monsieur

Guinaudie, also owns another vineyard in the Graves, as well as one in Fronsac.

Château Jean-Faure

Under the same ownership as Ripeau, this is a property of 9 hectares, producing 3,400 cases. For some years, the wine has been the monopoly of Maison Dourthe, the well-known Bordeaux merchants.

Château la Dominique

The property adjoins Cheval Blanc. The vineyard of 17 hectares produces 6,000 cases. This growth often produces exceptional wines in outstanding vintages. I particularly remember the 1929, 1945 and 1971. In lesser years, it is somewhat variable but always worth looking out for. The wine is rich and generous in style, with a touch of firmness in some years.

Château la Marzelle

This once formed part of the large estates of the Abbaye de Faize. It is a vineyard of only 6 hectares, producing about 3,000 cases. It has a very good reputation in France, and had the distinction of being served to Pope John XXIII when he visited Lourdes for the consecration of the underground basilica. The proprietors are the Carrère family.

Château la Tour-du-Pin-Figeac (Belivier)

This well-known growth is divided into two parts, one belonging to the Belivier family, the other belonging to A. Moueix & Fils. They are of roughly similar size. Production here is about 5,500 cases. The vineyard is almost opposite Cheval Blanc.

Château la Tour-du-Pin-Figeac (Moueix)

This part of the vineyard seems better known in England than the Belivier portion. The proprietors, A. Moueix & Fils, are important proprietors in both St Emilion and Pomerol, and *négociants* specializing in the wines of these two regions, but they should not be confused with J.-P. Moueix, who are the leading *négociants* of the Right Bank.

The wine has a tendency to be rather firm at first and seems to lack the roundness and mellowness of the best wines of the Graves.

An average of about 3,800 cases is made. There is a second wine, Clos La Fleur-Figeac, which tends to be lighter in body.

Château la Tour Figeac

This large property with 16 hectares under vine, producing some 8,500 cases on average was, until 1879, a part of Figeac. A good deal of work has recently been done on *cuvier*, *chais* and château. For one reason or another, the wine is not well known in England. The property is managed by Monsieur Louis Rapin, the proprietor of La Maison Blanche, a large vineyard in the Montagne-St Emilion.

Château Ripeau

This well-known growth consists of 30 hectares producing some 12,750 cases. The wine is typical of the region, full-bodied and fleshy, but sometimes a little hard. It enjoys a good reputation, and is well known both in England and in the USA where it was for some years distributed by Alexis Lichine.

Château Yon-Figeac

This is a large property producing very good, consistent wines. The vineyard of 21 hectares produces 10,200 cases. Although they are not among the top wines, I have always found the wines of Yon-Figeac solid, attractive and dependable, developing and holding up well in bottle. The proprietor is Madame Lussiez-Collet.

All these wines, classified in 1954 and 1969, lie within the commune of St Emilion. There are, however, two growths, one classified in 1954, the other in 1969, which lie outside the commune.

Château Haut-Sarpe

This vineyard lies in the commune of St Christophe des Bardes and was first classified in 1969. It lies on a hillside just at a point where the commune of St Christophe des Bardes adjoins that of St Emilion, so that geologically it can be said to be identical to the wines of the St Emilion Côtes. It actually adjoins the classified vineyards of Trottevieille, Balestard la Tournelle, and Sansonnet. Some 4,250 cases is an average production. Export markets include Belgium, Holland and the United Kingdom. The proprietor, Monsieur Joseph Janoueix, also owns several other lesser properties in St Emilion.

Château Larcis-Ducasse

Lying in the commune of St Laurent des Combes, this property had the distinction of being the only growth outside the commune of St Emilion to be classified in 1954. In fact, part of the vineyard lies in the commune of St Emilion, adjoining Troplong-Mondot. Some 5,100 cases of wine are made. The wine enjoys a good reputation; it is light but fine, in the manner of the wines of the Côtes. The proprietor is Madame Gratiot.

ST EMILION GRANDS CRUS

Some confusion exists about this *appellation*, introduced in 1954 along with the *Premier Grand Cru Classé* and the *Grand Cru Classé*. No actual list of St Emilion *Grands Crus* exists, in fact, because in theory all the remaining growths of the region are eligible for this classification on the results of an annual tasting, once it has been established that the minimum 11·5° of alcohol has been reached.

In his *Encyclopaedia of Wines and Spirits* (see Bibliography), Alexis Lichine lists over 500 growths in this category from the commune of St Emilion, who make declarations currently of the area under vine and the yield. The St Emilion satellites provide a further 200 names—a truly formidable list. There would obviously be little point in reproducing such a catalogue here, and many of these properties, of course, produce very small quantities.

Below, therefore, is a short list of some of the more important properties whose wines are worth looking out for:

From St Emilion

Château	Cases
Bellefond-Belcier	3,600
Cardinal-Villemaurine	5,100
Cormey-Figeac	3,650
de Ferrand	12,600
Grangeneuve	6,700
Fombrauge	12,750
Franc Pourret	4,150

Château	Cases
Grace-Dieu	3,000
la Tour-Peyblanquet	1,800
la Tour-St Pierre	4,700
Lavallade	4,750
les Basilliques	2,550
Monbousquet	12,250
Montlabert	3,400
Pailhas	4,350
Peyreau	6,375
Pressac	7,650
Puyblanquet	7,150
Simard	6,300

In addition, there is a large Cave-Coopérative responsible for vinifying some 210,800 cases. Some of these wines can, however, be declared with château names, provided they have been separately vinified.

From the St Emilion satellites

In the St Emilion satellites, the most important growths to look for are:

Château	Commune	Cases
Beauséjour	Puisseguin	4,950
Bel-Air	Puisseguin	4,650
Calon	Montagne	6,000
Corbin	Montagne	5,500
Guibeau	Puisseguin	10,600
la Tour de Grenet	Lussac	12,750
les Laurets	Puisseguin	31,900
de Lussac	Lussac	7,500
Lyonnat	Lussac	18,500
Maison Blanche	Montagne	12,750
Maisonneuve ⎫ St Georges-Macquin ⎭	St Georges	4,600
Plaisance	Montagne	3,900
Roudier	Montagne	12,750
St Georges	St Georges	11,900
Teyssier	Puisseguin	10,200
des Tours	Montagne	23,350

The most important Cave-Coopérative in the region is that of Puisseguin. There is a smaller, but nevertheless useful one, at Montagne.

9

Pomerol

In terms of area and of production, Pomerol is, by a fair margin, the smallest of the principal regions of Bordeaux. Its area is rather less than that of Margaux, while its production averaged 29,375 hectolitres in the ten years 1970 to 1979. But the quality and originality of its wines ensure for Pomerol a place among the great wines of Bordeaux.

Curiously enough, Pomerol did not establish a clear identity and fame for itself until comparatively recently. Early editions of Cocks & Féret treat it as no more than an appendage of St Emilion. The neglect which we noticed of the wines of St Emilion in the nineteenth century extended equally to those of Pomerol. The recognition of the separate personality and excellence of the wines of Pomerol is usually dated from 1878, when Pétrus gained a gold medal at the Paris Exhibition. But even after this, the fame of Pomerol still spread slowly and has continued to be hindered by the small production of the *appellation* in general, as well as by the small yield of many leading growths. In addition, there has never been any classification of Pomerol wines, so that no sort of official guide to the many growths exists.

English writers on Bordeaux tend to have given even less space, *pro rata*, to Pomerol than to St Emilion, and very few of its growths appear among the many wines they mention and describe. The reputation of Pomerol first seems to have gained a firm footing in Belgium, among the export markets, and it is interesting to note that Georges Thienpont, a Belgian wine merchant, acquired Vieux Château Certan in 1924. When I first visited Bordeaux in the early 50s, I was surprised and interested to find that there was considerable interest in and enthusiasm for Pomerol among leading Bordeaux houses such as Calvet & Cruse, but that very few of them were being shipped as yet to England. Certainly most English wine merchants at this time listed hardly any Pomerols, and restaurant wine lists were even more conservative. Among the pioneers at this period who bought and shipped fine Pomerols for their more discerning customers were Ronald Avery of Avery's and Harry Waugh of Harvey's—both firms, of course, based in Bristol. Another curiosity is that Pomerol's leading growth, Pétrus, was virtually unknown in England before the Second World War. Even after that, its reputation was better known than the wine itself, and it was only during the 1960s that this great wine was at all widely distributed on the English market.

In fact, the origins of Pomerol are as ancient as any in Bordeaux. It seems certain that it was the Romans who first planted the vine there. After this, the Hospitaliers of St John of Jerusalem established a *commanderie* in the Libourne area in the twelfth century, and the Church remained an important influence, as can be seen today in many of the names of the various growths. The region suffered considerably from the Hundred Years' War, and was slow to recover afterwards.

Much more recently, Pomerol suffered very severely from the 1956 frost, and many growths had to be largely reconstituted as a result. It was noticeable that many growths had still not sufficiently recovered to give of their best in the 1961 vintage, and usually 1962, and still more 1964, were more generally successful in the region. The grape varieties used and the *encépagement* is similar to that found in St Emilion. The Cabernet Franc (here called 'Bouchet') is much more important than the Cabernet Sauvignon, the Malbec (here called Pressac) is more widely used than in the Médoc, while the Merlot now tends to be the most important variety.

It is often conveniently said that the wines of Pomerol are a sort of halfway house between St Emilion and Médoc. But such a description does scant justice to the originality of these wines. In terms of alcohol, they tend to be less powerful than St Emilion but more so than Médoc. The *appellation* requirement is 10·5° as against 11° for simple St Emilion, and 11·5° for the *Premiers* and *Grands Crus Classés* and the *Grands Crus*. In Médoc, the minimum is 10° for Médoc and Haut-Médoc, and 10·5° for the communal *appellations* (Margaux, St Julien, etc). On tasting, one finds

Pomerol to have something of the same fullness in the mouth as the St Emilion Graves, but with less alcohol and more finesse and balance. It is also very noticeable that Pomerol is more tannic than St Emilion; all the best wines tend to have a characteristically firm finish when young, but this tannic mask seems to slide away more rapidly than would be the case in the Médoc. This results in very harmonious wines, enjoyable when comparatively young (say at five years), but nevertheless lasting well. I have often heard it said that Pomerol does not last as long as St Emilion, but I have found no evidence for this assertion. I have drunk good middle-range wines, such as Nenin and l'Enclos, of the 1928 vintage, when thirty to forty years old, and they were still highly enjoyable, while the best growths can certainly do every bit as well. The Pétrus 1895 was as fine when around seventy years old as any of the great Médocs of a similar age.

We have measured the characteristics of Pomerol in familiar terms and compared it to other districts, yet, of course, in the final analysis it is impossible, as with all great wines, to convey in words the essential nuances and subtleties which make this a unique and memorable district. It is impossible to pin down that tantalizing hint of the oriental and exotic about the perfume of a mature Pomerol, or that special savour at once spicy, mellow, yet with a touch of the austere, the power mingled with delicacy, the warmth balanced with an invigorating freshness, which goes to make up the flavour. I only hope that those who know and love Pomerol will recognize in these words something of what they too have experienced, and that those who have not will be drawn on to discover these glories for themselves.

Pomerol is the only one of the great red wine districts never to have produced a classification of its wines. This leaves the way clear for the commentator to express his own views and, at the same time of course, to note the various traditions and opinions which exist on the subject.

On one point there is no dispute. Pétrus has for long been recognized as *Hors Classé* in Pomerol, and in recent years, this has been reflected in the price, which is usually similar to, and sometimes higher than that of Cheval Blanc. Thus Pétrus has firmly taken its rightful place among the great first growths of the Gironde. It is after this that the problems begin. Professor Roger (see Bibliography) says that the leading growths after Pétrus are

280

usually accepted as being, in alphabetical order: la Conseillante, l'Evangile, la Fleur-Pétrus, Gazin, Lafleur, Latour-Pomerol, Petit-Village, Trotanoy and Vieux Château Certan; with la Conseillante, and possibly l'Evangile, in a different class from the others. They can, and do, produce wines which on occasion rival the first growths, and the others produce excellent and sometimes great wines, comparable to the second growths of the Médoc. After this, there is a larger group, such as Beauregard, Nenin, Clos-l'Eglise, la Pointe and Clos René, consistently producing wines of good average classified growth standing. Finally, there is a third group corresponding to the lesser *Grands Crus Classés* in St Emilion, and some of the *Grands Crus*, or to some lesser class growths and top Bourgeois growths of the Médoc. But it would take years of tasting and study to turn such general outlines into anything so definite as a list of names.

The real centre of Pomerol lies in a commercial sense in the old town of Libourne. In the Middle Ages this was an important port where wines from the length of the Dordogne were assembled and shipped to England. The town was fortified and frequently changed hands during the Hundred Years' War. Today, it has the air of a provincial market town with its grey stone houses, and well laid-out but hardly bustling streets. There is a fine old stone bridge, breached in the last war, but well restored, and below the bridge and along the river-front are the *chais* and offices of most of the *négociants* of the region, with the important firm of J.-P. Moueix at their head. This is really the only firm of the region which is large and important enough to take its place among the leading Bordeaux merchants.

The little village of Pomerol lies at the centre of the Pomerol vineyards; it is no St Emilion in terms of historical interest, buildings or size, but rather a village of the scale of a St Julien. The central plateau around the church and going towards the St Emilion Graves contains all the best growths, with its mixture of clay and gravel. This area is intensely cultivated so that there does not seem room for another vine, and the properties tend to be small—around 30 tonneaux is an average yield, with Gazin (80 tonneaux) as the largest property by a good margin. Then the land falls away and breaks up somewhat; here, the wines tend to be a little coarser with less finesse, the soil becoming more sandy. There are some larger properties here, notably de Sales with 110 tonneaux, and Nenin and la Pointe with 80 tonneaux each.

The leading growths in terms of interest and quality now follow. After the first few names, I have arranged them in alphabetical order for the sake of simplicity.

Château Pétrus

'Premier des Premiers Crus'; so ran the motto on an old cork from Pétrus, which I remember seeing once; and, indeed, few would quarrel with this confident assertion. While Cheval Blanc has to share its privileged position in St Emilion with Ausone, Pétrus stands proudly alone, not according to any official classification, but by universal consent.

Pétrus's position in the area first became clear when it won a gold medal at the Paris Exhibition of 1878, the first wine from Pomerol to gain this distinction, and in an era when such awards really carried weight. But its modern reputation was the work of Madame Loubat on the one hand, and of Monsieur Jean-Pierre Moueix on the other. It was Madame Loubat who steadily built up the quality of the wine with meticulous husbandry and impeccable vinification. Like a very great cook, she ensured that attention was paid to every detail, the vineyard was tended with the care of a garden, the *cuvier* and *chais* were so immaculate that it seemed impossible that any work was ever carried on there. While Madame Loubat ensured that the quality of Pétrus matched that of any wine in the Gironde, Jean-Pierre Moueix ensured that, for the first time, it was distributed in such a way that it would acquire the international reputation it deserved. Monsieur Moueix is not only a very successful *négociant*, he is also a great connoisseur of many things that make life noble, and it has been his judgement and discernment, recognized and appreciated by his many customers, which have done much over the last thirty years to place Pétrus where it is today. First, he arranged for Pétrus to be regularly distributed in the USA by the Leeds Import Co., then in 1963 he entrusted the UK distribution to International Distillers & Vintners via their Bordeaux subsidiary, Gilbey S.A., at Château Loudenne. The present distributors are the old City firm of Corney and Barrow. Now, as auction prices at Christie's and Sotheby's testify, Pétrus is as keenly sought after as Lafite or Mouton. What has this remarkable success story been built on? The vineyard itself is very small, originally 7 hectares producing on average around 25 tonneaux, or 2,100 cases, now extended to 11 hectares producing up to 40 tonneaux, or 3,800 cases, so that after Ausone, it is the smallest of the great wines of the Gironde in terms of quantity. Fortunately, the set-back in 1956 was not as grave as in some vineyards, and a rapid recovery was made, as the quality of the 1959, 1960 and 1961 testify.

The buildings themselves are minute but beautifully kept. *Cuvier* and *chais* are very small, with scrupulously clean and well-raked gravel on the floor. The *salle de réception* can only hold a very modest sized party at one time to sign the visitors' book which is kept there. I shall always remember my first visit there in the early 1960s, in Madame Loubat's time. She always wore a charming hat, and looked as it she was just going out to tea. After her death, her niece, Madame Lacoste-Loubat, carried on the same tradition for a while, and her hats helped to remind one of the great lady who had gone. Now, Monsieur Jean-Pierre Moueix has become the controlling partner in the property as well as arranging its distribution.

Since the early 1970s, Monsieur Christian Moueix has been very much engaged in the actual management of Pétrus, as part of his duties in supervising the Moueix properties in general. In this he is fortunate to have the assistance of one of the leading young oenologists of the region. Monsieur Jean-Claude Berrouet. With the extension of the vineyards, some sceptics thought that Pétrus would no longer be the same, and I asked Christian Moueix how he had maintained the quality. The answer is that each year they taste the different vats blind. Usually there are five vats, three from the original vineyard and two from the new portion. In all their tastings, a wine from the new portion has never actually come last, an interesting commentary on how well the new part fits in with the old. With such a small vineyard, many things are possible which could not be attempted on a larger scale. For instance, in 1976, when the vintage was interrupted by rain, Christian Moueix was able to bring in his workers to pick in the afternoons, when conditions were at their optimum.

It is not always realized that Pétrus is par excellence the wine of the Merlot. About 95 per cent of the vineyard is planted with this variety—a monument to what Merlot can achieve when circumstances really suit it. What is so interesting about the wine itself is how distinctly different it is from its neighbours. As one looks out across the modest vineyard, one sees it closely bordered by Vieux Château Certan on the one side, and by Gazin on another, yet this small parcel of land produces something unique. As usual with vineyards, it is that individual combination of soil and sub-soil, isolated by chance, rather than incorporated in some larger parcel, which is responsible. At Pétrus, the combination is 80 per cent clay, covered with a superficial layer of gravel.

In composition, it has certain points of similarity with Cheval Blanc. There is an unctuousness and almost a chewy quality of richness and power in common. But Pétrus has in all good years an exceptional depth of colour and a much clearer definition of flavour, that touch of firmness I have mentioned as so characteristic of Pomerol, but which is less marked than in some other growths. The bouquet is also better defined, while just as powerful, as Cheval Blanc, and it develops remarkable nuances with age. Curiously, some of the lighter vintages of Pétrus, years like 1954, and 1960, seem to have a character more reminiscent of Ausone than of Cheval Blanc. One of the marvels of Pétrus seems to be its ability to begin life with all the exuberance of a great St Emilion, yet to mature with all the finesse of a great Médoc. It is this balance and finesse, the combination of so many qualities in a single wine, that make Pétrus such a great wine.

I have been fortunate in having been able to taste a number of old vintages of Pétrus, and these confirm that great wines were being made here at a time when its glories were still unsung, and comfortable, bourgeois Bordeaux still thought of Pomerol as an untutored peasant not fit to mix with the nobility of the Médoc. The 1895 vintage was interesting because it was successful in St Emilion and Pomerol but not in the Médoc. The Pétrus of that year was still a great wine, deep in colour, rich and vigorous when over seventy years old. The next landmark was the 1917, which I found superior in almost every way to the 1928 when they were drunk together in 1963 at a dinner organized by Mr David Wolfe at the restaurant he owned at the time. The 1917 was deep in colour, still full of fruit and vigour, while the 1928 was very pale in colour and was drying up.

But the great age of Pétrus really began after the Second World War. The 1943 was the prologue; post-war visitors to Bordeaux were surprised and interested to be told by many fine judges in the trade that the almost unknown Pétrus was the outstanding wine of this war-time vintage. As a footnote, many years later I came across a bottle of the 1940, which was still delicate and delicious although nearly thirty years old. The 1945 was still of deep colour, rich and powerful when thirty-five years old. The 1947 would no doubt have become as famous as the Cheval Blanc had it had the same exposure to trade and public alike. On the occasion when I had the chance of comparing the two, I thought the Pétrus was the finer, although opinion at the table was divided. It has certainly been a more slowly developing wine and will, I believe, last longer. It may have lacked Cheval Blanc's overpowering presence at the beginning, but now that this exultant youthfulness has been shed, there seems to be more to the Pétrus. The 1949 was only a little behind the 1947, the vintages of the 1950s were on form, but the 1955 proved rather a light-weight for the vintage, while the 1954 was a very successful off-vintage. The 1960 was of a similar style, and then came a succession of great wines, 1961, 1962, 1964, 1966, 1967 (then perhaps the wine of the vintage), 1968 (one of the few successes of this vintage outside the Médoc), 1969 (probably the wine of the vintage again), 1970, 1971, 1973, 1975, 1976, 1977, 1978 and 1979. All are certainly among the best half-dozen wines in their respective vintages.

Château la Conseillante

I shall always remember visiting this château for the first time in March 1961, when I was travelling around looking at the very mixed results of 1960. I was deeply impressed by the 1960 here, and noted that this and the Latour were the two best wines I had seen in this vintage. I had not then seen the Pétrus or the la Mission, but time has, I believe, upheld my initial judgement that this was one of the best wines of its year.

The wines of la Conseillante are big, firm and rather closed at first, slow to develop and long lasting. There is more Bouchet in the vineyard than at Pétrus, and the wines are less fleshy and attractive to begin with, but with their power, concentrated fruit and great breed, they do develop into very fine wines and sometimes into outstanding ones.

The vineyard lies in the best part of the plateau of Pomerol where it adjoins the St Emilion Graves, actually opposite Cheval Blanc. For generations it has belonged to the Nicolas family, who still tend it with the greatest care. Like several of the best

Pomerols, I found it was virtually unknown in England when I first bought it in 1961, although in fact Harry Waugh had bought the 1955 for Harvey's. It is still not as well known or appreciated as its great quality deserves. Successful vintages which I have tasted include: 1947, 1955, 1960, 1961, 1962, 1964, 1966, a great 1970, 1973 (unusually rich for the year), 1975, 1976, 1977, 1978 and 1979. This is always one of the best three or four wines in Pomerol. The production averages around 3,500 cases.

Vieux Château Certan

One of the few growths of Pomerol to boast a fine château. The oldest part is seventeenth-century and the whole building is very pleasing, with its two squat towers of differing ages and proportions at either end. It is beautifully kept by the Thienpont brothers, Belgian wine merchants whose father bought the property in 1924. Originally, it had belonged to the Demay family, who sold it in 1850 to Charles Bousquit.

This has always been regarded as one of the top growths of Pomerol, and in recent years its reputation has spread to England and the USA, while the excellence of the wines has been equalled by their consistency. The vineyard adjoins the St Emilion Graves in the best part of the plateau of Pomerol and lies very close to Cheval Blanc, la Conseillante and Pétrus.

The wines of Vieux Château Certan have a very individual style. In colour they are lighter than Pétrus or la Conseillante, but are of a beautifully clear and ruby hue which retains its youthfulness longer than that of many Pomerols. The bouquet is especially marked, and on the palate the wines have a delicacy and breed unsurpassed by any Pomerol, although often markedly firm at the beginning. As with the bouquet, the flavour is very individual, penetrating and fine. Although lacking the flesh and richness of Pétrus, they always seem to have sufficient fruit and body for the tannin, and usually, indeed, the wines are remarkably long on the palate.

1952, 1953 and 1955 were all very successful. After the frost, 1961, 1962, 1964, 1966 especially, 1967 (a great success), 1970, 1971, 1975, 1976 and 1978 have all lived up to the considerable reputation which this growth has built up. It is consistently one of the best wines in Pomerol today. The average production is 5,800 cases.

Château l'Evangile

This important property lies close to la Conseillante in the best part of the Pomerol plateau. It enjoys an excellent reputation as one of the very best growths of the region, but unfortunately my own experience of the wine has been very limited. As with a number of the fine wines of Pomerol, l'Evangile does not seem to have been very widely distributed in England, so its reputation here does not correspond with its undoubted worth. In style, the wines rather resemble those of la Conseillante. They are powerful and vigorous with a good deal of tannin to start with, requiring quite a lot of ageing. When I saw the 1964 vintage at eight years old, it was still quite unready to drink. Since then, very fine wines have been made in 1966, 1970 and 1971. L'Evangile belongs to the Ducasse family and produces 3,450 cases on average.

Château la Fleur-Pétrus

A wine of very high quality and reputation—some would place it among the very top growths. It adjoins Pétrus and produces about 3,200 cases of wine on average from 9 hectares of vines. It has an extraordinary label which suggests it might belong to a private shipping company, but it would certainly be a shame to serve it on even the most luxurious of yachts. The property is run by the firm of J.-P. Moueix.

While the wine lacks the great depth of Pétrus itself, it nevertheless has considerable breed and a fine bouquet. It is also very consistent. In quality it is close to Latour-Pomerol.

Château Gazin

One of the best-known Pomerols on the English market, Gazin is the largest of the leading growths of Pomerol, with some 25 hectares producing about 7,500 cases. Monsieur de Baillieucourt is the proprietor. Once belonging to the Knights Templar, the vineyard of Gazin lies in the best part of Pomerol and borders Pétrus, Vieux Château Certan, la Conseillante and l'Evangile.

Its wines have plenty of colour, they are rich and generous, fleshy, and have sufficient tannin but without exaggeration. Although consistently one of the leading wines of the region, I feel they lack the finesse, breed and distinction of Vieux Château Certan or la Conseillante. They are undeniably attractive wines, but just perhaps lacking that spark which makes for greatness, and with a certain underlying coarseness.

The 1945 rightly had a great reputation and was widely distributed in England. After that, 1947 and 1953 were good but not exceptional and, since the frost, 1962 and 1964 have been up to form. The 1970 is a good example of the merits and shortcomings of this growth.

Château Latour-Pomerol

This property lies just opposite Pétrus and is owned by Monsieur Jean-Pierre Moueix of Pétrus fame. The average yield is 3,500 cases. Because the name is naturally liable to cause some confusion, it is always hyphenated with that of Pomerol. The reputation of the wine is high, but I must confess to having been rather disappointed by it on a number of occasions when mature vintages were opened. I had the feeling that the lovely wines I tasted in cask were not translated into great bottles. But since it joined the Moueix stable there have clearly been improvements in handling the wine, and throughout the 1970s wines of the highest class have been made. They are characterized by their beautiful flavour, vigour and fine balance. 1971, 1978 and 1979 are especially impressive.

Château Trotanoy

This leading growth is now enjoying the acclaim it so rightly deserves. It is the property of the family of Monsieur Jean-Pierre Moueix, Pomerol's leading proprietor and *négociant*. Only some 2,500 cases are produced from 9 hectares of vineyard, which is very well placed.

In style, the wine is more reminiscent of Pétrus than the other leading growths, with its dense colour, rich, enveloping bouquet, and mellow, fleshy body which develops a flavour of great charm and breed. This is another example of how a predominantly Merlot wine can look remarkably like a Médoc at times, in spite of the difference in grape varieties. The 1949 was a marvellous wine, the 1961 a great, slow-developing one, and the 1962 one of the most attractive and successful in the region. Since then, after a fine 1966, came an exceptional 1967, a typical 1970, followed by a delicious 1971. After a light-weight 1973, 1975 and 1976 are typical of the years, and 1978 is one of the top wines of the vintage.

It is a pity that the production is so limited, or the fame of Trotanoy would surely be even more widespread.

Château Petit-Village

An important growth formerly belonging to the Ginestet family and distributed through their Bordeaux house, this is now under the management of Bruno Prats of Cos d'Estournel. The vineyard is well placed, behind Vieux Château Certan, and produces some 4,030 cases. Although it is regarded as one of the leading growths of Pomerol, I have a certain personal lack of enthusiasm for this wine. On the occasions I have tasted it, it seemed to lack something of the charm and finesse of the best Pomerols, and to be unduly austere and dry. The best mature vintage I have tasted was the 1961 which was concentrated and very rich, certainly a very fine wine when nearly twenty years old. The 1970 is rather moderate, and the 1971 is certainly superior if not in the very top class.

In the mid-1960s, Ginestet introduced a non-vintage wine under the name of 'Selection du Maître de Chais', but this has now been discontinued.

The above growths are the undisputed leaders of the region; some would add one or two names, but none would subtract any.

Below, in alphabetical order, follow the other growths of note:

Château Beauregard

This is an important property, with 13 hectares under vine producing some 4,500 cases in favourable conditions. Under the present proprietor, Raymond Clauzel, the property is very well run, and a wine of excellent quality and consistency is made. It deservedly enjoys its reputation as one of the leading growths of the region.

The château, dating from the seventeenth and eighteenth centuries, is distinctive for its square, squat towers and terrace above a moat. After the First World War, it caught the fancy of an American architect, who designed a replica which was built on Long Island, NY for the Guggenheim family, and is known as 'Mille-Fleurs'. In style, the wine is rich and full-flavoured; it develops fairly quickly, showing considerable breed and charm.

289

Château Certan de May

The small production (1,500 cases), together with the fact that little of the wine has in the past been château-bottled, have combined to prevent this wine from being as well known as its position would suggest. The vineyard is very well placed and the growth has a reputation for quality. However, a recent tasting suggested a slightly rustic quality, less fine than the best growths.

Châteaux Certan-Giraud and Certan-Marzelle

These are adjoining properties on the plateau de Certan, close to Vieux Château Certan and Certan de May. Since 1955, both have belonged to the Giraud family, the owners of Château Corbin in St Emilion. Certan-Giraud averages 1,150 cases, Certan-Marzelle 1,275.

This is a good example of the unfortunate effects of the excessive division of properties in Pomerol. The situation is one of the best in the region and, to be fair, a good wine is made. But if these two properties were joined together and really well run, we might well have another growth of the quality of Vieux Château Certan. The only example I tasted in maturity was the 1961 Certan-Giraud. It was a generous, fleshy wine with a touch of firmness at the end.

Château Clinet

This property belongs to the Audy family, *négociants* in Libourne, and produces 3,300 cases on average. The vineyard is situated on the plateau of Pomerol near the church. I once had the opportunity of tasting several vintages of the 1950s. We actually bought some of them, but I must confess to having been disappointed with them. There was a hardness which did not seem to mellow, and a lack of charm. I have not seen the wine in recent years.

Château la Croix

The average production is 2,000 cases and it belongs to the Janoueix family. The vineyard adjoins Nenin, Petit Village and Beauregard. This is a good middle-of-the-road growth, which enjoys some reputation in England.

Château la Croix-de-Gay

This is another smallish property (2,900 cases average production) making an attractive, sound wine which is seen from time to time in England. The ownership has remained for several generations with the family Barraud-Ardurat-Raynaud.

Château l'Eglise-Clinet

One of the three properties lying near to the church of St Jean at Pomerol, this was built by the Knights Templar in the thirteenth century. It belongs to Madame R. Durantou, whose family have owned it for many generations, and Monsieur Lasserre of Clos René is the administrator. The average production is 1,700 cases. I particularly remember a 1952 from this château that had body and breed; the wine enjoys a good reputation.

Clos l'Eglise

This belongs to the Moreau family, who also own Château Plince, and it produces 2,050 cases on average. At its best, this can be a very fine wine, rather more delicate than some Pomerols, with a lovely bouquet. The 1964 and 1966 were especially good, but the 1969 proved a disappointment, as with so many wines of this meagre year. More recently the 1979 is especially fine, and initially looked better than some more famous growths.

Domaine de l'Eglise

The production is 1,700 cases and the proprietor is Monsieur Emile Castega. The wine is exclusively marketed by the Maison Borie-Manoux. It is rather light in style, but fine.

Château l'Enclos

I shall always remember this wine for its wonderful 1929. The examples I saw were bottled by Calvet, and were for some years on the list at the Bell at Aston Clinton. This was just the sort of wine with which Gerry Harris would delight his guests in the 1950s, when he was building up his reputation. It was velvety and delicious, a real elixir, which remained fresh and charming to the end. The property is one of the larger ones of Pomerol, making 2,900 cases on average, and it belongs to the Carteau family. I have not seen the wine very often in recent years, but its reputation remains good.

Château le Gay

A wine marketed by the firm of J.-P. Moueix, and one for which I have a special affection, having selected it for a number of years in my Loudenne period. It is an interesting wine, always very big and firm when new, sometimes almost clumsy, but developing a mellow richness fairly quickly. The 1962 was especially good, better than the 1961, and the 1964, 1966 and 1967 all proved most consistent. The proprietors are Mesdemoiselles Thérèse and Marie Robin, whose father and grandfather both won awards for the manner in which they ran the property. The average production is 2,100 cases.

Château la Grave-Trigant-de-Boisset

An old property, which has maintained its identity longer than most in the region, this was formerly the property of the Bouché family, and has recently been acquired by Monsieur Christian Moueix. The average production is 2,100 cases. This is not a wine I have often seen, but it enjoys a good reputation and is sometimes seen in England. The 1979 is a very big wine of great promise and marked character.

Château Lafleur

This is an exquisite little property which, like le Gay, belongs to the Robin sisters. Unfortunately, the tiny vineyard of 4 hectares, producing no more than 1,200 cases, prevents the wine from being as widely known and appreciated as its quality deserves. The wine itself is marketed by the firm of J.-P. Moueix, and is noted for its lovely bouquet and great finesse and charm.

Château Lafleur-Gazin

This small property lies in the heart of the best part of the plateau of Pomerol. The vineyard is adjoined by Gazin, Lafleur and La Fleur Pétrus. The owner is Monsieur Borderie, but the property has come to more prominence since the firm of J.-P. Moueix became 'fermier' in 1976. The wines have elegance and breed, without quite the power of the leading growths. An excellent 1979 was made. The 4 hectares of vineyard produce an average of about 1,200 cases.

Château Lagrange

Another growth producing wine of very high quality, but in very small quantities—only about 2,500 cases on average—the vine-yard is situated in the best part of the plateau of Pomerol, and is owned by Jean-Pierre Moueix and distributed by his company. The wine is very fine, only just below the very top growths in quality and reputation.

Château Moulinet

This is an old established growth of above average size for the region, its 13 hectares of vineyard yielding some 4,250 cases. There is also some woodland near the château. Moulinet has some reputation in England and produces a sound, fleshy wine of the middle rank. The 1970 was a rewarding mouthful.

Château Nenin

One of the largest and best-known properties of Pomerol. A vineyard of 20 hectares yields around 7,300 cases of wine, and the estate is very well run by the present proprietor, Monsieur Despujol. The finest wines of Pomerol come from the plateau, where the soil is clay and gravel, while towards Libourne the soil is sandy and the wines lighter but fine, maturing earlier. Nenin combines in its large vineyard elements of both.

I have found the evolution of Nenin interesting to follow. Its first tasting is nearly always very flattering, full-bodied and fleshy. Then, for a year or so after bottling, the wine is often dull with a rather common taste and lack of finesse. But after several years, the quality reappears, and when mature, the wine is suave and flattering, if not quite in the top class. Nenin has long been a firm favourite in England and is often to be found here. The quality is very consistent and the wine lasts well.

Château Plince

This is the sort of growth which used to be sold by English wine merchants in the early 1950s for about eight shillings a bottle. I well remember Plince with its Calvet label—my father had bought the 1947 and then the 1953. We drank them young and found them delicious, but never thought of them as anything more than charming small growths, the equivalent of a small *Bourgeois* from the Médoc. Recently, we unearthed a bottle of the 1947 and found it fresh, rich and full-bodied, with a wonderful bouquet and a long, silky elegance worthy of any aristocratic classified growth. Admittedly, it was a 1947, and this was one of the greatest years for Pomerol. If the price reaction of 1971–3 went too far too quickly, so the old prices of the 1950s did not reflect the true value of wines like Plince.

The production is now about 2,900 cases and Monsieur Moreau, the proprietor of Clos l'Eglise, is the owner. The growth is well known in England, though not as often seen now as it used to be. The quality has been a little variable in recent years, but tends to pull out the stops in really good vintages. This is not in the top flight of Pomerols, but at its best is the equivalent of a fifth growth of the Médoc and as a general rule of a *Grand Bourgeois*.

Château la Pointe

This important growth with its distinctive label has long been a favourite in England. The large vineyard of 20 hectares produces some 7,500 cases on average, and is most carefully run by Monsieur d'Arfeuille, the proprietor. My first acquaintance with the wine was a 1943 shipped as a concession wine by my father. It was one of the most agreeable examples of that uneven year. In style, la Pointe is on the light side, but with a typical Pomerol flavour, and fine bouquet and a finesse and delicacy which show real breed. If not quite in the top flight, it is one of the best and most consistent of the secondary growths of Pomerol. Among later vintages, the 1955 was a particular success. The 1970 was unusually big and powerful, the 1971 typically graceful.

Château Clos-René

This wine was for many years offered by Calvet to its English customers and bought by them with great regularity. The yield of 4,675 cases places it among the important growths of Pomerol, and under the care of its proprietor, Monsieur Lasserre, it enjoys a good reputation for consistency. Like Nenin and la Pointe, it has never been considered to be in the top flight of Pomerols, but is among the best of the secondary growths. Very good 1976, 1978 and 1979s were made.

Château Rouget

This growth is chiefly memorable for me as one which had a string of old vintages to offer at one time. Unfortunately, they never came my way. But a recent bottle of 1964 confirmed the frank character and solid virtues of this wine. The vineyard of 11 hectares produces 3,400 cases. It is also long established, having belonged to the mayor of Pomerol in 1804. In early editions of Cocks & Féret, it was placed among the leading growths, a position it no longer enjoys. The owner is Monsieur Marcel Bertrand.

Château de Sales

This is much the largest property in Pomerol. A fine château of the eighteenth century is surrounded by a domaine of around 100 hectares, including extensive woods, which encircle it. The vineyard of 31 hectares produces 9,350 cases of wine. It has belonged to the de Laage family for four hundred years.

As might be expected from such a production, the wine is widely distributed and is well known in England. When I first tasted it, the quality was only average, and I found a certain coarseness of character and lack of true Pomerol breed and distinction. But in recent vintages, there has been a marked improvement. The 1970, 1971, 1973 and 1976 are all in their differing ways successful examples of these vintages, with a marked bouquet and fine flavour.

Château Taillefer

This is the principal property in Pomerol of the important firm, A. Moueix & Fils, who make their headquarters here. It has a vineyard of 10 hectares which can produce as much as 4,250 cases in a good year. There is a lot of iron in the subsoil, as the name suggests. This is a carefully made wine, which is rather firm at first, but ages well—a good secondary growth.

There are a great many small growths in Pomerol, many producing wines of excellent quality. The 12th edition (1969) of Cocks & Féret lists over a hundred other growths in addition to those detailed above. Some, of course, go into generic blends, others are sold direct in France by the proprietors or are shipped through *négociants* to different markets, mostly to Belgium and northern France, but also to England. *Château le Bon-Pasteur* (production 2,250 cases) is just such a wine; it produced a magnificent 1970, full of Pomerol opulence.

Other growths worth noting are:

Château	Cases
Bourgneuf-Vayron	3,050
Feytit-Clinet	1,275
Gombaude-Guillot	2,550
Tailhas	4,600
Vraye-Croix-de-Gay	1,100

Attached to Pomerol, rather like the satellites of St Emilion, lie the communes of Lalande de Pomerol and Néac. Originally both had their own *appellations*, but now the growers of Néac are allowed to use the commercially more attractive name of Lalande de Pomerol. In character, the wines resemble the lesser growths of Pomerol, but unfortunately they are not always so carefully made.

The outstanding growth is probably Château Siaurac in Néac, the property of Baronne Guichard. The large vineyard produces about 8,500 cases. An outstanding 1964 was produced here, but there were also good wines in 1966, 1967, 1970 and 1971. Other growths of note are:

Château	Cases
Bel-Air	4,250
Perron	4,250
Grand-Ormeau	2,100
de la Commanderie	4,250
Belle-Graves	4,250
Teysson	4,250
Moulin à Vent	3,400

10

Fronsac, Bourg and Blaye, and other red wines of Bordeaux

Because Bordeaux is such a vast producer of *appellation* wines, it is almost inevitable that many of its less well-known wines suffer by exclusion from the limelight in which Médoc, Graves, St Emilion and Pomerol bask. I have often thought that if these wines had been situated elsewhere in France, they would have been hailed as great finds. So often when, in recent years, the hunt has been on for 'lesser known wines', these lesser Bordeaux have been forgotten, and wines of less intrinsic merit and interest have been successfully 'discovered' and promoted, simply because they lay outside the Gironde. Yet the best of these wines deserve recognition in their own right as wines of charm and character, which have the advantage of reaching maturity earlier than the great growths of the leading *appellations*. It is not surprising that wines like Bourg and Fronsac were preferred to those of the Médoc in the eighteenth century, when wines were not aged in bottle, but drunk young after cask maturation.

I firmly believe that the wines that follow have a very definite place in the cellar of anyone who loves Bordeaux red wines. I, for one, would much prefer to drink a mature Fronsac, a young Bourg or Blaye, even a young Premières Côtes, than an immature Médoc. It is true that a young, voluptuous St Emilion has great appeal, but only for certain occasions and with certain food. The more modest charms of these often delightful wines can sometimes prove more versatile.

FRONSAC

This relatively small district of hilly, partly wooded country, lies just to the west of Libourne. In effect, it consists of a giant bluff overlooking the Dordogne, and this special geographical feature is of much importance for the district. In 1956, for instance, the great February frost caused less damage here than anywhere else in the Gironde, because of the elevation of its vineyards. The centre is a small, medieval town of Fronsac, a mere two-and-a-half kilometres from Libourne, which lies at the junction of the Isle and the Dordogne. The River Isle forms the western boundary of the district. There are actually two separate *appellations*, Fronsac and Côtes de Canon-Fronsac, which is less confusing than it used to be when Fronsac was known as Côtes de Fronsac. There are just under 700 hectares of Fronsac vineyards, averaging some 30,000 hectolitres a year, while the Côtes de Canon-Fronsac has just under 300 hectares of vineyards producing, on average, just over 12,000 hectolitres a year. So the whole district is about the same size as Pauillac.

The distinction between Fronsac and Côtes de Canon really serves no useful purpose. While it is true that the outstanding growths are in the Côtes de Canon, it is equally true that the best of Fronsac is as good as the remaining growths of the Côtes de Canon, and that they share common characteristics.

When I first began to taste young Fronsacs in cask regularly, in the early 1960s, I was soon attracted by their very individual character. It is that early aroma of the new wine which develops in bottle into a charmingly distinctive, perfumed bouquet that is the characteristic which singles out Fronsac as certainly the finest wine outside the great districts. It is predominantly the perfume peculiar to Cabernet Franc, which is here the most important grape variety, demonstrating yet again that in different places, different *cépages* develop differing nuances of character. These wines have a breed and distinction of flavour which sets them apart from the best of Bourg or Blaye. In the past, they were noted for their body and firmness, but less rustic vinification has produced wines of finer texture, emphasizing their distinctive fruit. Some years ago, when a most interesting tasting of Fronsacs was held at Christie's, it was noticeable that many wines were parched, because kept too long in cask. In those days, most

properties kept their wines in cask as long as possible, hoping for
bulk sales to *négociants*, and only château-bottled what was left
when sales ceased. This was often too late for the good of the wine.
Recently, there has been a noticeable improvement in standards
in the district, so that more properties are now bottling wines
which really show the full potential of the area. So it is high time
that these wines received the recognition they deserve.

The principal growths are:

Côtes de Canon-Fronsac

Canon
Canon de Brem
Junayme
Vrai-Canon-Bouché
Vray-Canon-Boyer

These are, today, probably the leading wines. Then come:

Belloy
Constelle
Gaby
du Gazin
Grand Renouil
Haut Mazeris
La Marche (the largest property with Gazin)
Mausse
Mazeris
Mazeris Belle Vue
Moulin Pey Labrie

Fronsac

The following are the leading growths, which are on the same level
as the second group of properties in Côtes de Canon:

Bourdieu-La-Valade
de Carles
La Dauphine
Jeandeman (the largest property)
La Lagüe
Mayne Vieil
Rouet

Tasta
des Tonnelles
Trois Croix
Villars
Vincent

BOURG AND BLAYE

These two adjoining areas are of roughly similar standing, although the best growths of Bourg are certainly superior to those of Blaye. Geographically they are opposite the Médoc, with Bourg being partly on the Dordogne and partly on the Gironde. But the countryside is quite different from the Médoc, with its picturesquely rolling hillsides and mixed agriculture. The two old ports of Bourg and Blaye were once important for the control of the river, especially in the days when the kings of England held sway in Aquitaine, and a medieval fortress at Bourg forms the foundation for Vauban's seventeenth-century fortress, which complements his other one at Lamarque in the Médoc. Today, a ferry operates between the two, as a reminder of how much more important the river used to be.

While a glance at the map will show that the district of Blaye is far larger than Bourg, the vineyards of Bourg are the more extensive. In Blaye, only some 2,100 hectares are planted, of which just under 1,700 are for red wine production, while there are just over 2,700 hectares of vines in Bourg. Although some white wines are made in both districts, with some of the Côtes de Blaye being quite good, it is the red wines that give them their importance.

The best growths of Bourg are on slopes near the Gironde and are noticeably rich and fleshy in texture, with a good colour and pleasantly fruity bouquet. These are attractive, straightforward wines which develop quickly and are usually delicious to drink when three or four years old, but will hold well for another three or four years in good vintages. As an indication of the intrinsic quality of these wines, I have frequently found that a good Bourg will often be superior to many wines from the St Emilion satellites.

The wines of Blaye have less body and often used to be rather astringent. Now, with improved vinification, they are lighter but with an engagingly vivid fruitiness. However, it must, unfortunately, be emphasized that in both districts there are still poor wines to be found due to careless vinification.

Bourg

There are many châteaux, some of them with very large productions. Among the best-known are:

de Barbe (has long had a reputation as one of the best growths, consistent and fine)

Guerry (since it was acquired by Bertrand de Rivoyre, the leading *négociant* who also administers Fourcas Hosten, this has become one of the very best growths; a wine of richness and charm)

du Bousquet
Coubet
Croute-Charlus
Eyquem
Guionne
Haut Combes
Mendoce
Mille-Secousses
Plaisance
Poliane
Rouselle
Rousset
de Samonac
Sauman
Tayac
Verger

Blaye

Again, there are many châteaux, only a few of which are yet much known on export markets. Among these may be noted:

Barbé
Bourdieu
Chante-Alouette
Grand-Barrail
des Graves
Les Gruppes de Pivert
Haut Sociondo
L'Escadre

Loumede
Le Menaudat
Puy-Benet-Boffort
Segonzac
Videau

PREMIÈRES CÔTES DE BORDEAUX

This district extends south along the right bank of the Garonne from just above Bordeaux itself for nearly 50 kilometres, but is never more than two or three kilometres in depth. It is an extremely attractive, hilly area, in sharp contrast to the flat countryside on the opposite bank of Graves, Sauternes and Barsac.

The white wines are covered in the following chapter on Sauternes and other white wines. Whereas the best white wines are to be found in the southern part of the district towards Loupiac and Ste-Croix-du-Mont, more and more red wines are to be found as one goes north. It is also a district where the balance between red and white has been changing in the last decade. In the first five years of the decade, the average yield for whites was 66,267 hectolitres against 36,957 of red wines. But in the second half of the decade, the shift away from white wines has been dramatic, so that the average yields for the whites between 1975 and 1979 fell to 33,530 hectolitres, while that for reds rose to 46,377. It is obviously quicker to pull up vines than to bring new ones into production, and in the next few years the production of red wines will certainly rise. In 1979, just over 76,000 hectolitres were produced, just about twice as much as in 1970. The wines themselves have, like many of the lesser reds, much improved in the last few years. The best are very perfumed and attractively fruity, of light to medium body and usually delicious drinking when three to seven years old. Château names here still mean very little, and the best advice is to try any red wines you find under a property name. You have a good chance of having a pleasant surprise at a modest price.

CÔTES DE CASTILLON

This is the only other area of importance which is not completely hidden behind the anonymity of a Bordeaux Supérieur or Bordeaux *appellation*. There are actually two *appellations*—plain Bordeaux Côtes de Castillon, and Bordeaux Supérieur Côtes de Castillon—but almost all the wine of the district is now declared as Bordeaux Supérieur. This hilly, pleasantly rustic area lies behind the ancient market town of Castillon-la-Bataille, and used to be called St Emilionnais until it was excluded from the name by the *appellation*. In truth, when well vinified, the style of these wines is very close to the St Emilion satellites and not far behind in quality. There is a touch of roughness and coarseness at first, but this very soon gives way to a pleasantly robust fruitiness.

Production is tending to increase, and the average for the five years, 1975–9, was nearly 78,000 hectolitres, while the 1979 vintage topped 100,000 hectolitres for the first time. There are a great many properties now selling under their own label, but none has really established a reputation yet. The great problem has been to find properties which are consistent. Again, the best advice is to try any château wine you come across; often those selected and bottled by a good *négociant* can be more reliable than a château-bottling, since few proprietors in the district have the facilities or experience necessary for good *élevage* and bottling.

OTHER BORDEAUX AND BORDEAUX SUPÉRIEUR

Because a wine does not bear the name of one of the districts with its own *appellation*, it does not mean to say that it will be ordinary or without interest. More and more such wines are appearing on the market, and if well made and carefully selected, can prove excellent as early drinking, everyday claret. The main source is now the Entre-deux-Mers, where more red wines are now being made, and sold as Bordeaux or Bordeaux Supérieur, since the Entre-deux-Mers *appellation* applies only to white wines.

Another area without its own *appellation* should also be mentioned—the Cubzaguais. This is a corridor of land astride the Paris road, centred on St André de Cubzac, and lying between Bourg and Blaye to the north, the Dordogne on the west and south, and Fronsac to the east. The *appellation* is Bordeaux or Bordeaux Supérieur. There are three important properties with very big productions. Château de Terrefort-Quancard belongs to Les Fils de Marcel Quancard, the well-known *négociants* at St

André de Cubzac. It makes an attractive wine which can age very well in good vintages. There is the even larger Château Timberlay, which often produces over 42,000 cases of sound, straightforward wine. Then, more for its architecture than for its wine, there is Château de Bouilh, the magnificent mansion designed by Victor Louis, architect of the Théâtre in Bordeaux, for the La Tour du Pin family. Only a fragment of this grand design was completed when the Revolution interrupted the work, which was never to be resumed.

The area also has two properties which are best known for bearing the same names as two classified growths of the Médoc: the Domaine de Beychevelle, close to Timberley and Bouilh, and the Cru Cantemerle at neighbouring St Gervais. They are both decent enough wines, but their names have obviously been useful in selling their wine, especially on export markets.

For the sake of completeness, mention must also be made of several *appellations* which have little commercial importance on export markets:

Sainte-Foy-Bordeaux lies in the extreme north-east corner of the Entre-deux-Mers, with the Dordogne river running between it and the *département* and wines of Dordogne. Twice as much white as red wine is produced.

Graves de Vayres is a small enclave in Entre-deux-Mers opposite Libourne. The commercial advantage of being confused with the Graves district south of Bordeaux does not seem to have brought the area any notable *réclame*. About twice as much white as red wine is produced.

Côtes de Francs is the area to the north of and immediately adjoining the Côtes de Castillon and producing similar wines, but the *appellation* does not seem to have gained wide acceptance.

In conclusion, it must be emphasized again that many pleasant, useful wines are to be found under the simple Bordeaux and Bordeaux Supérieur *appellations*. For the minute difference in price, it is usually worth going for Bordeaux Supérieur. These are excellent wines for drinking when two or three years old, when their youthful fruit still shows to advantage. There has been a great improvement in recent years in *négociants'* generic blends, and many of the wines sold under individual château names are also excellent value. At this price, one can afford to experiment.

11

Sauternes, Barsac and other white wines, both sweet and dry

If one were to ask the most occasional wine drinker to describe Sauternes, the chances are strongly in favour of a reply that it is a sweet white wine. Such is the fame of this *appellation* that it is probably more widely known than any other district name in Bordeaux, and it is certainly one of the most famous of all French wines.

Yet the area producing Sauternes is very small, confined to the five communes of Sauternes itself, Barsac, Bommes, Fargues and Preignac. The district forms an enclave in the Graves, with the Garonne as its north-eastern boundary, some 40 kilometres south-east of Bordeaux. The production is also small, accentuated by the much lower yield resulting from the method of production from shrivelled grapes infected with *botrytis cinerea* or noble rot (*pourriture noble*). (For a description of the vinification of Sauternes, see Chapter 2.) The *appellation* permits only 25 hectolitres per hectare, compared with 40 hectolitres for other Bordeaux white wines, such as Graves or Loupiac.

Unfortunately, the fame of Sauternes has led to widespread fraud, and to the unhappy practice of many producers of sweet wines from countries such as Spain, Australia and the USA adopting this name for their own products. This practice of using a geographical name which has gained world-wide fame for the excellence of its product and then trying to give it a generic significance for the benefit of lesser-known wines—usually inferior in quality and always cheaper in price—is to be deplored. Happily, international agreements, and especially the EEC, have banished such malpractices from Europe now, but they are still to be found in the USA and have also spread to new wine-drinking countries such as Japan.

Historically, Sauternes is a relatively modern wine. In the eighteenth century, the wines of this region seem to have been dry or at best semi-sweet, and much red wine was also produced. It was only in the nineteenth century that the effects of allowing the *botrytis* to develop as widely as possible were evolved, and the technique for vinifying such wines was perfected.

As has been explained earlier, the selection of grapes with an unusually high concentration of sugar gives a must which even the vigorous yeasts of the Gironde cannot fully ferment, resulting in a naturally sweet wine. The *appellation* insists on an alcoholic strength of not less than 13° in the finished wine. Although no minimum is laid down for the sweetness of the wine, in practice it has to pass a tasting test, and one could say that 2·5°–3° Baumé was the practical minimum, with the fine growths producing 5° Baumé or more in good years.

The wines of Sauternes have often been compared with those rarities produced so much further north in the German vineyards. Although the basic principle of the selection of grapes infected by *botrytis* is similar, all the other conditions are so different as to make comparison of doubtful validity. Without going into great detail, it is worth pinpointing two factors of importance. The Beeren- and Trockenbeeren-auslese are essentially the products of special circumstances, prized rarities produced at admittedly uneconomic cost, as prestige wines—the apotheosis of the German vintners' art. In Sauternes, on the other hand, the conditions for making such wines on a large scale are the norm, and not the exception. Sauternes is unlucky if its ration of failure is any higher than for the red wines of the Gironde, though the record for the 1960s was below average, with four bad or poor years, one more than for other areas in the Gironde, and the 1970s have been no better. Two or three poor years in a decade is more typical. Whereas a large German estate of, say, 30 hectares, will in a very favourable year make perhaps 5 per cent, or at most 10 per cent of its production as Beeren- or Trockenbeeren-auslese, in Sauternes a property will in a normal year be able to declare nearly all its production as good enough to sell under its château label. On the debit side, though, is the sad spectacle of musts of insufficient weight being enriched through chaptalization. Such practices are surely the negation of all that Sauternes stands for, and would be unthinkable in Germany for Beeren- and Trockenbeeren-auslese.

The second point which is worth stressing is the tolerance of yeast to sugar. In the conditions under which German wines are fermented, which are very much cooler than those usual in the Gironde, the alcoholic fermentation usually stops somewhere between 9° and 10° G. L. In Sauternes, the fermentation continues until at least 13° and often up to 14° or 15°, if the conditions are favourable. This still leaves 4° or 5° Baumé, that is, of un-fermented sugar. In other words, the original musts in Sauternes are richer than in Germany and more sugar is converted into alcohol. If the must of a potential Trockenbeeren-auslese were to be transported down to the Gironde and placed in a Sauternes *chais*, its appearance would be quite transformed and one would end up, I suspect, with a much drier wine with more alcohol, but lacking much of that wonderful elegance and harmony which characterizes such wines. So it is not only the soil and climate which shape a wine, but the whole milieu in which it is afterwards reared.

The essential point about the Sauternes region is that nowhere else in the world do conditions exist to produce natural, sweet white wines on such a scale or with such consistency, though recent developments suggest that such wines may be produced with some regularity and in some quantity—but from the Rhine Riesling—in parts of northern California. The grape varieties used are exactly the same as for other white wines produced in the Gironde—the Sémillon, Sauvignon and Muscadelle—but here they reach perfect ripeness by late September, and then the warm, slightly humid climate, typical of this area, encourages the growth of the *botrytis cinerea*. This rather unattractive, furry mould rapidly dehydrates the grapes, thus greatly enhancing the con-centration of sugar. It is to be found in other parts of Bordeaux— at its best in Ste-Croix-du-Mont and Loupiac, in parts of the Premières Côtes, in neighbouring Cérons, and down the Dordogne at Monbazillac—as well as up to the Loire and, of course, in Germany. But nowhere else is its growth so uniform and exten-sive, year in and year out, or the resulting wines so unctuous and vigorous. It is the unique balance of alcohol and sweetness which gives Sauternes its special quality. Other wines may be more elegant or delicate, but Sauternes has an overwhelming bouquet of ripe fruit and a richness of savour and mellow perfection of sweetness not to be found in any other. Yet at its best it should not, and does not, cloy. The acidity and the alcohol are sufficient to balance the great sweetness.

It is not surprising that poets have been inspired by such a wine. One of the happiest and aptest sentiments is 'l'extravagance du parfait'. But, by the same token, Sauternes has found itself an unfashionable wine in recent years. It is not surprising, perhaps, that the great days of Sauternes were in the nineteenth century with its extravagant and flamboyant way of life, nor that the Russian Grand Dukes were among its greatest devotees. Then Yquem was the most expensive wine in Bordeaux, surpassing the great red wines of the Médoc. In recent years, the price of the great Sauternes (apart from Yquem itself) has been no more than that of a good *Bourgeois* Médoc or St Emilion. Such is the whim of fashion.

One is possibly tempted to think of Sauternes as a wine made for a more leisured age. Although the great châteaux have often demonstrated that different Sauternes can be served throughout a meal, this is not to the taste of most of us. It has to be confessed that Sauternes is really too rich, both in alcohol and sugar, to drink in this way. Yet, served at the end of the meal as an accompaniment to fresh fruit, especially strawberries, raspberries or peaches, or with any sweet dessert which does not incorporate chocolate, it is incomparable. Indeed, it is the only wine which can be drunk with such sweet dishes with complete pleasure. Many of the finest German wines are better drunk on their own, and seem too delicate beside really sweet and strongly-flavoured dishes.

In Bordeaux, there are many advocates of drinking Sauternes at the beginning of a meal with *pâté de foie gras*. The combination is certainly a very rich one and, although undoubtedly successful, it does pose the problem of what to do next. Ideally, a consommé is needed to clean and refresh the palate before going on to a red wine. A glass of Sauternes can also be magnificent with Roquefort cheese, the combination of lusciousness and saltiness being unusually delicious and satisfying.

But even if one has to admit that this is a luxury wine, the total quantity produced for the whole world is not, after all, large in an age of rapidly rising living standards. It would indeed be a sad day if there were not a place for such an exquisite luxury. The most recent signs have been encouraging after a long period in the wilderness. In the early 1950s, the leading growths of Sauternes commanded a rather better price than the second growths of the Médoc. But when prices for red wines improved in 1955, and again in 1959, the Sauternes were left behind. Right through the sixties the price of Sauternes remained static, with the leading classified growths well below the level of the second growths of the Médoc. It was not until the great price explosion of 1971 that Sauternes at last reaped some reward for its labours, and it began to look as if the lean years were past. The 1976 first growths opened at similar prices to the second and third growths of the Médoc. But it still needs to be stressed that even at today's prices the leading growths of Sauternes still represent the finest value of any of the great wines of France.

No survey of Sauternes would be complete without a word on the keeping qualities of the wine. One hears very conflicting views expressed on this. It is sometimes said that this is a wine which must be drunk young, that it is at its best when, say, five to seven years old, and generally begins to decline after ten years. In my view, this is both misleading and mistaken.

The chief enemies of Sauternes are oxidation and volatile acidity. Sauternes is prey to both, even more than other white wines, because the tradition of ageing up to three years in cask before bottling is still followed by some producers. With all we know now about the treatment and clarification of wines, and with the lack of real cellars which command a constant low temperature in summer, this long ageing in this wood is almost certainly a mistake. In the last few years, we have seen many of the leading châteaux abandon this tradition in favour of much earlier bottling, early during the second winter—if not before—with a corresponding benefit to the wines. What happens at the moment is that, in years when the concentration of sugar is exceptional, the resulting wines may be slightly unbalanced and will darken in colour rather rapidly, as indeed Trockenbeeren-auslese often do. The sugar caramelizes. The deep mahogany colour which results is, in fact, pleasing to the eye and is quite unlike the horrid browning of a normal oxidized white wine. The wine is still deliciously rich and mellow on the palate in such a state, because the sugar and alcohol have allayed the usual effect of oxidation.

Volatile acidity, on the other hand, is more insidious. Because of present methods, most Sauternes tend to have a rather high volatile acidity, but this is not readily detectable on the palate because of the sweetness of the wine which effectively masks it. However, after some years of maturing, one can begin to discern a hard, astringent taste at the finish of the wine in place of the mellow, velvety texture which usually gives Sauternes such a long, lingering flavour. This is the volatile acidity asserting itself, and after this the flavour will shorten and the wine will appear to lose fruit as well as sweetness. I remember a good example of this in the 1959 Yquem. At a banquet in Bordeaux in 1965, Edouard Cruse said he thought the Yquem 1959 being served had an excessive volatile acidity. It was not readily noticeable, but I remembered what he had said and when, about a year later, a customer returned a bottle of the same wine with some trivial complaint, I asked our laboratory to test the volatile acidity. It showed up well above the level that could be expected. The sequel came at a dinner at Loudenne in 1972. We compared the 1959 Yquem against the Suduiraut of the same year. The flavour of the Yquem was shortened by a hard, almost tannic taste, while the Suduiraut finished long and honeyed.

When discussing this problem recently with Monsieur Pierre Meslier, the *régisseur* at Yquem, I was interested to learn that Yquem has been collaborating with the University of Bordeaux on the whole problem of volatile acidity in sweet wines, and one of the results has been the discovery that two differing types of volatile acidity are found in sweet wines. One comes from yeasts and does not normally damage the taste of the finished wine. The second type comes from bacteria, and this is the sort that gradually masks and eventually spoils the flavour of the wine. To prevent this, great care is needed in the actual picking of the grapes, and there is a real hope that the problem can now be prevented.

I think it is this apparent drying-up of a wine, due to high volatile acidity, which the advocates of early drinking have in mind when they say that a wine should be drunk before it is ten years old. There is also the problem of wines which are really too luscious. The concentration of residual sugar causes such wines to colour rapidly and maderize prematurely. This is happening to some 1975s—notably the Rieussec. In fact, a well-balanced wine of a good year can be extremely long-lived. I have drunk wines of the famous 1893 vintage when they were around seventy years old, and they were still of good colour—deep golden, but not mahogany, and sweet and delicious. More recently, it was interesting to find that the 1890 Yquem—a rather light wine, never really luscious—was perfectly preserved when over seventy years old, while examples of the great years of 1867 and 1868 were well past their best and only interesting ruins. Generally speaking, though, I would say that a good vintage from a good growth could be expected to last for twenty to thirty years without disappointment—provided always, of course, the wine is well stored. Such wines will usually become drinkable when five to six years old. The sugar in the wine is not usually sufficiently in balance to make for enjoyable drinking much before this, and sometimes sulphur can spoil the nose initially.

One point in the naming of Sauternes often causes confusion. I said at the beginning of this chapter that Sauternes is produced in five communes, one of which is Barsac. When the *appellation* system was introduced, a separate *appellation* was given to Barsac, because for generations its wines had been sold under their own name. But, at the same time, they were given the right to use the name of Sauternes, so that a Barsac can always be a Sauternes, but a Sauternes need not be a Barsac. More recently, the habit has grown up in Barsac of labelling their wines Sauternes-Barsac, thus making clear the double allegiance. While dealing with names, it is worth pointing out that the terms Haut Barsac and Haut Sauternes have no official validity whatsoever. They were often used by growers in the best situated vineyards before the introduction of the *appellation*, and by merchants both before and after the *appellation* to indicate a superior brand. Some châteaux still preserve the anachronism on their label blocks, as in pre-*appellation* days.

During the lean years for Sauternes, there was much heart-searching as to how the wine could be more successfully promoted, and as to how fraud on the French and German markets could be stamped out. It was pointed out that many wines were of poor quality and many growers were chaptalizing their wines (concentration of the must is forbidden by the *appellation* regulations), resulting in heavy, dull wines unworthy of Sauternes. It seemed obvious that better prices could only come from a better control of quality. The result of several years' deliberation was a Groupe-

311

ment de Producteurs, officially recognized by government law in 1967. This established that the Union des Syndicats, which formed the Groupement, would only sell in bottle, and that all bottles should carry the numbered vignettes of the Groupement, guaranteeing that this was true Sauternes which had passed the surveillance of the Commission de Dégustation. Like nearly every such Bordeaux scheme, it was only partially successful, but did a certain amount of good for the standard of generic wines at the time. The entry of the UK into the EEC effectively ended the abuse of the Sauternes name on the British market.

Another development of these lean years was the so-called dry Sauternes. The attraction of the idea was that by picking a part of the crop early, the danger of damage from bad weather was alleviated, and a larger yield ensured. The resulting wine, however, could only be called Bordeaux Blanc and not Sauternes. Some growers aimed to produce a full-bodied, drier wine, preserving some Sauternes characteristics. Ygrec (from Yquem) and the dry Filhot were examples of this style, but over the years the experiment enjoyed a very limited success, being really neither one thing nor the other, a disappointment to those wanting a sweet wine, but not dry enough for those seeking dry wines. On the other hand, some growers have concentrated simply on producing a really dry wine as well as possible. The dry Doisy-Daene is an excellent example of this, and has proved successful over a number of years. But of course the real solution to this problem is to allow growers to use the Graves *appellation* for their dry wines. This would enable them to obtain a decent price for their dry wines, and so help to prevent the production of ersatz Sauternes through chaptalization. It is already allowed in Cérons, and it is hard to think of any logical reason why such dry wines should not be allowed the name of Graves.

The wines of Sauternes were classified in 1855, along with those of the Médoc. It is a commentary, perhaps, on the comparative neglect of the region that, whereas there has been much speculation for years on a re-classification of the Médoc, there has been none at all in Sauternes. Yquem clearly deserves its special position as the sole *Premier Grand Cru Classé* of the region, and few would quarrel with the eleven *Premiers Crus*. Of the fifteen *Deuxième Crus Classés*, however, while one or two may be thought to deserve elevation, there is little now to distinguish most of them

SAUTERNES AND BARSAC

As in the Médoc, the Sauternes vineyards were officially classified in 1855. This classification is known as the Official Classification of the Great Growths of the Gironde.

The total production from these vineyards represents approximately 25 per cent of the total Sauternes production, amounting roughly to 350,000 cases per year.

The following figures of production are approximate, and indicate average annual output, as given by the communes and taken from their Déclarations de Récoltes records.

TONNEAUX

Premier Grand Cru (First Great Growth)

Château d'Yquem	80

Premier Crus (First Growths)

Château Guiraud	120
Château La Tour-Blanche	50
Château Lafaurie-Peyraguey	50
Château de Rayne-Vigneau	120
Château Sigalas-Rabaud	35
Château Rabaud-Promis	75
Clos Haut-Peyraguey	25
Château Coutet	75
Château Climens	65
Château Suduiraut	110
Château Rieussec	90

Deuxieme Crus (Second Growths)

Château d'Arche	80
Château Filhot	50
Château Lamothe	25
Château Myrat	50
Château Doisy-Védrines	60
Château Doisy-Daëne	20
Château Suau	15
Château Broustet	30
Château Caillou	40
Château Nairac	25
Château de Malle	40
Château Romer	15

313

from a number of excellent *Crus Bourgeois* which today command prices which are just as favourable and sometimes superior.

Since the differences between the wines of the five communes are certainly no more marked than the differences between leading growths, I have adopted the practice of listing the leading growths in alphabetical order, rather than under their respective communes.

Château d'Yquem   *Premier Grand Cru Classé*

The supreme Sauternes and one of the most famous wines of the world. Appropriately, Yquem lies in the commune of Sauternes itself, occupying the most superb position, with the great medieval château dominating the splendid slopes below it and commanding an unrivalled view over the surrounding countryside. The château itself is a real castle in the English sense—indeed, one of the finest examples of a medieval fortress in the whole Gironde. While the massive towers remind us of its original purpose, the elegant windows which now adorn even the exterior walls are witnesses of more tranquil times, when civilization was permitted to beautify the fortress. The spacious courtyard of the château is a perfect setting for the concerts given here during the Bordeaux Festival each May.

The property has only changed hands by marriage since the sixteenth century. The family were related by marriage to their celebrated neighbour, Montaigne, the sixteenth-century essayist and philosopher. It passed to the present occupants, the family of the Marquis de Lur-Saluces, in 1785. The old Marquis, who died in 1970, had an exceptionally long reign, and has been succeeded by his nephew, Alexandre de Lur-Saluces.

In one sense, Yquem remains a very traditional growth. The wines are still kept for a full three years in cask. But, in another way, they have broken from tradition by introducing a dry wine sold under the name of Ygrec (this is the French for the letter Y), but still using the traditional Yquem label. This bastard was conceived during Sauternes' lean years, the first vintage being 1959. A number of leading growths in the region started to produce dry wines at this time, but there were two schools of thought as to what the style of the wine should be. Some argued that the wine must be full-bodied and fairly rich in alcohol, with even a suspicion of residual sugar to preserve the identity of the wine against other Bordeaux. Others thought that the object should be to produce as good a dry white wine as they could, and that the wine should bear no resemblance to the original Sauternes at all. Ygrec belongs to the first and more traditional school. The wine tends to go golden in colour rather rapidly, and to be heavy and rather flat, with a hard, dry finish, but with some Sauternes style on the nose. The experiment has not proved very successful, judging from the stock which often lies heavy on the hands of the Bordeaux *négociants* who habitually deal in Yquem. It also caused confusion with the label so closely resembling that of Yquem and with the similarity of names; it is easy for the unknowledgeable to be deceived. I was once on the receiving end of this when ordering a glass of Yquem at a famous London restaurant offering Yquem by the glass. It was late, and the sommelier had evidently left. I had great difficulty in persuading the young waiter on duty that the bottle of Ygrec from which he had poured my glass was not the Yquem I had ordered. Ygrec is produced spasmodically, not in every vintage.

A good vintage of Yquem is the quintessence of Sauternes. The nose is marvellously perfumed and flowered, the flavour incomparably luscious, yet fresh and invigorating. The harmony seems perfect, very sweet, yet with the concentration of great fruitiness, and without any hint of cloying. In comparison with other leading Sauternes, Yquem is both richer and has their virtues, only to a more marked degree. In some years, it can attain as much as 7° Baumé after an alcoholic fermentation which has produced over 15° G. L.

Unfortunately, there was a period when Yquem far too often failed to produce wines worthy of its best traditions. But the marvellous 1967 vintage, followed by the arrival of Alexandre de Lur-Saluces and some changes in staff—notably the appointment of Monsieur Pierre Meslier—have ushered in a new era. Once more, Yquem is producing wines which are worthy of its great reputation.

The domaine itself is very extensive, comprising 148 hectares; 100 hectares are actually under vine of which 80 produce wine and the rest are young vines. But such is the nature of Sauternes that these 80 hectares yield on average only about 7,500 cases of the precious wine, while a property in the Médoc could expect to produce about 21,000 to 25,500 cases of red wine from a vineyard of similar size. The vineyard is planted with 80 per cent Sémillon and 20 per cent Sauvignon.

At Yquem, there are no short cuts. The botrytized grapes are individually picked by the experienced staff drawn largely from the fifty-seven full-time workers on the estate. The aim is to pick the grapes when the refractometer shows a reading of not less than 20°, but not more than 22° Baumé. Pierre Meslier believes it is most important for quality not to allow the Baumé degree to rise too high, as many producers did in 1975. This leads to unbalanced wines. He finds that by following this rule, the fermentation will stop naturally at between 13·5° and 14°, thus giving the wines all the richness they need in terms of high residual sugar, without making them too rich in alcohol. The 1971 and 1975 are tributes to the success he has achieved by adhering to these yardsticks. Most of the best Sauternes châteaux produced fine, elegant 1971s, but few could claim these qualities for their 1975s. Yquem can; the 1975 is a worthy successor to the great 1971.

Some of the great vintages of Yquem made in the nineteenth century are legendary, and fetched enormous prices. Such a wine was the 1847. The only nineteenth-century wines I have tasted are the 1867 and 1868, both a long way past their best, and the 1890, a light wine still holding up well and enjoyable. Between the wars, the great vintages were 1921, still remarkably good when fifty years old, the 1928 and the 1937, one of the finest Yquems I have tasted—it was at its greatest in the 1950s but is now past its prime. After the Second World War, 1945, 1947 and 1949 all produced magnificent wines. In recent years I have found the 1945 and 1947 still so, in their differing ways. During this and earlier epochs, Yquem also produced some remarkable off-vintages, a careful selection producing a small quantity of wine worthy of being bottled under the famous label. Examples of this were 1922, 1931 and 1936 between the two wars.

In the 1950s and 1960s, however, the record was far too irregular. The 1955 did not last as it should, and is now disappointing and past its best. The 1959 went the same way, spoiled by too much volatile acidity. The 1960 was a disappointment after the quite acceptable 1954, throwing a heavy deposit in bottle and ageing rapidly. The 1961 was rather clumsy and heavy like many 1961s, but is probably good wine for the year, if lacking finesse. The 1962 was more successful, probably the best wine

316

made for several years. Then came 1963 and the astonishing decision to offer an Yquem from this vintage. The wine was quite frankly a disgrace and totally unworthy, not only of Yquem, but also of Sauternes. Yquem is unusual among Bordeaux châteaux in never offering its wine until it is in bottle, so there could be no excuse that a rash decision was made too soon—they had had three years to think about it! Most English merchants I know who had automatically reserved the wine when it was first offered, cancelled their orders when they saw the sample. It is said at the château that the 1963 was intended only for the French market and not for export, but the *négociants* did not keep to this agreement. One had hoped that Yquem would have learnt something from this, but apparently not, because the 1968 was nearly as bad. Fortunately, the magnificent 1967 has proved in retrospect to be the beginning of better things. The wine itself is luscious, yet with great elegance and panache. One has the feeling that like some other great Yquems of the past, its greatest period may lie between ten and fifteen years of age. The 1970 is a powerful heavyweight, the 1971 all elegance, a worthy successor to the 1967 which could perhaps prove to be even finer. Finally, there is the magnificent 1975, an object lesson in how to overcome the problems of the year.

THE *PREMIER CRUS CLASSÉS*

Château Climens

One of the two great wines of Barsac, this is always among the finest wines of Sauternes, and one of the few that can rival Yquem for the perfection of its flavour and breed, if not for its power. It has long enjoyed an outstanding reputation on the English market, where a small but consistent following for these fine wines has been maintained, even in the bleakest years for this district.

The vineyard of Climens consists of about 30 hectares which produce some 6,000 cases on average. It is interesting to note that the entire vineyard is planted with Sémillon, which is said to suit the chalky soil. From 1885 until 1971, Climens was the property of the Gounouilhou family, who then sold it to Monsieur Lucien Lurton of Brane-Cantenac. Continuity has been provided by Madame Janin, the *gérante* and *maître de chais*, who has been there for thirty years.

317

There have been some wonderful vintages of Climens. I think the finest I have tasted must be the 1947, certainly as fine a wine as was produced in that great vintage. The wartime vintage of 1943 was also particularly good. More recently, the 1952, 1955 and 1962 were particularly successful. At a tasting in 1979, it was very encouraging to see that there has been no lowering of standards, and that really classic wines are still the rule here. Thus beautiful wines were made in 1971, 1975 and 1976. These wines combine liquorousness with freshness and balance. The 1971 is one of the top wines of the year with a really beautiful bouquet and flavour, a wine of the highest class. The 1975 has more elegance and finesse than most wines of this year, and the 1976 will be another great wine.

Château Coutet

This is the inseparable twin of Climens, as the other great wine of Barsac. It has been a favourite in England for many years. The relative merits of the two wines have often been debated. In general, it can be said that Coutet has rather more delicacy than Climens, but that Climens is the more powerful. But when I was last able to compare the two side by side, the 1975 Climens had more finesse than the Coutet, so no generalization is sacrosanct. Curiously, the great years of Coutet often do not coincide with the great years at Climens. Thus Coutet was renowned for its 1949, while the 1947 was the great vintage at Climens.

For thirty years the proprietors of Coutet were the Rolland-Guy family, who tended it with the greatest care. They sold in 1977 to Monsieur Baly. At the time of the 1855 classification, it belonged to the Lur-Saluces family. About 6,500 cases is an average yield. The château dates in part from the end of the thirteenth-century, part is fourteenth century, the rest more recent, but harmonizing well with the older parts. The vineyard is planted with 80 per cent Sémillon and 20 per cent Sauvignon.

Since the Second World War, Coutet has enjoyed a fine record for consistency. The 1949 has already been mentioned—it was still in peak form in 1972. The 1950 was perhaps the outstanding wine of the vintage, certainly better than the Yquem. Since then, 1955, 1959 and 1962 were all excellent; then came 1966 which was rather light, but perfumed and elegant. The 1967 has disappointed; it is not one of the best examples of the year. But Coutet was back to

318

form with the 1971, the 1973 is one of the few fine Sauternes of this very mixed vintage, and the 1975 is a classic—much better than most, if carrying a little too much colour for comfort. In contrast the 1976 is pale in colour, perfumed and beautifully balanced. A typical wine of the year which should improve and last for years.

Château Guiraud

This is the only *Premier Cru*, apart from Yquem, wholly in the commune of Sauternes itself. It is an important property producing some 11,000 cases, and Monsieur Paul Rival is the enthusiastic proprietor. Curiously, this is the only one of the *Premiers Crus* to have changed its name completely since the 1855 classification, when it was known as Château Bayle.

I remember Guiraud as a light, elegant and attractive wine, not one of the outstanding growths today, perhaps, but still consistent and fine, if less vigorous than the best wines. But recently, the wines have been sweeter and fuller, perhaps because after fermentation in cask, the wine is kept in vat and not cask. The 1975 had already taken on a lot of colour when only three years old, and was heavy and clumsy. The vineyard is planted in the proportion of 70 per cent Sémillon and 30 per cent Sauvignon. In addition to the Sauternes, a dry white wine is made, sold under the name of Pavillon Sec, as well as a red—Pavillon Rouge. Vintages I remember with particular pleasure are the 1953, 1955, 1957 and 1962. But the most remarkable wine of all was the 1893, still fresh and sweet when seventy years old.

Château La Tour Blanche

The commune of Bommes produced four *Premiers Crus* in 1855, more than any other commune. La Tour Blanche was considered the finest of these and, indeed, was placed at the head of all the *Premiers Crus* in the classification. At that time, the name appeared as Latour Blanche. In 1910, the proprietor, Monsieur Osiris, gave the estate to the French State to be run as an agricultural school. Since then, it has been run in a number of different ways, but since 1954 has come directly under the Ministry of Agriculture. A good deal of experimental work is carried out, both in viticulture and in the vinification of wines, with the aim of assisting the growers of the region to improve their methods. The school receives many students wishing to do practical work.

One might have thought that, as a result of all this, La Tour Blanche would produce one of the outstanding wines of the region. But for some reason this does not seem to be so. The wine has not been seen much on the English market for some years, and its local reputation does not stand very high. Whether this is local prejudice against a property run by the state, or the students experimenting too much, is difficult to say. On the few occasions I have tasted the wine, it did not seem to be at all outstanding. At present, about 30 of the 65 hectares of the domaine are planted with white grape varieties, of which 26 are Sauternes *appellation*, and 4,800 cases is the average yield. Some red wine is also made.

Château Lafaurie-Peyraguey

In 1855, there was one domaine, Château Peyraguey, belonging to Monsieur Lafaurie, which is now divided between this property and Clos Haut-Peyraguey. Situated in the commune of Bommes, Lafaurie-Peyraguey is notable for a particularly impressive château. The gatehouse and towers date from the thirteenth century and are in a style described as Hispano-Byzantine. The main living quarters date from the seventeenth century. The domaine now belongs to the Cordier family, the important Bordeaux *négociants*, who are also considerable vineyard proprietors in the Médoc and St Emilion. The 17 hectares of vineyard produce as much as 4,800 cases. The vineyard is planted with 70 per cent Sémillon and 30 per cent Sauvignon. Apart from the Sauternes, a pleasant, dry white wine is also made. It is one of the more successful examples of its type.

In the past, Lafaurie-Peyraguey has made some magnificent wines—I remember especially the 1921, which used to be on the list at the Bell at Aston Clinton. The 1937 was a worthy successor. I must confess, though, that some recent vintages have been very disappointing, quite lacking the savour and distinction associated with a leading Sauternes. One suspects that too much wine is being made from the vineyard—it is noticeable that all the most successful growths today are producing lower yields than those now achieved here.

320

Clos Haut-Peyraguey

This is the other portion of the former Château Peyraguey of the 1855 classification. The proprietors are Monsieur Eugène Garbay, who is responsible for running the property, and the Pauly brothers. The wine is not very well known, chiefly because the production is very small, only about 2,200 cases being produced. But when I have tasted it, I have found the quality to be really fine.

Château Rabaud-Promis

The history of this property has already been given under Sigalas-Rabaud, up until the sale in 1903 to Monsieur Adrien Promis. When he acquired the property, Monsieur Promis built a château for himself on the dominant hilltop of the estate, and this commands a magnificent, unrivalled view over the whole region. The present owner, Monsieur Lanneluc, manages to produce as much as 7,000 cases from his 28 hectares of vineyard, considerably more, it will be noted, than is made at Sigalas-Rabaud. The vineyard of Château Peixotto, classified in 1855 as a *Deuxième Cru Classé*, is now also incorporated in Rabaud-Promis. The wine is not seen in the trade because Monsieur Lanneluc pursues a policy of selling in bottle direct to consumers all over France. But the wine does not enjoy the same reputation as Sigalas-Rabaud.

Château Rayne-Vigneau

The fourth of the *Premiers Crus* of Bommes. In 1855, it was known simply as Château Vigneau, the Veuve de Rayne (*née* de Pontac) being the proprietor. Even the few bottles of the 1893 in the Château Loudenne cellar were only marked as Vigneau on the bin card. It remained in the hands of the de Pontac family until 1961, and since 1971 has belonged to a syndicate of local merchants. But the château still belongs to and is lived in by the Viscount de Roton, a de Pontac. The estate is a huge one of 90 hectares, of which 55 are under vine, producing about 11,000 cases of wine. Rayne-Vigneau is famous for the semi-precious stones which have been found in its vineyard. These include onyx, agates, quartz and white sapphires.

In the past, some magnificent wines were produced here. I especially remember the 1893 and 1911, and the 1923 which my father bought on his first visit to Bordeaux. We had some half-bottles of the 1923 which continued to keep its colour—a pale golden—and was marvellously perfumed, with a glorious, honeyed flavour of great breed and delicacy when nearly forty years old. Unfortunately the wine does not enjoy the same reputation today. But a good 1976 was made, though the 1975 is rather unbalanced—very sweet, but ungainly. A dry wine is sold under the name Raynesec.

Château Rieussec

This is the only *Premier Cru* in the commune of Fargues. The vineyard is actually partly in the commune of Sauternes and partly in Fargues, but the château and *chais* are in Fargues, so the property is usually credited to this commune, although in the 1855 classification it was ascribed to Sauternes. The name was also spelt with only one 's'. This is an important domaine of 75 hectares, of which 55 are under vine, producing up to 8,500 cases. The vineyard is planted with 75 per cent Sémillon, 22 per cent Sauvignon and 3 per cent Muscadelle. The wine has long enjoyed a very good reputation on the English market, where it is a firm favourite. During the very good post-war period, Monsieur Baluresque was the proprietor, but in 1971 it was sold to the present owner, Monsieur Albert Veuilley. In spite of, or perhaps, because of being the owner of a supermarket chain, Monsieur Veuilley is a believer in traditional methods when it comes to Sauternes. He is the first owner for many years to live in the château, and casks rather than vats are still used here.

In style, the wine is quite distinct. The bouquet is very marked, and the wine used to be rather less liquorous than some, with a most individual flavour, concentrated and powerful, but elegant. There was a notable consistency for many years, certainly in Monsieur Baluresque's time. But at the moment, the new management does not seem to have got things quite right. Both the 1975 and 1976 have taken on a lot of colour very quickly. When I first tasted the 1975 in November 1978, it already had a fair amount of colour, but the flavour was complex and distinguished. By October 1979, the wine was dark in colour and smelt distinctly maderized. On the palate it was hard, with a tarry taste. In short, it shows all the signs of too much sugar through excessive *pourriture noble*, and I cannot believe it will last. The 1976, on the other hand, was really dark in colour, the bouquet had opened out but showed far more age than one would have expected, while the flavour was really raisin-like, reminiscent of an old Trockenbeeren-auslese—very rich and liquorous, but somehow unbalanced. There can be no doubt that Rieussec is one of the best growths in Sauternes today, and one hopes that this will prove to be only a temporary setback.

Château Sigalas-Rabaud

This is another story of a divided domaine, also in the commune of Bommes. The domaine of Rabaud (or Rabeaud, as it appears in the 1855 classification), has a long history. It takes its name from the de Rabaud family, who owned it until 1660, when Madame Peyronne de Rabeau married Arnaud de Cazeau, a member of the *noblesse de robe*. It remained in this family until 1819, when it was sold to Monsieur Deymes, the proprietor at the time of the 1855 classification. But it was under Henri Drouilhet de Sigalas, who acquired it in 1864, that the great reputation of the wine was really built. It was his son, Gaston Drouilhet de Sigalas who, in 1903, sold about half of the property to Monsieur Adrien Promis. Since then, the remaining portion has been known as Sigalas-Rabaud and ownership has stayed with the same family. The present owner, the Marquise de Lambert des Granges, is a grand-daughter of Monsieur Drouilhet de Sigalas. There was a brief period, from 1929 to 1952, when the property was again reunited, but the Promis part was then again sold, this time to Monsieur Lanneluc. In this short period, I particularly remember the Rabaud 1950 as a delightful wine, perfumed and elegant.

The production of Sigalas-Rabaud today is only about 3,000, but the wine is excellent and enjoys a very good reputation. It has a particularly fine bouquet, is liquorous, and has great breed. The 1967, 1971 and 1975 are among the most successful wines of the vintage, but the 1976 in contrast is rather disappointing.

Château Suduiraut

This is the most important domaine in Sauternes, even surpassing Yquem in the size of its magnificent estate. Of the 200 hectare estate, 85 hectares are at present under vine, and the average yield is given as 10,000 cases. But much depends on the final selection of what makes up the *Grand Vin*, and in 1975, 4,160 cases were made, and in 1976 only 2,900 cases, so meticulously are the traditions of Sauternes observed. The vineyard adjoins that of Yquem, lying partly in the commune of Sauternes and partly in that of Preignac, whose only *Premier Cru* this is. The vineyard is planted with 95 per cent Sémillon and 5 per cent Sauvignon.

This ancient domaine takes its name from the family of Suduiraut, who were proprietors until the Revolution. One of the Suduiraut daughters married a Monsieur du Roy, and the property briefly bore his name before reverting to its original one. Hence, the rather misleading motto 'ancien cru du Roy', which appears on the label, and which I had always supposed meant that the château had once been royal property! The lovely château and its delightful gardens were laid out by Le Nôtre, the famous architect of many such splendours in the age of Louis XIV, and are among the finest to be seen in the region. The *chais* is massive and cavernous.

This famous property had reached a stage of sad decline and neglect when it was acquired in 1940 by Monsieur Fonquernie, who has been responsible for reconstructing the vineyard and restoring the name of the wine until it today enjoys the reputation of one of the finest of all the great Sauternes. Monsieur Fonquernie insists on the most meticulous standards, and has been fortunate in several able and dedicated *maîtres de chais*. I remember visiting the château during the gathering of the 1966 vintage. There had been some rain the previous day, which had caused the must readings to fall to 15°, whereas they had been obtaining around 20°. Monsieur Fonquernie had immediately given instructions for picking to stop until conditions improved. At Yquem, which I visited on the same day, exactly the same thing had occurred, but picking continued.

When I first entered the wine trade, Suduiraut was unknown on the English market. The 1955 which I bought must have been some of the first Suduiraut to be shipped to England after the reconstruction of the vineyard. Since then, its reputation has climbed steadily, until today it enjoys a wide following. In tastings of the *Premiers Crus* over a period of years, I usually found that Suduiraut came first, and it consistently fetched a higher price on the Bordeaux market than the other *Premiers Crus* for a number of years.

I must preface my remarks on modern vintages by recalling the

1899 vintage. I owe this to Martin Bamford's generosity. The bottle had come from an impeccable cellar in Paris. We were all astonished by the wine's fine, golden colour, the absence of maderization, and the velvety sweetness which still pervaded it. The wine was just eighty years old, but one could not have placed it further back than the 1920s: a very great bottle of Sauternes. The first vintage produced under Monsieur Fonquernie's régime I saw was the 1943. It was good, but had not lasted so well as the Château Climens, and was not outstanding. Then came 1955, certainly one of the best wines of the year; 1957 was elegant and fine; 1958 quite exceptional in its balance, fruit and sweetness. The 1959 was a great and classic wine. The 1961 was almost too overpowering—I have always preferred the more elegant 1962, which is in the mould of 1959. The 1965 was a charming off-vintage, light but fine; the 1966 was good for the year but not special; the 1967 was again outstanding. The 1969, like most Sauternes of that year, was not of any special note. Then came the 1970, an outstanding example of the year, with more elegance and balance than many examples. In contrast, the 1971 was not so good, probably because at this time the château started economizing and cutting corners. The wine was kept in vat instead of cask and, perhaps more serious, the *deuxième vin* was added in to the *grand vin*, increasing the quantity by damaging the quality. This led to a final breach between Monsieur Fonquernie and Gilbey's of Loudenne, who were at that time his main distributors. This bad period at Suduiraut unfortunately affected the 1975 vintage which, while more balanced than some 1975s, lacks the distinction of the best Suduirauts. However, with yet another change of policy, the 1976 showed a clear improvement.

The characteristics of Suduiraut deserve special note. In colour, it is usually golden rather sooner than most Sauternes, the bouquet is exquisite and especially perfumed and penetrating, the flavour is very rich and vigorous with a most distinctive and beautiful savour, honeyed, suave, but of great finesse and breed. The richness of Suduiraut is rivalled only by Yquem; even the 1958 had 4·9° Baumé, and in good years it can easily exceed 5° Baumé.

THE *DEUXIÈME CRUS CLASSÉS*

As already indicated, they are a very mixed bunch, and many are much less important today than they were in 1855. At that time, eleven growths were actually classified as seconds; of these, one has disappeared (Peixotto integrated into Rabaud-Promis), while the remaining ten have grown to fifteen through the division of properties. Myrat (at present without vines), d'Arche, Filhot, Caillou, Suau ánd de Malle remain as they were, but Doisy has been divided into three, while Broustet-Nérac, Romer and Lamothe have all been divided in two.

Of the fifteen growths today descended from the original ten, I shall describe only the nine most important:

Château d'Arche

One of the three growths in the commune of Sauternes which were classified as *Deuxième Crus* in 1855. The property takes its name from the Comte d'Arche, who was owner from 1733 to 1789, and who was responsible for establishing the reputation of the wine.

I suspect that there is some confusion in many people's minds between this wine and that of Château d'Arche-Lafaurie. This is increased by the fact that they belong to the same proprietor, Monsieur Bastit-Saint-Martin. In fact, d'Arche-Lafaurie was once part of the same property. Today, the properties are run together, but the wines are marketed separately—d'Arche producing about 7,500 cases and d'Arche-Lafaurie about 4,300 cases. Curiously, d'Arche-Lafaurie seems rather better known in England, at least, than d'Arche. In effect, d'Arche-Lafaurie is the second wine of d'Arche. Both wines are sound and rather liquorous, consistent, but lacking the breed of the *Premiers Crus*.

Château Doisy-Daëne

This growth, with the charming name, belongs to one of the most *avant-garde* vinificators in the region. Monsieur Pierre Dubourdieu is a tremendous enthusiast who is always trying to improve his wine. He believes that the consumer today wants wines which are fruity, but light and fresh. He is also a great advocate of drinking wines young.

One of the most successful dry wines is made here. It is intended for early drinking, bottling taking place when the wine is about nine months old. But a few bottles of the 1964, which I kept to observe their development, have lasted very well, taking on some body but remaining fresh and acquiring a delicate flavour, not unlike a good Graves. It is made from the unusual combination of 50 per cent Sémillon, 20 per cent Sauvignon, with the balance comprising Muscadelle, Riesling and Chardonnay. The Sauternes is also bottled earlier than at most properties and has a delicious fresh fruitiness and a really distinguished flavour, always beautifully balanced. Its quality is certainly on a par with the *Premiers Crus* today, and it enjoys an excellent reputation. It is well known on the English market.

The vineyard of 14 hectares lies in the best part of Barsac. Only some 1,900 cases of the Barsac are produced, and usually 4,500 cases of the dry wine. Originally, this formed part of the Château Doisy, the single property of the 1855 classification. The proprietor at that time was Monsieur Daëne, an Englishman.

The special methods of vinification and *élevage* developed and used by Pierre Dubourdieu are certainly worthy of particular note. The sweet wine is made entirely from Sémillon. Modern, horizontal presses are used, and the juice from each pressing is fermented in stainless steel vats at a controlled temperature of not more than 18°C. After fifteen to twenty-one days, when the balance between alcohol and residual sugar is judged to be correct, the temperature is lowered to 4°C, which stops the fermentation. The wine is then filtered and racked into new casks, where it remains for only two or three months—in other words, only during the coldest part of the winter. Then the final *assemblage* is made, not later than March and, after another sterile filtration, the wine goes into stainless steel vats and is bottled about a year later. Before bottling, the temperature is again lowered to 4°C and the wine is bottled with a sterile filtration. All this enables Doisy-Daëne to be bottled with far less sulphur than any other Sauternes, and results in a light, fresh style which is a revelation. It also makes the young wines seem easier to drink and much fresher than other Sauternes, besides enhancing their finesse. But it would be a mistake to think that because of this precociousness, they will not keep. The superb balance often ensures a longer life than for many heavier, less balanced wines.

The only old vintage of Doisy-Daëne I have seen is the 1934, a lovely wine which has lasted very well. More recently, the 1953 was a great success and has lasted well, as were 1959, 1961 and 1962, followed by 1967, 1970, 1971, 1975 and 1976. The 1975 is certainly one of the best wines of this difficult vintage.

Château Doisy-Védrines

This is the parent trunk of the original Château Doisy of the 1855 classification. The Védrines comes from the Chevaliers de Védrines, who owned the property for several centuries until 1840. The present administrator, Monsieur Pierre Castéja, comes from a very old Bordeaux family of proprietors, and is connected with the families through which the property has passed by marriage since 1840.

The vineyard of 30 hectares lies between Coutet and Climens, and can produce as much as 5,700 cases, as well as some 750 cases of red wine sold as Latour-Védrines. The wine enjoys a good reputation and is well known and appreciated in England. In style, the wine tends to be fuller and heavier than the Doisy-Daëne, but lacks its finesse and breed. This is a property where the 1975 is better balanced than the 1976, against the general run.

Château Filhot

A beautiful property of 300 hectares, with a magnificent eighteenth-century mansion set among fields and woods. It belonged to the Lur-Saluces family for many generations, until the owner, the Comtesse Durieu de Lacarelle, herself a Lur-Saluces, sold to the present owner, Monsieur Henri de Vaucelles.

Situated in the commune of Sauternes, the vineyard of 55 hectares produces about 4,000 cases. It is planted in the proportion of 70 per cent Sémillon, 25 per cent Sauvignon and 5 per cent Muscadelle. The wine is distinctly drier than the other *crus classés* and for a long time enjoyed a great following in England. One has the impression that this following is now less strong than it used to be. I remember a glorious bottle of the 1928 I had with Dr (now Professor and Master of Christ's College) Jack Plumb at Cambridge, but in recent years I have been unable to be enthusiastic about this growth. It is interesting to note that both the 1975 and 1976 are decidedly more liquorous and fat than older vintages used to be. But the wine lacks the delicacy of Doisy-Daëne, while failing to achieve the elegance and harmony of Climens or Coutet.

Sichels originally pioneered the marketing of a dry wine which is of the Ygrec type but, I thought, more successful. However, its appeal has proved limited.

Château de Malle

The Château de Malle is one of the delights of the region. Unfortunately it was allowed to sink into a sorry state of disrepair, but has now been meticulously restored. The formal garden is also famous, but is of the sort likely to disappoint an English visitor. Apart from some fine statuary, little remains apart from indications of the original layout. The property is in the commune of Preignac.

The production is around 3,700 cases from 45 hectares planted in the proportion 70 per cent Sémillon, 25 per cent Sauvignon and 5 per cent Muscadelle. The château belongs to the de Lespinasse de Bournazel family. It is now very well looked after and carefully run by Comte Pierre de Bournazel, who has supervised it since 1956.

In the past, I have seen some rather disappointing vintages from de Malle, but in the last fifteen years there has been an improvement; the 1966 for instance, was most attractive, elegant and fruity, with a very marked character of its own. Indeed, the wines of de Malle are marked by a very definite personality and savour, elegant, but only moderately liquorous. It enjoys a good reputation today, and is certainly worthy of its classification.

Château Doisy-Dubroca

This is the smallest part of the original Doisy property. It was purchased in 1880 by the Dubroca family, and became connected with Climens when one of the family married a Gounouilhou daughter. Then, just after the First World War, it was bought by Monsieur Gounouilhou. Since then it has effectively been used as the second wine of Climens. When Monsieur Lucien Lurton bought Climens in 1971, Doisy-Dubroca was included in the sale.

The vineyard is only 3·5 hectares, and lies between Climens and Coutet. It is planted mainly with Sémillon, and only about 400 cases are made on average. The wine is now exclusively and appropriately distributed by Louis Dubroca, an excellent firm of *négociants* owned by one of the most respected members of the Bordeaux trade, Monsieur Bertrand de Rivoyre. The wine is liquorous and fine. After a beautiful 1971, a remarkably good 1972 has been produced—a surprise indeed from that meagre year—followed by an elegant 1973. The 1974 is full-blown and forward but remarkable for the year, while 1975 is elegant and classic yet powerful.

Château Myrat

This is indeed a sign of the times; the vineyard at Myrat was pulled up after the 1975 vintage was completed. The proprietor, Comte de Pontac, still lives in the château, but decided he could no longer afford the luxury of a Barsac vineyard. Prior to this, the wine had for some years been sold only in cask to *négociants*.

Château Nairac

This is another Barsac property. After writing of the demise of one vineyard, it is good to be able to record the renaissance of another. Originally the property was joined to that of Broustet, and in the 1855 classification it appears under the name of Broustet-Nérac, just to confuse matters. Nairac was the name of the eighteenth-century owners of the estate. In 1971, this run-down property was bought by a young American enthusiast, Mr Tom Heeter, now married to the daughter of the proprietor of Château Giscours. Desiring to dedicate his life to wine, Tom Heeter had gone to work for Monsieur Tari to learn his trade, and had not only done well in his new *métier*, but also succeeded in carrying off the lovely Nicole Tari from under the noses of numerous Bordelais admirers. Together they have rebuilt the vineyard and restored the charming château. There are now 15 hectares under vine, planted with 90 per cent Sémillon, 6 per cent Sauvignon and 4 per cent Muscadelle. The production rose in 1976 to 2,000 cases. The ubiquitous Professor Peynaud has been called in to advise and, although methods are still much more traditional than at Doisy-Daëne, the use of Vitamin B_1 during fermentation helps to inhibit oxidation and much reduce the use of sulphur. The wine is now beginning to build a reputation for itself. There are good reports of the 1975 vintage, and this must certainly be a name worth watching.

Château Romer

A complicated situation surrounds this small, Barsac property, for it has three owners, Monsieur André du Hayot and his mother, and Monsieur Fargesin. But Monsieur du Hayot makes and sells the wine for both his mother and himself under the name of Romer du Hayot. This is the best-known section of the vineyard.

The vineyard of 12 hectares is planted with 50 per cent Sémillon, 40 per cent Sauvignon and 10 per cent Muscadelle, producing on average 1,300 cases. The wine is little-known and the only vintage I have seen is the 1976 Romer-Hayot, which I found very liquorous and rich, but well-balanced with a pleasing freshness: elegant and fine, certainly a pleasant surprise.

The other *Deuxième Crus Classés* are as follows:

Château Broustet, proprietor Soc. Civile, production 2,700 cases.
Château Caillou, proprietor Monsieur Bravo, production 3,700 cases.
Château Lamothe, proprietor Monsieur Despujols, production 2,000 cases.
Château Lamothe-Bergey, proprietor Bastit-Saint-Martin, production 1,500 cases.
Château Suau, proprietor Monsieur Biarnes, production 1,300 cases.

CRUS BOURGEOIS

The majority of these wines seldom see the light of day, certainly on export markets, under their own names, but are bought by *négociants* to be made into generic blends of Sauternes and Barsac. When this is carefully and conscientiously done, the resulting wines can be excellent. A few growths have, however, established a reputation for themselves and are often found—especially on the English market. The most notable of these are:

Château d'Arche-Lafaurie (Sauternes), see under Château d'Arche.
Château Bastor-Lamontagne (Preignac), 8,500 cases.
Château Dudon (Barsac), 2,000 cases.
Château Gilette (Preignac), 2,700 cases.
Château Lafon (Sauternes), 1,500 cases.
Château Liot (Barsac), 2,500 cases.
Château Roumieu (Barsac), 4,000 cases.
Château Roumieu-Lacoste (Barsac), 1,000 cases.

Château du Mayne (Barsac) 1,700 cases.
Château Raymond-Lafon (Sauternes), 300 cases.
Château St Amaud (Preignac), 1,700 cases.
Château de la Chartreuse (Preignac), 800 cases.

STE-CROIX-DU-MONT AND LOUPIAC

It seems sensible to take these two communes together, because they adjoin one another, their wines are very similar, and they are the closest in style and quality to Sauternes and Barsac.

In contrast to the flat, rolling countryside of Sauternes and Barsac on the left bank of the Garonne, the vineyards of Ste-Croix-du-Mont and Loupiac rise high above the river, sometimes steeply sloping, sometimes on vertical ledges on the hillsides, with the best high up, commanding magnificent views over the Sauternes-Barsac and Graves vineyards across the river. These wines have suffered much the same fate as their peers, Sauternes-Barsac, only the rewards offered for producing good wines are even more meagre. Geographically, Ste-Croix-du-Mont and Loupiac form an enclave in the Premières Côtes—that attractive, hilly, wooded district which, rising steeply from the Garonne, forms the south-western border of the Entre-deux-Mers. But although some modest sweet wines are produced in the Premières Côtes, the wines of Ste-Croix-du-Mont and Loupiac have far more in common with their illustrious neighbours across the water than with their more immediate neighbours.

In practice, there is no meaningful distinction to be made between the two districts. They owe their separateness purely to their being in different communes. Indeed, it would be far more logical if all sweet wines made in Sauternes, Barsac, Cérons, Ste-Croix-du-Mont, and Loupiac were allowed the Sauternes *appellation*, with worth while alternatives available for the production of the good, dry white wines which can also be made there. Then we might have better and more genuine sweet wines and more prosperous growers.

I have on a number of occasions tasted good Ste-Croix-du-Mont and Loupiac in the company of Sauternes, and experienced Bordeaux tasters have agreed with me that it has in practice been impossible to distinguish these wines from Sauternes. While they lack the sheer liquorousness of the top Sauternes, they have a fruitiness and savour very reminiscent of some Barsacs. Unfortunately, relatively few of these wines reach export markets, so few of the property wines are in any way familiar. But there are a handful which deserve to be singled out.

Château Ricaud (Loupiac)

I first came across this wine in Monsieur Choyer's cavernous cellars near Tours. The vintages were 1943 and 1947, both marvellous wines of great breed, very fruity, rich but not really liquorous. Because of the special balance of these top Loupiacs, they age marvellously well and keep their colour. This discovery sent me in search of the château, and I ended up by buying the 1970. This very compact, stylish wine is still maturing slowly after nine years and promises to have all the qualities, including longevity, of those vintages of the 1940s that I first found in the Loire.

Today the château has 40 hectares under vine and produces 7,500 cases of white wine and 900 cases of red. Some of the white wine is dry. The owner is Madame Maurice Wells, whose family has now owned the property for nearly a century. The château itself looks so fairy-tale-like on the label as to be hardly believable, but for once the label does not lie.

Château Loupiac-Gaudiet (Loupiac)

This is another well-situated vineyard with origins going back to the fifteenth century. From 10 hectares, some 4,000 cases of high quality wine, with elegance and breed, are most carefully made by Monsieur Marc Ducau, the proprietor. The 1970 and 1971 are both delightful and, while giving much pleasure when young, will age well.

Château Loubens (Ste-Croix-du-Mont)

This is a property with a deserved reputation. 10 hectares produce some 3,000 cases. The château stands on the site of a sixteenth-century fort, and has always been one of the leading growths of the region.

Château de Tastes (Ste-Croix-du-Mont)

I shall always remember drinking a memorable bottle of 1920 de Tastes at Château Margaux, with Pierre Ginestet. This property goes back as far as 1230, and for many years belonged to, and was distributed by, the Ginestets. Today, it belongs to the Prats family of Cos d'Estournel. There are now only 6 hectares under vine, producing about 1,500 cases.

CÉRONS AND PREMIÈRES CÔTES

There are two other major categories of sweet wines: Cérons, which adjoins Barsac and has already been mentioned in the chapter on Graves, since its dry white wines have the right to the Graves *appellation*; and the Premières Côtes, immediately to the north of Loupiac.

Because of the declining interest in sweet white wines, and because the growers of Cérons have a lucrative alternative at their disposal, there has been a marked decline in the amount of wine declared as Cérons in the last decade. Thus in 1970 and 1971, repectively 20,916 and 19,162 hectolitres were declared. But in the abundant harvests of 1978 and 1979, the figures were 5,041 and 5,069. At the same time, the production of white Graves and Graves Supérieur increased significantly. Most Cérons is sold under *négociants'* generic labels in France. The best-known château is de Cérons, owned by Monsieur Perromat, president of the INAO. It produces a very fruity wine of real breed. A good Cérons is very like a small Barsac, and ages well—even if it is not quite as fine as the best of Ste-Croix-du-Mont or Loupiac.

In the Premières Côtes, an attempt was made in 1973 to create a superior category of sweet wine by allowing the best communes in the southern part, adjoining Loupiac, the right to a new *appellation*—Cadillac. The name comes from the commune of the same name, where one of the finest châteaux in the whole Gironde is to be found. This ill-conceived proliferation of *appellations* has met with little success. In the first vintage of 1973, as much as 15,482 hectolitres was declared. But the lack of interest shown by the market in yet another *appellation* for sweet wine, when everyone knows that what is really required is a simplification, was soon felt. In 1978 and 1979, the average has been just under 2,000 hectolitres.

The wines of the Premières Côtes are markedly lighter than Sauternes and all too often are little more than simple sweet wines, with no *pourriture noble* character and certainly none of the style

334

of the better *appellations*. More and more growers are now turning to the production of red wines as the figures amply demonstrate. The white wines are mostly used for generic blends, and in the UK were generally used to supply the need for cheap 'Sauternes' shipped in bulk, before the day of the enforcement of AC. Today, these relatively inexpensive blends—now correctly labelled—still have a certain place on the market, though the wines are seldom more than acceptable.

Although strictly speaking outside the scope of this book, mention should also be made of *Monbazillac*. Being in the neighbouring *département* of Dordogne, it is not in the Gironde at all, but those wines produced on the north-facing hills just south of Bergerac clearly belong to the Sauternes family of botrytized sweet wines. The conditions are similar, as are the grape varieties and methods of production. A good, properly made Monbazillac can certainly hold its own with all but the best of Bordeaux's sweet wines, but unfortunately, because of the meagre financial rewards, more and more wines are simply sweet and characterless, made without the benefit of *pourriture noble*. Again, many growers are turning to the production of dry white wines, as well as reds.

From the very heart of Sauternes itself, right through the lesser areas, we have noted all the signs of decline in production, often in quality, certainly in consumer interest. Yet no one who has enjoyed the delights of drinking fine Sauternes can doubt that this is one of the great wines of the world, or would wish to see it disappear.

In Germany, there is a buoyant market for the great Beeren- and Trockenbeeren-auslesen. The quantities produced are tiny and the price much higher than for all but Yquem. Even in the more favourable conditions of the Gironde, botrytized wines can never be cheap to make. At the same time, wines so rich in both alcohol and residual sugar can hardly be everyday wines. In Germany, the producers of the great sweet wines effectively subsidize them from their much larger production of more commercial wines, so that they are in no sense dependent on them in the way that most Sauternes producers are on their sweet wines.

The logical solution seems clear enough, then. What is needed is a smaller production of top-quality wines. But in order to achieve this, producers must be able to make other, more commercial,

335

everyday wines from the same vineyards. Let us hope that the authorities respond to what is a crisis situation with some common-sense solutions. Sauternes and the other great sweet wines of Bordeaux cannot survive much longer on philanthropy.

OTHER WHITE WINES

Entre-deux-Mers

After Bordeaux Blanc, this is by far the most important *appellation* for white wines in terms of quantity. And against the general tendency, it has been gaining ground instead of losing it over the last decade. Between 1970 and 1974, the production of Entre-deux-Mers averaged 74,463 hectolitres, which represented 6·5 per cent of all Bordeaux white wines. But between 1975 and 1979, production averaged 104,911 hectolitres, representing 10·5 per cent of all Bordeaux white wines. To put it another way, production of Entre-deux-Mers increased by just over 40 per cent at a time when white wine production as a whole was falling by over 12 per cent. A good part of the reason for this increase lies in the fact that it has become gradually more interesting to sell Entre-deux-Mers than Bordeaux Blanc. In the past, much of the production was only declared as Bordeaux Blanc, because sales of Entre-deux-Mers were not sufficiently buoyant to utilize all the white wine produced in the area. But in the last few years, sales of this *appellation* have increased considerably, by 132 per cent in the ten years 1969 to 1978.

Geographically, Entre-deux-Mers is a large wedge of land lying between the Garonne and the Dordogne. On the Garonne side, the Premières Côtes, together with Loupiac and Ste-Croix-du-Mont, occupy the whole of the south-western side of the district, while St Macaire forms a further enclave in the south, Ste Foy a large enclave in the north-eastern corner, and Graves de Vayres a small enclave in the north, opposite Libourne. Scenically it makes up for its lack of vinous distinction with hilly, wooded countryside dotted with quietly decaying châteaux, some of the most picturesque in the whole region.

Although the area contains many large properties, this is *par excellence* the district for cooperatives, and it is improvements in the vinification of white wines at such cooperatives which are

336

largely responsible for the gradual revival of the fortunes of Entre-deux-Mers. On the British market, Bordeaux white wines for many years had a poor reputation as sulphurous and therefore mawkish. It has taken a long time to overcome this legacy, and the effects of it are indeed still with us. In addition, it used to be the custom to sell medium sweet wines under the Entre-deux-Mers name in Britain. As a result, when the *appellation* laws were at last enforced here, it took a long time before customers would accept the fact that Entre-deux-Mers was a dry wine.

A good Entre-deux-Mers should be light, crisp, fresh and dry. The wines are usually bottled when three or four months old, and are intended to be drunk within the year. As in other parts of France recently, there is a tendency to increase the proportion of Sauvignon, and some properties produce pure Sauvignon wines. This seems to me to be a mistake. In the Gironde, if the Sauvignon becomes fully ripe, it tends to lose its special aromatic character rather quickly. On the other hand, if it is picked too early, the wine has an unpleasant acidity. It is not for nothing that the Sémillon has for so long been the backbone of Bordeaux white wines, and it is interesting to note that in California, they are beginning to experiment with the blending of Sémillon with their Sauvignons, and that in Australia distinguished dry wines are now being made from the Sémillon. I feel sure that in the long run, Sémillon-Sauvignon blends made with slow, cold fermentations are likely to give the best results, and the sooner the Sauvignon fad passes, the better for Bordeaux white wines. Other places can do it so much more successfully.

St Macaire

Of the other *appellations* adjoining Entre-deux-Mers, the sweetish wines of St Macaire have declined considerably in importance. In 1970, nearly 12,000 hectolitres were made, but by 1979 this had fallen to under 3,000 hectolitres. Graves de Vayres, with its dry wines, having rather more body than Entre-deux-Mers, still has some following in Germany, but even this has declined slightly in recent years, in spite of the name. Ste Foy, on the other hand, with its close affinity to Dordogne wines, has maintained and even marginally improved its position, but production is really very small.

The white wines of Blaye are more important than those of

Bourg. It is confusing to find that white wines in Blaye can be declared as Blaye or Blayais, Côtes de Blaye or Premières Côtes de Blaye. In fact, most of the white wine is declared as Blaye or Blayais, a much smaller quantity as Côtes de Blaye, and only a few hundred hectolitres as Premières Côtes de Blaye. But taken together, the white wine production of Blaye is second only to Entre-deux-Mers, and more important than Graves, which is surprising, so that one wonders what becomes of it all. The production of white Bourg is now commercially unimportant.

This leaves, of course, the enormous production of simple Bordeaux Blanc. Most of it is produced in the Entre-deux-Mers, but it is produced all over the region, including the Médoc and Sauternes. The variation in quality is considerable. Some of it is sweetish, mostly it is dry. Often there is little difference in quality between a good Bordeaux Blanc and an Entre-deux-Mers. Some property wines are certainly worth looking at. As a glance at the figures will show, the decline in production has been steady and clear over the last decade, due to the fall in demand, and the increasing difficulty in selling such wines. Doubtless, in a few years, there will be a shortage.

12

The Evaluation
of Bordeaux vintages

Anyone unfamiliar with Bordeaux and its wines might wonder
why so much time is spent discussing the merits of different
vintages. In all wine districts situated in temperate climates,
vintages are important to a greater or lesser extent, especially
when the wine grower is striving to produce something really fine
to mature over a number of years. Like people, wines develop
character and individuality with the passage of time. What makes
vintages of particular interest in Bordeaux is the very diversity of
the regions. We have already seen why it is that a good year for the
Médoc may not be a good one in St Emilion, and why a fine year
for red wines may not be echoed in Sauternes. When these
differences are added to the climatic instability of the region as a
whole, it is easy to see why vintages should assume such
importance here.

Whenever a new vintage is born, everyone attempts to find
some analogy with a previous one. The history of the weather
conditions from flowering to picking is examined in much the same
way as the parents and relatives look at a newly-born child, in an
attempt to discern its likely character. The process probably
works rather better than for human beings, but only up to a
certain point. It will usually establish the type of vintage which
has been produced, but will only give a hint as to its eventual
character. One has only to read the prognostications of experts
made at the time to see how wide of the mark they can be on
occasion. The only thing that is certain is that every year does
develop its own personality, and the better the vintage, the
stronger this character becomes. This is the reason why many
experienced tasters can often work out the vintage of a particular

wine when given it blind, but will often be floored by an off-vintage, especially if it has some age.

As far as red wines are concerned, vintages can roughly be divided between those which mature fairly rapidly, and the more tannic, slow developers—although with modern techniques for controlling the fermentation, this distinction can become blurred. It is a popular fallacy that hard vintages last and light ones do not. In the past, the light vintages have usually been the well-balanced ones, and for this reason have lasted well and often better than the tannic ones. In the end, it is the harmony of fruit, acidity and tannin that matters most. 1900 was a classic example of this, being considered too attractive too soon, in comparison to the 1899. (See Ian Maxwell Campbell *Wayward Tendrils of the Vine*, p. 53.) More recently, some 1945s have disappointed, while 1949 and 1953 have lasted much better than was expected.

I realize that very few will have the opportunity of drinking a bottle of claret from a vintage prior to 1920 as that, after all, is sixty years ago. Nevertheless, a few notes on the historic vintages of the nineteenth century may be of academic interest at least. In the cellars of Bordeaux, or indeed of British stately homes, as some sales at Christie's and Sotheby's have proved, the best examples of these historic vintages are still good. Usually, as at Lafite and Mouton, these wines have been regularly recorked. Even so, a sense of perspective needs to be kept. Most of these very old wines certainly provide what one would call 'interesting bottles'. That is to say, they are past their best, but are still alive and interesting to connoisseurs. Only the exceptional wine is still in top form, displaying the full character of its vintage and its château. I remember, after drinking one such exceptional wine, the 1869 Mouton, at the château, remarking on its exceptional preservation to one of the two Blondin brothers, the *maîtres de chais* at Mouton at that time. He told me that of all the great collections of old vintages stored there, the 1869 and 1870 vintages were now much the best preserved and most consistent of the nineteenth-century wines. Many others were still very interesting but had not retained their full vigour and character to the same degree.

13 September 1798: The first vintage to be matured in bottle to any degree. There is an example in the collection of Lafite. Cocks & Féret noted 'very celebrated for 70 years after'.

23 September 1802: A very good year, but inferior to 1798.

14 September 1811: An exceptional year; they were known as Comet wines.

15 September 1815: Small quantity, remarkable wines equal to 1798 and 1811.

20 September 1819: Plentiful harvest, very good wines.

31 August 1822: White wines especially good, the reds took a long time to mature.

11 September 1825: A celebrated year which did not quite live up to its early reputation. The white wines were the best.

15 September 1828: A fine year for the first growths.

14 September 1831: A great year, both red and white wines of remarkable quality. Yield reduced by hail in August.

9 September 1834: Considered a great year. Frost and hail resulted in a very small crop. Prices very high.

17 September 1840: Very good white wines, large crop.

18 September 1841: An excellent year, but white wines not as rich as in 1840.

14 September 1846: After a very hot summer, a vintage producing very big wines which just missed greatness, but the white wines were excellent and fetched very high prices.

25 September 1847: A large crop, classified as a great year. Reds light, but with a fine bouquet and very attractive. Whites very successful. Among the great years.

20 September 1848: A good crop but smaller than in 1847. Red wines more full-bodied than in 1847, wines of remarkable quality which developed very well. 1847 and 1848 are the first examples of a pair of outstanding but complementary vintages which occur from time to time in Bordeaux.

27 September 1851: A very hot summer produced hard, slow-developing wines which were only appreciated as they developed. White wines were excellent.

341

1853–6: The oidium years.

20 September 1857: Vines still feeble after the oidium of previous years, but good conditions produced red wines that were truly ripe, delicate and fine—a good vintage.

20 September 1858: A very hot summer produced a celebrated vintage which set historically new high price levels. Red wines were perfectly ripe and lasted very well, though this is not one of the pre-phylloxera vintages which has survived in more than an occasionally 'interesting' form to the present day. The white wines were considered to rival the 1847s, and Yquem reached unheard-of price levels.

23 September 1859: Famous only for the white wines which rivalled, and in some cases, surpassed 1858.

22 September 1861: Another year for white wines which were very luscious. Red wines proved very ordinary.

17 September 1864: An outstanding year. Very large crop. Red wines noted for their flavour, delicacy and elegance. The white wines were also very successful. Lafite still superb in 1979.

6 September 1865: 1864 and 1865 are another noted Bordeaux 'pair'. The crop was even larger than in 1864, but prices reached new records; this was the most expensive vintage of the century. While it was certainly a great year, it is interesting to note that by 1899, Cocks & Féret were saying the wines 'have not entirely realized the great hopes founded on them at first'. They have lasted well, but not as well as the 1869s or 1870s. 1865 was a tannic wine that is sometimes compared to 1870.

7 September 1868: A large crop in spite of spring frosts and hail. At first the red wines seemed to have a beautiful colour, body and a fine flavour, and very high prices were paid for the first growths. However, the wines were hard and slow to mature and so lost favour. The Sauternes crop was destroyed by hail.

15 September 1869: A very great vintage. A very large crop was harvested in superb weather. At first, the trade was uncertain as to the quality, but the wines developed so well that it was later recognized as one of the great years. This is the oldest vintage from which I have tasted wines which were still perfectly preserved.

Both the Cos d'Estournel and the Mouton reached their centenary in superb condition and with all their faculties intact, a remarkable achievement. The white wines were also very fine.

10 September 1870: Another very great year, so that 1869 and 1870 were certainly the greatest 'pair' in the nineteenth century. The red wines were very full-bodied and had great vinosity, but they developed very slowly. As a consequence, this vintage was preserved in many cellars until modern times and often forgotten about. The greatest bottle I have tasted was a magnum of the legendary Lafite from Glamis Castle prior to the sale of the cellar at Christie's. Characteristically, the whites were good but did not match the reds.

8 September 1871: This was preceded by one of the severest winters of the century. From 1 to 4 January the temperature dropped to $-14°C$ and the Gironde was frozen to the sixth arch of the Bordeaux bridge. Nearly a third of the vines in the Gironde were frozen, and at the end of March, another severe frost did much damage. Although the ripening was irregular and the vintage took place under unfavourable conditions, so that the wines were written off as a poor year, they developed much better than expected and some of the best Médocs were excellent, but not on the whole long-lived.

14 September 1874: A very good year, the yield surpassing 1869. The vintage was heralded as a success even before the harvest was completed, and high prices were obtained. The finest 1874 I have seen was the Latour which was beautifully preserved and still completely characteristic of its origins (this was a bottle from the Rosebery cellar, tasted thanks to the kindness of Michael Broadbent prior to the auction in 1967). If this was typical, the 1874s have lasted better than the 1875s. The white wines were also very successful.

22 September 1875: The largest vintage of the century and a uniformly very successful one. 1874 and 1875 were the third and last outstanding 'pair' of Bordeaux vintages in the great period between the oidium and onset of the phylloxera and the mildew. Although the red wines were lighter than the 1874s, they possessed great elegance and charm and this was one of the most admired vintages of its day. Most surviving examples are very pale in

343

colour and have faded, but an occasional bottle still conveys the elegance and breed of this year—I particularly remember the Margaux and the Rauzan. The white wines were not in the same class as the 1874s.

20 September 1877: Some light and very attractive red wines were made, possessed of a charming bouquet, race and elegance. They have not lived, although a number of examples were unearthed to present to André Simon on his ninetieth birthday. The white wines were ordinary.

19 September 1878: The last reasonable vintage before the onset of phylloxera and the mildew scourge. The wines were not highly thought of at first, but developed a good bouquet. To some extent their reputation as a good year, if nothing more, was enhanced by the poor years which followed.

1879–86: Years mostly of low yields and poor quality. The vines were debilitated by phylloxera and mildew, and *coulure* was also very prevalent. Very occasionally drinkable bottles do appear, I recall a pleasant Palmer 1880.

28 September 1887: The first ray of hope after the lean years, but the yield was very small. The wines had the reputation of being rather graceless.

28 September 1888: The largest crop for a decade. Produced pleasing light red wines, but only ordinary whites.

6 October 1889: Red wines of more colour and body than the 1888s. I have drunk the Mouton and the Langoa which were both well preserved and attractive.

28 September 1890: A vintage which was welcomed and enjoyed some reputation, but the wines tended to be hard. Some good whites were made and I have a pleasant recollection of the Yquem.

16 September 1892: Just missed being a really good year, a very hot, dry wind, a sort of sirocco, causing much harm in August. Nevertheless, the only example I have seen, the Lascombes, was a great wine when over seventy years of age, comparable to an 1899.

18 August 1893: The first unqualified success since the lean years of phylloxera and mildew. The crop was almost as large as the prolific 1875. The flowering was finished by 20 May, a good three weeks earlier than usual, and the heat and drought of the summer were the most intense since 1822. The wines provoked enormous interest and, being offered at moderate prices, business was so brisk that by Christmas, all the classified growths were sold—a case of early buying if ever there was one! The wines were very ripe, fruity and attractive and lasted well, but in my experience have tended to decay seriously in the last decade. The Lafite, in particular, was a beauty, reminding me of an 1829 in style, but it suddenly faded. Some of the Sauternes were wonderfully balanced and preserved their fruitiness and sweetness for an unsual period. The Rayne-Vigneau is the finest example I have seen; it was still superb and not maderized when nearly seventy years old.

19 September 1895: This might have been a great year if controlled vinification had been understood or had even been possible. As it was, the wines were rich in sugar and many turned volatile or 'pricked'. However, there were some notable successes; I have drunk a remarkable Pétrus, and I know Maxwell Campbell records that the La Conseillante was also very fine, although he characterized the vintage as a whole as fat and flabby. In the Médoc, both Mouton and Lafite were successful.

20 September 1896: Due to very mixed weather conditions, the red wines varied considerably in quality. The successful wines were described as light and elegant but they have been faulted as being dry. In spite of this, the Loudenne of this year was still fresh and well preserved when nearly seventy years of age, while the Lafite was a most beautiful wine, only just beaten by the 1899 when they were drunk together in 1954.

24 September 1899: The old century went out in a blaze of glory as if to prove that phylloxera and oidium were finally beaten. Although 1893 had been a great success in many ways, some claret lovers still had their reservations about the vintage as a whole. There was no doubt that 1899 was a vintage fit to take its place beside the great pre-phylloxera years, and time has certainly vindicated this judgment. In their prime they were described as full-bodied, vigorous, sweet and generous. In old age these wines held their colour very well and the best of them, such as the Lafite and Latour, have remained marvellously vigorous and complete.

In general, however, most wines now show signs of going dry and are fading. Also a great year for white wines. The Suduiraut when nearly eighty years old was one of the finest Sauternes I ever tasted.

24 September 1900: If the old century went out in a blaze of glory, the new century was not to be outdone, so that these two years provided one of the greatest Bordeaux 'pairs', long to be compared and discussed. In size this was the largest vintage since 1875, proving the recovered vigour of the Bordeaux vineyards. What is so interesting about 1900 as a year is that, when young, the wines were described as 'light, very light in body, but just as sweet as 1899 and soft and gentle, almost too much so to age well' (Ian Maxwell Campbell *Wayward Tendrils of the Vine*, p. 53). If ever there was a vintage to prove that light wines last, this was it, for today the rare survivals of this year are still magnificent—in fact I have never had a single disappointment. Of the first growths, I have drunk Lafite, Margaux and Mouton, and they were all superb and apparently ageless. But, one of the greatest wines of the year must have been Léoville-Lascases. When I first drank the wine in 1962, it was superb and was certainly of first growth standard, and the last time I saw it in 1970, it was equally fine, and did not seem to have aged at all in the interval. The outstanding character of the year seems to be its mellow fruitiness which has continued into old age, fresh and completely unfaded.

1901–3: A run of poor vintages and a great let-down after 1899 and 1900. After the failure of 1903, the Loudenne diary noted that nothing marketable had been made since 1900.

19 September 1904: Hopes were high at first for this year, and it was compared to 1887 and 1890; however the wines tended to be light, firm, but lacking fruit. The only example I have seen was Batailley. It was mellow but still firm and was decidedly at the end of its life in 1965. Maxwell Campbell recorded that the Ausone was more smooth and supple than most wines of the vintage. It is interesting to note that the 1922 edition of Cocks & Féret placed this vintage on a par with 1899 and 1900, and above 1906, a rating repeated uncritically in subsequent editions which place 1904 as the best vintage between 1900 and 1920. This is a judgment which I would suggest few of those competent to pronounce would endorse today.

346

18 September 1905: Attractive and useful wines which do not seem to have lasted, and certainly not in the top flight.

17 September 1906: A hot summer produced a crop of only average size. In style, they were big, beefy wines with a tendency to coarseness at first which later mellowed, to make this one of the best vintages in the period 1901–19. Haut-Brion, Cheval Blanc, Brane-Cantenac and La Lagune all enjoyed a good reputation. I found that Lafite lacked graciousness.

23 September 1907: The largest vintage since 1900. Wines made towards the end of the vintage were adversely affected by rain. At their best, the 1907s were 'deliciously delicate and flavoury in youth', but lacked staying power, so that by the early 1930s, Maxwell Campbell noted that they had become 'plain and rather "vacant".' All the examples I have tasted were distinctly too old, with the exception of a single bottle of Margaux in 1962 which, while being very light, still drank very well.

15 September 1908: A year of no reputation as far as the red wines were concerned. They were considered hard and unattractive, but the white wines seem to have been better, and I once enjoyed a bottle of Guiraud which was still sweet and attractive, with no sign of maderization.

23 September 1909: A generally successful year, although there was some trouble with rot. The wines were light and pleasing, somewhat in the style of the 1907s, but with rather more substance. During the early 1960s there were still a fair number of examples in the Loudenne cellar, and most of them still had great charm, fruit and finesse. The best were Latour, Margaux, the two Laroses, Cos d'Estournel, Rauzan-Gassies and Léoville-Barton. Although mostly just past their best, they were still immensely enjoyable.

1 October 1910: A notoriously poor year and not worth mentioning were it not for the Haut-Brion.

15 September 1911: The vintage was generally regarded as following 1909 as a good if not exceptional year. I tasted several examples just past their fiftieth year which showed that the year possessed charm and plenty of fruit, though none were quite as good as the 1909s. With the exception of a lovely bottle of

Batailley which had not stirred from its original bin at the château, and a remarkable bottle of Bel Orme, all the wines, including Cheval Blanc, were clearly well past their prime. The whites were fine, and I have had a bottle of Doisy-Védrines which was still full of fruit and richness.

20 September 1912: A large vintage. The red wines seemed attractive at first, but many suffered from the effects of mildew and did not last. I have not myself had the opportunity of tasting an example of the vintage.

25 September 1913: Again, contemporary accounts in Cocks & Féret speak favourably of the year, but Maxwell Campbell says 'nor have I seen a '13 that did not have fatal resemblance to 1910'.

20 September 1914: A very large crop, the biggest since 1907. Evidently attractive, supple wines at the start. According again to Maxwell Campbell, these wines seemed most attractive by 1920 when serious claret drinking resumed after the war, but they suddenly folded up 'and died as it were in a night'. The only bottle I have drunk was the Lafite, which was light but charming when first opened, but then quickly died in the glass, and that had come straight from the Lafite cellars.

20 September 1915: A year affected by *coulure*, oidium and mildew, so that the crop was the smallest since 1886. The year has a poor reputation, though surprisingly the only bottle to come my way— the Léoville-Barton—had survived forty years, although it was somewhat unbalanced.

25 September 1916: Oidium reduced the vintage to below average in size, but in spite of this, it proved the most successful vintage of the war years, and one of the relative peaks in this lean period between 1900 and 1920. For long it was understandably criticized as being too hard, although Cocks & Féret say that it was considered less hard than the 1906. All the examples I have seen still showed signs of this excess tannin when already around fifty years old. On the other hand, these were all wines of character and interest. The best were Cantemerle, Larose-Sarget and Lanessan. All were very deep in colour.

17 September 1917: This is cited as a vintage which might have had a greater success had it not been for the war. In the event, it proved uneven. As it happens, the two examples I have seen were both from the other side of the river, so it could be that St Emilion and Pomerol outshone the Médoc. Both the Pétrus and the Clos Fourtet were big, dark wines, full of vigour and life; while the Clos Fourtet was a shade too alcoholic in style, the Pétrus had fruit and great charm.

23 September 1918: An average crop of very unequal quality. Maxwell Campbell called them leathery. The quixotic behaviour of the vintage was typified for me in some Léoville-Lascases tasted over the years at Loudenne. When first drunk in 1962, it seemed a little tired, but still hard and ungracious. The following year it seemed equally unsympathetic. However, in 1967 came a bottle with a gloriously perfumed bouquet far more typical of this growth, and with a lovely long, rich, harmonious flavour to match. The change was extraordinary. The Lafite tasted the same year had gone into a graceful decline and was a shade 'watery' at the finish.

20 September 1919: A light year abundant in quantity which did not live long enough to acquire any lasting reputation.

15 September 1920: With this vintage there began one of those periods of bounty which nature permits from time to time. Different claret lovers will have their own favourites, but it is undeniable that for anyone who has enjoyed drinking fine claret in the last fifty years, the most frequent pleasure will perhaps have derived from the clarets of the 1920s. The crop was of good average size and good, if not exceptional; things were thought of it from the start. There were good judges who thought the wines would not last and were lacking fruit, but for the most part, these judgments have proved erroneous. Like all the best vintages of this decade, the 1920s have a lot of personality. I noted when drinking one of them that it was more robust than a 1929 and had more elegance than a 1926, and that seems not a bad assessment of the character of the year. I have not had the good fortune to drink the Latour, which was always famed as the outstanding wine of the year, nor the Cheval Blanc, which was overshadowed by the 1921. Probably the finest example I have tasted was the La Mission Haut Brion, which in 1966 was still in full vigour, with a

349

wonderful flavour, rich and powerful. The other outstanding bottles were the Montrose, Rauzan-Gassies, and that most dependable of wines, Lanessan.

15 September 1921: This exceptionally hot summer produced one legendary wine—the Cheval Blanc—and some great Sauternes, but very few other red wines were really successful because of the inability of the *vignerons* of the day to control adequately a fermentation made in hot weather of a must unusually rich in sugar. As a result, many wines turned acetic—notably the Lafite—while others suffered from the grapes being scorched, which gave the wines a roasted smell and a heavy, but tough, texture. The Haut-Brion was such a wine, still unyielding and graceless when over forty years old, though when I again tasted it in 1979, it had improved remarkably. The Mouton, on the other hand, was surprisingly attractive when I drank it at the château with Philippe Cottin in 1966. It had more delicacy than the 1926, plenty of fruit and finesse, and a strong, assertive nose that was only just beginning to fade. Also enjoyable was the La Lagune, though there was just a little coarseness about it which was perhaps almost inevitable in this year. The Cheval Blanc was the precursor of the 1947; its remarkable sweetness and almost overpowering flavour, placed this wine firmly among the first growths of the Gironde. The Yquem was equally renowned, and indeed, all the great Sauternes had remarkable richness which has lasted very well.

19 September 1922: The largest vintage in the history of the Gironde. Not surprisingly, the wines were on the light side and proved something of a drug on the market. However, I suspect that today we should have heralded it as a distinctly 'useful' vintage. The only two red wines I have seen, Léoville-Barton and Rausan-Ségla, had both lasted forty years and still managed to be well balanced, fruity and pleasantly flavoured, although by then gently faded. On the other hand, I have had several Sauternes which were very well preserved, although curiously the Yquem was the one wine to have gone completely dry.

1 October 1923: Another large crop, if not quite so abundant as 1922. The wines were light, with much elegance and breed. With so much good wine about and claret drinking in decline, this was an underrated year. These were certainly wines of a style that would be highly appreciated today, much as the 1950s were. Both the Clos Fourtet and the Larose-Sarget lasted very well, with a lovely flowery bouquet and a pronounced sweetness on the palate. I have also drunk the Loudenne over a period of years and note that we never had a disappointing bottle. Again, the wine was notable for its sweetness at the finish, and freshness and delicacy of flavour.

19 September 1924: 1922 apart, one has to go back to 1900 to find such a prolific year as this. From the beginning, they enjoyed a fine reputation and were generally preferred to the 1923s and thus more widely bought by the English trade. This is a vintage I always associate with Château Margaux because, while still at Cambridge, I attended the then famous Lebègue tasting through the good offices of Harry Waugh, then of Harvey's, in the year that they showed a range of Margaux of the century. I was very struck by the excellence of the Margaux 1924 compared to other vintages of that famous decade, but then both the 1928 and 1929 Margaux were disappointing. Both Lafite and Latour were good, but the finest bottle I have enjoyed, after the Margaux, was a magnum of Calon-Ségur which was full of vitality when forty years old. Generally speaking, though, the 1924s have faded markedly in the last twenty years, and bottles tend now to be very variable. At their best, these wines had great charm and plenty of fruit, but in the end lacked the staying power of 1926s, much as the 1929s compared to the 1928.

3 October 1925: Another prolific year, only slightly less wine than in 1924, but the quality was totally unremarkable. An example has never come my way or, if it has, I have failed to note it or remember it.

4 October 1926: Easily the smallest vintage of the decade. At Latour the yield was a mere 7 hl/hectare. I once asked Baron Philippe de Rothschild why it did not enjoy a greater reputation, as I had just enjoyed a really great bottle of the Mouton of that year. He replied that 1926 held unhappy memories for the Bordeaux trade. There had been a very small crop, difficult to gather, due to cochylis. (At Mouton, they had gone through the vineyard and filled several barrels with maggots before the vintage.) Prices had opened at record levels—and, indeed, 1926 was to remain the most expensive claret vintage until the last decade—and then the market had collapsed, resulting in very serious losses. Baron Philippe actually cancelled all his contracts and then resold to his original buyers at half the opening price, but one *négociant* at least was made bankrupt. Although decried at first as too tannic, the 1926s have developed into wines of great power and balance. Their tannin was matched by more fruit and sugar than was the case with most 1928s. In recent years I have found them to be the most consistently fine of all the great vintages of the 1920s, with more weight and power than 1929s and more fruit and charm than most 1928s, as well as being more dependable now than the 1920s. Although these wines are undeniably tannic and robust, they have an outstanding ripeness about them which gives them a richness and finesse denied to most tannic years. I think the Mouton and Haut-Brion were certainly the finest 1926s I have drunk, but the Calon-Ségur, Cos d'Estournel, Lascombes, La Mission, Pichon-Lalande, Cantemerle and Ducru-Beaucaillou were all excellent, while many *Bourgeois* growths like Bel Orme and Loudenne have lasted and developed well.

27 September 1927: A year which vies with 1925 as the poorest vintage of the decade. I have never seen an example.

25 September 1928: A large vintage which enjoyed a very great reputation at the beginning, but has somewhat disappointed since. This is not to say that there are not a number of great wines, but the quality is more mixed than had been expected. Maxwell Campbell noted that his first impression of the 1928s was that 'they seemed so well-balanced and well-bred, full to the taste and, at the same time supple, ... there was a touch of tannin and roughness about them ... but it seemed to me to be counterbalanced by a sufficiency of fruit and sugar.' In the event, some wines turned out to be much more tannic than this description suggests, and some, like the Gruaud-Larose, seem to have dried up. In the Médoc, the great wines for me have long been the Léoville-Lascases and the Léoville-Poyferré, both wines of great depth and intensity of flavour, gloriously balanced and without a discordant note; another St Julien, the Beychevelle, was not far behind. These are rivals even for the great 1900s, but Latour, fine as it is, will always surrender pride of place to the glorious 1929. Outside the Médoc, the Ausone was a great wine, outshining even the Cheval Blanc, I thought, while the Pétrus clearly foreshadowed the great reputation it now deservedly enjoys. On the whole, the St Emilions and Pomerols have shown more harmony and regularity in their development than many Médocs, but among the Médocs, Brane-Cantenac, Calon-Ségur, Palmer, the two Pichons and Pontet-Canet all reached maturity still possessed of enough fruit to give them balance and life. This was a particularly fine year for the great Sauternes. The Yquem produced one of its greatest vintages, which lasted very well. Generally, 1928 Sauternes were better balanced and lasted better than the 1929s.

23 September 1929: 1928 and 1929 were very well-matched years. In terms of size, they were as near identical as nature is likely to allow. At the same time, proprietors and *régisseurs* spoke of them in the same breath as 1899 and 1900. Certainly they proved the most celebrated pair of years since that time. To turn to Maxwell Campbell once more, he records his first impression of the vintage as finding in them 'a small taste of over-ripe grapes, . . . the wines seemed . . . soft, mellow, and very sweet, sweeter than the '28s.' If he, and most of his contemporaries, were over-optimistic about the 1928s, they were broadly right about the 1929s as wines too pretty and ethereal to make old bones, wines to be drunk while they still gave such pleasure. Certainly, many 1929s have been fading in the last decade. Yet no one who has had the pleasure of drinking a 1929 anywhere near its best can doubt that this was a great vintage. Their quality lay in a bouquet of outstanding brilliance and penetration. The Latour was probably the most famous wine, and rightly so, although for some years there has been a degree of variation from bottle to bottle.

Although my father has always been most generous with me, I was rather surprised when I received at Cambridge in the early 1950s, several bottles of Latour 1929 in response to a request for more supplies. I rested the wine for a month or two until my parents came to dinner in my rooms. The wine proved magnificent, and my father then confessed he had had a bottle with Allan Sichel which they had judged to be in decline and Allan, in pessimistic mood, had said he felt the wine should be drunk. We never had a bad bottle again for many a long day! The Mouton was also a famous 1929, but was, I thought, in decline when I last drank it in 1965. One of the most famous wines of the year was the Pontet-Canet, a quite exceptional wine for the growth, far above its class. As in 1928, the Léoville-Poyferré was a great wine with more richness and staying power than many 1929s. Other outstanding wines were the Cheval Blanc, Montrose, Nenin, Pichon-Lalande and Siran. Some beautiful Sauternes were made, but they tended to go very dark—to caramelize. The Guiraud and Rayne-Vigneau were particularly good.

29 September 1930: The first of three dire vintages! 1930 was small in quantity and I have never heard any exonerating point in its favour. Not since the 1880s had there been such a trio, and not until the 1960s was their like to be seen again—and then not in succession.

21 September 1931: This was a larger crop, spoilt by rain during the vintage. A few tolerable wines were made, notably at Latour, Margaux and Domaine de Chevalier, while the Yquem was surprisingly acceptable. 1931 was the best of the terrible trio.

14 October 1932: A good-size crop, but one of the latest vintages ever recorded; the quality was 'execrable'. Teddy Hammond of Edward Young always told the story that it was because of these three vintages (1930, 1931 and 1932) that the idea of Mouton Cadet was born, as a method of using the Mouton and Mouton d'Armailhacq of those years.

20 September 1933: A moderate yield. A year which deserved a better reputation. Certainly these were the sort of wines which would have been very popular today—light, fruity and most attractive; they were what was then described as 'luncheon claret'. The Latour, Mouton (still fine in 1979), Beychevelle and Canon (St Emilion) are four fine examples which have come my way.

17 September 1934: The largest recorded, good vintage, only exceeded by the rather ordinary 1922s. This is a vintage which enjoyed a great reputation at the start and then went through a dull period. I am inclined to think it has now come good, and those few 1934s that survive tend to have plenty of fruit and depth of flavour, and to be generally reliable, while seldom perhaps scaling the heights of the greatest years. It is certainly the best vintage of the 1930s, and perhaps more regular than 1928, but without the flair of 1929 or 1926. The Ausone was particularly lovely, one of the last great wines from this famous château before the lean years began. The Cheval Blanc was also an outstanding success. With the exception of Latour, the first growths were rather disappointing, the Lafite being one of the few really dull wines from this great growth, and Margaux also curiously lacking in breed. The Mouton, which was for years hard and uncouth, has now come good. The Pichon-Lalande, Léoville-Barton, Talbot and Calon-Ségur are all examples of leading Médocs which have truly fulfilled their promise. Among *Bourgeois* growths, the Lanessan was particularly fine, but one of the best of all 1934s was the La Mission Haut-Brion, a marvellously balanced wine of great breed and attraction. This was a good year for Sauternes, although the Yquem was not in the same class as the 1928 or the 1937.

25 September 1935: A big crop suffered from poor weather during the vintage, and this particularly affected the white wines. Another very poor year.

2 October 1936: A medium-sized crop of clean, sound wines which lacked ripeness and therefore style or attraction. Exceptions I have seen were the Latour, which was attractive and vigorous when thirty years old, and clearly superior to the 1931 which we drank at the same meal, and La Mission Haut-Brion, still very attractive when over forty years old. The Domaine de Chevalier also had something of a reputation. I have also seen a sound Yquem.

20 September 1937: This, the first vintage to take place under the new *Appellation Contrôlée* regulations, was rather modest in size, about the same as 1933. It was bottled just in time to be shipped before the fall of France in 1940 cut Bordeaux off from her export markets for five years. For the most part, 1937s have been found to be stubborn and tough, a recognized vintage which has disappointed, yet I would plead several important qualifications to this rather unfavourable verdict. All 1937s have a certain distinction of flavour which marks them out as wines of breed and individuality—in other words, this is decidedly a class vintage.

Then, most St Emilions and Pomerols, as well as some Graves, have more harmony than the Médocs, and have developed better. Finally, even some of the top Médocs have in the last decade mellowed sufficiently to give real pleasure. A good example of this is the Latour. I first drank it when it was twenty years old and found it hard and ungracious. I wondered if it would get any better. Eight years later I noted that it was now full in flavour, rich and long on the palate—fairly balanced and still developing well. It has continued to do so, and when compared with the 1934 in 1979, was clearly superior. The Lafite has also come through well, and I certainly find it preferable to the 1934. Other good 1937s I have seen in recent years are the Léoville-Poyferré, Pichon-Lalande, Branaire and Siran, while in the Graves, the Haut-Bailly is really fine. Only Montrose proved to be a disappointment. Certainly these are very masculine wines, but I suggest there could be much enjoyment to be had in the next few years for those fortunate enough still to have some salted away. This was a great year for Sauternes, and the Yquem will always be one of my favourites—in the 1950s, it was at its glorious best at a time when the 1921 had become undependable and the 1928 was showing signs of maderization. While now past its prime, it is still possible to find enjoyable bottles.

26 September 1938: A vintage of approximately the same size as 1937, overshadowed by the war. Unlike many of the wartime vintages, most 1938s seemed to have been bottled at the right time. The wines were on the light side, attractively fruity and quite fleshy. Only a very few were subsequently shipped after the war as 'concession wines', during the period of the limitation of imports into the UK. They are just the sort of wines we should have been very glad to have today. I think the first 1938 I drank was the Talbot, which was such a pleasant surprise that I always looked out for 1938s after that. The Latour was still at its best when nearly thirty years old, and smaller growths like Chasse-Spleen and Loudenne made delicious wines which lasted well.

20 September 1939: A very large crop of light wines which, for the most part, disappeared during the war. The only example I have ever seen, the Margaux, was quite finished when less than twenty years old.

356

25 September 1940: A rather small crop which, but for the war, might have enjoyed some fame. I first came across the Clos Fourtet—bottled, as were many wartime vintages, in Sauternes bottles—when it was around ten years old. It was deliciously fruity and soft. Since then I have noted that Latour, Haut-Brion, La Mission and Pétrus were all excellent.

30 September 1941: A small and poor year of light wines which lacked maturity. Very few can have survived the war, let alone been shipped afterwards.

22 September 1942: Another small year which did enjoy something of a reputation, at least in Bordeaux. I remember examining the cellar of a member of the diplomatic service who had served in France just after the war, and returned with a number of 1942s, bought on the advice of that sound and experienced judge, Henri Binaud. Professor Plumb of Christ's, now Master of the College, once gave me a Lafite 1942, but it was very light and faded when little more than ten years old. It seems probable that these light wines suffered from poor handling and especially late bottling, due to the war.

15 September 1943: In size, just a little smaller than 1937. In quality, it was on the whole reckoned to be the best of the wartime vintages. Generally, the St Emilions and Pomerols were more successful than the Médocs, and Pétrus was universally accounted the wine of the vintage. I have not seen it now for over a decade, but it was then a really memorable wine. Also successful was the Cheval Blanc, and I have particularly pleasant memories of the Trottevieille. In the Médoc, the Latour was outstanding, but I have tasted several wines which showed clear signs of having been kept too long in cask. Generally, partly due to their handling, the Médocs tended to be rather tough and lacking vinosity and style. This was a very good year for Sauternes—the Climens and Suduiraut being especially fine.

24 September 1944: A fairly large vintage. Rain during the gathering made for variations in quality. A year not unlike 1960. At their best, the wines were light and very attractive. I remember the Cruses being enthusiastic about them, and unlike the rather cruder 1943s, they were most enjoyable when young. The Latour was particularly good, the Lafite faded rather early, but the Haut-

357

Brion was again light and delicious. Pontet-Canet was also delicious when young.

10 September 1945: A tiny crop—only twice in the previous fifty years had there been a smaller yield. This was due to an unusually late and severe May frost, but the coming of peace was heralded by a vintage of outstanding quality. These are majestic wines, inclined, it is true, to be rather too tannic to begin with and very slow to develop but, as with the best 1928s, they have a depth and intensity of flavour only found in exceptional years. Until the coming of the 1961 vintage, 1945 was generally regarded as the finest post-war vintage, although some would advance the claims of 1947, 1949 and 1953 to have been, in their different ways, at least as good, and certainly more enjoyable for longer. Of the first growths, only the Margaux disappoints. Both Lafite and Latour are outstanding examples of these two, very different wines, as is the Mouton. In Graves, both Haut-Brion and La Mission are exceptionally fine. In St Emilion, half the crop at Cheval Blanc was *piqué* and had to be pasteurized, but generally the St Emilions and Pomerols were superb and could be drunk long before most of the Médocs. I particularly remember la Dominique and Gazin. Of the Médocs, it is only since these wines passed the twenty-year mark that one began to drink them without a feeling of committing infanticide. Two exceptions were Lynch-Bages and Calon-Ségur, both more supple and less tannic than most. There were some fine Sauternes, especially the Yquem, but generally they were outshone by the 1947s.

28 September 1946: A rather moderate yield, but higher than 1945. Very much an off-vintage, although both Latour and Mouton made good wines. It was so surrounded by successful years that practically none was shipped and the vintage has been forgotten.

15 September 1947: A plentiful year which produced wines which were immediatly attractive. After the small crop of slow-maturing 1945s, this was greeted with much enthusiasm by the trade, heavily bought, and generally drunk too early. It could be, however, that in many cases this proved to be the right thing to do, because many 1947s, especially in the Médoc, have not lived up to their early promise. However, some good judges in Bordeaux at one time considered the 1947s to be superior to the 1945s. The style of the wines was so completely different that this really resolves itself into a question of taste. The peaks of 1947 certainly vie with 1945, but in general the vintage was not so consistent, although more generally attractive when young, and it has not developed so well. The most famous wines of the vintage appeared in St Emilion and Pomerol. Cheval Blanc was early proclaimed as the wine of the vintage, and has held its position as the most expensive of the 1947s, but on the two occasions I have had the opportunity of comparing the Cheval Blanc against the Pétrus— at Monsieur Jean-Pierre Moueix's table—I have thought the Pétrus to be even finer. But at that time of course, Pétrus was not nearly so well known as Cheval Blanc, and with its much smaller production there were fewer opportunities of seeing it. The Cheval Blanc itself is a wine of almost overpowering richness, and was probably most generally drunk in this state when between ten and twenty years old. More recently it seems to have come into better balance, but is probably now at its best, if not a shade past it. I found the Pétrus a more balanced wine. In the Médoc, my favourite 1947 has long been the Margaux, the finest wine from this château for many years. The Mouton is also very fine, but the Latour disappoints, and the Lafite is less remarkable than its 1949. Many 1947s seem to have lost colour in recent years and to have become rather 'edgy'—a sign of a rather high temperature during the fermentation. Among wines which have come through with honours, I would place the Calon-Ségur, Ducru-Beaucaillou, Grand-Puy-Lacoste and Ducasse, Gruaud-Larose, and Langoa-Barton, with Lanessan as an outstanding *Bourgeois* growth. La Mission is an outstanding Graves. The Sauternes were especially memorable, wines of great richness, yet graceful and possessed of remarkable finesse. Both the Yquem and the Climens were very great wines.

22 September 1948: This produced a yield of average size. This vintage suffered from coming between two other outstanding years, 1947 and 1949, and at a time when the demand for fine claret was nothing like so keen as it is now. As a result, very little 1948 was shipped to the UK for bottling here, and it was only later that Château-bottled examples began to find their way to this country. An early torch-bearer for 1948 was Ronald Avery, of the famous Bristol firm. The 1948s have less breed than 1947 or 1949, but are more robust, tannic and masculine. After the initial crudeness had mellowed, they proved to have a pleasing depth of flavour, while lacking the fruit of 1947 or 1949. However, they have lasted better than some 1947s and are certainly finer wines than the more highly praised 1952s, for example. One of the best was the Cheval Blanc, while the Calon-Ségur was actually better than the 1949 from the same château. The Lafite was notably better than the Latour, which proved a rather sullen, dull wine. St Julien did particularly well, all three Léovilles being especially good.

27 September 1949: In volume, this was a year almost identical to 1948, another hot year. As with 1947, the wines were very attractive very early and were much in demand in all markets. At the time, there was a tendency to think that 1947 would turn out to be the greater year, but most of the examples I have seen in the last few years suggest the opposite. The great Médocs are marvellous examples of all the virtues of these remarkable wines at their best. Lafite and Mouton are generally considered to be the best, with Latour not far behind, and certainly superior to its 1947. On the other hand, I have generally preferred the 1947 Margaux to the 1949, which is a shade top-heavy. The Pétrus and Cheval Blanc are also very fine, only just behind their remarkable 1947s, while the La Mission Haut-Brion outshone Haut-Brion, but this was a rather disappointing period for Haut-Brion. Once more, the St Juliens were very fine, and generally the 1949s have proved wonderfully consistent; with their fine colour, body and fruit, they are beautifully ripe, attractive wines with plenty of life and vigour in them still. This was certainly one of the great post-war vintages. It was also a fine year for Sauternes, but like some of the 1945s, they tended to have almost too much sugar and gained colour rather rapidly. The Yquem was again very fine, after which the Coutet was generally considered to be the best.

17 September 1950: This, the largest vintage since 1939, marked the beginning of a steady recovery in the scale of production in the Gironde, which has continued with only the temporary setback of the 1956 frost. After a rather wet summer, no great hopes were held out for this vintage, but in the event it turned out much better than expected, and the wines, being both plentiful and cheap, were widely bought. The first growths were generally most

360

successful, on the light side, but full of charm and quick to mature. Margaux and Lafite, also the Carruades, were particularly delightful, the Latour took longer to mature but turned out very well indeed, and only the Mouton disappointed. In the Graves, La Mission was one of the successes of the vintage, and firmly established the reputation of this fine wine in England, where it had been surprisingly neglected until then. Pétrus and Cheval Blanc were also great successes. Generally, these delightful wines which gave so much pleasure in the 1950s and early 1960s are now past their best and are fading; but a magnum of Margaux I had in 1978 was still marvellous. Some Sauternes were elegant and very well balanced, the Coutet being particularly successful.

4 October 1951: The year was average in quantity, but very poor in quality, due to a very wet summer. This was the first year that chaptalization was permitted in Bordeaux, but even this could do little for the wines. Only one or two drinkable wines were made, notably Cheval Blanc, Latour and Mouton, but they were no more than decent, ordinary wines.

17 September 1952: This was another vintage of average yield. The trade had high hopes of 1952 at the start, but it has proved a disappointment. The wines are solid and well constituted, but dull. Even as they have slowly mellowed with age, this dullness seems to persist. In the Médoc, although both Lafite and Latour have their advocates, I have found both disappointing, while the Margaux is really poor and graceless. Lynch-Bages is one of the few Médocs I remember with any pleasure; it was surprisingly fruity and well balanced. On the other hand, Cheval Blanc and Pétrus are decidedly better, and Figeac, La Conseillante and Magdelaine all made fine wines. In the Graves, La Mission was particularly rich and fine. In the next few years, it is quite possible that a few bottles of some growths will be unearthed which will show that there was something to wait for after all, but I doubt that it will ever prove to be another 1948, less still a 1937. There were some good Sauternes, although Yquem had a blank year due to frost and hail. Climens was particularly fine.

28 September 1953: This was a plentiful vintage, on a par with 1950. It was a great Médoc year, but the top St Emilions and Pomerols were less successful. Perhaps this is why 1953 has always been very highly rated in England, but less highly so in Bordeaux. From the very beginning, these wines were immensely attractive, delicate, elegant and finely bred, with a very pronounced bouquet. It was the bouquet which reminded many claret lovers of the 1929s, but they lacked the sugar and depth of that great year. Still, it is probably true to say that the 1953s gave more continuous pleasure than any other vintage since the war, until the arrival of 1961. When they first began to be drunk at only four years, it seemed that their life would be brief but beautiful. In fact, they surprised everyone by going through a change, after which they seemed to take on added depth—almost a new dimension. From the beginning, the Lafite was hailed as the wine of the vintage. Then there was a tendency to decry it, to say it was faltering. In 1967, I had a wonderful bottle with Jean-Pierre Moueix and was surprised to learn that he had got up to decant it at 7 am for lunch, because he had been disappointed with the wine the last time he drank it. A few months later, I tried the same experiment at home, decanting the wine five hours before it was to be drunk. The result was again magnificent, and several friends who knew it said that they had never had a finer bottle. But Lafite has been dogged by inconsistency between bottles. For some strange reason, the Latour has always seemed disappointing, less good than the 1955. The Margaux and Mouton are both superb in their contrasting ways, and have lasted well, while in the Graves both Haut-Brion and La Mission were to be seen at their most attractive. 1953s which have lasted well included Beychevelle (a real beauty), Cantemerle, Ducru-Beaucaillou (one of the very best), Giscours, Gloria, Grand-Puy-Ducasse and Lacoste, Lascombes, Lynch-Bages, Montrose, Palmer (a glorious wine), the two Pichons and Siran. In St Emilion, the Cheval Blanc was light and most attractive, as was the Ausone, while in Pomerol the Vieux Château Certan developed slowly to produce an outstanding wine. The Sauternes have style and a lovely balance. Yquem came back into its own after two blank years, and I particularly remember the Doisy-Daëne for being a real 'peaches and cream' affair.

4 October 1954: Average yield. This was a year spoilt by poor weather. In the event, however, a few surprisingly pleasant wines were made, and while it was less good than 1958, it was decidedly superior to 1951 or 1956. I remember 1954 as the first time I had a hand in buying an off-vintage, and the pleasure it gave when the few reasonable wines that had been picked turned out well. Latour and Mouton, Cheval Blanc and Pétrus all produced very pleasing wines which lasted remarkably well, easy, fruity, agreeable wines that they were. Other agreeable wines were Beychevelle and Calon-Ségur. Rather surprisingly, the Yquem also turned out well, although, of course, it was very light.

21 September 1955: A large crop, on a par with 1953 and 1950, producing very consistent wines. At the time, it was heralded as a really top vintage, more solid than 1953 but with plenty of fruit. Generally, they have proved sound and reliable, well balanced, but dull—somehow lacking that indefinable spark which makes a great year—a quality which 1953 had but 1955 missed. Yet, when the wines were looked at analytically, they seemed to have all the components which go to make up a fine year. This is perhaps the last mystery of wine which, for all our scientific knowledge, remains beyond our grasp. The Latour is almost certainly the outstanding wine, better than 1953 or 1959, while in the Graves, La Mission was quite outstanding, more reminiscent of 1953 than 1955, and in a different vein the Domaine de Chevalier was also fine. Both Cheval Blanc and Pétrus were good, and Figeac and Belair especially so. Having said this, few of the other wines will let you down, but few will excite. The Sauternes were also good but not outstanding.

9 October 1956: Easily the smallest vintage since 1945, due to the disastrous February frost which froze the sap in many wines, especially in St Emilion and Pomerol, and damaged many more. This was a serious set-back, after the promise of a return to real prosperity with 1953 and 1955, something Bordeaux had not known since the mid-1920s. It was not until 1962 that Bordeaux was to enjoy another good vintage in quantity. The wines were green and small, and are best forgotten. One of the few drinkable wines, oddly enough, was the Lafite which, for once in an off-year, was better than Latour.

3 October 1957: The yield was just as poor as in 1956, and a poor summer resulted in imperfectly ripened grapes, so that the wines tended to be hard and short of fruit. Nevertheless, they were widely bought after the disastrous 1956s. With a few notable exceptions, the 1957s have been cold, closed wines short of sunshine, although they have always had their champions, among whom was the late Allan Sichel, who used to say they were claret lovers' claret. If, by this, he meant that only the most devoted of claret drinkers would be able to perceive much merit in them, he was probably right. The successful 1957s had a lot of character, a notable flavour and even a certain charm. One of the finest was Beychevelle, followed by Ducru-Beaucaillou, Brane-Cantenac, Cantemerle, Lynch-Bages, Cos d'Estournel, Léoville-Poyferré, Gloria and Siran. The first growths tended to disappoint, except for Lafite, which was much better than Latour, but Mouton was acceptable. In the Graves, both La Mission and Haut-Brion were most attractive and really untypical of the year. There were a few good Sauternes, particularly the Suduiraut.

7 October 1958: The third October vintage in a row, and I can see no other instance of this occurring before. It happened again in 1977, 1978 and 1979. The yield was only slightly better than 1956 and 1957, due to spring frosts, and rain during the vintage which caused some rot, but the market was getting short of wine and the growers were becoming more skilful in handling difficult vintages, with the result that this was the first off-vintage since the war to be widely bought on the English market. Although the wines were light and have not lasted, they were elegant, fruity and charming, if lacking somewhat in substance and personality. As an off-vintage, it was of sufficient quality to be a most acceptable stop-gap. Latour and La Mission were the most successful wines, I thought, but Ducru-Beaucaillou and Cos d'Estournel both made very pleasing wines, as did Cantemerle. There were a few good Sauternes, of which the Suduiraut was outstanding, surprisingly rich and complete in flavour.

21 September 1959: Another small yield, only slightly more wine being made than in 1958, but the quality was good, and from the beginning the vintage enjoyed a great reputation and was much sought after. It is probably fair to say that the reputation of 1959 suffered from over-extravagant praise at the start and then by the arrival of 1961. However, this is a classic vintage; the wines are both attractive and fine, but probably lack a little backbone to make them really great. There is considerable concentration of fruit and richness as would be expected from a very hot year, but most wines were rather soft to start with. Nevertheless, they have generally developed well, but many now seem rather dry. The only disappointments were in St Emilion and Pomerol, where many vineyards had still not recovered from the 1956 frost. All the first growths were good, with Haut-Brion being one of the best. Lafite and Mouton were very fine, and Latour is a slow developer. The Margaux, while better than the 1955, is not quite in the 1947/1953 category for this château. Cheval Blanc is a strange, rather unbalanced wine, but Pétrus is magnificent. This is such a fine all-round year that it is really invidious to single out individual wines. 1959s today are either at their peak or beginning to fade, but there should be few disappointments. The Sauternes are rich, luscious and well balanced. I confess, though, to finding Yquem disappointing, and when I tasted it against Suduiraut in 1972, the Suduiraut was clearly the winner.

9 September 1960: The biggest crop since the 1956 frost, but still well below the level of 1950/1953/1955. The vintage was endangered through a wet September, which caused a good deal of rot. As a result, the quality varied considerably. In general, the wines turned out to be very similar to 1958. Although the reputation of the vintage was poor at first, it was quite well bought owing to the increasing shortage of wine, and prices were higher than for the 1958s. In the end, there were probably rather more successful wines in 1960 than there had been in 1958, and again it proved a very useful stop-gap off-vintage, especially after the results of the tiny 1961 vintage were known. I remember looking at the 1960s very well, because at that stage my company needed more wine, and stocks of 1959 were very short. The wines which impressed me most in my first journey round Bordeaux in March 1961 were Latour, La Mission Haut-Brion and La Conseillante, and all have lived up to their early promise. Subsequently, I found the Mouton and Margaux to be very good. Both Lafite and Haut-Brion were most attractive, flowery wines, but really too light and ethereal to last. In St Emilion and Pomerol, most châteaux still seemed to be suffering from the effects of 1956, and the Cheval Blanc was not as good as the 1954, but the Pétrus did show better form, although I think the La Conseillante was better. In the Médoc, Léoville-Lascases and Palmer were two of the most successful wines. The

Sauternes were not very successful, and the Yquem quickly threw a deposit.

19 September 1961: A very small yield due to *coulure*, but a perfect summer and autumn resulted in wines with a great concentration of fruit and extract. Because of more carefully controlled fermentation, the growers avoided making another 1928 or 1945, and the wines were very supple from the beginning. I shall always remember the first tastings of 1961s in Bordeaux because of the remarkably characteristic bouquet which nearly all wines had right from the start. They seemed to possess an extra dimension compared to any other vintage I had seen. One result of the. elimination of excess tannin during the fermentation is that there has been an understandable tendency to drink many 1961s too early—people found it difficult to believe that such attractive wines could last. There are some wines which are too soft and lack the characteristic intensity, rather like some 1929s, and these wines were at their best already at the end of their first decade of life. Another point worth making—1961 was a wonderful year for the small *Bourgeois* growths of Bordeaux. There were scores of delightful wines like this well above their usual class and wonderful drinking after five or six years. All the top wines are marvellous, and at last Cheval Blanc and Pétrus seemed to be back to their pre-frost best. My early notes indicate a bewildering array of wonderful wines. Haut-Brion and Margaux both showed well early, Lafite and Mouton and Latour promised to be great, and La Mission, as usual in recent years, was very well up the field. My own favourites among so many wonderful wines, were Palmer, Haut-Bailly, Gruaud-Larose, Léoville-Lascases, Brane-Cantenac and Pape-Clément. Many of what one might call the second-line classified growths are quite outstanding—Batailley and Croizet-Bages are good examples of these, while Gloria, Villegeorge and Loudenne were marvellous *Bourgeois* growths. Like Cheval Blanc, many St Emilions and Pomerols were back to their old form, or nearly so. Some had to wait until 1964 to produce of their best again. Figeac, Magdelaine, Trotanoy and Beauregard are among the most successful.

In May 1978, thanks to the generosity of Dr Taams, I was able to taste nineteen of the leading 1961s blind, and this was a splendid opportunity to re-assess the vintage. It clearly confirmed

1961's claim to be the best vintage since the war, and also underlined the extraordinary consistency of the leading growths. In the first group of ten, I placed Léoville-Lascases and Lynch-Bages top, closely followed by Ducru-Beaucaillou and Beychevelle. Then came Pape-Clément, Léoville-Poyferré and Lascombes, with Calon-Ségur and Léoville-Barton not far behind. Only the Montrose disappointed. The tasting as a whole placed the Ducru first, just 0·26 ahead of Beychevelle. Unfortunately one bottle of Lascases was corked, which put it out of the race, or the result might have been different. So Ducru went into the second tasting.

In that final run-off, there was little to separate the top wines, but we were nearly unanimous in placing Palmer top. Then came the Latour, surely the 1961 of the future, followed by Mouton, Ducru, Trotanoy and Margaux, with Gruaud-Larose and Haut-Brion close on their heels. The Cheval Blanc was just behind these leaders, and Lafite trailed disappointingly last, another case of inconsistency from bottle to bottle, since we had a much better magnum at lunch. The Yquem 1961, served also at lunch, was almost overwhelmingly luscious and powerful, but rather top-heavy for my taste.

A few months later in Switzerland, with the Palmer not present, I placed Lafite, Latour and Haut-Brion equal top—all very great wines in their differing styles. The Latour was absolutely true to the form shown at the Taams Tasting, but the Haut-Brion and Lafite were much finer examples. Mouton and Margaux were again very fine, while the Calon-Ségur, was much better than in Holland, with the Ducru not as good and showing a little over-glown.

Taken as a whole, it is clear that the top 1961s are still improving and will repay keeping. But many are marvellously rewarding wines to drink and enjoy now, although they will surely live and even improve for many years to come. There can be no doubt that 1961 has taken its place, as it promised to right from the start, among the very greatest Bordeaux vintages, undisputed champion of the post-war years, and worthy to be placed beside the great wines of the 1920s, and to be mentioned as a true successor to the legendary wines of an earlier era.

1961 is always said to be a great vintage for Sauternes, but I must confess that in nearly every case where I have been able to compare the two vintages, I have preferred the 1962 to the 1961. It is really a question of style; the 1961s have a rather hard, alcoholic finish for the most part, and the 1962s seem more liquorous and better balanced.

1 October 1962: A very large crop, larger indeed than any vintage of the 1950s, and the largest vintage also of the 1960s, although slightly more red wine was to be produced in 1967. The summer of 1962 was not particularly good, but then Bordeaux was blessed by an Indian summer and, as a result, the vintage turned out to be far better than anyone had dared hope. From the start, the wines had a very good colour, and the quality was remarkably consistent in all districts. In cask, the 1962s were deceptively flattering and fruity, in bottle they have developed much more slowly than had been expected due, I suspect, to just a touch of unripeness in the grapes. Again, the smaller wines were excellent. Although the 1962s have had their detractors, I have always been a firm believer in their merits, and each year that passes seems to confirm this. They have developed a very classic flavour and have a very marked personality. They have a wonderful colour, and the acidity in them is ensuring a long life. While having no pretensions of being a 1961 or a 1966, 1962 is a very good vintage indeed, which is so well constructed that I believe it will have a very long life, giving great pleasure over many years. All the first growths were good, only Cheval Blanc and Margaux falling rather below the standard of the rest. Lafite has always been my personal favourite, the Pétrus is a beauty, the Latour the last wine made there under the *ancien régime*, and a worthy example. There are many fine St Emilions and Pomerols; the Ausone was the best for years—I preferred it to the Cheval Blanc—and Magdelaine was deliciously rich and attractive, while Trotanoy was one of the best Pomerols. In Graves, La Mission is outstanding, and both Haut-Bailly and Pape-Clément were excellent. It was a fine year for St Julien: Beychevelle, Léoville-Lascases, Léoville-Barton, Ducru-Beaucaillou and Gruaud-Larose all made excellent wines. There were many other successes, though, especially Palmer, Montrose, Mouton-Baron-Philippe and Pichon-Lalande. The Sauternes were also extremely fine, rich yet well balanced and with a fine savour. The Yquem was very successful and the Suduiraut especially fine.

3 October 1963: A large crop ruined by persistent rain during

September, which caused widespread rot. After the comparative success of 1958 and 1960, the growers refused to believe that the 1963s could turn out as badly as they first appeared—but indeed they could. I shall always remember the unpleasant experience of tasting these wines in wood, looking for the good ones which never really came. They had an unhealthy orange tinge to them, and a sickly hint of rottenness on the nose. Far too many wines were château-bottled, and in the end the only drinkable wines were Latour (easily the best), Mouton, La Mission, Domaine de Chevalier (a remarkably sound wine), and Léoville-Lascases— and that is probably being generous! The only Sauternes to see the light of day was the Yquem, probably the worst wine ever to go out with this great name. Most English merchants refused the sample when the wine was first offered.

21 September 1964: Another large vintage; almost as much red wine was made as in 1962. Unfortunately, torrential rain fell from 8 to 17 October, and many of the larger properties in the Médoc, especially in Pauillac and St Estèphe, had not completed the vintage. The best wines are to be found in St Emilion and Pomerol, Graves and St Julien. At their best, the 1964s are very ripe, fruity, elegant wines, but with a tendency to be soft. Because of the exceptional summer, the then French Minister of Agriculture made the mistake of proclaiming it the 'Vintage of the Century' before the picking had started. Inevitably there was a reaction, but there has, I think, been a tendency almost to underrate the 1964s in recent years. Certainly there are many disappointing wines in the Médoc, such famous names as Mouton, Palmer, Calon-Ségur, Lynch-Bages and Pontet-Canet among them. But, on the credit side, the Pétrus is a great wine, probably the wine of the vintage, the Cheval Blanc a worthy successor to the great pre-frost wines and much better than the 1962, while La Gaffelière, Figeac and Magdelaine all made outstanding wines. In Graves, the Haut-Brion is very fine, La Mission one of the best wines of the vintage, Domaine de Chevalier, Haut-Bailly and Pape-Clément are all highly successful. In the Médoc, Latour is generally regarded as the best, while Margaux is honourable but no more. There are more good 1964s to be found in St Julien than anywhere else in the Médoc, the outstanding wines being Léoville-Lascases and Beychevelle, but Léoville-Barton, Ducru-

369

Beaucaillou and Branaire were also successful. Lower down the Médoc, both Cantemerle and La Lagune made good wines, while Brane-Cantenac is good but light and forward. In Pauillac, Pichon-Lalande and Batailley are two of the most successful wines. To summarize, 1964 is a very different style of year to 1962, certainly less consistent, yet at its best producing wines of great class. But recently, some Médocs have gone very dull and dumb. Because of the October rains, the Sauternes harvest was ruined and many châteaux wisely did not sell their wine under the château name.

2 October 1965: A year of average size which produced some of the poorest wine since 1930–2. 1963 was the year of rot, in 1965 the grapes were simply unripe, and the wines were green and acid, although they had a better colour than the 1963s. Even Latour failed to produce a reasonable wine—indeed the only passable example I have seen was La Mission while, by some miracle, the Calon-Ségur turned out more drinkable than the 1963. A year to be quickly forgotten, even in these wine-hungry days. It is reassuring, perhaps, to know that for all our technical cleverness, we still cannot make a decent wine in the finest vineyards if grapes are rotten or unripe. But now we know much more about preventing rot in the first place.

26 September 1966: A good average yield in this decade of high yields. Conditions were almost perfect and resulted in very ripe, full-bodied wines with a splendid colour. Like 1962, it was a very consistent vintage in all areas, but the wines were richer and had more sugar than the 1962s, resulting in full, powerful and harmonious wines of considerable charm. I have always believed that after 1961—which was *hors classé*—1966 will prove the best vintage of the 1960s, and so far their development has been everything that could be hoped for. The first growths are really fine, more consistent and more complete than the 1964s. Especially outstanding are Cheval Blanc, Pétrus and La Mission, while in the Médoc, Latour is developing into an outstanding wine. This is one of the better years for Lafite in a very uneven period, and Margaux—little regarded at this time—is also very fine. One of the great wines of the vintage is Léoville-Lascases, and the Beychevelle is a delight. On the other side of the river, the wines are also most consistent, with La Gaffelière a special favourite of mine.

For the next few years, 1966 should prove the most abundant source of fine bottles of claret at every level, the liveliness and warmth of the bouquet, the clean, fresh flavour leading to a completely harmonious finish of immense charm; all these are the qualities one looks for in classic claret, and of which 1966 provides an abundance. Most of us can only drink 1961s on rare and special occasions, but 1966s are still widely available and are excellent value. It is also a very good year for the smaller growths and the lesser areas like Côtes de Bourg and Fronsac. The Sauternes are fine and elegant, but lack the richness and completeness of the 1967s.

22 September 1967: A large vintage, similar in total size to 1964, but the largest crop of red wines of the decade, beating 1962. The wines developed slowly to start with, and it took longer than usual to assess the quality of the wines, which were marked by a certain acidity in the early stages. However, they soon showed a pleasing fruitiness, and seemed to have elegance and style. They are lighter than the 1966s and have something of the consistency of the 1964s.

This has proved to be a useful stand-by vintage. The wines have some class, but fall short of being really first-class, certainly inferior to 1962 and 1964, but better than 1969. The early fruit has tended to pass rather quickly and most wines have a slightly bitter aftertaste, which is very typical of the vintage. Though mostly still enjoyable, this is a vintage which needs drinking and most wines will not benefit from further keeping. At a tasting of 1967s in 1979, all the wines showed these characteristics, with the exception of the Léoville-Lascases, which was *hors classé*, with the Pichon-Lalande, more harmonious than most, as the runner-up.

It should be noted that in general, Pomerol produced the best wines this year, with the Pétrus outstanding. In St Emilion, the wines of the Côtes were superior to those of the Graves, and good St Emilion Côtes are usually superior to most Médocs. It is often also said that the St Emilion 1967s were superior to the 1966s. While it is true that 1966 on this side of the river fell a little short of the success registered in Médoc and Graves, I do not share this view. Most 1967 St Emilions are now showing their age, while the 1966s, for the most part, are much fresher.

The Sauternes are outstandingly successful, easily surpassing the 1966s—the best vintage since 1962. The most successful wines were Yquem—probably the best since 1949, Suduiraut and Sigalas-Rabaud. The wines combine a rich lusciousness with great style and breed.

23 September 1968: An average crop, spoilt by rain. This time, a number of proprietors made a much more severe selection than had been the case in 1963 or 1965, and the grapes were riper than had been the case in 1965. The result was that, although overall the vintage was poor, more drinkable wines were made in 1968 than in 1963 and 1965 put together. They were naturally light, small wines, but had fruit and charm, ideal wines for early drinking. Among the most successful wines were Pétrus, Latour, La Mission Haut-Brion and Domaine de Chevalier. In the Médoc, Haut-Batailley, Ducru-Beaucaillou and de Pez showed well. This was another blank year for Sauternes, but unfortunately Yquem, unrepentant evidently after their 1963, again marketed a wine which does no credit to their famous name.

22 September 1969: A small vintage, indeed the smallest of the decade after 1961. A poor flowering ensured that the crop would be small from the beginning, but the summer was indifferent and the autumn brought only sporadic spells of good weather. The growers were optimistic that the vintage would turn out to be good, and the low yield resulted in high prices. But the wines, after a good start, developed disappointingly in cask, suddenly taking a turn for the worse during the second winter, and there was a rush to get them into bottle. Indeed, many châteaux assisted their wines with a touch of the prolific 1970s before bottling. In general, the wines are dry, short, with a mean, rather acid aftertaste. When the wines were mature in the mid-1970s, one of the most notable characteristics was quite simply a lack of district and château character—a sure sign of a poor year. One trusts that most of these wines are by now dead and buried. At a tasting of a wide range of 1969s in 1977, the best wines were Pétrus, Gruaud-Larose and Magdelaine.

21 September 1970: Unusual for its combination of quantity and quality, this was the year when everything went right. The flowering began on 5 June in ideal conditions and the season proceeded in copy-book fashion, so that a large crop was brought to perfect maturity and the vintage was gathered in perfect weather. Not since 1934 had there been such a prolific vintage of such quality. But 1970 can also be seen as a watershed, ushering in a decade when there was a marked switch from white to red wines, when the area under vine was to increase (especially in the Médoc), together with the yields. Thus the yield of red A.C. wine achieved in 1970 was to be surpassed in 1973, 1974, 1976, 1978 and 1979, but its yield of white A.C. was to remain the highest of the decade, so that finally, 1970's total A.C. yield was only to be surpassed in 1973, 1976 and 1979. In early tastings, the 1970s had a fine, deep colour, a powerful aroma, and were rich and velvety on the palate. The fruit and richness masked the tannin and led to the mistaken notion that these wines would develop rapidly. Actually, their evolution has been steady but rather slow, and the best wines have often gone through a dumb stage when their real virtues lay obscured. Many of the lesser growths showed their paces much sooner and have provided robust and delicious wines which have been excellent drinking for several years. But many of the best wines are still not at their best when ten years old.

This is a great all-round vintage of marked consistency as between different districts and different categories of wine, as great a year for the small growths as for the first growths. The wines have the sort of balance and harmony seen in 1966, but are more tannic and have been slower to evolve, while lacking the remarkable power and beauty of 1961. But beneath a rather shy exterior, 1970s at every level have that depth and complexity of flavour only found in the best years. In recent tastings, I have found Mouton and Latour outstanding in the Médoc, with Lafite good but not great. In Graves, La Mission is a prodigious wine of great intensity, remarkable for its sheer beauty of flavour and harmony. In St Emilion, both Ausone and Cheval Blanc are very fine in totally different ways, but the palm on the Right Bank must go to Pétrus. La Conseillante and La Fleur-Pétrus are also outstanding. What is certain is that many years of pleasurable drinking lie ahead for this vintage.

This is a good, but not outstanding, vintage for Sauternes. The wines have great power and richness, but in most cases I prefer the 1971s. An exception was Suduiraut. The Yquem is good, if lacking the style of 1967 or 1971.

25 September 1971: 1970 and 1971 are yet another of Bordeaux's famous pairs of vintages, and provide the most interesting contrast since 1961 and 1962. This was a rather small crop, caused by poor flowering, the smallest of the decade in terms of red A.C. wine of the decade, but producing more white wine than the other small vintage, 1977.

The wines provide a complete contrast to those of 1970. They had an immediate charm soon after bottling, rather reminiscent of the 1953s. They are very fruity, precocious and showy. There is also about them a distinction of bouquet and flavour which marks a fine vintage. Above all, they have a seductive quality which misled many good judges into believing them to be better than the 1970s. But the one flaw in their make-up is a low fixed acidity, which makes the comparison of 1971 against 1970 that of the brilliant 800-metre runner against the long-distance runner. This is why, in many early comparative tastings, the 1971s were preferred to the 1970s.

Another difference is that the red 1971s are far less consistent than the 1970s, especially among the lesser growths. When only three or four years old, it was possible to find *petits châteaux* going brown in colour and beginning to oxidize. Perhaps the greatest wine of the vintage is Pétrus, rather reminiscent of some Cheval Blanc of the immediate post-war period, almost overpoweringly fruity and headily perfumed. None of the Médoc first growths reached the same level, with Latour probably the best. Palmer and Ducru-Beaucaillou are outstanding among the other leading growths.

This is a great year for white wines. The Graves have great finesse and breed, the Sauternes enormous elegance and richness—the Yquem is exceptional.

3 October 1972: A year of unhappy memories; there was poor weather during the flowering, which was protracted, and not enough sun, so the late harvest resulted in wines lacking fruit and with too much acidity. At the same time, the growers demanded even higher prices than for the 1971s. This affront to common sense led in a few months to the market crisis which many had feared, and a very difficult period for Bordeaux wines which was to continue for nearly three years.

With cold weather during the vintage, more experience of how to prevent rot by spraying, and making more rigorous selections both in the vineyard and the *chais*, the wines were sounder than might have been expected. But in bottle the colour fell away quickly, there was a lack of clear characteristics on the nose, and the wines were short and mean on the palate, with at best a meagre fruitiness. Probably the most successful wine was Cheval Blanc, which had a mellow richness not found elsewhere. Latour and Lafite in their different ways were the most acceptable Médocs. Curiously enough, many lesser growths were more acceptable than most of the big names. But overall, this is certainly a year Bordeaux will be happy to forget. Many top châteaux would have done better not to have bottled under their own label.

20 September 1973: This year probably deserves a better reputation than it has. The weather was favourable, hot and exceptionally dry, and the crop exceeded in volume that of 1970. Only 1979 in this decade produced more wine.

The characteristics of 1973 are fruit, charm, a low fixed acidity and a certain irregularity due to very high yields where Merlot is heavily planted. Unfortunately, this large crop of attractive, precocious wines came at a bad moment for the Bordeaux trade, and although prices were very low after the rapid rise beginning in 1970, which reached its final absurdity with the 1972s, trade had virtually come to a standstill. But when the wines were in bottle and trade had recovered, 1973 proved an ideal vintage for early consumption, cheaper than the 1971s, much more attractive than 1974, and capable of giving much enjoyment while waiting for the 1970s to mature. There may be no great wines in 1973, but there are plenty of good wines, and very few poor ones have seen the light of day because they found their way into generic blends at an earlier stage. Haut-Brion and La Mission Haut-Brion had the misfortune to be hailed on the very eve of the vintage, and lack the charm of the year.

While some lesser wines are now past their best and beginning to fade, most 1973s are about at their best, but should probably be drunk before 1983–5. This was a mixed year for Sauternes, with wines of only moderate quality. Coutet is one of the best.

20 September 1974: Another large vintage whose quality was adversely affected by a wet, cold September. The vintage as a whole was slightly smaller than 1970, but produced more red A.C.

wine than in that year. The red wines tend to have held their colour rather better than the 1973s, due to better fixed acidity, but totally lack that vintage's charm and vinosity. Generally, there is something cold, charmless and austere about them, though they are certainly sounder and more balanced than the 1972s. The best results seem to have been obtained in St Julien and St Emilion. Among the few examples to give pleasure that I have noted are Langoa-Barton, Beychevelle and Figeac. Due to the sheer quantity produced, I suspect that bottles of 1974 will crop up for some years to come, and no doubt there will be the odd pleasant surprise.

22 September 1975: After the problems of 1972, 1973 and 1974, Bordeaux needed a top quality vintage to restore morale, and 1975 provided just what was wanted. After a cold spring, the summer arrived suddenly, the flowering passed in excellent conditions, to be followed by a very dry, hot summer. In September, there was just the right amount of rain to adjust the situation. Following two exceptionally large vintages, it was only to be expected that 1975 would be smaller, especially after such a dry summer. Actually, the yield was slightly larger than 1972 or 1971 overall, but the yield of red A.C. wine was significantly higher than in either of these years, again demonstrating the shift in emphasis from white to red, which was occurring throughout the decade.

Due to the dryness of the year, resulting in rather moderate *rendements*, alcoholic degrees were relatively high, and thick skins resulted in tannic, powerful wines. When I first tasted the young wines in the exceptional heat of the summer of 1976, they seemed massive but disappointingly flat. But in better conditions in the autumn, the remarkable aroma—the most striking in a young vintage since 1961—was again evident. The wines had a lot of fruit, but this was to some extent masked by tannin. In bottle, they seem to have shaken off what had appeared to be an excessive tannin content in cask, so that the fruit is now showing through to great advantage. As in 1970, this is a year when lesser growths show especially well, and many *petits châteaux* were already becoming enjoyable after two years in bottle.

One of the many things 1975 will be remembered for is the rebirth of Ausone. The 1975 is certainly one of the top wines of the vintage, and when compared with Pétrus and Cheval Blanc in

1979, came out top. In the Médoc, Lafite, Latour and Mouton all promise to develop to great wines. After that, I single out Léoville-Lascases and Palmer. In Graves, the contrast in style between Haut-Brion and La Mission Haut-Brion is especially striking, with Haut-Brion being much more forward than the other top growths and La Mission needing a lot of time.

Much has been written about the comparison between 1975 and 1961. Several differences of importance must be noted. In 1961, the *rendement* was much smaller, and the wines were characterized by a remarkable and singular aroma when in cask. Occasionally I noted something similar when tasting a few of the 1975s, but this vintage characteristic was not nearly so marked or so uniform. Then the 1961s were far more flattering in cask than the 1975s which, in my opinion, lack the extraordinary harmony of the older vintage. There will certainly be some great wines in 1975, but it is still too early to be certain of their development and final stature.

In Sauternes, wines of extraordinary sweetness and power were produced, but many lack balance and may oxidize early. Yquem is an exception to this; other successes are Climens, Coutet and Doisy-Daëne.

13 September 1976: In many ways, this was a most unusual vintage. From April to July, the weather was unusually hot and dry. This resulted in an early flowering and *véraison*. August provided two days of heavy rain, but apart from that was again very hot and dry, so that by the end of the month, the grapes were extremely small and the conditions resembled 1921, 1947 and 1949. The vintage started very early (13 September), but there was considerable rain in September which had the effect, at this stage, of diluting the quality. The resulting wines had a deep colour, were fairly rich in alcohol, and were very low in fixed acidity, with unusually high pHs. This suggested fragile wines, but the thick skins produced wines higher in tannin than early tastings had suggested, so masked was it by fruit.

In the lesser districts, delicious, elegant, fruity reds have been produced which are already drinking well. It is too early to say just how well the top growths will develop, but the overall results may well prove superior to what was at first predicted. Certainly, the year will provide a fascinating contrast to 1975, another pair of vintages to watch and compare. If 1975 was notable for the first offering of a new régime at Ausone, so 1976 will surely be remembered for a similar occurrence at Lafite. Early tastings in bottle showed Pétrus, Cheval Blanc, Haut-Brion, Mouton, Latour, Lafite, Léoville-Lascases, La Mission, Pichon-Lalande and La Couseillante as front runners.

There are some fine white Graves, and this was another good year for Sauternes, producing much more elegant wines than in 1975, with Yquem especially notable.

3 October 1977: Notable as the first of four unusually late vintages. By early September, there were dire warnings of an impending disaster, of a degree of unripeness far exceeding anything known in 1972. Then came an exceptional September, with more hours of sunshine (but not the highest temperatures) and the lowest rainfall recorded for a hundred years. Because of serious frost damage at the end of March (especially in Pomerol and St Emilion), the vintage was easily the smallest overall in the Gironde in this decade, although slightly more red A.C. wine was produced than in 1971.

Many *petits châteaux* have produced attractive, light, fruity wines for early drinking, especially in the Médoc, Bourg, Blaye, Fronsac and the Premières Côtes. The best results are to be found in St Julien and Margaux in the Médoc, and in Graves. At their best, they have charm and breed, but in some areas, such as St Estèphe and parts of Pauillac, there is too much acidity and greenness. Essentially a vintage for early drinking. No good Sauternes was made.

9 October 1978: After the 'miracle' vintage of 1977, it seemed impossible that another autumn such as that could be hoped for. In fact, the autumn of 1978 was even more remarkable. If March was the wettest since 1870, the months of July, August and September were notable for their lack of rain, and the heat was even greater than in 1977. This time there was a good-sized crop to bring in; the quantity of A.C. wine was situated between 1972 and 1974, but the quantity of red A.C. wine was actually slightly more than in 1974.

First impressions confirm that the 1978s have an excellent colour, considerable richness and natural glycerine, which masks their tannin. These are sumptuous wines, certainly finer than 1976 and more harmonious than 1975 at the same stage. It will be fascinating to see how they develop. There will certainly be some great wines and, generally speaking, it is a remarkably regular vintage. Only in the St Emilion Côtes are the wines below the general level of quality. There are many delicious wines for relatively early consumption in the lesser areas and among the *petits châteaux*.

Tastings in cask suggest that Margaux, Latour, Mouton, Lafite, Palmer, Léoville-Lascases, Ducru-Beaucaillou, Pichon-Lalande, Lynch-Bages, Cos d'Estournel, Montrose, Gloria and Prieuré-Lichine in the Médoc, should be among the most successful wines of the vintage. In Graves, Haut-Brion, La Mission and Domaine de Chevalier promised well. In Pomerol, where there were many fine wines, Pétrus, La Conseillante, Trotenoy, Vieux Château Certan and Latour-Pomerol were the leading growths. In St Emilion, where there are fewer successes, Cheval Blanc, Ausone and Figeac looked the pick of the bunch.

This was a freak year in Sauternes because, although the grapes achieved an excellent ripeness, there was no *pourriture noble* due to the fine weather and lack of humidity. Doisy-Daëne made their final picking in December.

2 October 1979: The third in this remarkable quartet of October vintages was also the largest vintage in the Gironde since the war, and the first time that over 3 million hectolitres of red A.C. wine had been made. The 3,315,124 hectolitres produced was a huge increase on the previous best—2,479,382 in 1973. After a mild, wet winter, April was unusually cold, and this held back the vegetation. May began with heavy rain which gave way to periods of better weather, so that by the end of the month, vegetation was rapidly making up for lost time. June provided warm, sunny weather for the flowering which began on the 12th and passed quickly with excellent setting of the fruit. July was equally beneficial, but with August came a setback. Temperatures were below average and there was much rain. The development of the vegetation was blocked during an important phase. There followed, however, a warm, generally sunny September, and an October mainly favourable for bringing in the vast crop. There were outbreaks of rain and misty mornings, but the weather remained warm. The state of the grapes was generally healthy, with very little rot.

In spite of the record harvest, this was not a year of enormous *rendement* as in 1973; rather, yields resembled those of 1970. Most of the classified growths in the Médoc reported producing between 25 and 35 per cent more than in 1978. This was balanced by the careful selection most of them made.

First impressions were that the St Emilions were unquestionably better than the 1978s, confirmation that this is a Merlot year. All the leading growths on both sides of the river had a depth of colour and individuality which are the hall-mark of a fine vintage. First tastings in casks showed uniformally high quality from St Estèphe down to Margaux; among the most impressive wines at this stage were Lafite, Mouton, Margaux, Pichon-Lalande, Montrose, Léoville-Lascases and Ducru-Beaucaillou, while on the other side of the river Pétrus, Ausone and Cheval Blanc were outstanding, with Figeac, Belair, Canon and Magdelaine not far behind.

6 October 1980: We had thought that three late vintages in a row was remarkable, then came 1980. After a typical Bordeaux winter, humid but without extreme cold, the first buds broke on 2 April, which is about normal, and ten days earlier than in 1979. April was dry but cold, May wet and cold, and the cold weather persisted into June which was the coldest since 1946. As a result, the flowering, which began on 6 June, was very prolonged and widespread *coulure* and *millerandage* followed. July was the coldest since 1954. At this stage, conditions were comparable to those of 1969 and 1971 and a drop of 40–50 per cent in yield compared to 1979 was forecast. Then fortunes changed. The sun shone in August and through September. The *véraison* began on 18 August, three weeks later than normal, and eight days later than in 1979. September was the hottest since 1964. In early September, the vintage was still forecast for 15 October. During the heat of September, there were also some serious storms and on 20 September, 70 mm of rain fell in some places in 24 hours. During the vintage, the weather was unsettled and rather cold. Some of the best growths delayed their picking and recorded the latest vintage since 1922. At Mouton they did not begin until 18 October, when 700 pickers brought in the whole crop in eight days. At Ausone the picking did not begin until 20 October.

The total yield of A.C. wines was the smallest since 1969, at

2,918·083 hectolitres, but the production of red A.C. wine, at just over 2 million hectolitres was, in fact, larger than that recorded in 1977, 1975 or 1971. The shortfall was in white wine, which at 866,607 hectolitres, was the smallest for many a long day.

This will certainly go down as a vintage saved by modern treatments. Until very recently, rot would have crippled quality. In fact, because of widespread treatments, there was scarcely any rot at all. Then, carefully controlled fermentations made the best of the quality that had been harvested.

The first analysis of both the composition of the new wine and subsequent tastings revealed several interesting points. The Merlot did better than the Cabernet Sauvignon. The alcohol level was better than in 1977 for the Merlot, but similar for the Cabernet. Acidities were low for both *cépages*. Selection of vats was very important, as was the time of vintaging. First tastings revealed supple, fruity wines, light and forward in style but with sufficient tannin and good balance. But some wines are clearly too light and unsubstantial and the wines are generally short. This is a year when each wine must be carefully tasted and where the range of qualities is likely to be wide.

Professor Pascal Ribereau-Gayon's evaluation of the year (made in May 1981) was that it is clearly superior to 1977 and also better than 1974 and 1973. Tastings I made in July 1981 confirm the year's superiority over 1977, and in my opinion, over 1974, but I would prefer to reserve judgment as to whether it will be better than 1973, whose wines have, I believe, often been undervalued.

Appendices

APPENDIX I

Rainfall registered by the regional meteorological services at Merignac

1945: no measurement during the war period

	mm		mm		mm		mm
1946:	709	July:	24	August:	56	September:	42
1947:	866	July:	43	August:	71	September:	67
1948:	661	July:	59	August:	75	September:	31
1949:	778	July:	4	August:	2	September:	88
1950:	863	July:	21	August:	87	September:	49
1951:	1111	July:	73	August:	97	September:	80
1973:	788	July:	114	August:	23	September:	100
1974:	922	July:	15	August:	70	September:	115
1975:	780	July:	11	August:	51	September:	120
1976:	1018	July:	113	August:	136	September:	111
1977:	960	July:	100	August:	83	September:	4
1978:	894	July:	37	August:	20	September:	31

Yearly average for the last thirty years: 900 mm

For 1976, the important rainfall in July and August was due to three or four very big thunderstorms, whereas these two months on the whole were very dry.

385

APPENDIX II

Comparison of weather conditions, ripening cycle of the three late harvests of 1977, 1978 and 1979

METEOROLOGICAL CONDITIONS FROM APRIL TO END AUGUST				
Year	Rainfall level (mm)	Total temperatures	Number of very hot days	Hours of sunshine
1963	299	2,500°	7	1,096
1969	305	2,646°	14	1,054
1975	250	2,707°	16	1,089
1978	300	2,496°	10	952
1979	315	2,501°	10	1,083
last 25 years average	275	2,624°	13	1,090

It will be seen from the above table that meteorological conditions in 1978 and 1979 were not significantly different from those in 1963 and 1969.

Year	Flowering date	*Véraison* date	Maturity date
1977	27 June	2 September	12 October
1978	26 June	2 September	12 October
1979	21 June	25 August	8 October
Last 20 years average	15 June	20 August	3 October

The French term *véraison* is more or less untranslatable by a single English word, and for this reason it is normally used even in English. It refers to the moment when the grapes change colour.

The above table shows the lateness of each stage of maturation, from flowering to ripening, in comparison with the average in the last twenty years.

Dates of tests	1977 10.10	1978 02.10	1978 09.10	1979 01.10
Merlot				
Weight for 100 g (g)	148	134	130	137
Probable alcoholic strength	10°6	10°9	11°7	11°3
Total acidity grams per litre	5·9	6·1	5·5	5·1
Cabernet Sauvignon				
Weight for 100 g (g)	117	113	114	115
Probable alcoholic strength	10°2	10°8	11°3	10°4
Total acidity grams per litre	6·5	6·6	5·2	5·9

The comparative performances of Merlot and Cabernet Sauvignon in the above table, show the very clear differences which were registered in the three years. Thus, in 1979, Merlot had reached a stage of ripeness comparable to that reached eight days later in 1978. On the other hand, the Cabernet Sauvignon was nearly as ripe on 1 October 1979 as on 2 October 1978. The other point to note is that the acidity was significantly lower in 1979 for both grape varieties compared with the same date in 1978.

APPENDIX III

Rendement for the 1978 and 1979 vintages

The 1974 revision of the *Appellation Contrôlée* system introduced several new concepts.

Rendement de base: this indicates the basic yield allowed by the decrees for each *appellation*.

Rendement annuel: this is the yield fixed each year following proposals from each wine-growing *syndicat* and the INAO. This can be above or below the *rendement de base*.

Plafond limité de classement (PLC): this is a fixed percentage given in the decrees controlling the *appellations*, which when applied to the *rendement annuel*, gives the maximum permitted yield for that year. Anything over this figure has to go for distillation. Below is a comparison of the *rendement annuel* and the maximum permitted yield for all the Bordeaux *appellations* in 1978 and 1979. This gives a good idea of the wide differences which are now possible from year to year according to the individual circumstances of each vintage.

388

(A)
RED WINES: 1978

APPELLATIONS	Annual *rendement* Ho/ha	Maximum permitted yield Ho/ha
1. *Bordeaux & Côtes*		
Bordeaux	55	66
Bordeaux Supérieur	48	57·6
Bordeaux—Côtes de Francs	48	57·6
Bordeaux—Côtes de Castil	48	57·6
Bordeaux, Clairet & Rosé	55	66
Blaye or Blayais	55	66
1° Côtes de Blaye	55	66
Côtes de Bourg & Bourgeais	50	60
Graves de Vayres	48	57·6
1° Côtes de Bordeaux	50	60
Ste-Foy-Bordeaux	50	60
2. *Libournais*		
St Emilion	45	54
Lussac	50	60
Montagne	50	60
Puisseguin	50	60
St-Georges	50	60
Lalande de Pomerol	42	50·4
Pomerol	42	50·4
Fronsac	45	54
Canon Fronsac	45	54
Parsac	50	60
Néac	42	50·4
Bergerac	55	66
Côtes Bergerac	55	66
3. *Médoc, Graves*		
Médoc,	48	57·6
Haut-Médoc	48	57·6
Listrac	45	54
Margaux	40	48
Moulis	40	48
Pauillac	45	54
St Estèphe	48	57·6
St Julien	40	48
Graves	50	60

RED WINES: 1979

APPELLATIONS	Annual rendement Ho/ha	Maximum permitted yield Ho/ha
1. *Bordeaux & Côtes*		
Bordeaux	65	78
Bordeaux Supérieur	55	66
Bordeaux—Côtes de Francs	55	66
Bordeaux—Côtes de Castillon	55	66
Bordeaux, Clairet & Rosé	65	78
Blaye or Blayais	65	78
1° Côtes de Blaye	65	78
Côtes de Bourg & Bourgeais	65	78
Graves de Vayres	55	66
1° Côtes de Bordeaux	60	72
Ste Foy Bordeaux	60	72
Bordeaux Mousseux Rouge & Rosé	65	78
2. *Libournais*		
St Emilion	55	66
St Emilion *Grand Cru Classé*	50	60
St Emilion 1° *Grand Cru Classé*	50	60
Lussac	55	66
Montagne	55	66
Puisseguin	55	66
St-Georges	55	66
Lalande de Pomerol	52	63
Pomerol	52	63
Fronsac	55	66
Canon Fronsac	55	66
Néac	52	63
Bergerac	65	78
Côtes Bergerac	60	72
3. *Médoc, Graves*		
Médoc	55	66
Haut-Médoc	54	65
Listrac	58	70
Margaux	50	60
Moulis	55	66
Pauillac	50	60
St Estèphe	58	70
St Julien	50	60
Graves	55	66

(B)
WHITE WINES: 1978

APPELLATIONS	Annual rendement Ho/ha	Maximum permitted yield Ho/ha
1. *Dry White Wines*		
Côtes de Duras	50	60
Bordeaux	50	60
Bordeaux—Côtes de Francs	50	60
Blaye and Blayais	50	60
Côtes de Blaye	50	60
1° Côtes de Blaye	50	60
Côtes de Bourg and Bourg	50	60
Graves de Vayres	50	60
Enire-deux-Mers	50	60
Graves Secs	50	60
Bergerac	50	60
Ste-Foy-Bordeaux	50	60
2. *Medium-Sweet to Sweet*		
Bordeaux Supérieur	45	54
Bordeaux Sup. Côtes Franc	45	54
Côtes de Bordeaux St-Macaire	42	50·4
Graves Supérieures	40	48
1° Côtes de Bordeaux	40	48
Cadillac	40	48
Côtes de Bergerac	55	66
3. *Sweet Wines* (*Rendement* without PLC)		Coefficient
Cérons	40	1·5
Loupiac	40	1·5
Ste Croix du Mont	40	1·5
Barsac	25	2
Sauternes	25	2

The above *appellations* for sweet wines are without PLC but can, however, under certain conditions, benefit from a supplementary yield in other *appellations*. This supplement can be either Bordeaux or Bordeaux Supérieur Blanc but without overtaking the maximum yield permitted for these two *appellations*.

Example: a grower in Sauternes can declare:

- 25 Ho/ha of Sauternes
- by multiplying 25 Ho/ha by the coefficient 2 we obtain 50 Ho/ha
- the maximum permitted yield for Bordeaux being 60 Ho/ha,

this grower can declare 10 Ho/ha in AC Bordeaux Blanc.

WHITE WINES: 1979

APPELLATIONS	Annual *rendement* Ho/ha	Maximum permitted yield Ho/ha
1. *Dry White Wines*		
Côtes de Duras	70	84
Bordeaux	70	84
Bordeaux—Côtes de Francs	70	84
Blaye & Blayais	70	84
Côtes de Blaye	70	84
1° Côtes de Blaye	70	84
Côtes de Bourg and Bourg	70	84
Graves de Vayres	60	72
Entre-deux-Mers	55	66
Graves Secs	50	60
Bergerac	70	84
Ste-Foy Bordeaux	60	72
2. *Medium-Sweet to Sweet*		
Côtes de Duras	65	78
Bordeaux Supérieur	55	66
Bordeaux Supérieur Côtes de Francs	55	66
Côtes de Bordeaux St Macaire	55	66
Graves Supérieures	40	48
1° Côtes de Bordeaux	50	60
Cadillac	40	48
Côtes de Bergerac	60	66
Bordeaux Mousseux Blanc	70	84
3. *Sweet Wines*		
Cérons	40	*Rendements* without PLC but with the possibility of an additional allowance of 10 hectolitres per hectare in AC Bordeaux Blanc
Loupiac	40	
Ste Croix du Mont	40	
Barsac	25	
Sauternes	25	

APPENDIX IV

Average prices from the beginning of the *campagne* in December 1973 until November 1974

AOC	Average prices December 1973	Average prices November 1974	Approximate fall in %
Bordeaux	2,400	1,300	45
Bordeaux Supérieur	2,750	1,400	50
Côtes de Castillon	3,100	1,500	50
Côtes de Bourg	2,900	1,400	50
Côtes de Blaye	2,900	1,500	50
Côtes de Fronsac	4,000	2,150	45
Canon Fronsac	4,250	2,400	45
Sables St-Emilion	4,250	1,950	55
Lussac & Parsac St-Emilion	4,250	2,100	50
Montagne, Puisseguin & St-Georges St-Emilion	4,250	2,150	50
Graves	5,500	2,600	55
St-Emilion	5,250	2,400	55
Lalande de Pomerol	6,500	3,100	50
Pomerol	9,500	3,750	60
Médoc	5,250	2,600	50
Haut-Médoc	6,000	2,950	50
Moulis	6,500	3,250	50
Listrac	6,500	3,250	50
St-Estèphe	6,750	3,750	45
Pauillac	7,000	4,000	45
St-Julien	11,000	4,000	65
Margaux	9,500	4,000	60

These prices are per tonneau of 900 litres taken at the property. The above figures demonstrate vividly the extent of the fall in the Bordeaux market at the height of the crisis in 1974.

Evolution of the area under vines, number of growers who declare the vintage, the production and stocks in the Gironde, from 1946 to 1980

Years	Number of hectares declared			Growers declaring the vintage	Yields 25 November HL	Stocks 31 August HL	December availabilities HL	Rendement per ha
	AOC	CC	Total					
1946			136,482	57,907	2,883,329	895,464	3,779,393	
1947			137,694	59,122	4,139,687	1,529,952	5,669,639	
1948			134,493	58,843	3,358,932	1,142,999	4,501,931	
1949	97,329	38,392	135,721	57,621	3,306,261	1,185,989	4,492,250	24·3
1950	82,669	56,111	138,780	60,327	3,395,000	1,105,259	6,501,259	24·5
1951	69,587	62,296	131,883	56,601	3,574,603	2,350,427	5,925,080	27·1
1952	72,077	60,043	132,120	56,929	3,502,875	1,883,426	5,396,301	26·5
1953	71,537	62,261	133,798	58,024	5,459,216	1,668,924	7,128,140	40·8
1954	75,263	56,429	131,692	56,202	3,963,605	2,335,340	6,298,945	30·1
1955	76,290	56,047	132,337	55,969	5,396,595	1,723,229	7,119,824	41·1
1956	67,845	58,359	126,204	46,701	2,132,011	2,662,625	4,794,636	17·0
1957	68,867	45,135	114,002	46,278	2,057,254	1,736,183	3,793,437	18·0
1958	65,057	46,322	111,379	47,890	2,982,468	1,051,079	4,033,547	26·8
1959	67,557	43,045	110,602	46,883	2,979,596	1,280,787	4,260,383	26·9
1960	69,676	43,164	112,840	46,550	3,996,456	1,035,334	5,031,790	35·4
1961	71,592	37,019	108,611	45,685	2,789,650	1,613,620	4,403,270	25·7
1962	74,964	39,322	114,286	46,512	5,554,413	1,448,084	7,002,497	48·6
1963	70,750	41,751	112,501	45,870	4,984,636	2,479,263	7,463,899	44·3
1964	74,419	37,560	111,998					

	75,676	34,740	110,416	41,856	4,553,098	2,784,732	7,337,830	41·2
1966	75,676	34,740	110,416	41,856	4,553,098	2,784,732	7,337,830	41·2
1967	76,760	32,343	109,103	40,137	4,937,892	2,682,778	7,620,670	45·2
1968	75,171	33,137	108,308	38,437	4,897,560	2,837,850	7,735,410	45·2
1969	73,176	30,145	103,321	36,125	3,162,959	2,884,491	6,047,450	30·6
1970	69,628	35,154	104,782	35,263	5,508,449	2,083,221	7,591,670	52·6
1971	66,104	36,251	102,355	33,084	3,734,845	3,215,882	6,950,727	36·5
1972	69,471	33,165	102,636	31,810	3,977,997	2,476,471	6,454,468	38·7
1973	70,736	31,435	102,171	31,078	5,663,648	2,750,146	8,413,794	55·3
1974	67,364	35,475	102,839	30,029	5,472,789	4,213,920	9,213,920	53·2
1975	69,028	33,100	102,128	29,180	4,191,988	4,828,091	9,020,079	41·0
1976	70,844	33,824	104,668	28,630	5,515,705	3,701,046	7,223,102	52·7
1977	76,001	21,575	97,576	25,372	2,492,396	4,385,492	6,877,888	25·4
1978	78,439	18,565	97,004	25,703	3,980,143	3,080,093	7,060,236	40·9
1979	74,290	24,321	98,611	25,561	6,230,720	3,359,081	9,589,801	62·9
1980	76,271	20,187	96,458	24,346	3,664,532	4,883,623	8,548,155	37·8

These figures illustrate a number of interesting points:

1. It will be noted that there is a very rapid change in the proportion of AC to *consommation courante* area under vines between 1949 and 1951. This is due to the fact that, after the war, it was discovered that many vineyards which had been declared as AC, contained unauthorized varieties of vines and, therefore, had in future to be declared in *consommation courante*; in other words, they were incorrectly classified.

2. It will be noted how the steady build-up of the area under vine received a severe set back with the 1956 frost. The fluctuation in figures in the 1960s and 1970s reflect the reconstruction of many vineyards and particularly in the 1970s, the switching from white to red varieties.

3. There has been a very steady decline in the amount of CC produced in the region, and a dramatic decline in the number of growers making declarations.

4. A look at the stocks available in December, when the new vintages are added to existing stocks, demonstrate very clearly the massive increase in stocks held during the crisis years of 1973, 1974 and 1975 and how rapidly these began to fall in 1976 and 1977.

APPENDIX VI

Yields of the vintage in the Gironde from 1970 to 1980: quantities in hectolitres

RED WINES

AOC	1970	1971	1972	197
Blaye or Blayais	575	378	394	
Bordeaux	443,964	289,479	384,561	588,
Bordeaux Supérieur	354,921	230,423	308,177	405,
Bordeaux Clairet	3,413	3,671	1,263	2,
Bordeaux Supérieur Clairet	—	—	—	—
Bordeaux Côtes de Castillon	—	6,151	—	
Bordeaux Sup. Côtes de Castillon	65,728	40,151	55,790	91,
Bordeaux Côtes de Francs	3,349	2,359	4,814	—
Bordeaux Sup. Côtes de Francs	—	—	—	5,
Bordeaux Rosé	6,152	3,810	3,839	4,
Bordeaux Supérieur Rosé	158	—	—	
Côtes de Blaye	—	—	—	—
Côtes de Bourg, Bourg, Bourgeais	126,377	74,510	92,275	159,
Fronsac	32,135	17,545	25,100	38,
Côtes de Canon Fronsac	13,871	8,711	10,031	13,
Graves	40,958	25,084	35,912	41,
Graves de Vayres	2,386	3,123	6,238	8,
Haut-Médoc	77,158	43,875	64,071	98,
Lalande de Pomerol	37,327	17,364	20,947	38,
Listrac	13,046	9,283	14,255	21,0
Lussac St Emilion	42,994	23,827	36,274	58,6
Margaux	35,486	19,329	24,743	38,3
Médoc	88,432	45,296	67,387	109,1
Montagne St Emilion	50,844	25,077	33,084	75,0
Moulis	10,648	6,649	8,240	12,3
Néac	18	2	—	
Parsac St Emilion	9,339	5,040	6,792	
Pauillac	45,265	21,535	30,141	47,7
Pomerol	39,284	21,333	22,060	41,7
Premières Côtes de Blaye	46,077	25,081	35,934	69,9
Premières Côtes de Bordeaux	38,275	17,679	29,550	49,8
Puisseguin St Emilion	27,492	16,624	20,859	34,7
Sables St Emilion	8,039	4,844	5,379	7,5
St Emilion	293,344	161,901	187,828	306,0
St Estèphe	58,507	33,165	49,950	60,5
Ste Foy Bordeaux	—	—	219	1
St Georges St Emilion	10,928	4,446	7,484	10,2
St Julien	34,443	14,945	22,773	35,3
Bergerac	266	238	468	
Côtes de Bergerac	—	—	—	—
Côtes de Duras	1,385	1,373	1,990	2,6
TOTAL: AOC	2,061,991	1,223,951	1,620,408	2,479,3
TOTAL: CC	624,375	385,733	391,071	460,9
TOTAL GENERAL	2,686,366	1,609,684	2,011,479	2,940,3

.974	1975	1976	1977	1978	1979	1980
1,724	749	289	210	265	312	111
16,410	513,656	805,698	411,510	658,258	1,168,727	685,293
28,734	283,795	286,329	188,435	357,271	382,916	282,358
1,973	2,063	3,621	1,542	5,622	3,949	2,572
—	—	—	8	—	—	—
9,090	—	149	404	—	—	—
66,054	68,294	83,334	42,215	86,447	108,351	75,686
—	—	84	2,547	90	—	—
3,957	4,904	5,718	—	6,260	7,099	6,469
4,977	6,016	7,541	4,625	6,651	6,638	4,626
42	197	46	8	244	148	55
—	—	—	—	—	10,236	—
22,758	99,421	144,174	58,807	99,729	155,756	86,721
31,759	27,563	32,434	20,013	29,357	40,543	25,833
15,979	10,848	14,086	9,585	10,791	16,024	10,951
52,861	41,278	57,760	31,935	59,457	89,748	62,098
4,998	6,549	6,661	3,858	7,016	8,167	5,452
88,270	61,662	100,171	53,175	99,321	154,851	94,323
36,151	22,452	37,361	11,304	28,394	45,355	24,249
19,657	12,330	21,190	9,746	18,059	29,498	15,298
40,718	35,286	45,784	15,153	43,540	57,590	32,847
39,825	28,189	37,972	21,827	34,615	46,724	34,512
96,729	66,595	110,006	64,610	108,086	154,904	95,106
59,254	43,855	59,394	23,097	53,429	76,010	43,617
12,251	8,326	12,788	7,420	12,020	16,926	11,332
195	—	—	—	—	—	—
41,319	30,553	38,450	25,375	34,438	48,789	32,733
37,856	21,110	33,445	13,543	27,216	36,188	23,283
59,590	56,387	93,228	63,099	91,017	134,782	68,292
49,385	32,352	52,842	27,501	42,496	76,697	41,723
24,785	21,949	27,626	11,152	28,184	33,795	22,519
	—					
270,117	193,324	245,883	113,397	213,251	287,985	187,051
53,893	33,883	49,855	32,583	47,483	59,413	40,904
166	314	868	1,049	4,509	3,675	2,136
7,378	5,647	7,878	4,001	6,659	9,509	5,724
35,916	23,604	30,124	17,978	26,207	36,534	23,580
213	321	422	154	343	432	277
—	—	—	—	—	65	31
2,360	2,601	3,690	1,884	5,298	6,788	4,314
237,354	1,766,073	2,456,901	1,293,750	2,252,023	3,315,124	2,052,076
558,786	401,576	539,163	145,845	255,198	461,837	191,184
896,140	2,167,649	2,996,064	1,439,595	2,507,221	3,776,961	2,243,260

WHITE WINES

AOC	1970	1971	1972	1973
Barsac	16,535	14,640	14,066	14,5
Blaye or Blayais	90,709	38,245	16,620	25,1
Bordeaux	796,134	569,024	648,491	896,9
Bordeaux Supérieur	31,291	17,265	22,801	21,3
Bordeaux Mousseux	—	—	—	—
Bordeaux Côtes de Francs	—	227	403	—
Bordeaux Sup. Côtes de Francs	—	—	—	1
Cadillac	—	—	—	15,4
Cérons	20,916	19,162	17,840	13,0
Côtes de Blaye	12,778	4,545	3,140	8,9
Côtes de Bordeaux St Macaire	11,855	8,602	11,267	11,3
Côtes de Bourg, Bourg, Bourgeais	12,578	6,428	4,082	6,0
Éntre-deux-Mers	71,096	58,713	90,840	81,6
Graves	10,095	10,973	8,305	4,8
Graves Supérieures	45,558	32,021	29,280	45,5
Graves de Vayres	24,342	17,744	16,702	19,9
Loupiac	13,946	11,336	14,045	13,5
Premières Côtes de Blaye	2,859	905	886	1,1
Premières Côtes de Bordeaux	76,597	62,061	83,931	68,2
Ste Croix du Mont	16,008	14,675	15,614	12,5
Ste Foy Bordeaux	5,796	1,773	5,459	5,3
Sauternes	43,661	24,514	26,439	19,4
Bergerac	788	229	196	1
Côtes de Bergerac	—	250	154	—
Côtes de Duras	9,702	1,764	6,530	11,1
Monbazillac	—	—	—	—
Montravel & Côtes de Montravel	309	243	100	1
Bergerac Côtes de Soussignac	—	—	—	—
TOTAL: AC	1,313,553	915,339	1,037,091	1,296,7
TOTAL: CC	1,508,530	1,209,822	929,427	1,426,6
TOTAL: VINS DE PAYS	—	—	—	—
TOTAL	2,822,083	2,125,161	1,966,518	2,723,3

1974	1975	1976	1977	1978	1979	1980
15,440	13,239	14,812	3,793	10,782	14,137	13,739
44,255	37,112	44,999	30,151	71,005	50,404	22,896
62,303	657,955	700,235	456,183	535,504	793,314	526,299
13,073	11,876	12,767	8,826	6,100	15,840	11,586
—	—	—	—	—	24	—
226	320	130	211	334	571	556
—	—	376	—	—	—	—
299	4,209	6,704	1,769	1,425	2,572	2,551
10,714	12,254	10,878	2,377	5,041	5,069	7,407
7,448	4,403	6,515	10,051	23,021	10,039	12,124
3,896	6,345	6,581	2,561	3,490	2,696	4,049
13,585	5,283	8,683	4,596	6,087	5,936	5,960
70,041	77,635	75,009	75,323	194,103	102,487	102,049
16,373	8,462	48,243	19,928	31,507	59,568	25,551
42,034	31,569	13,708	6,054	11,640	13,363	21,714
12,846	12,428	16,001	9,869	11,178	19,654	12,796
9,920	11,023	10,789	4,715	8,767	11,095	9,739
578	1,963	85	231	238	514	282
40,501	45,176	31,481	27,720	25,027	38,247	33,605
14,873	14,562	15,168	10,077	12,581	16,766	13,927
23,210	4,521	6,402	2,827	9,277	8,506	4,044
26,102	24,034	26,123	8,622	25,581	30,486	26,899
281	309	207	432	565	125	77
—	—	—	—	110	—	—
8,435	8,209	8,720	5,637	9,448	12,327	8,727
—	—	188	98	—	—	—
—	—	—	—	—	253	—
—	—	—	—	—	55	30
136,433	992,887	1,064,804	692,051	1,002,811	1,214,048	866,607
440,216	1,042,892	1,454,837	360,750	470,111	1,235,292	550,773
—	—	—	—	—	4,419	3,892
576,649	2,035,779	2,519,641	1,052,801	1,472,922	2,453,759	1,421,272

APPENDIX VII

Study of the areas under vine and the production in the different communes of the Médoc from 1972 to 1978

COMMUNES	1972		1973		1974	
	Sup. Ha	Prod. Hos	Sup. Ha	Prod. Hos	Sup. Ha	Prod. Hos
1. AOC 'Médoc'						
Bégadan	574	22,704	580	39,991	603	31,9€
Blaignan	93	3,567	93	4,369	94	4,5?
Civrac	23	745	24	1,357	25	1,2€
Couquêques	54	2,372	67	3,474	69	3,8€
Gaillan	7	352	8	484	9	4?
Jau-Dignac-Loirac	6	184	6	313	6·5	3?
Lesparre	7	286	9	341	8	2·
Ordonnac	190	7,461	193	11,910	193	9,9€
Prignac	234	7,570	231	11,816	232	9,8?
Queyrac	63	2,317	62	4,044	64	3,3?
St-Christoly	152	5,613	156	10,450	151	7,9?
St-Germain d'Esteuil	95	3,694	106	4,790	109	4,9€
St-Yzans	278	10,743	289	16,942	267	13,6?
Valeyrac	52	1,694	56	3,300	59	3,3?
Vensac	6	255	15	632	13·5	5?
St-Vivien						
Hors Communes	2	13	18	1,264		
TOTAL	1,836	69,570	1,913	115,477	1,903	97,3€
2. AOC 'Haut-Médoc'						
Arcins	95	1,613	85	2,112	56·5	2,6€
Blanquefort	42	1,428	43	2,458	43	2,07
Avensan	51	2,158	64	2,932	78	3,6C
Castelnau	2	85	30	247	28·5	44
Cissac	178	7,463	171	11,000	169	8,92
Cussac	122	3,721	144	7,221	165	6,€5
Lamarque	83	2,822	85	4,901	74	3,33
Le Taillan	15	447	19	641	15	67
Le Pian	30	698	28	1,382	32	1,5C
Ludon	110	3,244	109	2,385	110	4,50
Macau	22	458	22	641	20	78
Parempuyre	23	1,295	24	1,797	22	1,2€
St-Laurent	226	10,056	231	16,816	258	13,36
St-Sauveur	178	6,861	221	11,967	225·5	11,34
St-Seurin	301	11,950	308	20,695	296·5	16,83
Vertheuil	201	8,793	205	12,389	203	10,14
Hors Communes	61	1,433	35	1,357	19	1,2C
TOTAL	1,740	64,525	1,824	100,941	1,815	89,55

1975		1976		1977		1978	
Sup. Ha	Prod. Hos	Sup. Ha	Prod. Hos	Sup. Ha	Prod. Hos	Sup. Ha	Prod. Hos
612·17	21,968	758·97	34,936	795·30	21,114	804·97	33,770
109·87	3,814	115·65	6,171	138·28	3,618	171·30	7,781
26·34	704	26·71	1,096	28·66	798	37·21	1,547
61·33	2,564	74·24	3,847	79·87	1,810	82·76	3,663
8·45	398	13·75	729	14·63	331	14·88	625
5·75	178	10·35	362	16·61	320	17·69	473
22·49	563	26·68	1,248	37·58	1,122	37·58	2,004
199·18	6,750	201·67	10,718	214·63	6,419	221·44	8,641
240·23	7,801	304·35	11,866	325·77	6,924	384·90	13,880
71·53	2,795	76·46	4,030	84·70	1,861	96·42	2,890
163·21	6,679	169·83	9,177	179·40	5,076	204·33	8,906
123·38	3,337	130·21	6,413	149·87	3,805	158·59	5,785
335·98	9,319	300·06	15,300	323·21	8,937	334·59	15,781
64·57	2,019	66·17	2,721	78·27	1,720	80·25	2,199
15·96	456	17·15	702	15·24	264	33·49	931
				·40	110	·53	17
·83	18	17·73	606	52·23	556	—	—
,061	69,363	2,309·98	109,923	2,534·65	64,785	2,681·03	108,893
85·58	3,314	99·32	5,850	172·16	4,654	187·09	7,761
46·77	1,427	47·17	2,154	54·26	1,730	55·00	2,058
80·92	1,523	83·76	3,074	86·61	1,668	107·18	3,193
3·02	120	3·67	175	3·67	60	3·50	108
165·87	6,104	187·69	10,119	208·41	5,871	222·38	10,507
141·71	4,784	173·93	6,611	222·78	2,845	251·93	8,228
104·38	3,758	106·27	4,674	109·23	2,481	110·66	4,997
14·06	545	17·51	937	20·00	375	20·20	636
34·33	1,513	49·53	2,577	60·75	1,378	60·09	2,844
109·30	2,460	112·37	3,102	113·12	1,847	117·61	3,276
20·50	464	22·76	568	29·81	393	71·34	1,892
22·22	1,124	26·20	1,332	27·59	837	28·00	759
272·60	10,566	307·85	15,856	355·23	8,344	356·30	14,503
240·80	7,353	225·89	10,290	243·83	4,199	255·85	9,653
316·71	8,396	352·63	16,620	395·93	11,988	423·35	17,544
209·10	6,312	213·79	10,270	219·54	4,543	227·17	8,085
46·13	1,790	53·41	2,178	119·77	1,450	91·31	4,250
,914·—	61,583	2,083·75	96,387	2,442·69	54,663	2,588·96	100,294

COMMUNES	1972		1973		1974	
	Sup. Ha	Prod. Hos	Sup. Ha	Prod. Hos	Sup. Ha	Pr H
REPORT TOTAL AC MÉDOC	1,836	69,570	1,913	115,477	1,903	97
REPORT TOTAL AC HAUT-MÉDOC	1,740	64,525	1,824	100,941	1,815	89
3. *AOC Communales*						
Margaux	285	8,179	308	11,921	282	12
Arsac	63	1,231	69	2,248	81	2
Cantenac	316	9,091	309	15,073	307	13
Labarde	103	2,024	104	4,062	102	4
Soussans	105	3,175	115	4,917	114	5
Hors Communes	13	416	6	253	8	
Margaux (Total)	885	24,116	911	38,474	894	39
Listrac	381	14,462	398	21,067	382	19
Moulis	275	8,255	255	12,500	264	12
Pauillac	757	26,261	781	47,753	785	45
St-Estèphe	1,010	39,899	1,020	59,690	989	53
St-Julien	629	23,052	629	35,334	663	35
GENERAL TOTAL	7,513	270,140	7,731	431,236	7,695	393

APPENDIX VII

1975		1976		1977		1978	
o. **a**	Prod. Hos	Sup. Ha	Prod. Hos	Sup. Ha	Prod. Hos	Sup. Ha	Prod. Hos
·—	69,363	2,309·98	109,923	2,534·65	64,785	2,681·03	108,893
·—	61,583	2,083·75	96,387	2,442·69	54,663	2,588·96	100,294
7	8,295	315·11	11,025	324·25	8,205	326·90	10,046
5	1,594	80·08	2,531	81·37	1,207	82·49	2,027
5	9,170	244·19	13,722	379·53	8,082	377·70	12,717
)	3,930	115·15	4,677	118·29	2,918	115·79	3,939
)	3,820	123·71	5,268	139·49	2,797	144·22	4,805
8	370	9·68	451	10·36	297	17·09	653
5·—	27,179	887·—	37,674	1,053·—	23,506	1,064·19	34,187
8·—	12,156	415·—	21,336	471·—	9,910	495·42	17,538
5·—	8,576	291·—	12,768	340·—	6,974	334·15	12,023
2·—	28,201	931·—	38,526	934·—	24,686	958·88	34,006
)·—	33,837	1,304·—	49,451	1,104·—	32,433	1,107·61	45,291
8·—	23,677	702·—	30,179	687·—	18,015	746·06	26,206
·—	264,572	8,923·—	396,244	9,566·—	234,972	9,976·30	378,438

APPENDIX VIII

Study of the areas under vine, the *rendement* and the total quantity of the 1978 vintage in Médoc, illustrating the breakdown between classified growths, *bourgeois* and artisan growths, and *caves cooperatives* for the 1978 vintage

AC MÉDOC

	Crus Bourgeois	Crus Artisans	Coopératives
Areas under vine/hectares	1,096	438	1,137
Production in hectos	47,314	17,845	43,858
Rendements hectos/hectares	43·14	40	38
Average *rendement* of the *appellation*: 40 hectos/hectare			

AC HAUT-MÉDOC

	Crus Classés	Crus Bourgeois	Crus Artisans	Coopératives
Areas under vine/hectares	143	1,609	393	454
Production in hectos	5,892	59,061	16,265	18,100
Rendements hectos/hectares	41	36	41	39
Average *rendement* of the *appellation*: 38 hectos/hectare				

AC MOULIS

	Crus Bourgeois	Crus Artisans	Coopératives
Areas under vine/hectares	253	53	21
Production in hectos	8,992	2,046	734
Rendements hectos/hectares	35	38	34
Average rendement of the appellation: 35 hectos/hectare			

AC LISTRAC

	Crus Bourgeois	Crus Artisans	Coopératives
Areas under vine/hectares	326	49	119
Production in hectos	11,383	1,594	4,370
Rendements hectos/hectares	34	32	36
Average rendement of the appellation: 35 hectos/hectare			

AC MARGAUX

	Crus Classés	Crus Bourgeois	Crus Artisans
Areas under vine/hectares	721	256	87
Production in hectos	22,313	8,653	3,220
Rendements hectos/hectares	30	33	36
Average rendement of the appellation: 33 hectos/hectare			

AC ST JULIEN

	Crus Classés	Crus Bourgeois	Crus Artisans
Areas under vine/hectares	559	96	91
Production in hectos	20,505	3,367	2,332
Rendements hectos/hectares	36	35	25
Average rendement of the appellation: 35 hectos/hectare			

AC ST ESTÈPHE

	Crus Classés	Crus Bourgeois	Crus Artisans	Coopératives
Areas under vine/hectares	216	537	63	285
Production in hectos	6,950	21,328	3,199	13,856
Rendements hectos/hectares	32	39	50	48
Average rendement of the appellation: 41·18 hectos/hectare				

AC PAUILLAC

	Crus Classés	Crus Bourgeois	Crus Artisans	Coopératives
Areas under vine/hectares	753	88	13	185
Production in hectos	26,780	2,877	537	3,712
Rendements hectos/hectares	35	32	40	20
Average rendement of the appellation: 41·18 hectos/hectare				

ALL APPELLATIONS OF THE MÉDOC

	Crus Classés	*Crus Bourgeois*	*Crus Artisans*	*Coopératives*
Areas under vine/hectares	2,392	4,261	1,188	2,201
Production in hectos	82,440	162,975	47,038	84,630
Rendements hectos/hectares	34	38	40	38
Average *rendement* of the *appellation*: 41·18 hectos/hectare				

APPENDIX IX

Important dates in the cycle of the vine

Dates / Vintages	Budding	Flowering	*Véraison*	Vintage
1980	2 April	6 June	18 August	6 October
1979	12 April	12 June	10 August	2 October
1978	29 March	10 June	12 August	9 October
1977	5 March	15 June	1 August	3 October
1976	25 March	30 May	15 July	13 September
1975	28 March	2 June	21 July	22 September
1974	25 March	3 June	25 July	20 September
1973	1 April	1 June	28 July	20 September
1972	20 March	7 June	10 August	3 October
1971	30 March	1 June	27 July	25 September
1970	28 March	5 June	25 July	21 September

APPENDIX X

Study of the areas under vine, the average *rendement* and the actual yield in the different *appellations* of the Gironde from 1974 to 1978

RÉCOLTE	1974			1975		
	Hectares under vine	Average *rendement*	Approved volume	Hectares under vine	Average *rendement*	Approve volume
Bordeaux Rouge	9,870	56	559,841	10,528	48	506,86
Bordeaux Supérieur Rouge	7,020	46	329,095	7,871	36·7	288,96
Bordeaux Rosé	131	56	7,351	166	46	7,64
Bordeaux Clairet	39	61	2,335	56	49·7	2,78
Bordeaux Supérieur Blanc Moël	160	39	6,260	207	33·2	6,89
Bx Côtes de Castillon	1,151	47	73,791	1,660	41·5	69,00
Bx Côtes de Francs Rouge	104	47	4,919	159	29	4,61
Bx Côtes de Francs Blanc	5	44	223	7	45	32
Entre-deux-Mers	1,429	52	75,527	1,558	45·3	70,65
Graves de Vayres Blanc	240	53	12,897	275	44·5	12,23
Graves de Vayres Rouge	99	52	5,192	158	40	6,33
1° Côtes de Bordeaux Blanc	990	40	40,501	1,234	34·5	42,56
1° Côtes de Bordeaux Rouge	959	48	46,235	1,005	32·4	32,59
Cadillac	3	37	112	149	35·4	5,27
Ste Croix du Mont	—	—	—	—	—	—
Barsac	663	24	15,981	669	19·8	13,24
Sauternes	1,242	20	25,861	1,257	18·7	23,54
Cérons	345	31	10,714	388	29·1	1,32
Graves Blanc Sec, Graves Blanc Sup.	1,486	39	58,545	1,325	33·8	44,71
Graves Rouges	1,172	45	53,249	1,220	33·8	41,29
Côtes de Blaye Blanc	111	48	5,388	166	39·5	6,56
1° Côtes de Blaye Rouge	1,075	56	60,641	1,299	44·8	58,30
Côtes de Bourg	2,232	57	135,149	2,577	38·0	98,01
Fronsac	635	51	32,398	636	42·7	27,18
Canon Fronsac	290	49	14,340	278	38·8	10,80
Montagne St Emilion	1,123	51	58,251	1,145	37·5	43,00
Puisseguin St Emilion	529	49	26,267	552	41·7	23,02
Lussac St Emilion	836	48	40,263	889	39	34,69
St Georges St Emilion	127	58	7,395	131	41·5	5,44
St Emilion	2,290	52	120,201	2,300	36·8	84,78
St Emilion *Grand Cru*	—	—	—	1,864	42·8	79,56
St Emilion *Grand Cru Classé*	—	—	—	674	35·6	24,01
St Emilion 1° *Grand Cru Classé*	—	—	—	198	26·3	5,21
Médoc	1,900	50	96,394	2,061	33·6	69,35
Haut-Médoc	1,786	49	89,123	1,914	31·6	60,51
Listrac	382	50	19,401	398	30·5	12,15
Margaux	894	44	39,532	884	30·7	27,17
Moulis	263	45	12,062	285	30·0	8,57
Pauillac	784	52	41,368	902	31·2	28,20
St Estèphe	989	54	53,788	1,050	32·2	33,83
St Julien	688	54	35,926	668	35·4	23,07
Ste Foy Bordeaux Rouge	—	—	—	—	—	—

1976			1977			1978		
Hectares under vine	Average *rendement*	Approved volume	Hectares under vine	Average *rendement*	Approved volume	Hectares under vine	Average *rendement*	Approved volume
14,337	52	776,656	11,504	33·9	390,466	11,595	56	635,008
6,316	47	298,946	8,988	22·5	202,679	9,580	37·5	330,743
231	61	15,556	200	32	6,798	184	57	10,328
109	52	5,812	91	28	2,797	30	—	5,053
259	—	10,386	300	21	6,314	168·50	31	4,954
1,712	48	82,063	1,898	22	41,907	2,024	43·6	87,800
125	—	5,704	149	15·5	2,312	13,642	44·3	6,035
8	—	375	11	19	211	—	—	—
1,489	46	69,191	2,676	30	77,600	4,221	45·5	167,878
245	61	15,037	324	31·5	10,206	321·25	34·8	11,053
121	52	6,395	147	26	3,851	170	41	6,952
757	46	28,877	1,008	25	25,520	796·70	31·5	24,362
1,138	38	50,062	1,193	22	26,454	1,208·50	38	45,230
166	24	6,312	63	27·5	1,733	48·67	39·6	1,900
—	—	—	392	25·6	1,083	384·27	30·5	11,715
609	24	14,886	549	6	8,789	494·34	20·1	9,968
1,277	20	26,295	1,256	7	9,023	1,414	17·7	24,998
288	36	10,409	222	12·60	2,808	197·3	25·7	5,041
1,393	36	50,845	1,372	15·85	25,437	1,424·59	30·5	43,092
1,230	45	56,236	1,333	23·50	31,651	1,505·67	39·5	58,824
87	55	4,817	362	27	9,801	456	41·8	18,122
1,410	64	90,774	1,606	29	47,095	1,674	50	83,352
2,226	62	138,480	2,512	28·6	71,843	2,721	38·2	104,105
609	55	32,411	671	30·5	20,504	695	42	29,221
278	48	13,470	264	24	9,214	284·70	37·4	10,632
1,173	49	58,055	1,158	19	23,274	1,251·85	40·4	50,589
533	51	27,397	579	19	10,999	604	48·5	29,328
795	50	40,213	927	16	15,200	963·25	45·80	44,135
147	53	7,923	153	25	3,859	152·83	46·2	7,076
2,525	50	127,189	2,148	23·9	51,339	2,167·60	43·2	93,748
1,407	50	71,249	1,832	23·5	43,120	1,924·98	43	82,755
630	49	30,814	670	23	15,150	703	37·6	26,469
196	39	7,770	202	17	3,460	202·20	32·9	6,650
2,302	47	108,551	2,531	25·5	64,610	2,680	41	109,016
2,133	45	96,012	2,462	21·6	53,374	2,588	39·75	101,861
416	50	20,909	471	20·7	9,792	495	35·5	17,471
889	42	37,558	1,053	20·6	21,738	1,064	32·4	33,591
297	42	12,553	348	21·1	7,371	334	36	11,858
931	40	37,013	953	25·5	24,576	958	35·5	33,521
1,304	35	49,358	1,105	29	32,583	1,107	42·3	46,256
703	42	30,100	731	24·5	17,941	746	35·1	25,883
—	—	—	—	—	—	78	52·16	3,743

APPENDIX XI

Sales of Entre-Deux-Mers for the 10 years from 1969 to 1978 illustrating the progress that has been made in the sale of the *appellation*

MONTHS	1969	1970	1971	1972	1973	1974	1975	1976	1977	197.
January	2,465	2,231	2,984	3,768	6,464	2,003	4,005	2,615	4,233	4,0€
February	2,896	2,450	4,399	3,313	3,318	3,698	1,778	5,973	6,109	10,3⁊
March	2,508	3,646	1,723	2,882	2,622	1,992	2,685	3,773	3,647	6,4⁋
April	1,989	4,328	3,263	6,076	3,659	3,997	7,326	4,142	2,811	6,0⁏
May	1,220	1,098	1,282	1,676	6,082	4,654	6,349	3,945	3,583	2,6⁏
June	2,356	586	1,290	1,750	1,595	2,338	2,605	3,852	4,688	6,0⁊
July	2,767	—	1,908	3,056	769	3,123	2,081	2,218	868	1,3€
August	450	4,347	1,220	720	505	2,670	1,087	2,743	2,628	6€
September	1,519	357	2,238	4,169	3,361	1,981	5,634	2,522	4,127	4,64
October	1,798	1,762	1,303	2,122	502	1,660	3,424	2,303	1,316	5,3€
November	2,567	1,371	1,422	2,810	2,320	1,774	2,434	2,303	1,598	1,9⁋
December	770	1,394	3,477	3,100	1,160	3,065	4,776	6,007	6,724	4,3€
	23,305	23,570	26,509	35,442	32,357	32,955	44,184	42,396	42,332	54,07

APPENDIX XII

Leading Bordeaux *négociants*

At the beginning of 1980, there were no fewer than 200 enterprises which were members of the Syndicat des Négociants in Bordeaux, but this figure compares with 600 in 1950. These 200 enterprises employ 7,000 people and have a storage capacity of some two million hectolitres. Their turnover in 1979 was 4,400,000,000 Francs, and 1,800,000,000 of this comes from exports (41 per cent of the total).

Over 50 per cent of exports are accounted for by the 20 leading firms. In 1978 these were, in order of importance:

D. Cordier
Barton & Guestier
C.V.B.G (Maison Dourthe)
A. Delor & Cie
Alexis Lichine & Cie
Sté Distribution des Vins Fins
Calvet
Castel Frères & Cie
Cruse & Fils Frères
A. de Luze & Fils
Maison Sichel
Gilbey de Loudenne
J. Lebègue & Cie
Schroder & Schyler & Cie
Dulong Frères & Fils
Les Fils de Marcel Quancard
Borie Manoux
Louis Eschenauer
De Rivoyre & Diprovin/Dubroca
R. Joanne & Cie

Other important firms in the export trade include:

Pierre Coste
Nathaniel Johnston
Kressmann
A. Moueix
J. P. Moueix

Select Bibliography

This is a list of books for reference and further reading, and makes no attempt to cover all the books consulted, since many are out of print and generally unobtainable.

GENERAL

The World Atlas of Wine, Hugh Johnson, 2nd edition, Mitchell Beazley, 1977

Encyclopedia of Wines and Spirits, Alexis Lichine, 4th edition, Cassell and Christie's, 1979

Wines of the World, André Simon (edited by Serena Sutcliffe), 2nd edition, Macdonald U.K., McGraw-Hill U.S.A., 1981

Drinking Wine, Peppercorn, Cooper and Blacker, Macdonald and Jane's, 1979

History of the Wine Trade in England, André Simon, Holland Press, 1964

* *Guide to the Wines and Vineyards of France*, Alexis Lichine, Knopf U.S.A., Cassell and Christie's U.K., 1979

Great Vineyards and Winemakers, Serena Sutcliffe, Macdonald U.K., 1982, The Rutledge Press U.S.A., 1981

SPECIALIZED

Bordeaux et ses vins, Cocks and Féret, 12th edition, 1969

---

* The Lichine classification which appears in the text is taken from the French edition, *Les vins et vignobles de France*, published by Robert Laffont, which is slightly more up-to-date than that appearing in the English or American editions. Special thanks are due to the author and his publishers for permission to reproduce his classification.

Le Medoc, Fédération historique du sud-ouest, Editions Bière, 1964,

Histoire de Bordeaux (8 vols), Fédération historique du sud-ouest, particularly vol. III—*Bordeaux sous les rois d'Angleterre*; vol. V—*Bordeaux au XVIII siècle*; vol. VI—*Bordeaux au XIX siècle*

La Seigneurie et le vignoble de château Latour (2 vols), Fédération historique du sud-ouest, 1974

The Wines of Bordeaux, Edmund Penning-Rowsell, 4th edition, Penguin Books, 1979

The Great Wine Châteaux of Bordeaux, Hubrecht Duijker, Times Books, 1975

The Winemasters, Nicholas Faith, Hamish Hamilton, 1978

Connaissance et travail du vin, Prof. Emile Peynaud, Dunod, 1975

Lafite, Cyril Ray, Christie's, revised 1978

Mouton-Rothschild, Cyril Ray, Christie's 1974

Chateau Margaux, Nicholas Faith, Christie's 1980

Les vins de Bordeaux, Prof. J.-R. Roger, English translation 1960

Le Medoc—un grand vignoble de qualité, René Pyassou (2 vols), Tallaudier, 1980

Index

417

427